It was the time when there were no people on the earth. For four days the first man lay coiled up in the pod of a beach pea. On the fifth, he burst forth, falling to the ground, and stood up, a full-grown man. Feeling unpleasant, he stooped and drank from a pool of water, then felt better. Looking up, he saw a dark object approaching with a waving motion until it stopped just in front of him. It was a raven. Raven stared intently at man, raised one wing and pushed up its beak, like a mask, to the top of its head, and changed immediately into a man. Still staring and cocking its head from side to side for a better view, Raven said at last: "What are you? Whence did you come? I have never seen the likes of you." And Raven looked at Man, surprised to see that this stranger was so much like himself in shape.

Then Raven told Man to walk a few steps, again marvelling: "Whence did you come?" To this the Man replied: "I came from the pea-pod," pointing to the plant nearby. "Ah!" exclaimed Raven, "I made that vine, but did not know anything would come from it." Then Raven asked Man if he had eaten anything, to which Man replied he had taken soft stuff into him at a pool. "Well," said Raven, "you drank some water. Now wait for me here."

c.1

He drew down the mask over his face, changing again into a bird, and flew far up into the sky, where he disappeared. Again Man waited four days, when the Raven returned, bringing four berries in his claws. Pushing up his mask, Raven became a man again and held out two salmonberries and two heathberries, saying, "Here is what I have made for you. Eat them." Then Raven led Man to a creek where he took clay and formed two mountain sheep, which Man thought were very pretty. Telling Man to close his eyes, Raven drew down his mask and waved his wings four times over the images, which became endowed with life and bounded away. When Man saw the sheep moving away, full of life, he cried out in pleasure. Next Raven formed two other animals of clay, but because they were not fully dry when they were given life, they remained brown and white. Thus originated the tame reindeer. Raven told Man they would be very scarce. In the same way a pair of wild reindeer, or caribou, were made, being permitted to dry and turn white only on their bellies before being given life. These, Raven said, would be more common, and people could kill many of them.

"You will be very lonely by yourself," said Raven. "I will make you a companion." Going to a more distant spot and looking now and again at Man, he made an image very much like him, fastening a lot of fine water grass on the back of its head. After the clay dried, he waved his wings over it as before, and a beautiful young woman arose and stood beside Man. "There," cried Raven, "is a companion for you."

In those days there were no mountains far or near, and the sun never ceased shining; neither did rain fall or winds blow. Raven showed them how to make a warm bed of moss where they slept, while Raven lay nearby in the form of a bird. Waking before the others, Raven went to the creek and made pairs of sticklebacks, graylings, and blackfish. When Man arose and came to see them, Raven explained that the graylings would be found in the mountain streams and sticklebacks along the coast, and both would be good to eat. Next the shrewmouse was made, Raven saying that it would not be good for food but would enliven the ground and prevent it from seeming barren and cheerless.

*In this way, Raven continued for several days making birds, fishes, and animals, showing them to man and explaining their uses. After a while Woman gave birth to a child, and Raven showed Man how to feed and care for it. As soon as it was born, Raven and Man took it to a creek, rubbed it all over with clay, and then returned. Next morning the child was running about, pulling up grass and plants Raven had made, and on the third day it became a full-grown man.*

*After this, Raven thought that if he did not create something to make men afraid they would destroy everything he had made to inhabit the earth. So he went to the creek, where he formed a bear and gave it life, jumping to one side quickly as the bear stood up and looked about fiercely. He then told Man to avoid the bear or he would be torn to pieces. Raven then made different kinds of seals and explained their names and habits. He taught Man to make rawhide lines from sealskin, and snares for deer, but cautioned him to wait until the deer were abundant before snaring any of them.*

*Soon a girl was born to the Woman who was told she should marry her brother in order that the earth would be peopled more rapidly. . . .*

(Adapted from Raven Myth, Nelson 1899)

# inua

## spirit world of the bering sea eskimo

William W. Fitzhugh and Susan A. Kaplan

with contributions by Henry B. Collins
Thomas Ager
Dorothy Jean Ray
Saradell Ard Frederick

Published for the National Museum of Natural History
by the Smithsonian Institution Press, Washington, D.C.

1982

Edited by Jeanne M. Barry


This book was made possible in part by a generous grant from
Chevron U.S.A. Inc.

# contents

Edward William Nelson 1855–1934

# foreword

Life abounds in the magnificent collection of objects acquired from Bering Sea Eskimo communities more than a century ago for the Smithsonian Institution by Edward William Nelson. From 1877 to 1881, Nelson lived among the Eskimos in this remote region of Alaska, collecting every imaginable commonplace object, from intricately carved bag handles and earrings to elegantly fashioned wooden boxes, spears, and ceremonial masks. So persistent was Nelson in his quest for artifacts representative of the everyday life of these people that the Eskimos nicknamed him "the man who buys good-for-nothing things."

Indeed, many of the ten thousand objects collected by Nelson were of little intrinsic value at the time. But a look through the pages of this book will show how this has changed. The objects are, at the same time, both simple and elegant, and by studying them one can learn of the lifestyle, philosophy, humor, and spirituality of the nineteenth-century Bering Sea Eskimo peoples. The Nelson Collection breathes life into the past.

The merits of the Nelson Collection can also be considered from a somewhat different point of view. The main business of natural history museums is to acquire, preserve, and study collections. This vast assemblage of objects, brought together through the vision and hard work of Edward W. Nelson, has a special integrity because of its completeness. The fact that the Nelson Collection was acquired and well cared for during the past hundred years has made possible this volume and the related exhibition, "Inua: Spirit World of the Bering Sea Eskimo." The Smithsonian Institution has a strong mandate to preserve the integrity of this and other such collections, so that future scholars may be able to gain their own insights from these materials, and, of course, the general public can look forward to the time when future publications and exhibitions will be prepared.

Before turning to the magnificent substance of *Inua*, I am delighted to acknowledge the involvement of a large part of the Smithsonian family with this project. Mr. and Mrs. Thomas M. Evans, longtime friends of the Smithsonian Institution, generously provided funding to create a new and special gallery for temporary and traveling exhibitions. The exhibition of the Nelson Collection materials will have its debut in this gallery before it travels to cities in Alaska, the original home of these objects, as well as to communities in the "lower forty eight." The Smithsonian Institution Traveling Exhibition Service (SITES) provided encouragement and funding and developed the means for the exhibition to travel. The Contributing Membership, Smithsonian National Associates Program provided the major support necessary for production of this volume. To Chevron U.S.A. Inc., gratitude is extended for providing the funding that was necessary to add that extra measure of quality in design and photography that will make this publication a rich and lasting statement for years to come.

RICHARD S. FISKE
Director
National Museum of Natural History                    9

# acknowledgments

This book and exhibition program were inspired by the late Ann Stevens. In 1978 she visited the Smithsonian Institution and viewed its holdings of Alaska native artifacts. Upon doing so she inquired about the possibility of showing a portion of the collection in Alaska so that the beauty of the artifacts could be shared by all Alaskans.

A year later, during an Arctic museum training workshop supported by the Smithsonian Institution's Educational Outreach Program, Senator Ted Stevens of Alaska was invited to examine these same collections at the request of our Alaskan participant, Rachael Craig. Senator Stevens also urged us to prepare a traveling exhibition that would tour a number of the finer specimens to Alaska, where they had originated. We decided that the exhibition should concentrate on the collection of Edward Nelson, made one hundred years ago on the Bering Sea coast.

While still in the planning stage the project benefited from the advice of Ronald Senungetuk, Alan Munro, Robert Shalkop, Martha Cappelletti, Ruth Selig, Ann Bay, Anna Riggs, and Charlene James.

Dr. Richard Fiske, Director, National Museum of Natural History, decided that the first exhibition to be produced by the museum for installation in the new Thomas M. Evans Gallery should feature the Nelson Collection, one of the hidden treasures of the museum. Dr. Fiske's enthusiasm for and support of the project has made the entire exhibition and book program possible.

We would like to thank the many people in Alaska who extended assistance to us during two planning visits to the state. In Anchorage, Saradell Ard Frederick guided us through contemporary art collections, and Robert Shaw permitted us to use unpublished archeological specimens. For a pleasant and informative visit in Fairbanks we thank Wendy and Robert Arundale, Jean Aigner, Steve Jacobson, the Photographic Archives of the Elmer E. Rasmusson Library, William Sheppard, Ken Pratt, and the University of Alaska Museum. In Juneau we were assisted by the Alaska State Museum and by Lynn Price Ager.

Our two visits to Bethel provided an invaluable introduction to life along the Bering Sea coast. For this we are indebted to Phyllis Morrow and Chase Hensel and the Yupik Language Center of Kuskokwim Community College, who also aided us as interpreters and invaluable guides. Phyllis and Chase escorted us into the "Big Lake" country where we learned more about ongoing traditional life from Mary and George Andrews and Andrew Chicoyak of Nunapichuk, and advised on the use of Yupik terminology. James H. Barker of Bethel made available photographic materials, while artists Edward Kiokan and Kay Hendrickson provided modern ethnographic information.

In the Smithsonian's Department of Anthropology we have appreciated the strong support provided by Douglas Ubelaker, Chairman, and Clara Ann Simmons, Elizabeth Beard, and Carolyn Lewis. Jane MacLaren Walsh and Nigel Elmore followed many leads in a frustrating and still unresolved search for Nelson's Alaskan diary. This important document was never submitted to the Smithsonian and its location is unknown. Jane Walsh has also assisted in extracting Yupik terms from Nelson's dictionary manuscript. Jane Norman and Catharine Valentour supervised the conservation of objects. Aron Crowell prepared subsistence pattern data and Dosia Laeyendecker identified woods. Paula Fleming assisted in locating ethnographic photographs.

People in other departments have assisted the project. George Watson, Richard Vari, and Charles Handley provided taxonomic information. Roxie Laybourne identified feathers. Jean Smith lent office space. Suzanne Morris, Barbara Bridges, Wendy Bruneau, and Meredith Weber gave much to the project as student interns. The Office of Photographic Services, Development Office, and the Natural History Office of Exhibits provided excellent support.

Other institutions that generously loaned us material or supplied us with photographs are Alaska State Council on the Arts, Anchorage Historical and Fine Arts Museum, Visual Arts Center of Alaska, Atlantic Richfield Company, Henry E. Huntington Library and Art Gallery, United States Department of the Interior Indian Arts and Crafts Board, Indian Historian Press, Lowie Museum of Anthropology, Museum of the American Indian—Heye Foundation, National Museum of Denmark, Sheldon Jackson Museum, Alaska State Museum, Thomas Burke Memorial Washington State Museum, and University of Alaska Museum. We also extend thanks to individuals who have generously loaned materials from private collections.

We thank the two illustrators who have cheerfully prepared a number of fine pieces of work: Jo Ann Moore for the drawings and Molly Ryan for the charts and maps. Jeanne Barry has had the monumental task of editing this book under unusual circumstances. We thank her and the Smithsonian Institution Press for their efforts.

The contributors to the volume also assisted us in other ways. Henry B. Collins generously shared a lifetime of Alaskan experiences with the authors. Thomas Ager of the U.S. Geological Survey made available photographs and provided advice, as did Dorothy Jean Ray while studying the Nelson drill bows, and Saradell Ard Frederick who selected the contemporary art and initiated loan requests. Anthony Woodbury has contributed the opening section of the qasgiq essay and has made available Yupik texts from Chevak, Alaska. Linda Lichliter Eisenhart analyzed Nelson's grass baskets and contributed essay material on these objects.

Throughout the many months of intensive work on this project we have neglected family, friends, and professors, cutting phone conversations short and discouraging visits. We thank those who have been so understanding, especially Lynne Fitzhugh who created many evenings of cheer when she was able to tear us loose from "the Nelson lab."

Special thanks go to the Alaska State Council on the Arts and its Chairman, Anna Riggs, and its Director, John Blaine, for planning assistance, coordination, and advice. Jessie A. Brinkley of the Smithsonian National Associates Program, and Chevron U.S.A. Inc. have made this publication possible.

Alex Castro joined this project when it was in its formative stage. He participated in selection of materials to be illustrated, determined format, and designed an elegant book in keeping with the high quality of the Nelson artifacts. Joel Breger patiently, diligently, and with unending humor photographed the impossible. Were it not for their unstinting efforts this ethnography would be something less than visual.

# introduction

In 1877, when Edward William Nelson arrived in St. Michael, in what is now Alaska, to begin ethnological and natural history studies for the Smithsonian Institution, the Bering Sea Eskimos occupying the lowland regions of western Alaska, between Bering Strait and the Aleutian Islands, were the least-known Eskimos in the world. Living along the shallow coast of the Bering Sea, and along the lower courses and in the deltas of the salmon- and bird-rich Yukon and Kuskokwim rivers, Bering Sea Eskimos were largely ignored by explorers bent on reaching firmer ground, and by vessels seeking the summering grounds of the bowhead and other whales in the deeper waters of Bering Strait and beyond. The Bering Sea Eskimos' geographic isolation from events shaping the rapidly changing course of Alaskan history ten years after the purchase of the territory from Russia obscured a startling fact. Amid the marshy delta and along the coastal lowlands within an area of only three thousand square miles lived twelve thousand Eskimos—two-thirds of the Eskimo population of the territory and nearly a quarter of the Eskimo population of the entire world (Petroff 1884).

Bering Sea Eskimos are members of the larger family of Eskimo cultures extending from Prince William Sound on the Pacific Coast of Alaska to Bering Strait, and from there north and east along the Arctic coast into Canada, ultimately reaching as far as Greenland and Labrador. While occupying a larger region of the earth than any other ethnic group, they nevertheless share a common cultural and biological makeup, and speak a series of related languages, including *Inupiak* from Greenland to Norton Sound and *Yupik* from Norton Sound to the Pacific Coast. Culturally, they consist of regional groups known as Greenlanders, Canadian Inuit, North Alaskan Eskimos, Bering Sea Eskimos, and North Pacific Eskimos. The Aleuts, a related but distinct ethnic stock, do not speak Eskimo although in many respects their culture and way of life resembles that of Eskimos.

Most of what was known about Eskimos in 1877 came from contact with groups occupying the top of the continent from Bering Strait to Canada and Greenland. For nine hundred years Europeans—first Norse and later many others—had had sporadic contacts with eastern Arctic Inuit and Greenlanders. Theirs was the ultimate case of the spartan life, living much of the year in an unforgiving icy wilderness where starvation or death was a constant threat, where winter darkness reigned for months, where life was sustained by luck, ingenuity, and perseverance against inimical fortune.

Bering Sea Eskimos lived a very different life from that of their far-flung northern relatives. They occupied large, stable villages with substantial log and sod houses and commodious summer plank houses. Those living along the rivers enjoyed a plentiful supply of storable fish, while those on the coast had abundant supplies of driftwood, seals, walrus, fish, birds, and other game. They were equipped with finely made weapons and tools of wood, bone, ivory, and other materials, some of which were obtained by trade with outside groups, and they were well adapted to life in their region.

**Inua Mask**

Every natural object and living thing has a spirit, or *inua*, which has the capability of taking on a variety of physical forms. Usually, an *inua* will reveal itself to a person in the form of a small, humanlike face on the back, breast, or in the eye of a creature. The person will get just a fleeting glimpse of this semihuman image.

Masks, such as this one, are often the work of shamans who are the primary interpreters of the Bering Sea Eskimos' spiritual world. Such masks are worn on ceremonial occasions when encounters with animals and spirits are related to an audience of people, *inuas*, and supernatural beings.

South of Lower Yukon 33114, 48.5 cm

Social and intellectual life was complex, and during the long winter months they held large celebrations and festivals which were enlivened by intricate masks and theatrics. As Henry B. Collins has noted: "In the elaborate wooden dance masks of the Yukon–Kuskokwim region modern Eskimo art may be said to have reached its peak. No other Eskimo art products or handicrafts reveal so clearly the inner characteristics and the artistry of these gifted people. Here in a remarkable combination of abstract representation and grotesque fantasy we have evidence of the Eskimo sense of humor, both robust and subtle, of their sprightly imagination, and their technical virtuosity. Also, since the primary purpose of the dance festivals in which the masks were worn was to propitiate the spirits controlling the universe and bring success in hunting, the masks provide insight into Eskimo religion and cosmology" (Collins 1962:21).

Spirit life is manifested in religion and mythology as well as in hunting amulets, wooden serving bowls and ladles, clothing, and virtually everything made by man. Each of these artifacts, and all natural objects and living things, possessed a spirit, or *inua* (*yua* in the Yupik language), which was capable of taking on different physical forms but usually was revealed in a humanlike countenance. The *inua* of a bird might appear as a small semihuman face hidden among the feathers on its back, while that of a bear might be concealed under the long fur covering its body.

Spiritual transformation, symbolized by Man's first encounter with his maker, Raven, was at the heart of Bering Sea Eskimo life and culture. When an animal died its *inua* inhabited the form of an unborn animal of the same or similar species. Therefore, man needed to deal properly and respectfully with animals and objects so as not to displease the *inuas*, insuring that they would return to repopulate the earth with their kind. The Bering Sea Eskimo world was also inhabited by powerful spirits, including the *tunghät* who controlled the availability of game on earth. *Tunghät* as well as shamans—religious leaders—could take possession of *inuas* and use them for good or evil purposes. This world view, prominently displayed in material culture, makes Bering Sea Eskimo works some of the most complex, revealing, and intellectually challenging in the New World.

Surprising as it seems, the lifeways of Eskimos of this region of Alaska today continue to be poorly known to the public, whose attention remains largely fixed on the walrus and whale hunting Eskimos of North Alaska and their distinctive ivory carving, as well as on the Canadian Inuit who for many years have been featured in general educational programs and films and whose soapstone carvings and prints are widely distributed.

The purpose of this book and the exhibition which it accompanies is to correct this imbalance by reconstructing traditional nineteenth-century Bering Sea Eskimo life, stories, religion, and art as represented in the comprehensive collections and information gathered by Edward Nelson during his four years in Alaska from 1877 to 1881. Coming on the heels of the hundredth anniversary of the close of Nelson's field work, it is a fitting accolade to the memory of a remarkable scientist. Few, if any, other collectors or field ethnologists during the history of the Smithsonian Institution have acquired materials of such richness and depth.

In organizing Nelson's collections we have chosen to take the vantage point of an observer among the Bering Sea Eskimo during the time when Nelson conducted his field work. For this reason the form of the first person and present tense is generally used together with direct quotes from Nelson's notes, articles, and monographs and sections of myths and stories he collected. Where relevant the work of other ethnologists and students of

Bering Sea Eskimo culture is included, but no systematic attempt has been made to provide complete scholarly documentation or extensive citation, or to include data collected or reinterpreted in the intervening period. Certain errors made by Nelson have been corrected, but it has not been possible, nor deemed appropriate for this task, to reanalyze Nelson's research. In many areas, however, we have expanded upon his documentation, making interpretations and providing new insights where necessary to permit a fuller appreciation of the collections, especially in the areas of ceremonial life and art.

In addition to presenting a visual ethnography of the Bering Sea Eskimo, this book places their life in a regional and chronological framework. Contacts and influences from the Bering Strait and from North Alaska and Siberia are discussed, as are those with Indians to the east and Aleuts to the south. Features of European contact are everywhere noted. The significance of these contacts—economic, artistic, religious, and otherwise—is seen also in the perspective of time by the use of archeological materials touching upon the prehistoric roots of Bering Sea Eskimo culture and post-Nelson artifacts, which show the changing role of the Eskimo artist and the objects he has created.

WILLIAM W. FITZHUGH
SUSAN A. KAPLAN

For caption material, unless otherwise indicated artifacts were collected by Edward William Nelson and are housed in the Department of Anthropology, National Museum of Natural History, Smithsonian Institution.

Unless specific attributions are given, all ethnographic photographs are the property of the Smithsonian Institution and are housed in the Office of Photographic Services, Smithsonian Institution.

When known, the Yupik Eskimo term for an entry is set in italic next to the caption title. When more than one object has the same provenience, the provenience is not repeated.

Yupik terms with diacritical marks and syllabification are Nelson's original terms; others are modern Yupik transcriptions.

## The Way They Lived Long Ago

I will say a little
about the way people lived long ago,
about the life I was there to see,
the life I was lucky just to catch
when I was a boy,
down there in Qissunaq.

In the autumn around this time,
the women
used to fish for arctic tomcods
with dipnets.

Outside,
when it got cold, they used to wade, even
    when ice was forming,
and they wore only sealgut rain parkas,
tied around the waist like so.

Otherwise, the women
wore nothing,
Oh, how they endured back then,
those women!

They closed off their rain parkas
by tying them around their waists,
to keep their bodies
from getting cold.
But from the waist down
their bare skin was exposed,
since they did not have their pants on
    in the water.

They fished,
and the mud sometimes froze.

That is how it was
when they tried to catch fish for storage
in the autumn.

By themselves
the men,
the husbands of these women,
went off to hunt bearded seal down at the sea.
They speared them then,
they did not shoot them.

Whenever the weather was calm down at the sea,
they went after these seals in parties.

And by themselves,
the women
fished for sticklebacks, and

gathered vole-food from under the ground,
trying to get for food
the things
that voles will store there.

When it got cold, around this time,
the women got grasses they needed for the
    winter,
a sturdy flat grass for sleeping mats,
a long rough grass for storage baskets and
    partitions,
and regular grass for bedding and bootliners.
All of these were gathered.

Their houses were made of sod then.

I was lucky enough to have known
my grandmothers, who now are dead,
and who lived the way people did long ago.

Many people here now
were born after they picked things up from
    the white men,
after they began to get stoves for cooking,
stoves made at first of two five-gallon
    cans, or of washtubs.

When I was a boy the runners on the sleds
were made of the ribs of bowhead whales,
or else the runners
were made of ivory.

Sometimes the sleds
were made entirely of wood,
with runners of hardwood underneath.
In fact they even called those runners
    "hardwoods."

They had no saws back then,
and were just beginning to get axes,
so instead of sawing wood, they chopped it.
That is how it was done.

Whenever I come inside now I think
of my late grandmothers.
When it was cold
they covered the smoke window with ice,
and cleaned it with icepicks,
using the wood
of the handles.

16

When the cold let up,
they
put a cover of baby bearded seal gut on
   the smoke window,
in place of the ice cover.

After a while an ice cover cannot keep out
   the cold,
they used to say,
so they replaced them every so often
with another piece of ice.

The ribs and beams supporting the roof
stood out, because they alone were blackened
   with soot,
There was grass ontop of the ribs, with an
   outer layer of sod on top of that.

When the roof was covered on the inside
   with built-up frost,
they assembled wood
below
for a fire.

In winter the entranceway
was closed off on both sides
with woven grass partitions.

And they went outside only through the
    lower entrance,
for the upper entrance had no door leading
    through its covering.

Their plates were made of wood,
their water buckets were also of wood,
and they had wooden drinking ladles.

They had dippers
which they used in the winter
to get water
from the lake
whenever they ran out.

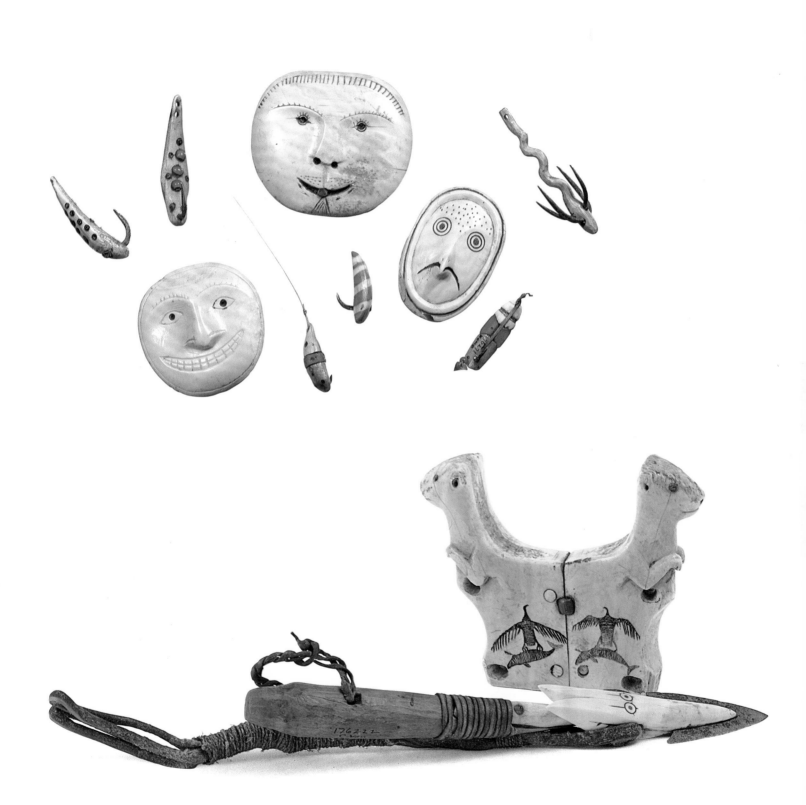

20

Very well now.
They used to cover their clothes
when the melting frost from the roof
    was dripping.

After the dripping stopped,
but before the embers burned out
in the fireplace
below,
they covered the smoke window.
And as soon as the window was covered, the
    house was warm.

Whenever it got cold in the evening,
black lumps of ice formed
where the drips had landed
on the sod
down on the floor.

And the lumps of ice
grew in height there on the floor,
and were black in color,
just as black
as the ceiling above.

In early spring
they started going in and out
through the upper entrance.

The qaygiq too
had an underground entrance-tunnel
in the wintertime.

And in the spring
they started using the upper entrance
   there, too.

They took baths early on
back then,
long ago,
when I was a boy.

As we do now,
they ate in the morning,
they had a midday meal,
and an evening meal, too.

That is how they ate.

During the Bladder Feast,
they had special meals.
That was when they
had ceremonies using the bladders
of certain animals.

On one side of the qaygiq,
light spears and heavy spears
were tied in bundles
from which the bladders were to hang.

Well,
when they were all done celebrating,
and it was time to take
the bladders outside,
they stood up the kagaciqaq, a
   wooden stake
with grass
wrapped around the top of it.

They lit it, and then put it up
through the qaygiq's smoke window.
The one who was to take it away
wore sealgut rainwear.

With the stake on his shoulder he took the
   fire down
from the roof of the qaygiq
and carried it off.

Behind him
the people with bladders took their bladders
   in hand and ran in pursuit.

And when they arrived down at the lake
where they were to put the bladders,
they took them,
punctured them,
and then put them into the water.

That is how it was when I was a boy.
Those are the things back then
that I used to see.
I was lucky enough to have caught those days.

When food got scarce in the early spring,
and the days were getting longer,
they tried to get sticklebacks for food,
from the rivers.

They got mostly sticklebacks up until
   springtime,
but from the sea
they got a few seals now and then
before it was time
for spring seal hunting.

Those are things you do not know about.
I am telling you about them,
since I caught those times.

Told by Tom Imgalrea of Chevak, 1978
Translated by Anthony C. Woodbury
and Thomas Moses

*At length a breeze arose, and during the pale twilight of the next midnight we forced a passage through a scattered ice-pack. During all of my experience in this region I never saw equaled the gorgeous coloring exhibited on this night by sea or sky. Along the northern horizon, where the sun crept just out of sight, lay a bank of broken clouds tinged fiery red and edged with golden and purple shades. Floating about us in stately array were the fantastic forms of the sea ice, exhibiting the most intense shades of green and blue, and the sea, for a time nearly black, slowly became a sullen green, on which the white caps chased one another in quick succession. As the sun neared the horizon the rosy flush spread from the clouds to the sky all around and a purple tint touched the sea and ice into the most gorgeous coloring, which lasted for an hour. The rush of the waves among the fragments of ice and the grinding of the pieces among themselves and along the side of the vessel made a strange monotone that blended harmoniously with the mysterious brooding twilight and the rare coloring of sea and sky.*

Edward W. Nelson
Upon his first approach
to St. Michael

the land

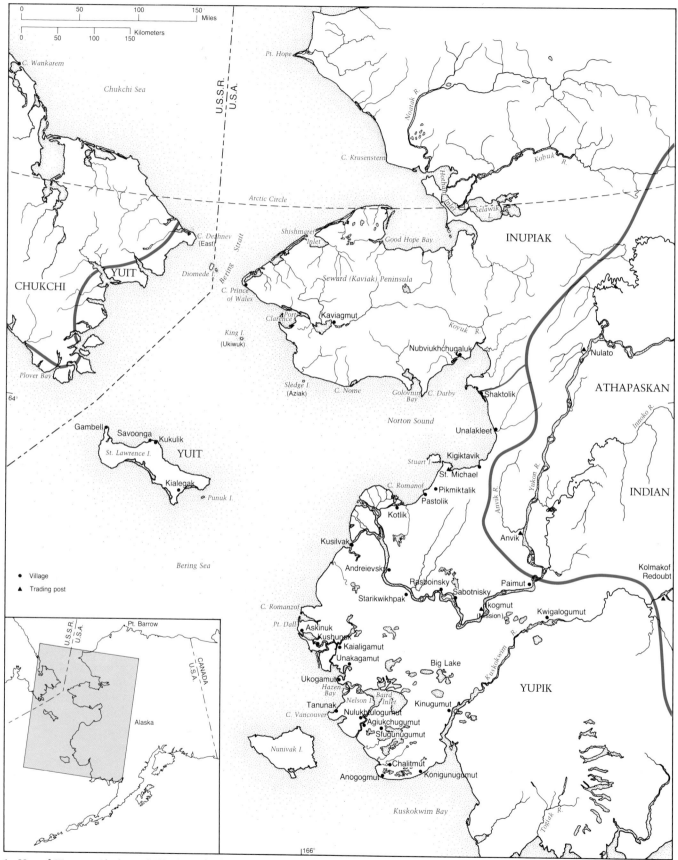

**1. Map of Western Alaska and Siberia with Place Names**

*In the morning after my arrival at Sledge island a knife was stolen from my box of trading goods, and on making this known to the headman he sent out a small boy, who returned in a few moments with the knife, everyone apparently knowing who had committed the theft.*

*A little later one of the King island men, who was sitting close by me, and who had traveled down the coast with the trader and myself the previous day, tried to steal a small article from me but was detected in the act, and I at once ordered him to leave the house. To this he paid no attention. I then seized him by the right arm, and when he saw that I was in earnest his face grew dark with passion, but he did not hesitate to take up his mittens and leave the room. He did not return during the day, but that evening when the people had left the room and the trader and myself were preparing for bed, we noticed that the headman of the village was still seated by the entrance way. . . . About 3 oclock the next morning I was awakened by a slight noise, and, raising my head cautiously, heard someone creeping in through the passageway. A moment later the head of the thief whom I had sent out and shamed before his companions the day before was thrust into the room. In an instant the watchful headman had taken him by the shoulder and spoken rapidly to him in an undertone. In a few minutes the King islander drew back and went away. The headman remained in his place until we arose in the morning. . . .*

*I have always considered that the watch kept by the headman during that night was all that prevented an attempt by the King islander to obtain revenge for my having offended him. (Nelson 1899:297)*

# the man who buys good-for-nothing things

HENRY B. COLLINS

The unfortunate incident involving the King Islander was one of the few unpleasant experiences Edward W. Nelson had with individuals during his four-year stay in western Alaska. Generally people treated him with kindness, and because of his desire to buy old objects, many of which they cast aside, they regarded Nelson with a good deal of amusement, asking, "Where is the buyer of good-for-nothing things?" (Nelson 1899:373; Hooper 1884:37).

In his early twenties and already an accomplished ornithologist, Edward W. Nelson arrived in Alaska in a roundabout way. He came to the attention of Spencer Fullerton Baird, assistant secretary of the Smithsonian Institution and director of the United States National Museum, when Nelson applied for a job at the Smithsonian Institution. Through Baird's efforts Nelson secured an appointment as a weather observer for the U.S. Signal Service at St. Michael on the Bering Sea coast of Alaska. In addition to his official meteorological tasks, Nelson was instructed by Baird to gather information and to make collections relating to the geography, zoology, and ethnology of this little-known region of Alaska.

Realizing that the Bering Sea coastal area was one of the least-known sections of the Arctic, Nelson responded to its challenge. This was indeed a naturalist's paradise though the cold and stormy weather was anything but heavenly. Myriads of waterfowl and other birds nested on the tundra and on the sea cliffs, and its water teemed with fish and sea mammals. Thousands of Eskimos, occupying small villages along meandering riverbanks and scattered along the coast and offshore islands, lived off these rich resources.

The Eskimos Nelson met differed in many ways from the stereotyped Eskimo who lived in snow houses on the frozen seas of the Canadian archipelago and subsisted on large sea mammals and caribou. Instead, here were Eskimos who lived in semisubterranean sod-covered houses made out of driftwood timbers. They hunted seals and occasionally walrus and caribou, and relied heavily on fish, birds, and small mammals. Indeed, some of their beautiful clothes were made from the skins of ducks, geese, ground squirrels, and even salmon.

When Nelson arrived at St. Michael in 1877, Alaska had been an American possession for only ten years. St. Michael, originally called Michaelovski Redoubt or Fort St. Michael, was established in 1833 as a Russian outpost to control the Yukon Eskimo and Indian fur trade. In the early nineteenth century the Russians sent several exploring expeditions to the Bering Sea region and established a few trading posts and missions on the Yukon, Kuskokwim, and Nushagak rivers. One of their explorers, Russian naval officer Lieutenant Lavrentii A. Zagoskin, wrote an excellent report on the land and people he saw along the Yukon and Kuskokwim. However, his work was not widely distributed and remained little known (Zagoskin 1967).

Twenty years after Zagoskin's travels St. Michael was headquarters for the members of the Western Union Telegraph Expedition who were studying the geography and ecology of the area, while searching for a route for a trans-Siberian cable. Their reports on the natural history and resources of Russian America, transmitted to Congress by Spencer Baird, were partly responsible for the purchase of Alaska. William H. Dall, who was part of the scientific staff, wrote the first description of the Alaskan Eskimos and Indians to be published in English (Dall 1870).

As an observer of Eskimo culture Nelson was fortunate in being assigned to St. Michael, for in no other place could he have met with such cultural diversity. St. Michael was a kind of Eskimo crossroads where, in addition to the resident population, other Eskimos from western Alaska and Indians from the Yukon came to trade their furs and other products for tobacco, metal, cloth, guns, beads, and other Russian trade goods available at this principal trading center.

Norton Sound marked a dividing line between two essentially different patterns of Alaskan Eskimo language, culture, and physical type. People living north of Norton Sound spoke the Inupiak language, to the south they spoke Yupik, and the northerners were linguistically more closely related to far away Greenland and Labrador Eskimos than they were to their Yupik-speaking neighbors (Jenness 1928; Swadesh 1951). Eskimo houses north and south of Norton Sound differed fundamentally in structure. Their clothing, hunting technology, art, and ceremonial traditions were also distinct. Nelson noted that northerners tended to have long and narrow heads, while people living south of Norton Sound had relatively shorter and broader heads.

### 2. Tribal and Linguistic Boundaries

During his travels throughout western Alaska and eastern Siberia, Edward Nelson observed that a number of different languages were spoken. At St. Michael he lived among Yupik and Inupiak speakers, for Norton Sound was a dividing line between people who spoke these two Eskimo languages. During a sled journey into the interior Nelson came in contact with Ingalik Indians who spoke an Athapaskan dialect. The Eskimos on St. Lawrence Island and those living along the east coast of Siberia spoke Siberian Yupik. Altogether different languages were spoken by the Aleuts and the Siberian Chukchi reindeer herders.

When possible, Nelson recorded the Yupik and Inupiak terms for many of the objects he bought during his stay in Alaska. These terms were eventually incorporated in an English-Eskimo, Eskimo-English dictionary in which several dialects were recorded, but which Nelson never published.

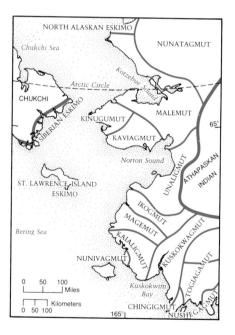

**3. Nelson's House at St. Michael**

While living at St. Michael between 1877 and 1881 Nelson worked for the U.S. Signal Service as a weather observer. His meteorological observations were as thorough as his ornithological and ethnographic observations. He recorded daily weather conditions and described the development of individual auroras in great detail.

St. Michael was a major trading center to which northern and southern Eskimos, Indians, and even Siberians came, so Nelson was able to learn a great deal about the land and its people while living in St. Michael. However, the lure of scientific investigation was too great to leave him content simply manning his weather station. Heeding Spencer Fullerton Baird's request for collections from Alaska, Nelson hired others to man his weather station at St. Michael while he traveled throughout the country for two to three months during his last three years in Alaska.

SI–6381

The Eskimos Nelson met in the St. Michael area were the Unaligmut, the original inhabitants, living on the southern and eastern shores of Norton Sound, and the Malemut and Kaviagmut, two groups of northern Eskimos who, earlier in the nineteenth century, had begun to move down and settle on the north and east coasts of Norton Sound. The Malemut and Kaviagmut were active middlemen in the extensive intercontinental trade between Siberia and Alaska in which Alaskan furs and other Eskimo and Indian products, mainly from the Yukon, were traded for skins from domesticated reindeer, tobacco, and other Russian trade goods from Siberia. As for the Unaligmut, they were the northernmost members of the Yupik-speaking Eskimo population of the Bering Sea region.

Nelson spent his first year in Alaska investigating the St. Michael surroundings while making meteorological observations. Beginning in December 1878 he started taking long sled journeys about the country that gave him the opportunity to assemble large zoological and ethnological collections while also carrying out geographic studies. When Nelson was away trader friends and their assistants carried on his work at St. Michael.

Nelson's most important and memorable trip began on the second of December, 1878, when, in company with a fur trader named Charles Petersen, and an Eskimo guide, he set out with four dog teams for a period of two months to traverse unmapped and unexplored territory, heading first for Andreievsky, Petersen's trading post on the Lower Yukon River. From there they proceeded west across the tundra to the Bering Sea coast, before turning southward and traveling along the low-lying coast and unknown area now called Nelson Island.

Along the way Nelson was greeted by villagers who invited him into the *qasgit*, or men's houses. Here Nelson traded tobacco, cloth, ammunition, beads, and needles, for wood, ivory, and stone implements. He spent

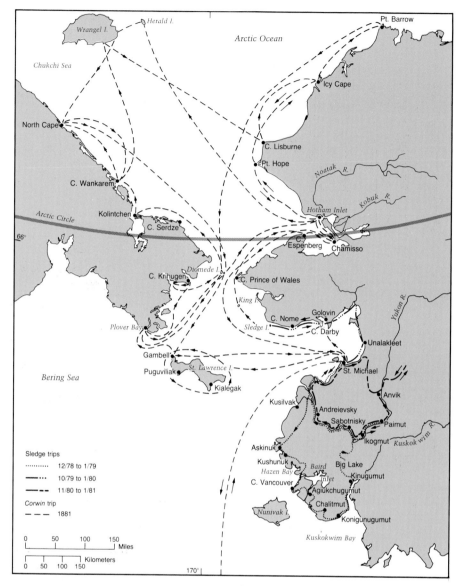

Sledge trips
·········· 12/78 to 1/79
———— 10/79 to 1/80
– – – 11/80 to 1/81

Corwin trip
— — — 1881

### 4. Nelson's Journeys

Nelson made a number of epic journeys along the coast and into the interior of western Alaska, traveling by dog sled, bidarka, and finally on the Revenue Cutter *Corwin*. On his journeys Nelson studied the wildlife, mapped unknown territory, and observed the daily life of people who were his hosts. As a result of his extensive travels he managed to buy ten thousand implements ranging from ceremonial masks to children's toys. He documented where each was collected, how it had been made and used, and what it was called in Yupik. While traveling he lived off the land, enduring the hardships and witnessing the beauty that made the Bering Sea region a special place to live. During the last few months of his term in Alaska, Nelson was the naturalist on board the *Corwin*, and he visited northern Alaskan and eastern Siberian peoples. During this voyage Nelson continued his detailed ethnographic work, with the result that his collection demonstrated the cultural diversity of the Bering Sea and Bering Strait regions.

his evenings writing in his journal while people practiced songs and told stories. At Kushunuk a hunting festival was in progress, and custom dictated that no one was to leave the village or work during this time. Nelson, in accordance with the foreign customs of his hosts, rested here for several days. This stopover afforded him the opportunity to make extensive notes and collections.

Throughout the last part of December the party encountered severe storms and covered treacherous terrain. In an account of a stretch of this journey Nelson stated that they left the village of Ukagamut on the twenty-first of December and

> made a hazardous passage for several miles along a narrow ice-foot which bordered the seaward face of the mountains. Finally we were forced to abandon this track, as the shelf narrowed so that it would have been impossible to avoid falling into the open sea, which surged back and forth below. We were caught in a terrific wind and snowstorm on the mountains, and by great fortune reached the village of Tanunak at Cape Vancouver, with only a few slight frost-bites. (Nelson 1882:667)

## 5. Nelson's Camp on the Yukon Delta

In May 1879 Nelson and his Eskimo companion Alexai hired a man to take them to the Yukon Delta in his bidarka. Here Nelson and Alexai set up a camp and began to study the habits of the magnificent emperor goose, which had its breeding grounds in the area. "Then followed about two weeks of the greatest misery it was my fortune to endure while in the north. Day after day the wind blew a gale from the ice-covered sea, and was accompanied by alternate fog, sleet, and snow. Without fire, and with no shelter but a small light tent made of thin drilling and pitched on a bare marsh facing the sea, the Eskimo and myself crouched in our scanty supply of blankets, benumbed with cold, and unable to better our condition. Finally, the weather moderated, and the geese, ducks, and other water-fowl flocked to their breeding grounds" (Nelson 1887:15).

The following year Alexai joined Captain De Long of the whaler *Jeannette*. The vessel was crushed in the ice and sank in the Arctic Ocean, and Alexai died during the crew's unsuccessful retreat over the ice. De Long's diary was recovered and relates Alexai's heroic hunting efforts and his insistence that the crew share the small amount of food he, as expedition hunter, managed to catch during their doomed southward march.

SI–6379

On the twenty-fifth they were drenched by a heavy rain which continued the following day accompanied by violent winds. They continued traveling through melting snow and pools of water, finally reaching Sfugunugumut where the travelers gave the villagers their clothes to wear and dry out with the heat of their bodies. On the twenty-eighth the weather was so bad that Petersen turned back, but Nelson and his Eskimo guide continued southward toward the Kuskokwim River.

They ascended the Kuskokwim for some ninety miles and then set out for the Yukon River. They crossed the marshy, lake-studded area known as the Big Lake region lying between the two great rivers. This desolate, treeless, wet country, lying a little above sea level, was nevertheless the most densely populated area of Alaska, or indeed of any part of the Arctic. This was possible because people had a stable food supply consisting mainly of fish. These included salmon and whitefish, but also blackfish (*Dallia pectoralis*) known only in Alaska. Blackfish is abundant in shallow lakes and sluggish streams, and because it is present throughout the year, has been the most dependable food resource available to the Eskimos. Nelson estimated that more than one hundred tons of these fish were caught annually.

Nelson observed that the people living here "are among the most primitive people found in Alaska, and retain their ancient customs, and their character is but slightly modified by contact with whites. They present one of the richest fields open to the ethnologist anywhere in the north. They retain their complicated system of religious festivals and other ceremonies from ancient times. Their work in ivory and bone bears evidence of great skill, and all their weapons and utensils are well made" (1882:670). On reaching the Yukon, Nelson and his companion went upstream as far as Paimut, the uppermost Eskimo village on that river, and then proceeded

downstream to the Yukon Delta and back to St. Michael, concluding a two-month journey of some 1,200 miles.

Some of the place names seen on present-day maps are those given by Nelson during this journey. Hooper Bay and Hazen Bay are named for Captain C. L. Hooper of the Revenue Cutter *Corwin* and General W. B. Hazen, chief signal officer, U. S. Army; and Baird Inlet and Dall Lake are named for Spencer Fullerton Baird, assistant secretary of the Smithsonian Institution, and William H. Dall, then of the U.S. Coast Survey and the Smithsonian Institution. Nelson determined that the large land mass east of Cape Vancouver was in fact an island. Later, Henry Gannett, geographer of the U. S. Census Bureau, designated it Nelson Island.

The ethnological results of this journey were equally noteworthy. At village after village in this unknown area, both along the coast and in the interior, Nelson met with and lived among the Eskimos, observing their way of life, describing their ceremonies, and collecting their tools and utensils. Nelson's observations show insight and sensitivity to a culture quite foreign to his own, and his descriptions lack the biases common for his time.

Shortly after his return to St. Michael, Nelson headed for the Yukon Delta to study the habits of breeding waterfowl, particularly the emperor goose. He and his Eskimo companion Alexai, along with a third man, traveled to the Delta in a bidarka, a three-man boat, where Nelson and his companion were left to camp. After enduring discomfort suffered from a gale blowing off the ice-covered sea, and downpours of sleet and snow, they managed to secure skins and eggs of the emperor goose. They then hired a man to take them to St. Michael. Unfortunately they were not equipped with gutskin garments, used to keep water out of the boat while also serving as raincoats. On the second day of their journey they encountered a storm and quickly headed for the mouth of the Pikmiktalik River.

> The water was icy cold, and as nearly every wave dashed over us and added to the water in the kyak, we were soon wet to the skin and sitting in water constantly increasing in the bottom of the boat. All three worked desperately at the paddles, and just as I began to despair of our reaching the river in time a welcome break in the shore line showed its vicinity. The kyak was at once headed for this opening, and we were soon among the breakers. As we neared the mouth the breakers became heavier, until one huge roller caught the stern of the kyak and lifted it high in the air, while the bow cut the water in the trough of the swell advancing at terrific speed. . . . The boat was run ashore among a large bed of drift-wood, and upon trying to get out I found that sitting in the icy water, which had covered my legs and hips for several hours, had deprived my lower limbs of the power of motion and of sensation. The men dragged me out and built a huge fire, before which I slowly thawed out and restored my circulation. (Nelson 1887:15)

In a letter to his good friend Robert Ridgway, a Smithsonian Institution ornithologist, Nelson recounted this experience, adding that he removed his wet clothes, hung them in the breeze, and "stalked about 'à la noble savage'," whereupon he spotted a *Freisga semipaluata* and, oblivious to his condition, became delightfully engaged in a study of the little bird and her nest of eggs (Nelson letter to Ridgway 1879).

Nelson embarked on a sled trip in November 1880, and headed north along Norton Sound and Norton Bay, and south along the coast of Seward Peninsula as far west as Sledge Island, where he was almost killed. This trip required three months to complete in stormy weather and intense

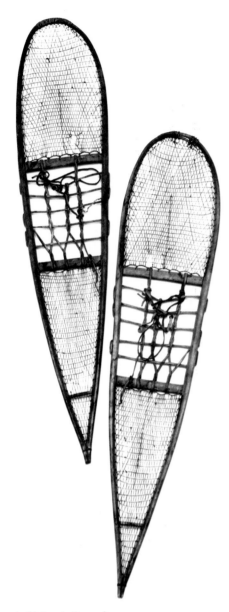

**6. Nelson's Snowshoes**

In a list of specimens brought back from Alaska Nelson made a note under the entry for this pair of Ingalik Indian snowshoes: "pair used by myself on two expeditions about 1800 miles." No other personal effects dating from Nelson's years have been identified, nor are there photographs of him at work. Personal reactions to and thoughts about his four-year effort can only be gleaned from Nelson's scholarly writings, for despite the fact that Nelson repeatedly made reference to a personal diary, extensive searches in archives have failed to bring this important document to light.

Nulato 49099 (pair), 131 cm

cold. Nelson, generally inclined toward understatements, refers to this trip as "an extremely rough journey, but the series of notes and ethnologic specimens obtained on this reconnaissance are extensive and valuable" (1899:20).

That same year, on an extensive inland journey, Nelson explored the Anvik River from its headwaters to its confluence with the Yukon, as well as the middle Yukon and Innoko rivers—all in Indian territory. On this trip he made valuable observations on the Ingalik, the westernmost of the Athapaskan Indians, including a detailed account of their religious ceremonies. His report shows that ceremonialism and other cultural features of the Ingalik, who lived in direct contact with Eskimos, were in large part a reflection of similar features of Eskimo culture. As Nelson's account of this Yukon trip dealt with Indians and not Eskimos, it was not included in his 1899 description of his Eskimo ethnological collection, and remained an archival document until only recently (Van Stone 1978).

In 1881 Nelson accompanied the *Corwin* on her annual northern voyage. He traveled to St. Lawrence Island where most of the population had been decimated by disease, also stopping at Big Diomede and points along the Siberian coast, before proceeding north along the American coast as far as Point Barrow. He scaled the cliffs of Herald Island and reached isolated, ice-bound Wrangel Island deep in the Arctic Ocean as well. Thus Nelson was able to buy northern materials, record house forms and customs, and take photographs of northern peoples, enriching his understanding of the diversity of the landscapes, animals, and cultures found on both sides of the Bering Sea and Arctic Ocean.

Nelson was a patient observer and a careful collector of all kinds of information. His detailed descriptions of birds, fish, and land and sea mammals, and even butterflies—"secured by means of my hat"—include the Latin and Eskimo names for the animal, its appearance, geographic distribution, and habits, as well as techniques by which Eskimos hunt and use the animal. A section of his description of the little brown crane (*Grus Canadensis*), called *lat-slhuk* by the Eskimos, is typical of his work.

> They come from the south toward the Lower Yukon, and on mild, pleasant days it is a common sight to see the cranes advancing high overhead in wide circuits, poised on motionless wings, and moving with a grace unexpected in such awkwardly-formed birds. As the weather gets warmer they become more and more numerous, until the drier parts of the wide flats and low, rounded elevations are numerously populated by these odd birds. The air is filled with the loud, hard, rolling k-r-roo, kr-r-r-roo, kû-kr-r-roo, and either flying by, with trailing legs, or moving gravely from place to place, they do much to render the monotonous landscape animate. The end of May draws near, and the full tide of their spring-fever causes these birds to render themselves pre-eminently ludicrous by the queer antics and performances which the crane's own book of etiquette doubtless rules to be the proper thing at this mad season. I have frequently lain in concealment and watched the birds conduct their affairs of love close by, and it is an interesting as well as amusing sight. (Nelson 1887:94)

Nelson related well to the people amongst whom he lived as a foreigner. He made efforts to learn their language, recording their myths and legends, games, and ceremonies, touching also on their political and social organization. He came to his observations of Eskimo lifeways with the same sharp eye and clear perception exhibited in his descriptions of Alaska's land and animals.

In the middle of September 1881 the *Corwin* left Arctic waters with Nelson on board. Not surprisingly, Nelson had contracted tuberculosis while in Alaska, and its effects were to plague him for the rest of his life. Upon his return he began to write his report on the natural history of Alaska but he had to let his Smithsonian friends assist in the final editing of the volume due to his poor health. For years thereafter he lived in the southwestern United States and in Mexico. In addition to his natural history reports, during this early period Nelson unselfishly disseminated information he had gathered regarding the numbers of people inhabiting the Bering Sea region and the character of the land and climate. His contributions were recognized in Ivan Petroff's report on Alaska (Petroff 1884) and in Captain Hooper's narrative of the *Corwin's* 1881 voyage (Hooper 1884).

Nelson's ethnological collection—numbering close to ten thousand specimens, each assigned a number with accompanying information on the village where it was collected—was deposited by Nelson at the Smithsonian Institution and is now housed at the National Museum of Natural History. The Nelson Collection is the largest, most complete, and fully documented single collection of Eskimo material culture from any part of the Arctic. Nelson's 518-page monograph, *The Eskimos About Bering Strait* (1899), describing the implements and the manner in which they were used, along with descriptions of houses, hunting techniques, mythology, religious ceremonies, and other aspects of Eskimo life, became at once a classic of Eskimo ethnology.

Edward Nelson continued his distinguished career, pioneering studies on the natural history of Mexico and the American Southwest. This led through a series of wildlife posts to his final assignment, that of chief of the Biological Survey of the U.S. Department of Agriculture from 1916 to 1927 (Goldman 1935; Lantis 1954). During these years he was a constant advocate of wildlife conservation, fostering bird-banding programs and becoming a key figure in negotiations leading to the Migratory Bird Treaty Act with Great Britain on behalf of Canada, a landmark in the history of wildlife conservation in North America. His interest in Alaska continued throughout his life nevertheless. He was instrumental in passage of the Alaska Game Law of 1925 and helped develop policies to improve conditions for domestic reindeer in the area. Although Nelson is known to have visited Alaska only once after leaving St. Michael in 1881, he corresponded with young naturalists such as Frank Dufresne, and his fond memories of his work there always remained fresh in his mind.

☆             ☆             ☆

The work of a naturalist in the north is one of almost continual hardship, yet the succession of novel experiences lends a peculiar zest to such a life. Many of the most enjoyable days of my life were passed on expeditions in which it was a constant struggle to obtain the bare necessities of life. One speedily comes to disregard the discomforts of such a life, and the changing episodes attending each day, together with the strange and often beautiful scenes, are all that linger in his memory. (Nelson 1887:21,22)

**7. Revenue Cutter *Corwin***

The U.S. Revenue Cutter *Corwin*, first under the command of Captain Hooper, and later of Captain Healy, made an annual voyage to Alaska beginning in 1880. The *Corwin* maintained order in Alaska, settling disputes and enforcing United States laws, as well as conducting studies of the geography, natural history, and ethnography of the area. During her 1881 voyage, of which Nelson was a member, the *Corwin* was searching for the lost whaler *Jeannette*. Hooper crisscrossed Bering Strait and penetrated north into the Arctic pack. The *Corwin* crew scaled the cliffs of Herald Island and were the first Westerners to set foot on Wrangel Island, while seeking the remains of *Jeannette* and her crew.

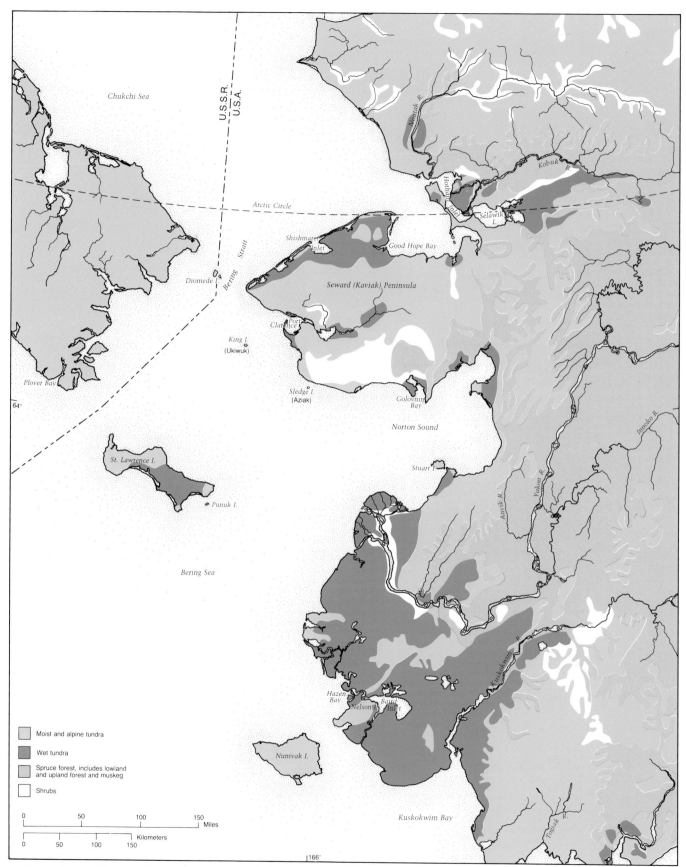

Chukchi Sea

U.S.S.R.
U.S.A.

Montak R.

Kobuk R.

Hotham Inlet

Selawik L.

Arctic Circle

Shishmaref Inlet

Good Hope Bay

Seward (Kaviak) Peninsula

Diomede I.

Bering Strait

Port Clarence

King I.
(Ukiwuk)

64°

Plover Bay

Sledge I.
(Aziak)

Golovnin Bay

Norton Sound

Innoko R.

Stuart I.

St. Lawrence I.

Anvik R.

Yukon R.

Punuk I.

Bering Sea

Hazen Bay

Baird Inlet

Nelson I.

Kuskokwim R.

Moist and alpine tundra

Wet tundra

Spruce forest, includes lowland
and upland forest and muskeg

Shrubs

Nunivak I.

0          50          100          150
                                        Miles

0      50      100      150
                         Kilometers

Kuskokwim Bay

Togiak R.

166°

**8. Vegetation and Topographic Map of Western Alaska**

*In the beginning there was water over all the earth, and it was very cold; the water was covered with ice, and there were no people. Then the ice ground together, making long ridges and hummocks. At this time came a man from the far side of the great water and stopped on the ice hills near where Pikmiktalik now is, taking for his wife a she-wolf. By and by he had many children, which were always born in pairs—a boy and a girl. Each pair spoke a tongue of their own, different from that of their parents and different from any spoken by their brothers and sisters.*

*As soon as they were large enough each pair was sent out in a different direction from the others, and thus the family spread far and near from the ice hills, which now became snow-covered mountains. As the snow melted it ran down the hillsides, scooping out ravines and river beds, and so making the earth with its streams.*

*The twins peopled the earth with their children, and as each pair with their children spoke a language different from the others, the various tongues found on the earth were established and continue until this day. (Nelson 1899:482)*

# raven's works

THOMAS AGER

During the last great glacial period, about 26,000 to 10,000 years ago, vast ice sheets and mountain glaciers covered northern North America and northern Eurasia, nearly all of Canada, and large areas of the northern midwestern and northeastern United States. In Alaska, glaciers were restricted to the mountainous northern and southern parts of the state. Central Alaska was too low and too far from the moisture sources of the ice-free Pacific Ocean to permit the growth of large glaciers (fig. 9). The enormous volume of water stored on land in the form of glacial ice lowered sea level about 90 meters over a period of several thousands of years, exposing very large expanses of the globe's continental shelves as dry land (Hopkins 1979). This sea level drop altered the northern landscape dramatically. The shallow sea floors of the Bering and Chukchi seas were exposed and formed a broad plain linking Siberia and Alaska. This land connection, sometimes called the "Bering Land Bridge," allowed periodic interchanges of animals and plants between eastern and western hemispheres over that long period when the land bridge was above sea level. The first humans to enter North America more than 11,000 years ago probably came by way of the land bridge.[1]

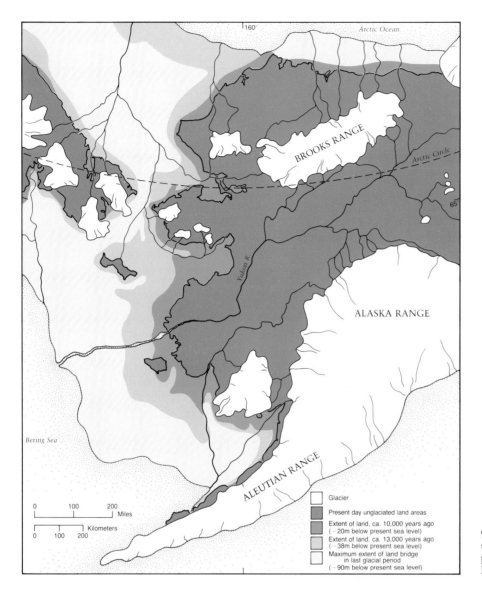

**9. Postglacial Land and Sea Changes, Thirteen Thousand Years Ago to Present** (compiled from Hopkins 1973, 1979; Ager 1982; Nelson 1980)

The history of vegetation change in western Alaska over the past 26,000 years is known primarily from the study of the minute but nearly indestructible grains of pollen that are preserved in the mud at the bottoms of lakes and in peat deposits.[2] These fossils tell us that the Bering Land Bridge and adjacent unglaciated parts of Alaska (together called Beringia) were covered with tundra composed of grasses, sedges, and a variety of herbs, most of which are found today in arctic and alpine regions. Small woody plants such as willows were the only common shrubs present, and the ground cover was interspersed with patches of bare soil.

The full glacial climate was continental, with colder winters, less snowfall, and cooler, drier summers than in the region today. Permafrost was much more extensive, underlying nearly the entire landscape.

As glaciers began to wane about 14,000 years ago, vegetation began to change significantly throughout Beringia. The alpine tundra of the full glacial period was replaced by a shrub tundra in which willows, dwarf birch, sedges, and mosses predominated. This vegetation change was probably a response to warmer temperatures and increased moisture associated with deglaciation. Some of that moisture increase was probably in the form of deeper winter snows.

During deglaciation from about 14,000 to 10,000 years ago, runoff from melting ice on the continents caused a rapid rise of sea level, inundating the exposed continental shelves. As central Beringia was drowned by rising sea levels the maritime climatic influence of the Bering Sea spread inland, bringing increased moisture to adjacent land areas. The first trees to appear in Alaska in postglacial times were hardy poplars about 11,500 years ago. They made their appearance in the Norton Sound region about 11,000 years ago, adding a new component to its shrub tundra vegetation. Another new element, alder shrubs, migrated into the area about 7,500 years ago, forming thickets with willows along streambanks and in protected hollows.

Spruce trees began to appear on the eastern fringes of the region about 5,500 years ago after migrating westward from northwestern Canada via interior Alaska. Today white spruce reaches as far west as Bethel on the Kuskokwim River (fig. 8) and the Andreievsky River in the Nulato Hills. White spruce and black spruce also now grow in the vicinity of the Bering Sea coast in eastern Norton Sound.

The reconstruction of past environments from pollen evidence and other data suggests that during the interval when Eskimo cultures probably developed in western Alaska (fig. 290) the vegetation and fauna were not dramatically different from that of the present day. Climatic oscillations have occurred since glaciers receded, but most were too small to change the regional vegetation dramatically. These climate changes may have had significant impact upon the human populations of the region, however, by changing the length of winters, influencing the duration and distribution of pack ice, and perhaps affecting the population size and timing of migrations of mammals, birds, and fish.

Ice Age animals once roamed the tundra of western Alaska and Beringia, and some of their remains are scattered around western Alaska. Among the few fossils in the Yukon–Kuskokwim region are the tusks, teeth, and bones of woolly mammoths, found by Eskimos in riverbeds and eroding from thawing river banks and coastal bluffs. Nelson recorded Eskimo myths that explained the occurrence of these impressive fossils:

> The bones of the mammoth which are found on the coast country of Bering sea and in the adjacent interior are said to belong to an animal known as the *kī-lûǵ-û-wûk* (*ko-gukh´-pûk* of the Yukon). The creature is claimed to live under ground, where it burrows from place to place, and when by accident one of them comes to the surface, so that even the tip of its nose appears above ground and breathes the air, it dies at once. This explains the fact that the bones of these animals are nearly always found partly buried in the earth. The Eskimo say that these animals belong to the under world and for that reason the air of the outer world is fatal to them. (Nelson 1899: 443)

Eskimos also told Nelson tales of these animals having been observed digging with their enormous tusks in the beds of rivers. The tales usually recount the experience of someone else, the man who actually saw the wonderful sights either having died or not being available for corroboration.

The remains of other Ice Age animals that once inhabited this region have been found in frozen ground and in cave deposits in other areas of unglaciated Alaska and parts of the Yukon Territory (Harington 1978). These animals include horses, large-horned bison, caribou, giant ground sloths, camels, Saiga antelopes, yaks, short-faced bears, lions, and muskox

(Péwé 1975; Harington 1978). Most of these species became extinct in Beringia before or during the waning phases of glaciation. Many that survived these large-scale extinctions live in Alaska today—wolves, moose, caribou, Dall sheep, grizzly bears, and wolverines (fig. 13).

The cause of these mass extinctions is still debated. In Alaska and the Yukon many of the extinctions coincide with dramatic changes in climate and vegetation, and also with the appearance of Early Man at scattered locations in Alaska between 12,000 and 10,000 years ago. Probably both environmental changes and hunting pressure by man contributed to the demise of many of these species. Native tradition holds that great tusked animals came in old times from the east and were later destroyed by a shaman from the river Kroichback. Others claim that the herd was merely driven into the earth, and that it comes back to graze and feed on earth only for one night each year (Hooper 1884:82).

## Land and Sea

> The belt bordering the Alaskan coast of Bering sea belonging to this district is mainly low, and much of it consists of broad, marshy tracts which are but little above sea level. This is particularly the case in the large, roughly triangular area lying between the lower Kuskokwim and Yukon rivers. To the northward of this the country is more broken or rolling in character, rising gradually in many places to low mountainous masses, several hundred feet in height and coming down to the coast at intervals as bald headlands. The islands of Bering straits are small and rocky and rise precipitously from the water, as does much of the adjacent Siberian shore. St. Lawrence island is large and has an undulating surface with rocky headlands at intervals along the coast. (Nelson 1899:23)

The present-day Yukon–Kuskokwim Delta is a vast coastal lowland with an area of about 75,000 square kilometers. Most of the Delta is composed of wetland tundra. Sedges, grasses, and a variety of herbs predominate. Willows are the most common woody plants in the wet tundra. On lowland surfaces with slightly better drainage other low woody plants occur together with willows—such as blueberry, bog cranberry, cloudberry, Labrador tea, and dwarf birch. Also important are mosses, sedges, grasses, and lichens (fig. 16).

Northern boreal forest occurs in the interior of the Delta as far west as Bethel on the Kuskokwim and St. Marys on the Yukon River (fig. 8). These forests are composed primarily of white spruce, but paper birch and poplar also occur. Forests extend into some valleys of the Nulato Hills and reach the vicinity of the Bering Sea coast in eastern Norton Sound. Poplar trees grow along the region's major rivers far beyond the western limit of spruce.

The Delta is laced by a myriad of rivers and streams meandering across the wetlands to the sea. A complex network of river, marine, lake, delta, and wind-blown sediments, the Delta is the product of two great rivers, the Yukon and the Kuskokwim. Of the two, the Yukon is by far the largest, contributing 88 million tons of eroded earth each year to the Bering Sea from a drainage basin substantially larger than the state of Texas. The Delta is a highly changeable environment, with frequent shifts in river channels and swift alterations in the shape of coastlines. The most abrupt and dramatic changes occur during severe storms in the Bering Sea and during spring breakup when ice jams divert the major river courses. The lowlands between river channels are sprinkled with thousands of lakes,

**10. Fishskin Bag**

Bering Sea Eskimos have identified the important qualities of the resources available to them. Fish, a major food resource of the area, also supply people with oil and strong, durable, waterproof skins. In addition to fashioning fish skins into garments, Bering Sea Eskimos have made them into mittens, boots, and elegant containers, such as this clothing bag.

Nushagak 37401, 33.5 cm high

ponds, and bogs (fig. 8) which cover between one-quarter to one-half of the entire surface area of the Delta. Permafrost underlies much of the region and contributes to the poor drainage by keeping water levels near the surface. Travel across this landscape is impossible except by boat during the summer, when one must follow meandering channels and lakes; it is easier when the land and waterways are frozen and straight courses can sometimes be maintained. Nelson, who traversed this country on foot during his epic sledge expedition in 1878–79, remarked many times on the unusual nature of this terrain and its Eskimo inhabitants:

> In all the coasting from the mouth of the Yukon to that of the Kuskokwim, excepting merely the small part covered by mountains . . . the country is so low that the tide flows up the river from 10 to 50 miles, and we were frequently unable to find a fresh-water stream or lake from which to obtain drinking water, even when 20 to 30 miles from the coast. Bushes are scarce, being found sparingly on some of the streams. Wood is an article of great scarcity and is frequently brought many miles by boat (in *oomiaks*) in summer. (Nelson 1882:10)

Within this huge expanse of marshy lowlands, framed by the Nulato Hills on the north, and the Kilbuck Mountains rising south of the Kuskokwim, one finds scattered low hills and mountain ranges emerging dramatically from the great expanse of wet lowlands covered with tundra and scattered thickets of willows and alders. Hardy alpine tundra occurs on the highest rocky ridges and steep slopes. Eskimos have used these uplands as sources of stone, copper pigment, clay, useful plants, and game, especially caribou. Some of these uplands, including St. Michael and Stuart islands and the Ingakslugwat Hills, in the central part of the Delta, are low volcanoes and lava flows probably less than a million years old. The volcanic history of this region contributed to its unusual character. Although most of this

43

activity preceded the appearance of man, some of the lava flows on Stuart Island and in the low hills southeast of St. Michael appear young enough to have been possibly witnessed by humans when they formed. On St. Michael Island there are several volcanic craters. Some are occupied by lakes, while others were drained when coastal erosion breached the volcanic deposits separating the lakes from the sea. Both the breached and unbreached craters are incorporated in the Eskimo legends of the *ă-mí-kuk*, a dangerous beast.

> The *ă-mí-kuk* is said to be a large, slimy, leathery-skin sea animal with four long arms; it is very fierce and seizes a hunter in his kaiak at sea, dragging both under the water. When it pursues a man it is useless for him to try to escape, for if he gets upon the ice the beast will swim below and burst up under his feet; should he reach the shore the creature will swim through the earth in pursuit as easily as through the water.
>
> Near St. Michael the people believe that these creatures swim from the sea up through the land to some land-locked lakes in the craters of extinct volcanoes and to similar inland places. Several dry lake-beds were shown to me in that vicinity as having been drained by these animals when they swam out to the sea, leaving a channel made by their passage through the earth. It is said that if the *ă-mí-kuk* returns the water follows from the sea and again fills the lake. The idea of this creature may have had its origin in the octopus. (Nelson 1899:442)

Thunderbirds, featured in many Eskimo legends, created and nested in dry craters in the tops of volcanoes:

> Very long ago there were many giant eagles or thunderbirds living in the mountains, but they all disappeared except a single pair which made their home on the mountain top overlooking the Yukon River near Sabotnisky. The top of this mountain was round, and the eagles had hollowed out a great basin on the summit which they used for their nest, around the edges of which was a rocky rim from which they could look down upon the large village near the water's edge. (Nelson 1899:486)

Nelson also recorded tales of apparent volcanic ash falls in the region that almost certainly had a factual basis, for on rare occasions southerly winds carry ash clouds from erupting volcanoes in the Aleutians and perhaps the Alaska Peninsula to the Yukon–Kuskokwim Delta.[3]

**11. Legendary Creatures**
Bering Sea Eskimo mythology includes descriptions of a changing world once covered with ice and showered with ashes. In distant times strange creatures inhabited the crater lakes of the Bering Sea regions' volcanoes. Today, slimy and dangerous creatures are said to frequent the Delta. Illustrated here are carvings of a large, fierce seal monster and a tiny, harmless-looking worm monster. The first is a socketpiece to a sealing dart, the second an amulet.
Kushunuk 36477, 19 cm; 36894, 3.8 cm

The Eskimo have various traditions of occurrences long past. One very old woman on the lower Yukon told me she had heard related by old people when she was a girl that showers of matter like ashes fell there very long ago. The first shower of ashes she heard of was quite deep, killing fish in the rivers and causing the death of many people by starvation.

At St. Michael an old man related that before the Russians came to the country he knew of one fall of a strange substance like ashes which covered the ground like a slight fall of snow and adhered to whatever it fell upon so that when rubbed off from wood it left a polished appearance. This man said that such showers were known to have taken place at widely distant intervals and that people were very much frightened by them.

These accounts undoubtedly refer to falls of volcanic ashes from eruptions taking place in the Aleutian islands and other points in this region, and are interesting as showing the manner in which occurrences of this kind are treasured in the memories of these people. (Nelson 1899: 449–50)

Human life in this region is also strongly affected by the Arctic climate and stormy weather, which often have severe consequences for people whose life is dependent on hunting and fishing. Violent storms sweep in across the Bering Sea from the southwest where they are spawned in the western Aleutian Islands. The most violent storms from this direction come between mid-August and the end of November. In winter, storms often strike from the north and northeast, and can bring frigid Arctic air with temperatures below − 40 degrees F.

During a dogsled journey across the Delta in December and January, 1878, Nelson experienced severe winter storms, which he later described:

The country in the region between the mouths of the Yukon and Kuskoquim is principally low and marshy, and during two weeks of the time spent in traversing it violent storms of snow, rain, and sleet accompanied by high winds prevailed. During this time my bedding became saturated with moisture, as did also my clothing, and day after day forced marches were made over a country covered with slush and water. At night a miserable shelter was improvised from our sledges or found in the underground huts of the natives. These storms finally culminated in a terrific gale as I approached the sea-coast south of Cape Vancouver, and just at sunset, by great good fortune, I reached a couple of huts built on a knoll about 5 miles from the coast. The best of them was flooded with water, leaving a space about 3 feet wide of bare ground around the sides, but in going out and in we were forced to wade through a foot of water all along the entrance passage. Here my interpreter and myself crouched against the wall in silent misery for two days, while one of the most violent tempests I ever witnessed swept over the desolate tundra. This wind was accompanied by a dense fog and, after two days, when we continued our journey to the coast, we found that the gale had caused an extraordinary high tide the previous day, and the rising sea, bearing a massive sheet of ice, had swept over all the low coast lands to the base of the small knolls where we had found shelter. Had we been delayed half an hour in reaching these knolls on the night of our arrival we must inevitably have missed them and been lost in the overwhelming mass of ice that covered the low land of all this district.

Such floods, covering the region along the Lower Kuskoquim at intervals of three or four years, usually raze some of the native villages, and in some cases people and all have been swept away. (Nelson 1887:14)

In late October ice begins to form in the northern Bering Sea and along the coast. Freeze-up usually occurs by mid-November, forming a broad shelf of shore-fast ice along the coast, beyond which pack ice drifts almost constantly in response to currents and winds.

In late December at this latitude, the duration of sunlight plus twilight is about 7 hours per day. By comparison, at Point Barrow in northern Alaska light is restricted to only about 3.5 hours of twilight per day.

Spring breakup of sea and river ice usually begins in mid-May, but some sea ice persists until mid-June in most years. Breakup of the river ice is accompanied by extensive flooding of lowlands, rapid erosion of river banks, and occasional major shifts in the course of rivers.

Summers in most coastal areas such as Nunivak and Nelson islands are cool and windy, with frequent fog and light rains. Inland from the coast, in places like Bethel on the Kuskokwim, the climate becomes more continental, with less wind and fog, and warmer summer temperatures (fig. 12). Sunlight plus twilight lasts twenty-four hours a day from late May to mid-July at this latitude.

Another atmospheric feature noted by all who travel in the north is the aurora borealis, or "Northern Lights." While not affecting weather, it nevertheless has a strong psychological effect on people, and is a common subject of mythology in the Bering Sea region as elsewhere in the circumpolar Arctic. There was a belief among people here that the shifting curtains of light of the aurora were caused by boys playing ball across the sky with a walrus skull, while the galaxy was the track made by Raven's snowshoes while walking across the sky. Nelson, revealing his Western background, described the aurora with a different intent, but in an equally elegant manner in his meteorological observations for the Signal Corps:

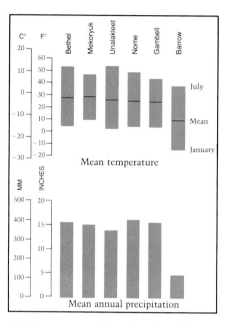

12. **Temperature Variation in Western Alaska**

> September 28 (8 to 11:30 p. m.).—An aurora of three arches arranged in the north. The middle arch gave out long pencils, streamers, and curtains of light in wavy motion and at times extremely bright, traversed with waves of green violet, and rose-red, besides straw-yellow and white. The display of colors was generally seen accompanying the waving, curtain-like masses of light which hung downward from the middle arch. The lower arch wavered and threw out streamers a few times, but held a very secondary place in the display, while the outer arch appeared like a pale reflection of one of the others, and the only changes it gave were a waxing and waning of the light as the lower arches brightened or faded. The bases of the two inferior arches were close together. Temperature fell the next day. (Nelson, in Hooper 1884:94)

## Living Things

Edward Nelson's energetic efforts as a collector were not restricted to ethnographic subjects. During his four years in Alaska he made significant contributions to the region's natural history (Nelson 1882, 1887), previously studied by Lavrentii A. Zagoskin (in Michael 1967), William H. Dall (1870), and Lucien M. Turner (1886). His collections included nearly 2,000 bird skins and 1,500 eggs, 370 mammal pelts and skulls, 50 species of fish, and small collections of butterflies and vascular plants, the latter probably originating from John Muir's work on the 1881 cruise of the *Corwin* (Muir 1917). In addition to describing these specimens, Nelson compiled information on species distribution, habitat, and behavior, with frequent reference to methods employed by the Eskimos in obtaining and utilizing them.

## 13. Mammals Commonly Utilized by the Eskimos of the Yukon-Kuskokwim Delta–Norton Sound Region

| COMMON NAME | GENUS AND SPECIES | ESKIMO NAME |
| --- | --- | --- |
| *LAND MAMMALS:* | | |
| Caribou | *Rangifer tarandus* | *tuntu* |
| Black bear | *Ursus americanus* | *tan'gerliq* |
| Grizzly or brown bear | *Ursus arctos* | *taqukaq* |
| Polar bear | *Ursus maritimus* | *nanuaq* |
| Wolf | *Canis lupus* | *kegluneq* |
| Arctic fox | *Alopex lagopus* | *qaterliaraq* |
| Red Fox | *Vulpes vulpes* | *kariaq* |
| Least weasel | *Mustela nivalis* | *teriaq* |
| Mink | *Mustela vison* | *imarmiutaq* |
| Wolverine | *Gulo gulo* | *qavcik* |
| River otter | *Lutra canadensis* | *cinkaq* |
| Snowshoe hare | *Lepus americanus* | *maqaruaq* |
| Tundra hare | *Lepus timidus* | *qayuqeggliq* |
| Arctic ground squirrel | *Spermophilus parryii* | *cikik* |
| Beaver | *Castor canadensis* | *paluqtaq* |
| Muskrat | *Ontatra zibethicus* | *iligvak* |
| Brown lemming | *Lemmus sibiricus* | *qilagmiutaq* |
| Porcupine | *Erethizon dorsatus* | *il'anquciq* |
| Shrew | *Sorex dorsatum* | *uugnaraq* |
| *MARINE MAMMALS:* | | |
| Bowhead whale | *Balena mysticetus* | *arveq* |
| Beluga whale | *Delphinapterus leucas* | *cetuaq* |
| Killer whale | *Orcinus orca* | *arrluk* |
| Northern fur seal | *Callorhinus ursinus* | *aataak* |
| Pacific walrus | *Odobenus rosmarus* | *asveq* |
| Harbor seal | *Phoca vitulina* | *nayiq* |
| Spotted seal | *Phoca largha* | —— |
| Ringed seal | *Phoca hispida* | *issuriq* |
| Ribbon seal | *Phoca fasciata* | *qasguliq* |
| Pacific bearded seal | *Erignathus barbatus* | *maklak* |
| Sea otter | *Enhydris lutris* | *arrnaq* |
| Steller sea lion | *Eumetopias stelleri* | *wi-'nûk* |

*Adapted from Nelson 1887*

## 14. Fish Utilized by the Eskimos of the Yukon-Kuskokwim Delta–Norton Sound Region

| COMMON NAME | GENUS AND SPECIES | ESKIMO NAME |
| --- | --- | --- |
| Arctic lamprey | *Lampetra japonica* (A) | *nemersaq* |
| Herring | *Clupea harengus* (A) | *iqalluarpak* |
| Sheefish (nelma) | *Stenodus leuichthys* (A) | *cii* |
| Whitefish, cisco | *Coregonus* spp. (A, F) | *qaurtuq* |
| Dolly varden or salmon trout | *Salvelinus malma* (F) | *iqallugpik* |
| Pink salmon, humpback | *Oncorhynchus gorbuscha* (A) | *tûkh-tûk!* |
| King or chinook salmon | *Oncorhynchus tshawytscha* (A) | *tarsaqvak* |
| Coho salmon | *Oncorhynchus kisutch* (A) | *chy-u-yak!* |
| Chum salmon | *Oncorhynchus keta* (A) | *nû-ka'!* |
| Sockeye or red salmon | *Oncorhynchus nerka* (A) | *uqurliq* |
| Grayling | *Thymallus arcticus* (F) | *culugpauk* |
| Rainbow smelt | *Osmerus mordax* (S) | *hl'-ko-ŏg'-û-nĭk* |
| Alaska blackfish | *Dallia pectoralis* (F) | *imangaq* |
| Pickerel | *Esox lucius* (F) | *cuukvak* |
| Burbot or losh | *Lota lota* (F) | *manignaq* |
| Bering wolf-fish | *Anahicus orientalis* (S) | *qaculluk* |
| Arctic cod | *Boreogadus saida* (S) | *iqalluaq* |
| Tomcod or saffron cod | *Eleginus gracilis* (S) | *iqalluaq* |
| Ninespine stickleback | *Pungitius pungitius* (S, F) | *i-luk-chugûk!* |
| Sculpin | *Cottus* sp., *Myoxocephalus* sp. (S) | —— |
| Arctic flounder | *Liopsetta glacialis* (S) | *naternaq* |

KEY: (A) Anadromous
(F) Freshwater
(S) Saltwater

Adapted from Turner 1886; Nelson 1887; Morrow 1974

## 15. Birds Utilized by the Eskimos of the Yukon-Kuskokwim Delta–Norton Sound Region

| COMMON NAME | GENUS AND SPECIES | ESKIMO NAME |
| --- | --- | --- |
| Pelagic cormorant | *Phalacrocorax pelagicus* | *agasuuq* |
| Whistling swan | *Olor columbianus* | *qugsuk* |
| Canada goose | *Branta canadensis* | *tuutangayak* |
| Brant | *Branta bernicla* | *leqlernaq* |
| Emperor goose | *Philacte canagica* | *nacaullek* |
| Greater white-fronted goose | *Anser albifrons* | *leqleq* |
| Snow goose | *Chen caerulescens* | *kanguq* |
| Mallard duck | *Anas platyrhynchos* | *uqsuqerpak* |
| Common pintail | *Anas acuta* | *uqsuqaq* |
| Old-squaw | *Clangula hyemalis* | *äh-lĭ-hlû-gŭk* |
| Common eider | *Somateria mollissima* | *metraq* |
| King eider | *Somateria spectabilis* | *qengallek* |
| Spectacled eider | *Somateria fischeri* | *ūng-ū'* |
| Rough-legged hawk | *Buteo lagopus* | *pĭ-tŏ'ghŭk!* |
| Bald eagle | *Haliaeetus leucocephalus* | *metervik* |
| Gyrfalcon | *Falco rusticolus* | *kă-gokh'-tŭk* |
| Willow ptarmigan | *Lagopus lagopus* | *aqesgiq* |
| Rock ptarmigan | *Lagopus muticus* | *ung-ă-'wĭk!* |
| Sandhill crane | *Grus canadensis* | *lăt-slhŭk!* |
| Glaucous gull | *Larus hyperboreus* | *kukisvak* |
| Herring gull | *Larus argentatus* | *naruyaqliq* |
| Murre | *Uria* spp. | *alpaq* |
| Crested auklet | *Aethia cristatella* | —— |
| Horned puffin | *Fratercula corniculata* | *qaterpak* |
| Tufted puffin | *Lunda cirrhata* | *qilangaq* |
| Snowy owl | *Nyctea scandiaca* | *ungpek* |
| Short-eared owl | *Asio flarnmeus* | *mengqucivak!* |
| Northern raven | *Corvus corax* | *tulukaruk* |

Adapted from Nelson 1887; Klein 1966; American Ornithological Union Checklist

## 16. Edible Plants Utilized by Eskimos of the Yukon-Kuskokwim Delta

| COMMON NAME | GENUS AND SPECIES | ESKIMO NAME | ADDITIONAL USES |
|---|---|---|---|
| Rockweed (seaweed) | *Fucus* sp. | —— | —— |
| Fern | *Dryopteris dilatata* | cetuguar | —— |
| Diamond-leaf willow | *Salix planifolia* | —— | sore treatment |
| Felt-leaf willow | *Salix alaxensis* | uqvigpak | chewing gum; added to tobacco |
| Willow | *Salix glauca* | enrilnguaq | many |
| Wild potato | *Claytonia tuberosa* | ulqiq | —— |
| Mountain sorrel | *Oxyria digyna* | quunartiarraat | —— |
| Sourdock | *Rumex articus* | quagciq | medicinal tea |
| Bistort | *Polygonum* spp. | soochluk? | —— |
| Seabeach sandnat | *Honckenya peploides* | —— | —— |
| Marsh marigold | *Caltha palustris* | allngiguaq | —— |
| Pallas buttercup | *Ranunculus pallasii* | kapuukaraq | —— |
| Roseroot | *Sedum rosea* | cuqlamcaraat | sore treatment |
| Spiked saxifrage | *Saxifraga spicata* | muchuktulak? | —— |
| Cordate-leaved saxifrage | *Saxifraga punctata* | —— | —— |
| Northern red currant | *Ribes triste* | —— | —— |
| Northern black currant | *Ribes hudsonianum* | —— | —— |
| Marsh firefinger | *Potentilla palustris* | pingayunelgen | —— |
| Cloudberry, salmonberry | *Rubus chamaemorus* | atsalugpiaq | —— |
| Nagoonberry | *Rubus arcticus* | puyuraar | —— |
| Fireweed | *Epilobium angustifolium* | ciilqaaq | medicinal tea |
| Dwarf fireweed | *Dpilobium catifolium* | angukoq? | —— |
| Mare's tail | *Hippuris* spp. | tayarut | —— |
| Wild celery | *Angelica lucida* | ikiituk | ritual; purification |
| Beach lovage | *Ligusticum scoticum* | mecuqelugaq | —— |
| Hemlock parsley | *Conioselinum chinense* | —— | —— |
| Bunchberry | *Cornus* spp. | cingqullektaq | —— |
| Crowberry | *Empetrum nigrum* | tan'gerpak | —— |
| Blueberry | *Vaccinium uliginosum* | curaq | —— |
| Lingonberry | *Vaccinium vitis-idaea* | kitngiq | —— |
| Cranberry | *Oxycoccus microcarpus* | tumagliq | —— |
| Labrador tea | *Ledum palustre (decumbens)* | ayuq | burned as a cure or to drive out ghosts; medicinal tea |
| Alpine bearberry | *Arctostaphylos alpina* | —— | —— |
| Red-fruit bearberry | *Arctostaphylos rubra* | —— | —— |
| Wooly louswort | *Pedicularis kanei* | —— | —— |
| Beach sunflower | *Senecio pseudo-arnica* | —— | —— |
| Cotton grass | *Eriophorum angustifolium* | iitaq | mats; socks; medicine |
| Horsetail | *Equisetum* spp. | qetek | —— |
| Legume | *Astragalus polaris* | —— | —— |
| Stinkweed | *Artenisia telesii* | qanganaruaq | wound dressing; medicinal tea |
| Avens | *Dryas octopetala* | kiyuk? | —— |
| False-camomile | *Matricana suaveolens matricarioides* | atsaruaq | medicinal tea |

*Some Other Utilized Plants:*

| | | | |
|---|---|---|---|
| Fungi | *Fomes pinicola* | iqmik | added to tobacco and snuff |
| Bluegrass | *Poa* spp. | evget | boot lining; diapers |
| Rye grass | *Elymus arenarius* | —— | baskets; mats |
| Compositae | *Petasites* spp. | qaltaruaq | added to tobacco and snuff |
| Moss | *Sphagnum* spp. | urut | lamp wicks; diapers |
| White spruce | *Picea glauca* | mingqutnguaq | many |
| Birch | *Betula papyrifera* | u'linguk | snowshoes; containers; canoes |
| Larch | *Larix laricina* | elriguq | bows; arrows; paddles |

Adapted from Oswalt 1957; Lantis 1959; Fries 1977; Ager and Ager 1980; Hultén 1968; Heller 1966; Ager, unpublished data; Young and Hall 1969.

**17. Polar Bears**

Polar bears are often associated with Eskimo subsistence. However, this animal is rarely found south of Norton Sound, preferring to stay north, where it hunts seals along the ice edge. Periodically polar bears appear in the south, having been carried down the coast on floating ice. However, upon reaching land the bears begin to travel north.

A drag handle has been carved in the form of a polar bear with a seal, a favorite food, in its mouth. The tiny polar bear may have been a charm which dangled from a woman's needlecase to protect her from possible attack by a bear that might mistake her for a seal.

Sledge Island 176217, 55 cm; 45184, 2 cm

**18. Forest-dwelling Animals**

The interior forest-covered regions of western Alaska support a variety of small mammals, including porcupines, ermine, and marten, which are not present on the treeless coast.

Koyuk 44070, 5 cm; Cape Vancouver 43578, 4 cm; Nubviukhchugaluk 44029, 2 cm

Nelson's work shows the biological resources of the Bering Sea coastal region to be abundant and diverse in comparison with Arctic regions farther north. However, most of this relatively rich resource base is available for only about five months of the year. The challenge is to survive during the long winter, when resources are very limited and the climate is severe.

Mammals heavily utilized by the Eskimo include seals, walrus, and beluga. Other sea mammals occur in the region, but are less abundant and are used on an opportunistic basis (fig. 13). On shore, small mammals abundant in the wetlands include muskrats, hares, weasels, and mink. Farther inland, particularly within the forested regions, black bears are common. Caribou, of primary importance to man for food and materials, were once present throughout the upland country during much of the nineteenth century. By 1877, however, they had disappeared and during Nelson's four years of residency and travel in areas of their former abundance not a single animal was seen, although their earlier trails, deeply worn into the landscape, were plainly evident. Only on Nunivak Island was a herd still extant. Nelson attributed this to the introduction of firearms and subsequent excessive and sometime wanton human exploitation, but natural cycles and disease may also have contributed (Nelson 1887:285; Burch 1972). In addition to these large animals, many others such as fox, wolf, wolverine, beaver, porcupine, and ground squirrel have been important resources for the Eskimos.

People living in the Yukon–Kuskokwim region depend to a great extent upon its rich fish resources (fig. 14). Some salt, brackish, and freshwater species, especially tomcod and blackfish, are available all winter long. During the summer months great numbers of salmon enter the region's rivers and streams from the Bering Sea and along with herring, lampreys, burbot (losh), blackfish, whitefish, needlefish, and grayling provide a large and relatively stable source of food and materials.

The vast wetlands of the Delta are a stopping-over point and nesting area for several million migratory birds (fig. 15). Waterfowl and shorebirds are the most numerous of these, arriving in early May and remaining until early autumn. Eskimos eat the meat and in some cases the eggs of geese, ducks, swans, cranes, shorebirds, seabirds, and ptarmigan. In addition, feathers, bones, and entire bird skins are often utilized for manufacturing a wide variety of utilitarian, ornamental, and ceremonial objects. Few bird species remain through the long winter. Snowy owls, gyrfalcons, ravens, ptarmigan, chickadees, and along the coast some sea ducks, such as eider and old-squaw, stay behind if patches of open water remain.

Of the 450 known species of vascular plants available, at least 38 have been used by the Eskimo population for food (fig. 16). Many additional species have been used for ritual and medicinal purposes, as raw materials for manufacturing utilitarian objects, tobacco additives, fuel for heating and for smoking fish, dyes for coloring hides or grass, and other purposes. Of these, grass is by far the most important. The only plant material of greater importance is driftwood. Driftwood logs of spruce and occasionally logs of paper birch and poplar float down the river channels and are carried out to sea to be deposited unevenly along the coast of the Bering Sea. Driftwood is critical for the survival of Bering Sea Eskimo culture as known, being a source of firewood, building material for dwellings and caches, fish-drying racks, kayaks, tools and weapons, bowls, ceremonial masks, and a host of other items.

Nonvascular plants such as lichens and mosses have been used for a variety of purposes, among them food, caulking, bandage pads, and diapers.

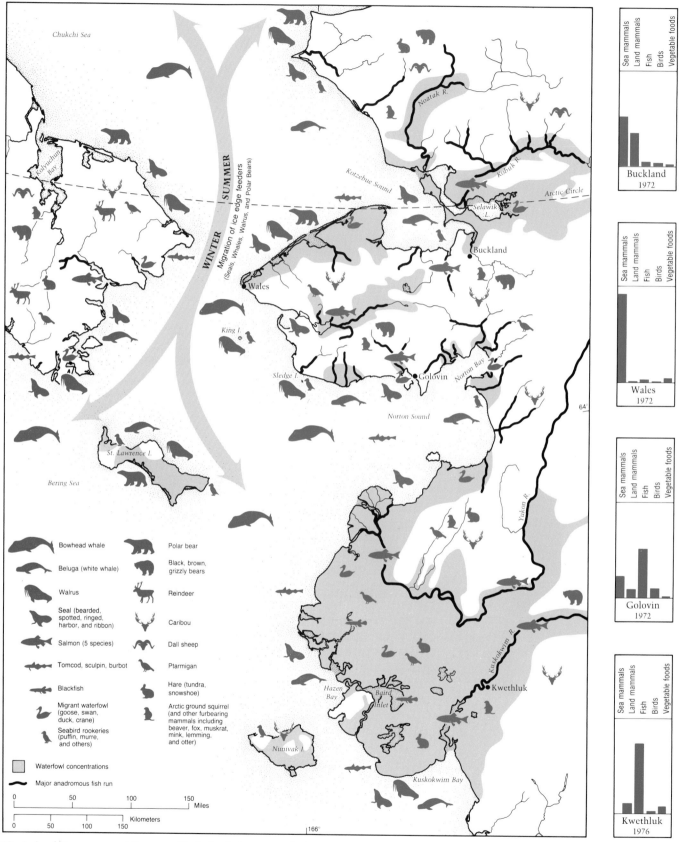

**19. Animal Resources and Resource Variation in Western Alaska**

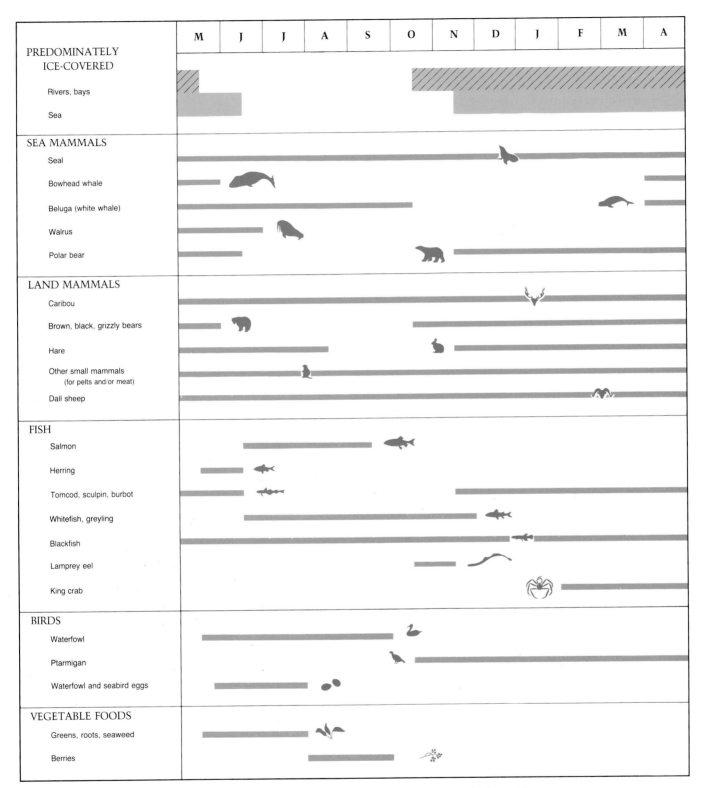

|  | M | J | J | A | S | O | N | D | J | F | M | A |
|---|---|---|---|---|---|---|---|---|---|---|---|---|
| **PREDOMINATELY ICE-COVERED** | | | | | | | | | | | | |
| Rivers, bays | | | | | | | | | | | | |
| Sea | | | | | | | | | | | | |
| **SEA MAMMALS** | | | | | | | | | | | | |
| Seal | | | | | | | | | | | | |
| Bowhead whale | | | | | | | | | | | | |
| Beluga (white whale) | | | | | | | | | | | | |
| Walrus | | | | | | | | | | | | |
| Polar bear | | | | | | | | | | | | |
| **LAND MAMMALS** | | | | | | | | | | | | |
| Caribou | | | | | | | | | | | | |
| Brown, black, grizzly bears | | | | | | | | | | | | |
| Hare | | | | | | | | | | | | |
| Other small mammals (for pelts and/or meat) | | | | | | | | | | | | |
| Dall sheep | | | | | | | | | | | | |
| **FISH** | | | | | | | | | | | | |
| Salmon | | | | | | | | | | | | |
| Herring | | | | | | | | | | | | |
| Tomcod, sculpin, burbot | | | | | | | | | | | | |
| Whitefish, greyling | | | | | | | | | | | | |
| Blackfish | | | | | | | | | | | | |
| Lamprey eel | | | | | | | | | | | | |
| King crab | | | | | | | | | | | | |
| **BIRDS** | | | | | | | | | | | | |
| Waterfowl | | | | | | | | | | | | |
| Ptarmigan | | | | | | | | | | | | |
| Waterfowl and seabird eggs | | | | | | | | | | | | |
| **VEGETABLE FOODS** | | | | | | | | | | | | |
| Greens, roots, seaweed | | | | | | | | | | | | |
| Berries | | | | | | | | | | | | |

**20. Seasonal Cycle of Food Resources from the Yukon-Kuskokwim Delta to Kotzebue Sound About 1880**

At least one type of marine algae (*Fucus*) is collected for food at low tide in spring and early summer when it is covered with herring eggs. Many other types of marine life including crabs, clams, and mussels are also utilized for food and decorations on clothing and ritual objects.

## Bering Sea Eskimo Economy

> The visit of the Walruses to the beaches of Bristol Bay occurs in June, and they remain there only a few days and sometimes only a few hours. I know of one party of hunters who camped a month on one of these hauling grounds waiting for the Walruses. Finally, becoming tired of staying in camp, all hands went egging one day and returned to find, much to their disgust, that the Walruses had been there and vanished again. (Nelson 1887:268)

In order to take advantage of the seasonal changes in wildlife Bering Sea Eskimos have developed a "seasonal round" that permits them to make efficient use of game available at different places and times during the year (figs. 19, 20). For the most part, these changes are broadly predictable from one year to the next, and this fact is the major determinant in establishing one's village location. Winter freeze-up reduces animal life to a minimum and makes any that remain difficult to catch; this creates the most serious challenge to survival for Eskimo people. With the coming of spring there is a huge influx of migratory animals that have taken refuge in southern regions, whose phased reappearance in the north is a marvel of orchestration.

For most Eskimo villages in this region late winter is a time of hardship occasioned by dwindling supplies of stored food, of oil for the lamps, and of driftwood for heating and cooking. When weather permits, women and children fish through the sea ice for crab, tomcod, flounder, and sculpin, and snare ptarmigan, while people living in the Delta live off blackfish from their traps. The men set seal nets under the ice, but there is little game stirring about. During the frequent spells of bad weather activity centers in the house and *qasgiq* where equipment and clothes are prepared for the coming spring hunts.

Finally, in early April, the signs of spring are at hand. Gulls appear, dipping and wheeling far out over the ice as cracks and leads begin to open toward the shore. Men load their kayaks on their sleds and travel out to the ice edge where they find seals gathering, fresh from their dens with pups, feeding on fish amidst the broken ice. Soon walrus and bearded seals appear, the former heading north through the broken ice to their summer ground north of Bering Strait, the latter working toward shore from their wintering places in the open ocean leads. In a successful year many animals are killed and brought home to provide the season's first fresh meat, and many hours will be spent processing food materials and blubber, making seal floats and air bladders for harpoons, cleaning intestines for gutskin clothing, and replacing worn harpoon parts with new ivory fittings.

By early May the lakes and rivers begin to thaw and snow melts from the land, revealing patches of ground and wintered-over berries which attract flocks of ptarmigan. The bays open and the sea is filled with drifting pack ice. At this time the first migratory birds arrive: loons, cranes, eiders, cormorants, and geese. Sealing slacks off with the disappearance of the pack ice, and murres, auklets, and other seafowl arrive to establish their rookeries. In the north, where caribou are still found, there is a spring hunt; bears are taken after leaving their dens, and ground squirrels are trapped for their fine fur, used in making summer parkas.

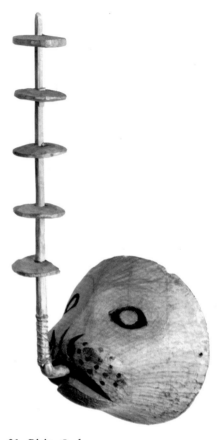

**21. Rising Seal**

While a hunter waits for a seal at the breathing hole, he remains quiet, listening for the sound of air bubbles rising to the surface, for they signal the seal's approach. This wooden hair seal maskoid, worn in a festival, has a shaft with five wooden disks attached to it representing air bubbles being exhaled as the seal rises. This imaginative piece, made of twisted sinew, wood, and blue, red, and black pigments, typifies the perception of nature and the wide-ranging creative talent of Eskimo artists and craftsmen.

Lower Yukon 33115, 11 cm (head length)

## 22. Birds

The Yukon-Kuskokwim wetlands are visited yearly by millions of migratory birds that arrive in early spring and breed in the area. Nelson and others have described the huge flocks that gather throughout western Alaska. While most species leave the north with the approach of winter, the landscape is never completely abandoned—some sea birds, snowy owls, ptarmigan, and ravens are among the birds that stay. Nelson's experience in Alaska must have influenced his later activities, for he played a major role in establishing some of the first international treaties which protect migratory birds.

St. Michael 49189, 2.4 cm; Kotzebue Sound 37722, 3.5 cm; Golovnin Bay 43313, 3.2 cm

## 23. Fish

Salt, brackish, and freshwater fish are the mainstay of Bering Sea Eskimo economy. During the summer rivers and streams team with salmon, as well as whitefish, blackfish, grayling, and herring. During the winter tomcod and blackfish continue to inhabit the inland waterways. The blackfish is particularly noteworthy, for this tiny fish has the capability of surviving being frozen!

Sfugunugumut 37179, 13 cm; Lower Kushunuk 176226, 8 cm; St. Michael 33366, 6 cm; Konigunugumut 37739, 12 cm

By late May the coastal rookeries swarm with roosting birds. Eskimo adventurers, hanging over the cliffs with nets, take hundreds of birds and eggs, many of each are eaten while others are packed in sealskin pokes and stored in the permafrost cache pits. The herring runs begin in early June, and by mid-June the first of the migratory fish strike the coast and enter the rivers where they are caught in great numbers. The king salmon appears first, followed over the course of six to eight weeks by dog salmon, king, humpback, coho, red, and others. Although present longer in the rivers, the main runs clear the coast by mid-August, leaving people there in a slack period when there are only a few seals and bottom fish. During this time fish are dried and stored, and vegetable foods like sour dock leaves and salmonberries (cloudberries) are harvested. A euphoric spirit pervades. It is a time for wandering about the land, for hunting the occasional caribou on Nunivak Island or the seal that chances by. Nets are made and repaired, and driftwood is gathered. Pods of beluga are hunted along the shallow shores and in the rivers whenever they appear, and their capture brings great rejoicing. Long trips are also made by umiak to visit relatives and to trade local materials and wares for needed goods.

During the summer months the villages along the major river channels are fully occupied with the fish runs. People from the lake country participate by moving temporarily to the rivers to fish and gather precious driftwood which they transport back into the tundra villages. Other tundra villagers remain at home fishing for whitefish, pickerel, pike, and other fish that have ascended the streams to spawn and feed on blackfish in the shallow lakes and streams. Here too, large numbers of waterfowl have gathered to nest, and are harvested with their eggs.

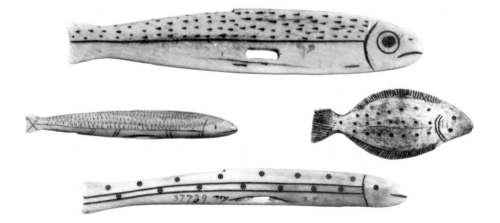

August is the time of the great bird drives on the lakes, with people from many villages teaming up to capture huge numbers of moulting ducks and geese with nets and spears. Along the coast and rivers silver salmon run and herring eggs are gathered. Throughout the land, in August and September, berries ripen and are gathered for mixing with meat and seal oil to make a delicacy known as *agoutak*. These and other vegetable foods are gathered and stored for winter use.

Despite increasingly stormy weather, coastal people continue to net seals in September, but at this time of year attention everywhere is riveted on the assembling of large flocks of migratory ducks, geese, and cranes and the stopping over of thousands of other nonresidents heading south from northern summer grounds in Alaska and Siberia.

> The last of July, and during August, the cranes frequent the hill-sides, and feast upon the berries growing there, and early in September the small flocks, which have been trooping about from one feeding ground to another, join into larger companies, until toward the last of the month—from the 18th to the 30th—they pass to the south, making the air resonant with their guttural notes as they file away toward the Yukon. The Eskimo say that once, very long ago, a pretty woman was out picking berries, when a great flock of cranes gathered near, and circling about suddenly closed about the unfortunate girl, and taking her upon their broad backs, soared away toward the sky, where they vanished, drowning the girl's cries meanwhile by their own hoarse chorus. Since taken the girl has never been seen by man, but the cranes to this day retain their habit of making a loud outcry, and soaring in flocks, in autumn, as a reminiscence of this abduction. (Nelson 1887:95)

At this time grass is cut and dried to be made into baskets, mats, and boot insoles, while driftwood collecting and fish drying continue. And in October, smelts and tomcod are caught, while the hunters make their last catch of beluga and attempt to intercept the southern walrus migration.

With the first snow huge flocks of ptarmigan congregate and fly south through the river valleys entering the eastern end of Norton Sound, where they are caught at twilight by hunters concealed on the tundra with long nets. As winter descends and the lakes and small rivers freeze, large numbers of whitefish are taken as they abandon the tundra ponds and lakes for the main river channels where they remain for the winter. Dried whitefish and summer salmon constitute much of the diet of the tundra Eskimos during the winter, when there is little fresh food other than the occasional small mammal, the ever-present but life-sustaining blackfish, and the ptarmigan.

December is the time to prepare for the festival season which continues throughout early winter when subsistence activities are curtailed by limited hours of daylight, scarcity of animals, and stormy weather. Fur trapping, important even before Europeans came, and long sled trips to visit relatives and to trade with neighboring groups or, lately, at European posts are also undertaken. As winter draws on, however, much of the festival atmosphere is dissipated as villages run out of food and fuel and can no longer proudly host the elaborate festivals of early winter. Time passes slowly, punctuated by periodic crises and hardship until the cycle is renewed by the spring seal hunt.

Although many animals are present in the Bering Sea region and its adjoining lands, few of these species occur throughout its range. Large differences in the upland and lowland ecology of the Delta, its rivers, and along the Bering Sea coast result in regional specialization on certain types

**24. Willow Root Basket**
Bering Sea Eskimos use nearly forty different kinds of vascular plants for food. Plants are also used for medicinal and ceremonial purposes and as fuel, and colors extracted from plants are used to dye skins. In addition, grass is woven into socks, containers, and mats, and spruce and willow roots are used as lashing materials and are made into coiled baskets. All plants are not available uniformly throughout western Alaska. Therefore, raw materials and manufactured items, such as this small willow root basket, are traded widely.

Cape Darby 48123, 8 cm (diameter)

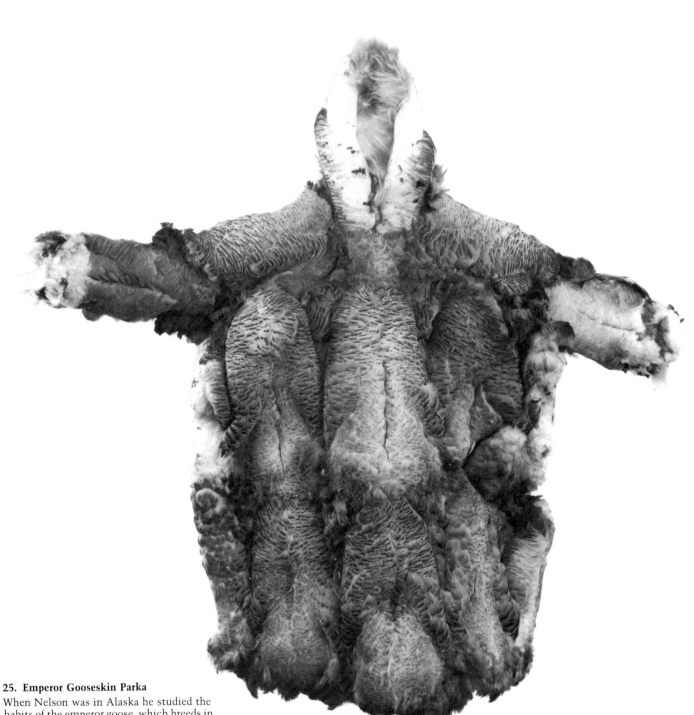

**25. Emperor Gooseskin Parka**

When Nelson was in Alaska he studied the
habits of the emperor goose, which breeds in
the area. Bering Sea Eskimos use the skins
of this bird to make parkas, such as this magnificent piece from Cape Vancouver. Transformations between men and animals figure
prominently in Bering Sea Eskimo mythology. Moving along the tundra, the man wearing this garment must have appeared to be
part man, part bird.

Cape Vancouver 48336, 148 cm

of game, and the need for exchange among peoples of different regions who require materials for tools and other goods not available in their districts. Large whales migrate past St. Lawrence Island, through Bering Strait, and along the coast of northwestern Alaska in the spring and early summer. They do not enter the shallow waters of Norton Sound off the coast south to the Kuskokwim, although dead whales may wash up there and are used. Walrus have a similar migration pattern following the receding ice pack north, but can be caught in many places in spring and fall, while beluga may be encountered along the shore and in river mouths throughout summer. Fish, birds, and other game have similar variations in regional abundance.

Regional patterns are reflected in subsistence hunting statistics comparing relative numbers of sea mammals, land mammals, fish, and birds utilized at four locations between Kotzebue and the Kuskokwim in the 1970s (fig. 19). Buckland, north of Bering Strait, derives nearly all its subsistence food from a combination of seals, walrus, white whales, and caribou and moose. The village of Wales, located at Bering Strait, specializes in hunting large sea mammals, often including large whales (although none were caught in 1972), with only meager contributions from other sources. Golovin, at the head of Norton Sound, depends on salmon and other fish combined with smaller amounts of birds, land game, and seals. Kwethluk, a village in the Kuskokwim Delta, takes seventy-six percent of its local food from fish and also has the highest vegetable values of the four.

During Nelson's time some of these differences would have been more accentuated since Wales would have been more involved in whaling and walrus hunting, while the dependency in Kwethluk on fishing would have been modified by increased takes of birds. The figures nevertheless provide a key to former economic variations that were important factors in maintaining regional cultural and linguistic diversity. Regional ecological variation also provided a buffer against the inevitable hunting failures that strike these localities at one time or another.

Notes

1. Many aspects of the geological and biological history of this land connection have been discussed in Hopkins (1967, 1973, 1979), and Hopkins and others (1982).

2. Important localities from which late Pleistocene and Holocene pollen assemblages have been described in western Alaska include several on Seward Peninsula (e.g. Colinvaux 1964; Matthews 1974; Hopkins and others 1982), St. Michael Island in Norton Sound (Ager 1982a, 1982b), Yukon Delta, and Bristol Bay (Ager 1982a), and the Pribilof Islands (Colinvaux 1981).

3. One such ash layer forms a useful marker horizon in lakes in the region (Ager 1982a, 1982b). Radiocarbon dates suggest that the ash fell about 5,000 years ago, somewhat earlier than the oldest known Eskimo cultures in the region (Giddings 1967). Other less dramatic ash falls probably occurred since that time but have not yet been documented in the region.

### 26. Caribou Herds

Herds of caribou once roamed throughout the upland regions of the Yukon-Kuskokwim. However in 1877, when Nelson arrived at St. Michael, the Nunivak Island herd was the only one in existence. The deeply worn caribou trails that crisscrossed the mainland landscape were all that remained to suggest the animals' former abundance.

The arrowshaft straightener is a vital implement in a hunter's tool kit, and is used to straighten the wooden shafts of arrows used to hunt caribou, birds, and fish. Arrowshaft straighteners are usually made out of tough fossil ivory which is found eroding out of thawing permafrost banks.

Hotham Inlet 64159, 17.5 cm

*When Raven reached the pea vine he found three other men had just fallen from the pea-pod that gave the first one [first man]. These men, like the first, were looking about them in wonder, and Raven led them away in an opposite direction from that in which he had taken the first man, afterward bringing them to firm land close to the sea. Here they stopped, and Raven remained with them a long time, teaching them how to live. He taught them how to make a fire-drill and bow from a piece of dry wood and a cord, taking the wood from the bushes and small trees he had caused to grow in hollow and sheltered places on the hillside. He made for each of the men a wife, and also made many plants and birds such as frequent the seacoast, but fewer kinds than he had made in the land where the first man lived. He taught the men to make bows and arrows, spears, nets, and all the implements of the chase and how to use them; also how to capture the seal which had now become plentiful in the sea. After he had taught them how to make kayaks, he showed them how to build houses of drift logs and bushes covered with earth.*

Nelson 1899:455–56

among the animals

# hunting the sea mammals

## Kayak and Umiak

Bering Sea Eskimos live in an unusually rich environment. Unlike most northern Eskimos, including Canadian Inuit, who live along a thin strip of Arctic coast, Bering Sea Eskimos live on major fishing rivers, near upland caribou hunting grounds, in marshy lowland tundras with rich fish and bird resources, and along the shores and islands of the Bering Sea, the most productive Arctic water body in the world. In order to tap its resources of fish, sea mammals, and birds, Eskimos have developed an ingenious technology centered around the skin-covered boat known as the kayak.

Skin boats are not unique to the Eskimo, but have been used in treeless areas of northern Europe and among the Plains Indians and some Asian groups. However, Eskimo kayaks are the most advanced of these forms, with the Bering Sea Eskimo designs being the most elegant and complex. The origin of the Eskimo kayak is not known, but it was probably developed along the southern rim of the Bering Land Bridge where people were learning to hunt large sea mammals in icy waters more than ten thousand years ago.

These circumstances require a boat that can be made with locally available materials and that is maneuverable and sturdy. It is especially important that such a boat be light enough to be hauled up on the land or onto the ice by a single hunter. The Eskimo kayak fits these criteria admirably. Its driftwood frame when enclosed in a tight skin covering produces a boat that is strong and flexible, weighing about one-third that of a comparably-sized wooden boat. It will not freeze or be cut by newly formed ice, and when handled by an experienced paddler equipped with a spray skirt tied around the cockpit it is virtually unsinkable.

A hunter's kayak is his most prized possession and symbol of manhood. In the course of its manufacture, a man not only pays attention to craftsmanship but also to symbolic and ritual matters. He begins by cannibalizing his old kayak, adding new pieces of driftwood as necessary, sometimes using naturally bent pieces of stumpwood saved for this purpose for several years. The frame is built up piece by piece and is fastened with pegs and

**27. Nunivak Island Hunting Kayak and Paddle** *qayaq, anguarun*
This kayak, with its painting of the mythological monster known as *palraiyuk*, is typical of the Nunivak Island region. Made of seal skins sewn over a wooden frame, the kayak has an enlarged cockpit capable of carrying a passenger sitting back-to-back with the paddler. Bering Sea kayak forms vary from region to region, and within a region a hunter's kayak is given personal identification marks, here seen as colored stripes on the projecting stern piece.

To protect him from the powerful and sometimes evil spirits that dwell in the sea the Bering Sea Eskimo kayak hunter carries charm images in the form of smiling male and frowning female faces lashed inside his kayak cockpit.

Nunivak Island 160345, 4.57 m; 340373a (H.B. Collins and T.D. Stewart Collection), 17.0, 17.5 cm; Norton Sound seal hunter, SI–3846

**28. Float Board Symbolism** *ă-chăl´-ûk*

Male and female symbolism may extend to the kayak float board, which usually has a hole in its center surrounded by crescents curving in opposite directions, like the male and female mouth imagery. These forms may also refer to lunar symbolism seen in dance masks.

Probably Yukon-Kuskokwim T–14611 (Collector unknown), 62 cm

lashings to make it flexible, for a rigid boat would break at the first encounter with stormy seas or ice. Then a cover of bearded seal skins is sewn onto the frame by the hunter's wife whose participation in the boat-building process has special importance.

The kayak is not ready for sea until it has been given personal and religious marks and symbols. Each man has his own identification marks, such as colored stripes or shape modifications given to bow or stern projections (Lantis 1960:85). These marks provide identification should an accident befall him at sea. Similar marks are painted on his paddles and other boat gear. To protect him from dangerous sea spirits he may paint a charm image, or *inogo* (Lantis 1946:239), along the side of his boat, while inside and known only to him or the shaman, he may place additional amulets consisting of the dried head of a loon or a carving of a sea beast that may have threatened him in the past. Finally, he secures two human face images beneath the cockpit rim on either side of his seat. One of these has a smiling male visage and the other a frowning female one. These charm images, or spirit helpers, are standard equipment for all boats in the Yukon–Kuskokwim region, linking the boat, the hunter, and his wife in a protective spiritual relationship similar to that observed in the use of male and female sea otter figurines in Aleut kayaks (Ray 1981:42). The hunter then may carve face charms on his paddle handles together with personal marks and sexual imagery.

61

### 29. Hunting Visor *sil´-kĭ-ûk´*

North of the Yukon, kayak hunters wear visors to shield their eyes from glare. This wooden visor from Pastolik is painted white and is bordered with broad red grooves. Its brim is embellished with ivory carvings of gull and walrus heads. A fan of cormorant and old-squaw tail feathers adorns the rear. South of the Yukon, visors are replaced by conical wooden helmets reflecting strong Aleut and south Alaskan Eskimo influences.

Pastolik 176207, 35 cm long

### 30. Spear Guards *nayiguyaq*

Spear guards often are carved into whimsical sea mammals and abstract forms. They are fastened to the kayak deck or to leather straps to prevent harpoons and lances from falling overboard while the hunter is approaching the quarry with his weapons at "ready" position. This group of spear guards includes a startled seal, a cormorant preparing to dive, and a beluga sounding—all portrayed in activities frequently observed from the hunter's vantage point.

Cape Darby 44300, 2.7 cm; Konigunugumut 37677, 4.7 cm; Chalitmut 37016, 3.7 cm

In addition to being a vehicle for personal and religious expression, a kayak is designed and outfitted as a complex piece of hunting technology. Its features have been developed to accommodate specialized hunting equipment used for different species of game and hunting conditions. Straps are used to retain the hunter's weapons while he paddles to the hunting place; spear guards prevent his lance from rolling off after it has been removed from the straps for ready use; and arrangements are made for holding the float board, line coils, and inflated skin floats. The kayak's cockpit is large enough to hold two paddlers if necessary, and to store extra harpoon heads, boat hooks, lance tips, lines, and meat for the homeward trip. When the kayak is used in bad weather, the hunter wears his waterproof gutskin garment, tying it over the cockpit rim, and around his face and wrists. This prevents water from entering the boat or running under the gutskin garment and makes it possible, under extreme conditions, for him to right himself after capsizing. Other modifications, such as provisions for carrying small sleds on the deck for transporting the kayak across ice pans, illustrate Eskimo ingenuity in developing technological solutions to enhance safety and efficiency while hunting large, dangerous animals under difficult conditions.

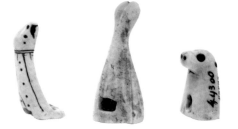

### 31. Kayak Paddles *anguarun*

When placed side-by-side the blades of these kayak paddles from Kushunuk form an image described by Nelson as a female phallic emblem, whose precise meaning he was unable to ascertain. The outer hoop and spurred hooks constituting the female portion of the image can be compared with similar motifs on women's wooden serving bowls and trays (fig. 125). Black bars and crosses on the blade and broad bilateral "Norton grooves" and double-spurred lines on the paddle shafts probably represent both regional and personal ownership marks. The rich symbolic content of the specimens is completed with smiling male and frowning female images, similar to those found on boat cockpit plaques, lightly incised on opposite sides of the paddle handles.

Kushunuk 36057 (pair), 150 cm, 149 cm

### 32. Cord Attachers *kâñ´-ĭ*

This miniature convocation of ivory cord attachers includes images of a fox, a sea parrot, and men and women whose faces are fringed with parka hoods. According to custom men are nearly always portrayed smiling while the women frown. This identification is confirmed here by the position of labrets, men's being worn under the corners of the mouth and women's in the center of their lower lip. In this group one of the female images has slit eyes, a motif sometimes used to denote a masked or false face image. Portrayed here on implements used to attach lines and tools to the kayak, the cord attachers show the pervasive use of male and female charm images in sea hunting equipment—also occurring on paddles, cockpit images, and float boards. This type of cord attacher made from the peglike teeth of walrus or beluga is found throughout the region. It is used strung on a short loop of line. The looped end of a second line is passed between the attacher and the end of the first loop and is secured in the groove around the neck of the piece.

Kushunuk 37063, 37054, 37065, 37067; Askinuk 37064; Kaialigamut 37229; Cape Vancouver 43624; Sabotnisky 48950; Sledge Island 44709 (all ca. 1.5–2.0 cm wide)

### 33. Boat Hooks *nĭkh-chú-i-ûk*

Large-pronged boat hooks are used to retrieve floating harpoon gear and captured animals at sea, while small hooks are used to extract items from inside the ends of the kayak. The King Island hook illustrated with paddles is decorated in the northern style with fluted surfaces and fine-spurred line engravings. Southern styles often portray animals, seen in this antler hook depicting a walrus from the coastal village of Askinuk. A land carnivore, probably a wolf, is portrayed on an antler hook from the interior settlement at Big Lake, which also bears the double-spurred mark commonly found on hunting equipment in the Yukon–Kuskokwim region.

King Island 45413, 149 cm; Askinuk 37939, 25 cm; Big Lake 36421, 25 cm

Kayaks are made in a number of regional styles—there being greater variation between those used between Bering Strait and the Kuskokwim than there is across the entire North American Arctic between Point Hope, Greenland, and Labrador. In many cases this variation is meant only to reinforce the identity of local social groups, while also serving to make the travelers' identity known at a safe distance. However, functional considerations are also important. Boats used in the quieter waters of Norton Sound or on the Yukon River are narrower and lighter than those used in open sea conditions around Nunivak Island or in Bering Strait. South of Nunivak Island, kayaks decrease in height and become longer and more slender, reaching their extreme in the Aleut area, where two- and three-holed boats, called bidarkas after their Russian name, are common.

In addition to kayaks, larger skin boats known as umiaks are used by Bering Sea Eskimos. These boats are also found among the St. Lawrence Islanders and Siberian Eskimos and are present in Canada and Greenland. Made with stout wood frames covered with walrus hides, their large storage

**34. Umiak Model** *angyaq*
Nelson had no way to transport a large u-miak to the Smithsonian Institution, so he commissioned this model of a Norton Sound vessel, accurate to the smallest detail of its frame and lashing, and equipped with marked paddles and a grass mat sail. European introductions of the period are evident in its square rig, halyard blocks, and oars. Care had to be taken in long voyages to dry and oil the umiak every few days or its skin and lashings would stretch and collapse from the frame. Long-distance travel was therefore potentially hazardous, especially for island dwellers in stormy seas.

St. Michael 38882, 119 cm

### 35. Seal Inua Mask

*Then [Raven] made different kinds of seals, and their names and habits were explained to man.* Raven Myth

The seal is the staff of life for coastal Eskimos, providing food, heat, light, and myriad materials for clothing and technology. To insure its continued abundance and availability the seal spirits are entreated in many ways. Upon killing a seal the hunter placates its thirsty departing spirit with a drink of fresh water from his flask. Seals are honored especially in the Bladder Festival, in mythology, and in storytelling. The *inua* of the bearded seal (*E. barbatus*) seen in the dance mask from the Lower Kuskokwim has a masked semihuman countenance. Special attention has been given to the seal's head, which has blackened eyes and red nostrils and a menacing tongue of baleen.

Cape Vancouver 37654, 29 cm

capacity and seaworthiness make them suitable for moving large groups of people and equipment, for hunting walrus and whales, and for trading and conducting war. Renditions of umiak scenes are favorite subjects of drill bow art.

Umiaks are traditionally propelled by paddles or by sails made of twined grass mats. Recently oars and cloth sails have been introduced by Europeans. In the rough waters of Bering Strait, additional buoyancy is achieved by erecting hide flaps above the gunwales and by lashing inflated seal floats along the sides of the boat. In this way even severe storms can be weathered. Voyages across Bering Strait are frequently made by Siberian Eskimos, who are much respected for their nautical prowess. In the past Siberians used their skills to great advantage raiding and waging war among the Alaskans. Like kayaks, umiaks can be drawn up on shore or upon ice pans with the aid of bone blocks and tackles. Their serviceability is only offset by the danger of their being blown far out to sea by storms. Unless land can be reached within a few days, the water-saturated walrus hide relaxes off the frame, drowning all on board.

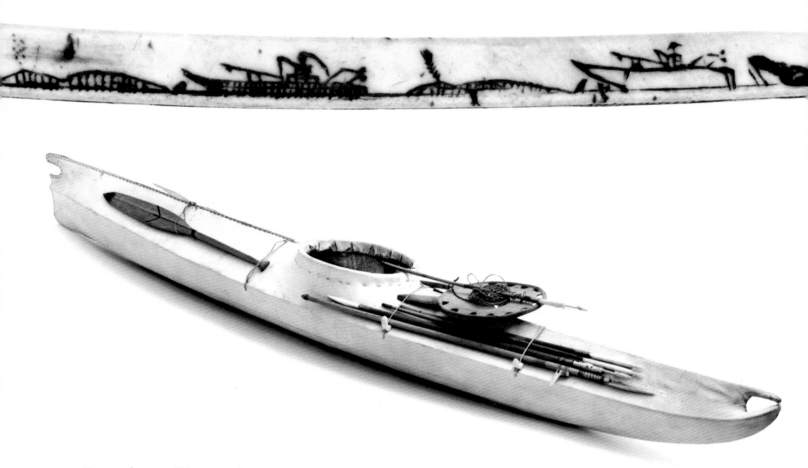

## Preparing to Hunt at Sea

By the time a man reaches adulthood he has been thoroughly trained by his father and other men in the methods of hunting various sea mammals. Long days and nights have been passed watching the men in the *qasgiq*, the men's house, make harpoons and darts and listening to tales of hunts and the habits of the animals. Experience has also been gained through practice, first with toy weapons and later with small versions of harpoons. It is important that a man not only understand hunting methods and equipment, developed over many generations by his ancestors, but also give attention to the spirits of the animals. Here the practices and counsel of the shaman and the oldest hunters, who specialize in these matters, are important, for it is easy to offend these spirits. Failing to perform certain rituals before, during, and after the hunt may endanger not only one's own safety, but can bring misfortune on the whole village.

In addition to one's weapons, proper personal attire is called for. A man's wife or mother will have made a young hunter a waterproof suit from transparent seal gut, inserting bits of feathers and auk bill parts into its seams for decoration. The hunter may also blacken his eyes to reduce the glare from the water, and he will customarily wear a visor or conical hat for the same purpose. Such items are treasured pieces of clothing that are decorated with ivory animals and birds and backed with an array of feathers, making the hunter's head resemble the body and fanned tail of a floating bird. These hats also may be painted with sexual imagery.

**36. Kayak Model** *qayaq*

This kayak is the finest in the Smithsonian Institution's model collection. It faithfully portrays the vessel and paraphernalia of a Norton Sound hunter with float board and harpoon, darts, lances, boat hooks, bird spear, spear guards, and spare paddle. The kayak's float board has two semilunar cutouts whose forms resemble the male and female face motifs found on other boating gear.

Similar shapes are often used at the entrance hole through the floor of the *qasgiq* where the shapes symbolize the interface between the land and the sea through which shamans and the spirits of dead sea mammals pass during the Bladder Festival.

Port Clarence (J.H. Turner Collection) 153656, 80 cm

# Eskimo Harpoons

The techniques used for hunting sea mammals have been understood by Bering Sea Eskimos from time immemorial. The essential implement is the harpoon head. This device has been developed especially for hunting large mammals and fish living in the oceans. These animals cannot be tracked or intercepted as land animals can. Nor is it easy to kill them in the instant when they appear at the surface of the water even if they are close to the hunter. To hunt sea mammals and fish one must first secure a line into their flesh or hide so that their escape can be impeded until death blows can be administered by another weapon. Two varieties of harpoon heads are used for this purpose: nontoggling or barbed harpoons, and toggling harpoons. The nontoggling form is probably the older kind and is commonly used in the ice-free regions of the southern Bering Sea and Pacific Ocean. This implement has barbed points and a line hole in its butt end and is thrown with a female-socketed harpoon shaft. Because the harpoon head is only held in the animal's flesh by its short barbs, it can easily be torn out. For this reason it is released from the hunter's direct control and set loose attached to inflated seal skins or bladder floats which tire the animal until it can be approached and killed with a lance or club. Similar harpoon heads are also used by peoples of the Northwest Coast and elsewhere for hunting sea mammals and large fish in ice-free waters. Their use diminishes north of the Aleutian Islands and is largely replaced by the toggling form north of Bering Strait.

Toggling harpoon heads are usually pointed on both ends and have their line holes near the midsection of the harpoon head. They are attached to the end of a slender foreshaft whose purpose is to thrust the head through the animal's skin and blubber and into its flesh. When the line tightens, the angled spur at the base of the harpoon head turns the head sideways toggling it beneath the blubber. This system holds the animal fast, and makes possible a direct connection to the hunter or his boat. It also insures that the animal cannot free itself by breaking off the line end of the harpoon on a block of ice or a rock. For this reason Eskimos living in areas of seasonal ice cover use this implement rather than the nontoggling form. The toggling harpoon head also makes hunting at breathing holes effective.

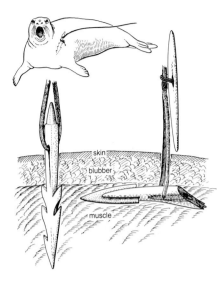

**37. Harpoon Point Forms**

Two forms of harpoon points are used by Bering Sea Eskimos. For hunting sea mammals in open water with float gear, Eskimos south of Bering Strait frequently use barbed harpoon points which hold the animal by catching beneath its blubber and hide. This type of harpoon is fine for hunting small sea mammals with drag and float equipment, but it can pull out of large animals if the restraining line is fastened to a boat or a man on the sea ice. Barbed harpoon points also fail when the animal breaks off the butt end against a rock or ice floe. The toggling harpoon point avoids these problems by being forced deeply into the flesh on the end of a slender foreshaft. When the line tightens and begins to pull the harpoon out, its oblique basal spur twists the point sideways, toggling it firmly beneath the animal's blubber. Barbed harpoon points are therefore used in summer and in open water; toggling forms in winter and when sea ice is about. Toggling points are the predominant form used north of Bering Strait, where sea ice persists throughout the year.

**38. Toggling Harpoon Sizes**

Different sized harpoons are used to secure different sized sea mammals. These harpoon heads from Bering Strait are graded for small seals, large seals and beluga, walrus, and large whales. They were tipped with stone, bone, or ivory points in early days, but by the time Nelson arrived iron and copper were in common use except in parts of Norton Sound where the prohibition against use of metal in beluga hunting was observed. The oblique spur at the base of the harpoon causes it to twist sideways under the animal's blubber and skin, safely toggling the line beneath the animal's blubber.

Cape Nome 44484, 7 cm; Sledge Island 44694, 10 cm; St. Lawrence Island 63230, 11 cm; 63492, 21 cm

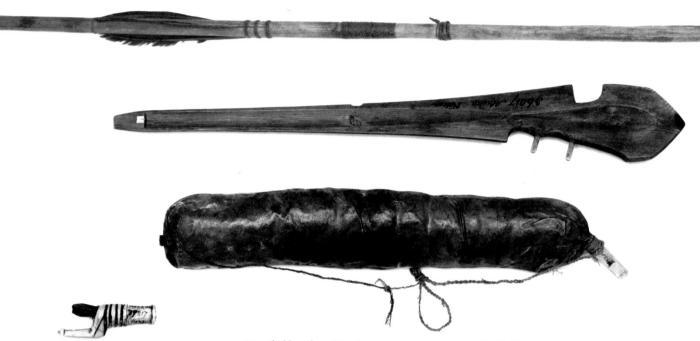

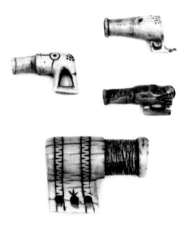

## 39. Bladder Float Nozzles

Floats for bladder darts are made from the air bladders or intestines of seals. They are fitted with ivory inflation nozzles displaying a wide range of forms and decorations. A concave plate serves to lash the nozzle to the dart shaft while the tube end is attached to the bladder. Three small nozzles illustrate forms typical of the Lower Kuskokwim. The larger nozzle from Norton Sound bears a decorative "tooth" pattern common in this region and a "raven's foot" totem mark. Another nozzle is carved in the form of a wolf's head. Similar predator effigies are found on bladder dart socketpieces south of the Yukon.

Golovnin Bay 33298, 5.5 cm; Konigunugumut 37818, 3.5 cm; 37814, 4 cm; 37817, 5 cm; Lower Kuskokwim 36977, 4 cm

## 40. Bladder Dart

Bladder darts are used by kayak hunters for capturing small seals. A bladder dart consists of a short round shaft fitted with a heavy bone or ivory socketpiece at its tip, into which is fitted a barbed harpoon whose line is fastened to the middle of the dart shaft. Sinew wrappings reinforce the shaft and bind its cormorant feather fletching to the butt end, which is marked with a single red-and two black-painted ownership stripes. The dart is propelled with the aid of a throwing board whose hook engages a concavity in the end of the dart. An inflated bladder made from a section of seal intestine normally is lashed to the shaft to keep the dart and dead seal from sinking. This dart is missing its bladder.

Using the throwing board, whose length is taken as the distance from the hunter's elbow to the end of his forefinger, increases the power and speed of the dart by effectively lengthening the arm. Designed to suit individual sizes and tastes, the throwing board is one of the handiest and most elegant of Eskimo tools and is frequently embellished with totem animals and personal marks.

Norton Sound (L. Turner Collection) 29806, 130 cm; Kaialigamut 36017, 49 cm; Chalitmut 36209, 40 cm

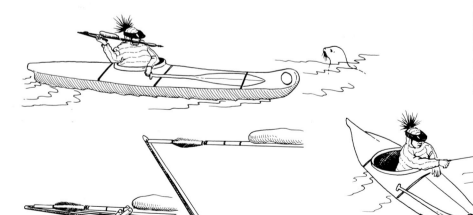

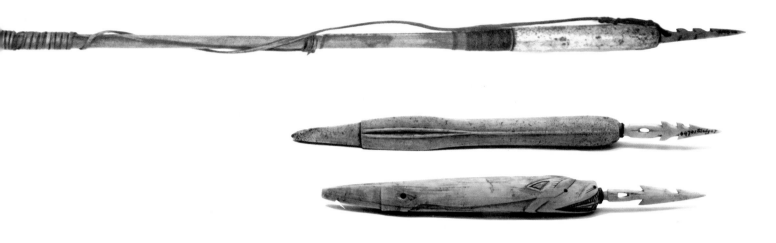

## Spring Hunt

**41. Bladder Dart Socketpieces and Points**

Bladder dart socketpieces often display land or sea predators whose cunningness is engaged spiritually to enhance the hunter's success. These harpoon parts portray a Kuskokwim wolf with green-pigmented eyes and ferocious red teeth, and an abstract (beluga?) form. They may be compared with the simple cylindrical northern form from Norton Sound. Points are mounted in inset split wooden plugs that help absorb the shock of impact. The bases of southern harpoons are pointed while northern forms are tongue shaped.

Lower Kuskokwim 38442, 22 cm; Konigunugumut 37746, 9 cm (point); Chalitmut 36339, 27 cm (socketpiece lengths only); Sledge Island 44701, 8.8 cm (point)

**42. Bladder Dart Hunting**

The bladder dart is thrown with either an overhand or sidearm cast, depending on the kind of game and the condition of the waves. When struck, the animal's escape is impeded by the dart shaft, which is rigged to drag crosswise, tiring the seal so the hunter can overtake it and dispatch it with a lance or braining stone. A hunter may carry several darts in case he encounters more than one seal at a time, or he misses his first cast, or his quarry begins to sink.

In May, with the coming of open water, hunters drag their kayaks across the shore ice on small sleds to the open leads and moving pack ice beyond. Here they find large numbers of seals basking on the ice and feeding on tomcod and other fish. Launching their kayaks they begin one of the most productive hunts of the year, for the seals are concentrated in a small area, and there are many young which have not yet learned to be wary of man.

The principal weapon used for the spring hunt and for capturing small seals in open water in summer and early fall is the bladder dart. This harpoon, only slightly longer than a man's arm, has an ivory or bone socketpiece into which is inserted a detachable barbed point fastened to the dart shaft with a short length of thong. An inflated air bladder made from a section of seal intestine keeps the dart from sinking should the hunter miss his target and also insures that the dead animal will float and be recovered. The bladder dart is thrown with the throwing board and may or may not have a feathered shaft. Norton Sound darts are featherless—those from Bering Strait and the Kuskokwim have only one feather, while Nunivak Island and Cape Vancouver darts have two. The bladder dart is found among the Pacific Eskimo and Aleut, and north as far as Bering Strait. Further north its function has been taken up by the light toggling harpoon.

Hunting magic and animal symbolism are prominent features of bladder dart hunting. Feathers of sea-hunting birds like cormorants and certain hawks are used for fletching, and socketpieces are embellished with the carvings of otters, ermine, and mythical wolflike beasts whose toothed mouths embrace the harpoon points and their sockets. Such figures sometimes represent the totem of the hunter or beasts intended to provide special power or fatality to the dart.

In addition to hunting seals from kayaks people take advantage of ring seals found basking in large congregations upon the ice floes. At such times a white shirt is worn to camouflage the hunter against the ice, so he can disembark from his kayak and rapidly approach the seals before they become alarmed. Ring seals are also hunted in the rivers as they commonly ascend the Yukon some 30–50 miles, well above the limits of tidal action, to feed on the salmon and other migratory fish.

69

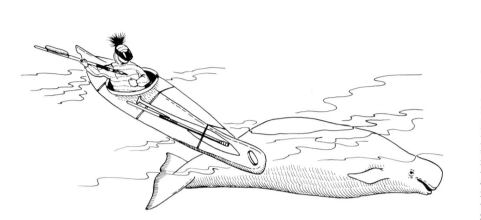

## Beluga and Mukluk

Another important quarry also known to ascend the large rivers is the beluga, or white whale. This animal has a special significance to Bering Sea people and is accorded the utmost respect. When a beluga is caught a song is offered to its spirit, and it is customary in many regions never to hunt for these whales with iron-bladed harpoons nor to cut them with iron knives. Beluga and bearded seals are hunted with large harpoons that are similar to but heavier than bladder darts. These weapons are thrown by hand, aided by intricately carved ivory finger rests, and their socketpieces are sometimes decorated with wolf effigies.

Beluga frequent the shores of Norton Sound and the mouths of the Yukon and Kuskokwim rivers from May until November, when they are forced south by the ice. They may be encountered in large numbers in the river mouths and sandy flats, at which time they are surrounded and driven into the shallow water and killed. Beluga are also taken with nets in the fall when stormy conditions and cloudy water make it difficult for them to see the mesh. Nelson records an encounter with these animals:

> Along the low, flat coast from Saint Michaels to the Kuskokwim River are many tide creeks running back into blackfish marshes. From midsummer until these streams freeze over they abound in tom-cods. In pursuit of these the White Whales go up these streams regularly every night after darkness has settled over the land an hour or two, and while camping on the banks of these streams I have heard dozens of them blowing with a quick, forcible, hissing or sighing sound as they hunted up and down the creek. They hunt about the Yukon mouths at night in the same way and are found just off shore among the flats and sand-bars during the day. (Nelson 1887:289)

**43. Throwing Harpoon Technology** *ăkh´-ĭ-līgh´-ut*

A throwing harpoon similar to but longer than the bladder dart is used to capture large seals and beluga. It has a bladder float and a heavier socketpiece with a detachable harpoon secured to the wooden shaft by a short length of thong. These harpoons are cast by hand without the throwing board, aided by an ivory finger rest. South of Bering Strait, ivory finger rests are often carved as seals, to the north they are shaped as polar bears. Shafts are tapered from foreshaft to butt end to reduce unnecessary weight and, in Norton Sound, have broad longitudinal grooves on each side—a stylistic feature of the area that also lightens the weapon. These harpoons are also used to attach a second float to an animal that is in danger of sinking. When the animal has been sufficiently weakened, it is killed with the lance and towed to shore.

Pastolik 33933, 150 cm

**44. Finger Rests** *tegumiarun*

While simple finger rests take the form of lugs and pegs, most are delicate carvings of animals, like this polar bear head with its brow furrow and eyes and nostrils of polished baleen from Cape Nome, or the seal with polished wood inlays from St. Michael.

Cape Nome 44532, 2.5 cm; St. Michael (J.H. Turner Collection) 129188, 2 cm

**45. Throwing Harpoon Socketpiece and Point**

To make long throws possible the throwing harpoon must be light yet still have enough punch to force the point through a thick layer of skin and blubber. This is accomplished by placing a heavy socketpiece at the forward end of the spear, into which the point is set in a cushioning plug of wood. This socketpiece from Shaktolik has been engraved into a wolf's head with pointed ears and eyebrows. The whiskers are shown, and the teeth reveal the stylized "tooth pattern" commonly found on artifacts from the Norton Sound region. The ivory point from Chalitmut illustrates an application of the skeletal/lifeline motif often found on weapon tips and other tools, and it may function both as a spiritual aid and as the hunter's identifying mark.

Shaktolik 38440, 13.5 cm; Chalitmut 37974, 16 cm

Extending his observations to the use of this animal by the Eskimo, Nelson continues:

> The flesh of a young beluga is tender and not unpalatable, but is rather coarse and dry. The fat, or blubber, is clear and white, and is considered to be much superior to seal-oil by the Eskimo and Indians. The intestines are made into waterproof garments or floats, and the sinews are very much prized. Their small ivory teeth are carved into toys or ornamental pendants. The skin is made into strong lines or very durable boot-soles. When well cooked the skin is considered choice eating and is really pleasantly flavored. This refers to the epidermis, which is nearly half an inch thick, soft, and has a flavor recalling that of chestnuts. (Nelson 1887:290)

Beluga and bearded seals are also captured with a large version of the toggling harpoon. This harpoon, which is not illustrated here, is similar to the light ice-hunting harpoon and may be used both from the kayak and from the edge of the fast ice in spring. The harpoon line is not attached to the harpoon shaft as in drag float hunting, but is joined to a long thong whose other end is fastened to a U-shaped apparatus known as the float board. This board, which is often decorated with crescentic male and female "mouth" motifs, detaches from the kayak and drags crosswise behind the fleeing whale or seal. If the animal is large, the hunter may attach another length of harpoon line and a large inflated sealskin float to the float board to insure that the animal does not escape.

The bearded seal, known as *mukluk* to Eskimos, is the largest and most important seal frequenting these waters. Full-grown males may weigh between 600 and 800 pounds. Nelson found its flesh "excellent eating when freshly killed, and the blubber is tasteless and much like very fat pork. If kept a few days, however the flesh and blubber become rank and repulsive to any but an educated taste" (1887:260). Its importance to Eskimos, in addition to food, is for the many products it provides, including rawhide thong, boot sole leather, kayak and umiak covers, bladder floats, and gut-skin for clothing.

71

**46. Lances** *kapun*

Lances used to dispatch sea mammals include a simple northern variety found around Bering Strait, seen here with a finger rest and a fixed blade of chipped stone. The shaft is made from hemlock wood, a Pacific Coast forest species that must have been imported into Norton Sound by Europeans. The more complex southern form has a tapered shaft with a finger rest and a heavy, ornamented socketpiece of ivory made to accommodate detachable lance points that remain in the animal after each thrust, enlarging its wounds.

Kigiktauik 33889, 198 cm; Anogogmut 36058, 175 cm

## Killing Lance

When a hunter has captured a sea mammal with his harpoon and it is weak enough to be approached without danger, he assembles his lance and prepares for the kill. The lance is slipped out from its restraining straps, and one of the detachable points is taken from its storage bag inside the cockpit and fitted into the ivory socket at the end of the shaft. A lance tip is made to fit snugly into the socket, but loosely enough so that when the lance is thrust into the thrashing animal the tip detaches and remains in the flesh, causing laceration and enlargement of the wound. Several lance stabs may be necessary to kill the animal, but should it escape for some reason it carries the hunter's marked lance and possibly his harpoon. Other hunters finding the animal dead or recapturing it can tell who struck the first blow and are obliged to present the animal to that hunter. In addition, should a number of hunters be involved in killing several beluga or seals, the marked lances identify the owners of the dead animals. In all cases, a hunter is obliged to share the meat and blubber according to carefully defined principles.

Lances, being the immediate instrument of death, are given special treatment, and like a hunter's harpoons, are made carefully and decorated with certain marks and symbols. Their wooden shafts are carved from spruce in the Yukon–Kuskokwim region where shorter, more robust shafts are used than in Norton Sound and the Seward Peninsula. Nunivak Island lances are the most elaborate. These pieces usually have ivory foreshafts fitted with slate or iron blades and small ivory spurs to keep the lances from dislodging from the animals' wounds. Sometimes these lances are decorated with *palraiyuks* or totemic animal symbols. Lances from the Yukon–Kuskokwim are also marked with green- or red-painted bands and

**47. Losh Box** *u-lú-tĭk*

This wooden box takes the form of a fat losh, also known as a burbot, or ling codfish. The losh has ivory eyes with wood inlays, an incised mouth, and gills. The tail is doubled back beside its bulging body. A lid opens the belly revealing a stomach cavity used for storing spear points.

Cape Nome 44459, 19 cm

### 48. Lance Tips

Changing times and environmental conditions are evident in these lance points from Norton Sound. Around Bering Strait contact with European whalers has resulted in iron and bottle glass replacing traditional stone points, though the points are still bound with baleen lashings. In the more remote shallow regions where there are no whales or whalers, slate and chipped stone points continue to be used, but in the absence of baleen are lashed with sinew. All, however, have ownership marks to identify the hunter's tools and quarry.

Cape Nome 45458, 39 cm; 44647, 36.5 cm; Unalakleet 38607, 42 cm; Cape Vancouver 37389, 27 cm

### 49. Lance with Decorated Sheath

Wooden sheaths protect lance tips from becoming dull or piercing the kayak covering. This fine specimen, made from a block of wood that has been split, hollowed out, and then rejoined, has the likeness of a whiskered wolf. North of the Yukon, lance tip sets are bagged in leather pouches filled with straw rather than in individual sheaths. Nunivak Island lance tips frequently have spurs to prevent the weapon from becoming dislodged from the wounded animal.

Nunivak Island (W.H. Dall Collection) 16350, 27 cm (lance), 20 cm (sheath)

have a variety of incised markings representing totems such as raven's feet, wolves, and, not infrequently, sexual symbols similar to ones found on the set of Kushunuk paddle blades (fig. 31).

In western and northern Norton Sound people use long and thin lance points. Northern people mark their lances differently than do southerners, preferring to use stylized wolf and raven totems, small notches, and inscribed rings and spirals. Their use of materials is also different. Northern lance lashings are of baleen, willow, and birch rather than of sinew, and lance tip shafts are made out of hardwoods like birch and willow. In one case a lance from Kigiktauik (381855) has been fashioned from Douglas fir. The wood was probably imported into Norton Sound by European traders or whalers from the Northwest Coast.

Whereas southern peoples use slate for their points, northerners use chert and slate and frequently will substitute these for chipped bottle glass, iron, and copper. In both areas the use of iron and copper is increasing with the relaxation of traditional taboos and the increasing abundance of metal.

Individual wooden lance sheaths protect the southern lance tips. These exquisitely fashioned sheaths are made from blocks of wood that have been split, hollowed out, and rejoined with lashings and skin coverings sometimes made from the penis sheaths of certain animals. These lance sheaths show considerable variation, probably expressing regional as well as personal styles. Northern lances are stored collectively in bags holding a dozen or so points. No special protection is given these points except for the grass padding within the bag.

## Eggs and Sea Birds

In the spring great flocks of waterfowl head north into the Bering Sea region to establish breeding colonies among the craggy islands or to mate and nest in the marshy tundra country of the Yukon–Kuskokwim Delta.

The arrival of waterfowl is eagerly awaited for, in addition to being a harbinger of spring, they provide meat and eggs, skins for winter parkas, colorful feathers and down for masks, and parts to ornament baskets and fishing hooks. Also, bird hunting is always a favorite activity among the Eskimo of this region, who have devised a number of ingenious ways to capture them.

> Along the northern coast of Norton sound the people gather the eggs of sea fowl from the cliffs by means of seal nets, which they roll into a cable and lash in that shape with cords; the nets are then lowered over the cliffs and the upper ends firmly fastened to rocks or stakes. The egg gatherer fastens a sash about his waist, removes his boots, and goes down the net, hand over hand, to the ledges below, the meshes of the net forming excellent holding places for the fingers and toes; the hunter then fills the inside of his frock above the sash with the eggs and clings to the top of the cliff.
>
> In a camp at Cape Thompson, on the Arctic coast, I saw many dead murres which had been caught by letting a man down by a long line from the top of the cliff to the ledges where the birds were breeding; there he used a scoop net and caught as many birds as he wished by putting it over them while they sat stupidly on their eggs. . . . (Nelson 1899:133)

**50. Bird Spears** *nuusaarpiit*
Delicate light spears are cast by hand or with the throwing board to capture waterfowl when they are moulting and are unable to fly. The special feature of these spears, two varieties of which are found in Norton Sound, is the set of three or four divergent prongs whose inner surfaces have rows of back-slanting barbs. The multiple points not only provide a wider striking circle than a single point but also gather up wing tips, feet, and necks, wedging them among the prongs. With such spears several birds may be caught in a single throw. Both specimens have flat butt ends to fit the throwing board. When cast sidearm they skim the surface sending up small jets of spray from the wavetops as they speed toward their target. Wary birds that would otherwise dive seem to be confused by the skimming action of the spears and do not realize the danger until too late.

Yukon Delta 33854, 160 cm; Unalakleet 33844, 142 cm

**51. Chukchi Duck Hunters**
Nelson photographed this group of Chukchi men at Cape Wankarem where he observed them hunting eider ducks with the bolas. At such times the Chukchi wear this implement on their heads, ready for throwing at an instant's notice should ducks come within range.

NAA–6924

In the spring and late summer, birds are caught by hunters with bird spears which can be thrown with great accuracy to distances of 30–50 yards. They are often thrown overhand, so as to strike from above, but if the birds are wary and dive quickly the spears are thrown underhand. For throwing at groups of birds, the hunter casts so that the spear twists sideways as it approaches, striking a glancing blow and gathering the necks, feet, or wings of several birds between its prongs.

North of the Yukon, Eskimos use the bolas sling to capture low-flying ducks and geese as they crisscross between points of land and islands. Being extremely fast in flight, the birds cannot be speared or shot with arrows, but their path often takes them within sling shot of hunters concealed behind rocks or in boats.

> When in search of game the bolas is worn around the hunter's head with the balls resting on his brow. When a flock of ducks, geese, or other wild fowl pass overhead, at an altitude not exceeding 40 or 50 yards, the hunter by a quick motion untwists the sling. Holding the united ends of the cords in his right hand, he seizes the balls with the left and draws the cords so tight that they lie parallel to each other; then, as the birds come within throwing distance, he swings the balls around his head once or twice and casts them, aiming a little in front of the flock. When the balls leave the hand they are close together, the cords trail behind, and they travel so swiftly that it is difficult to follow their flight with the eye. As they begin to lose their impetus they acquire a gyrating motion, and spread apart until at their highest point they stand out to the full extent of the cords in a circle four or five feet in diameter; they seem to hang thus for a moment, then, if nothing has been encountered, turn and drop to the earth. . . . if a bird is struck it is enwrapped by the cords and its wings so hampered that it falls helpless. (Nelson 1899:134–35)

### 52. Bolas

The bolas is a highly effective weapon for taking birds when they fly near a hunting blind or hide. Bolas slings used on land are generally made of stone, ivory, or similar heavy materials which give them greater range. This bolas was collected from St. Lawrence Island where it was used to hunt geese from boats. Its balls are made of conifer wood and will float, the cords are of braided sinew, and the handle is a bundle of bird quills.

St. Lawrence Island 63258, ca. 6.5 cm (ball length)

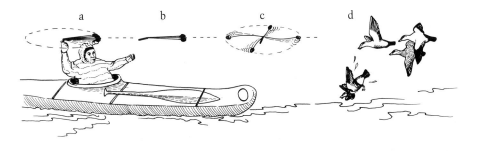

**53. Toggling Harpoon and Line** *ä-jä´-kut*

A light form of toggling harpoon is used for catching large seals and beluga from kayaks in summer and at ice holes or at the floe edge in winter and spring. This harpoon has a grooved, robust shaft with an antler ice pick, an ivory finger rest, and a bulbous antler socketpiece. The spurred antler toggling harpoon head is attached to the shaft by means of a rodlike foreshaft whose larger end is inserted in a shallow depression in the socketpiece. The smaller end fits into the socket in the base of the harpoon head.

Harpoon lines are made by cutting a continuous spiral strip from the hide of the bearded seal, whose skin is the proper thickness for such line. The width of the cut determines the strength of the thong—seal harpoon line generally being about 4 millimeters in diameter and having a tensile strength of several hundred pounds. This line, obtained at Nunivak, is 30 meters long and is composed of three separate segments: a harpoon loop (with foreshaft attached), a main thong, and a hand toggle grip. The grip indicates this line was last used for ice hole or floe edge hunting without the float. Each segment is attached to the other with ivory line fasteners.

Kigiktauik 33888, 186 cm; Nunivak Island 175673, 30 m

## Seal Hunt

Ice hunting for seals is only one of many activities that occupy Bering Sea Eskimos during the winter months. Unlike people of northern Alaska and northern Canada, who have fewer resources and a longer period of darkness, Bering Sea people have a wide range of subsistence alternatives and usually have stored supplies of fish or meat. For coastal groups, however, hunting and netting seals on the ice provide an important source of winter food and oil.

Breathing hole sealing begins as soon as the ice is firm enough for travel. Equipped with a light toggling harpoon fitted with an ice pick, and wearing ice creepers to keep him from slipping on the smooth new ice, a hunter sets out to explore for seal breathing holes. These are often visible from a distance by their domed appearance, the result of frozen spray and moisture from the seal's breath. Finding one, the hunter thrusts a long stalk of grass down through the dome until it comes to rest floating in the middle of the hole below. When the seal approaches, the hunter detects its presence by the sound of rising bubbles. He steadies himself, and when the straw begins to rise he strikes downward through the snow dome into the seal's

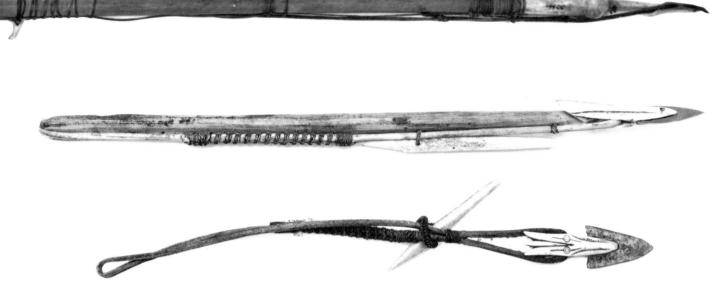

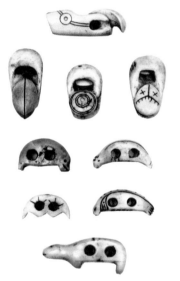

### 54. Line Attachers

Two types of attachers fasten loops at the ends of lines. Bar attachers have two parallel holes and are used to secure the detachable harpoon head to the float line. Block attachers have holes at right angles and employ a grooved lug as a fastening post to secure the line to the float, or to the toggle handle for ice hunting. Animal effigies tend to be used on the bar forms and are often positioned closest to the harpoon and its quarry. Geometric forms are more commonly found at the remote end of the line.

Block attachers: Nunivak Island 48317; Agiukchugumut 35999; Lower Kuskokwim 38563; Unalakleet 33445 Bar attachers: Cape Vancouver 43625; Paimut 37036; Kushunuk 37109; Chalitmut 37219; 37112 (all 3–4 cm long)

### 55. Harpoon Heads

Toggling harpoon heads display an elegance that results from combining art and technology. These two antler specimens show the basic functional features of the tool, seen in front and side views. The heads are fitted with short thong loops to which the float line is attached with a line fastener. Foreshafts are also attached to the harpoon thong. Until ready to be fitted on the harpoon shaft, the heads are stored neatly on slender wooden mounts.

Kigiktauik 38753, 8 cm; Chalitmut 37380, 7 cm (points)

### 56. Visual Pun: Polar Bear Meats Seal

This attacher is a humorous rendition of a close encounter between a seal and a polar bear. On the base, not seen, is the image of another bear, formed from parts of the first two animals. All of these images are functional components of the attacher. Location of visual tricks challenges the ingenuity of the artisan just as the tricks themselves surprise and delight the beholder.

Paimut 37218, 3.7 cm

skull, trying to kill it instantly. If not, a struggle ensues in which the seal tries to escape by pulling the hunter through the small breathing hole. The latter has only to hold firm to the line until the seal expires by drowning. He then enlarges the hole, hauls the seal up on the ice, and drags it home using a short towline with a drag handle formed in the shape of a seal, wolf, or polar bear.

Polar bears are rarely encountered along the mainland south of Norton Sound, where seal hunters may travel on the ice without fear of attacks that commonly occur around Bering Strait. In these areas, and further north, hunters never go onto the winter ice without their spears. Terrible tales are told of the fate of those who chanced to meet these animals while unarmed.

Seals are also caught by setting nets under the ice around points of land where the currents run strongly. Holes are made at right angles to the shore, and a long pole with a line fastened to one end is inserted through the first hole and passed from hole to hole until the final one is reached. Then the line is used to spread the net between the farthest holes under

the ice. Ivory or stone sinkers keep the bottom of the net down in the current. These nets are most efficient during the night when seals cannot see the mesh.

In the spring, when the days grow longer and warmer, the ice begins to break up and leads form along the shore, attracting seals and walrus.

> At this season, also, the people about St. Michael begin their usual spring hunting upon the ice. They leave the village, hauling their kayaks, spears, guns, and other implements on small, light sledges made specially for the purpose. Whenever open water is to be crossed the kayak is launched, the sled placed upon it, and the hunter paddles to the opposite side, where he resumes his journey upon the ice. The method of obtaining seals at this time is by the hunter concealing himself on the ice close to the water, and from this point of vantage shooting or spearing them as they swim along the edge. (Nelson 1899:128)

Spring is also the time of year when hunters stalk seals that are basking in the sun on top of the ice. The hunter wears a pair of knee protectors made from polar bear or dog fur and a pair of large mittens of the same material. Armed with his harpoon, the hunter walks toward the seal as far as is prudent, and then drops to his knees and proceeds to crawl, concealing himself behind his outstretched left mitten and dragging his harpoon behind with his right. Periodically the seal will awake, sensing the approaching form. To reassure it, the hunter scratches on the ice with an implement made of seal claws mounted on a wooden handle, imitating the sound of a seal working at his breathing hole. Usually the seal then falls asleep, allowing the hunter to approach within throwing range. A hunter who owns a rifle uses a small sled with a white cloth or skin shield mounted on its front end. Pushing his sled in front of him, the hunter sights his rifle through a hole in the middle of the shield. However, many seals that are wounded by rifle shots reach their holes and escape or are lost when they die and sink.

Before a hunter sets out hunting on the sea ice, he makes sure that his equipment is in proper order. It is important not only that he be warmly clothed and that he have his ice pick, extra harpoons and lines, his knife, and other tools, but that he also be prepared spiritually for encounters with

### 57. Seal Scratcher *cetugmiarun*

In late winter and spring seals come onto the ice to bask and sleep, and so can be hunted by stalking. As the hunter crawls forward, the seal wakes periodically, sensing danger. When he sees the seal's head rise, the hunter pauses, hiding behind one of his large dogskin or polar bearskin mittens, and rakes his seal scratcher on the ice, imitating the sound of a seal working at its breathing hole. Thus reassured, the seal dozes again and the hunter advances until within striking range with the harpoon.

This seal scratcher exudes "sealness" in more than audible dimensions. As with other elements of hunting technology it reflects the strongly rooted belief among Bering Sea people that effectiveness requires a combination of fine craftsmanship and technology with the use of spiritually compatible materials and appropriate imagery. This implement exemplifies that philosophy. In imitation of a seal's flipper, three bearded seal claws have been attached by intricate lashings to a beluga tooth on its bottom side. The lug penetrates the shaft and emerges on top looking as if it were a seal rising through its breathing hole. The seal's eyes are inlaid with soot-blackened wooden plugs, and the ears and nostrils with a sooty paste. A second seal head is carved with subtle elegance into the other end of the wooden handle.

Such a tool should indeed reassure seal spirits about man's reverential approach. The seal scratcher must have been effective and treasured in the tool kit of the Sledge Island hunter from whom Nelson obtained it.

Sledge Island 45060, 28 cm

### 58. Braining Stone and Drag Handle *kaugtuutaq*

This braining stone is made from a heavy dark rock containing speckled rodlike white fossils. It has been polished to a high sheen, partly through natural processes. A stout thong is passed through a tapered hole drilled from each side and is fastened in a chevron-pattern splice to the main line. There is a wrist loop at the other end. Use of the stone rather than a lance avoids making unnecessary holes in the skin.

In winter, game is brought home over the ice with the aid of drag handles. In Norton Sound handle loops are fastened to the animal with fancy attachers, such as this double-headed bearded seal with eyes inlaid with blue beads and wooden plugs. The attacher is made from a beluga or walrus tooth and has a semidetached beluga carving on its bottom.

King Island 43796, 65 cm (outstretched); Golovin 33663, 20 cm

### 59. Drag Handle with Pyrite

Nelson collected this rakish beast from Pikmiktalik, near St. Michael. Its eyes gleam with pyrites, as does an inlay on its brow. While possibly a wolf, it has the sagittal furrow depicted in carvings to identify polar bears.

Pikmiktalik 33664, 9 cm

potentially unfriendly spirits. Therefore, the hunter carries protective fetishes in pouches hung around his neck or sewn to his clothing. He may also carry one or more hunting charms—perhaps a seal's tooth or raven's beak—one to assist him in finding game and another to guide his harpoon. Symbolism extends also to the implements themselves. His harpoon may be decorated with an engraving of a wolf and have an ivory finger rest carved as a seal, walrus, or polar bear's head. Line fasteners may carry representations of people or animals, or simply of geometric designs. His drag handle may be shaped as a seal, polar bear, or a ferocious wolf spirit with gleaming pyrite eyes. His antler harpoon heads have double- and triple-spurred bases resembling tucked bird plumage, and their elegant fine-line incision and inlaid plugs appear as stylized faces whose zoomorphic roots have been long lost. A man's seal scratcher may be made with the claws of the seal and may also have carvings of seals set into its "palm" or engraved on its handle. This repetitive use of imagery reinforces the "sealness" of the implement, making it more effective at fooling the sleeping animal, as well as being visually pleasing and expressing the creativity of the craftsman.

The Ringed Seal is an abundant winter resident in the northern half of Bering Sea, its range reaching the mouth of the Kuskoquim River and extending thence in a westerly course across the sea in a line coinciding with the southern edge of the ice-pack. When the ice leaves the shore in spring, and the pack-ice is drifting along the coast in May and the early part of June, these seals are found in considerable numbers among the ice well offshore. They gather in large bunches on large ice-cakes and are hunted there by the Eskimo. The latter wear a shirt made of white sheeting and paddle cautiously up to a piece of ice on which the seals are gathered, and disguised in their white dress are able to land and get among the seals before the latter are alarmed. A stout club is usually employed on such occasions, and sometimes a man will secure a number. This style of hunting is practiced off the Yukon mouth and thence northward, at least to the northern shore of Norton Sound.

In Norton Sound the males become very rank after the last of March, and the Eskimo say that only a part of them are able to eat its flesh at this season, as it makes some of them ill. (Nelson 1887:262)

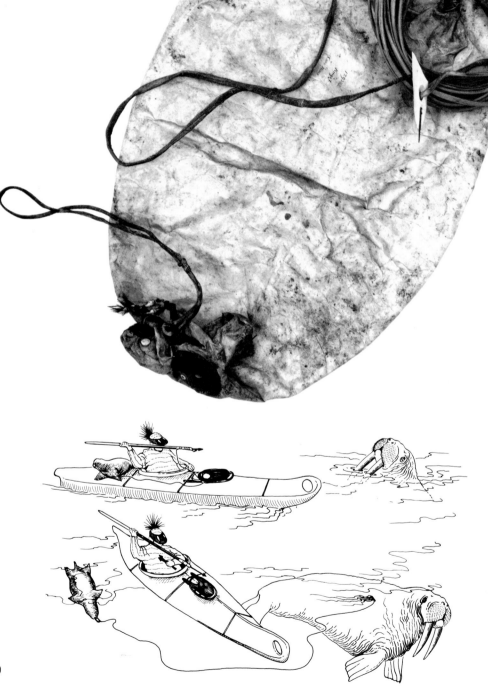

## 60. Walrus Harpoons and Line

Key features of the walrus harpoon are its robust shaft—here made of imported hemlock—its heavy weight, and its long foreshaft, all of which are needed so that the harpoon head can penetrate the animal's thick hide and blubber. This upper harpoon, obtained in northern Norton Sound, is fitted with an ivory seal head finger rest, a walrus tusk ice pick, and a heavy socketpiece made from walrus jawbone.

The lower specimen is from Nunivak Island and shows the form used south of the Yukon. It differs in having a larger ice pick which is made from a split length of walrus tusk. On the pick is incised a mythological toothy beast, probably a *palraiyuk*, with blue beads for eyes. The harpoon has a collared socketpiece and is used without a fixed foreshaft.

Floats used for hunting walrus and beluga are made from the tanned, dehaired hides of whole seals. This harpoon head, line, and float assembly were obtained by Captain Healy, skipper of the *Corwin*. The components are joined with sturdy fasteners and display intricate splices, ties, and line stops. The float is fitted with a toggle handle for grasping and has thong loops at both ends for fastening on other lines and floats. It is ornamented with a blue-eyed, ivory-toothed face and has tassels to which tufts of brown fur have been sewn.

Golovin 43346, 207 cm; Nunivak Island 48379, 134 cm; King Island (M.A. Healy Collection) 129582, 85 cm (float)

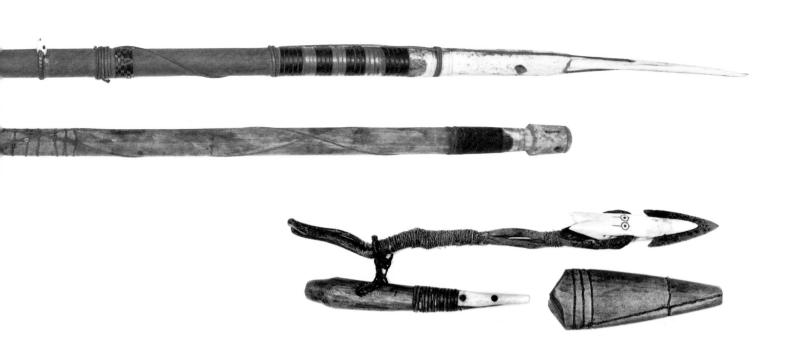

## Walrus Hunt

**61. Walrus Harpoon Heads**

Northern harpoon heads used on harpoons with fixed foreshafts are typified by the ivory head attached to the float line on the opposite page. The form of the harpoon head is basic and simple, having an oval cross section, a single undivided spur, and no decoration. The metal blade is pegged with an ivory rod. When not in use it is stored in a leather sheath.

Different forms of harpoons are used south of the Yukon. This ivory head from Cape Vancouver has a swallowtail spur and circle-and-dot with line ornamentation and when not used is stored in a split-wood sheath. Its foreshaft, a tapered rod with a wooden base and antler tip, is held in position between the socket and the head by a loose loop of thong. When an animal is struck the foreshaft detaches from the harpoon, not with the shaft as in northern harpoons.

Cape Vancouver 176222, 12 cm (point), 17 cm (foreshaft)

Nunivak Island people say that the shifting patterns of the Northern Lights are caused by men playing ball with a walrus skull. In addition to the walrus being featured in their mythology, many coastal Eskimos depend on this large, gregarious animal for food, heating oil, ivory for carvings and toolmaking, and hides for boat covers. Walrus are hunted in spring when they migrate north, following the retreat of the winter ice pack, and are commonly encountered around Nunivak Island and northern Norton Sound. They are also sometimes found in the shallow waters off the mainland between the Kuskokwim and Cape Romanzof. When encountered here they are driven toward shore until they reach water that is too shallow for them to escape by diving, and they are slain. They are also hunted when they pass on their southward migration, but stormy weather frequently makes this hunt less successful.

The spring hunt begins on an auspicious day chosen by the hunters and the shamans who have made special preparations for the event. At this time of year the weather is often still and warm, and as the men haul their kayaks out to the open water they feel keen anticipation. At the ice edge, there is not a breath of wind and the floes gleam in the bright sunlight, moving majestically in the current, silent except for the water dripping from their sides. Seals are spotted, as are ducks and murres, but the groups press on weaving among the ice searching for signs of walrus diving and feeding on clams, or basking in clusters upon the ice floes.

When walrus are found on the ice, the hunters approach quietly from downwind, avoiding the "sentinel" among the group. If they are successful, the hunters may be able to mount the floe and dispatch several animals with an ax blow to their spine, being careful not to be in the path of the stampede that follows as the other animals try to gain the safety of the water. Harpoons are secured to the wounded animals, and the hunt is completed by the kayak hunters.

When walrus are hunted from the kayak, a group of men will surround one animal and, using their heavy harpoons, secure it with several lines

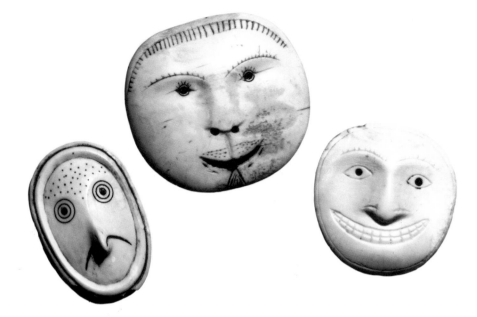

at the end of which are fastened large sealskin floats. As the animal struggles against the floats, returning to the surface occasionally to breathe, it is lanced repeatedly until it expires from drowning or loss of blood. Care is taken in approaching the wounded animal, which may weigh several thousand pounds, for its tusks can easily rip the kayak's cover and break its frame. The hunter's greatest fear is that the beast may surface directly beneath his boat, so the hunters alert each other as they see the direction taken by the moving floats.

Once secured, the animal is butchered with axes, meat hooks, and flensing knives and distributed to the hunters according to prescribed sharing rules. On Nunivak Island, the man who makes the first strike is the owner and receives half of the intestines, used for making waterproof garments, the hide, and the upper half of the body. The second hunter receives the lower half of the body; the third, the ivory tusks; the fourth, the remaining intestines; and the fifth, the stomach (Curtis 1930:31).

> One hunter told me of an instance in which he and a companion, both in kyaks, had an encounter with one of these animals. They were hunting among the drift ice off Cape Vancouver one day in spring, when his companion saw and killed a young Walrus without knowing that the old one was about. A moment later the parent arose from the water and catching sight of them uttered a hoarse, bellowing cry and swam rapidly towards them. Both hunters paddled for their lives to a large piece of ice close by and landed upon it just in time to escape their pursuer. Here they were kept prisoners nearly the entire day, and every time they tried to leave, thinking their enemy gone, they were pursued and forced to return to the ice again.
>
> The people of Bering Straits often meet vicious Walruses at this season. In one instance which came to my hearing a Walrus broke a hole in the top of a man's kyak with its tusks, but the man escaped. Numerous tales are told of their pursuing hunters. . . .
>
> I have heard the walrus-hunters say that these animals, when on shore, often keep guard by gathering in a body, and then as the leader falls asleep his head drops and he prods the next animal with his tusks; as the latter falls asleep he repeats the performance, and so there is one of the animals continuously on the alert. (Nelson 1887:269)

**62. Large Float Plugs** *khă-l'a´-chī-ŭ*

These decorated float plugs from the Nelson Island region are inserted in holes in the sealskin floats where seals' limbs and heads have been removed. The plugs have animal, human, and beastly images. The humorous, stupid-looking, short-eared owl, a common representation, is depicted here with speckled forehead and eyes inlaid with red-colored wooden plugs. It has pale green pigment in its beak and a border incision.

The central piece presents a moonlike, bisexual visage with female chin tattoos, male labret incisions, and a tattoo or mustache on its upper lip. Eye circles have been cut by slashes, and one contains the remnant of a crushed green glass bead. Lashes, eyebrows, and hair are also seen. A wooden plug between the teeth emerges on the reverse side at the apex of an incised "raven's foot" motif, perhaps the clan mark of the owner who might possibly be one of the village shamans, many of whom acquired special powers from their social and behavioral peculiarities.

The third image has almond eyes and a large toothy grin, features that are common on dance masks from this region. The hooplike border, seen on the owl too, also suggests that these plugs may be representations of masks of *inuas* rather than of real animals or people, as in the case of the moon shaman.

Cape Vancouver 43509, 5 cm; 43510, 6 cm; Agiukchugumut 37329, 4.5 cm

**63. Small Float Plugs**

This group of small ornamented plugs includes a cormorant from Cape Vancouver, a short-eared owl with green eyes and a red forehead plug from Kaialigamut, and a mild-mannered wolf with delicate eyelashes, linked to a collared plug from St. Michael. They are made from beluga or walrus tooth.

Cape Vancouver 43508, 3 cm; Kaialigamut 37528, 2.5 cm; St. Michael 33476, 5 cm

### 64. Sealing Harpoon Heads *nän-ûkh´-pûk*

These sealing harpoon heads illustrate stylistic variation from Bering Strait to the Lower Kuskokwim. The differences are not related to function as all heads are equally efficient at catching seals. Rather, the heads reflect individual and regional differences between the villages where they were collected. Greatest change is seen between the simpler, undecorated forms collected north of the Yukon, an area occupied by Inupiak language speakers, and the more delicate, decorated multipronged forms to the south, where people speak the Yupik Eskimo language. At least at this level, harpoon head variation and language boundaries correspond closely, probably reflecting deeply rooted cultural differences between these linguistic groups. Nelson's large and systematically gathered collection from both sides of this boundary provides an unusual opportunity to study the effects of language and social groupings on stylistic variation in material culture and art.

Left to right as photographed: Sledge Island 45144, 7 cm; Golovin 43316, 8.5 cm; Kushunuk 36343, 7.7 cm; Sfugunugumut 37955, 8 cm; Kaialigamut 37953, 7.5 cm; Lower Kuskokwim 176173, 8.8 cm

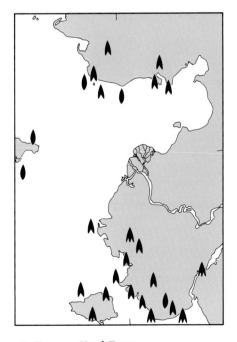

### 65. Harpoon Head Types

## Harpoons and Hunters' Marks

More so than any other implement, the harpoon head form is bound by functional considerations and is close to the spiritual core of hunting activities. Harpoon head patterns are passed down from father to son with few changes, and the "right" way to make a harpoon head is constantly being reinforced by social and religious values. Few alterations are introduced during a man's lifetime, and only minor, perhaps barely distinguishable, changes are seen between the work of adjacent generations. For this reason archeologists can trace the development of Arctic cultures by studying the changing forms of harpoon heads much in the same way pottery is used as a handy guide of cultural history among other peoples.

Within a village hunters may use a number of standardized harpoon head forms and decorate them in traditionally acceptable ways. Nearby villages have different, but related, forms and decorations. More distant villages or those isolated by geography, language, or social barriers such as war exhibit more divergent patterns. Divergence in form and decoration, therefore, may imply either social or geographic distance or changes in traditions through time.

Variation related to spatial and social factors is illustrated by differences in harpoon heads used by Eskimos between the Kuskokwim and Bering Strait. Bering Strait toggling harpoon heads tend to be made with single basal spurs and have cylindrical cross sections. They are frequently undecorated and are often made of ivory. Norton Sound harpoons often are made of antler and have bifurcated basal spurs. Their bodies are sculptured but frequently lack incised line and inlaid decoration. South of the Yukon, harpoon heads have flat cross sections and are made of antler. They have bifurcated and trifurcated bases, and are decorated with ivory inlays and fine-line incision incorporating spurred lines, circle-and-dots, and other motifs. In many instances the latter are portrayed in pairs as though to represent eyes. This technique recalls the raised circles and bosses found on two-thousand-year-old harpoon heads from the Old Bering Sea culture, while their spurred bases resemble tucked bird wings also found in these

**66. Harpoon Head Marks**

Most harpoon heads are incised with marks beneath the line hole. Sometimes they occur on the base or on one of the faces. Similar identifying marks are found on lance tips and arrows.

Golovin 43316, 8.5 cm; Nunivak Island 48242, 7 cm; Kaialigamut 37951, 7.5 cm; Sfugunugumut 37955, 8 cm

early forms. The harpoon heads made by Bering Sea Eskimos are the finest produced by Eskimos of the historic period anywhere in the north, and suggest a direct link with the harpoon head styles of the ancient cultures of the Bering Sea.

Marks are commonly found on a man's tools and weapons and on many other artifacts used by Bering Sea Eskimos. These marks serve a variety of purposes, designating ownership by persons or clans and representing charms and other images. The first category, that of personal identification, is illustrated by the "otter's trail" mark found on a set of wooden wedges from Ikogmut (fig. 76). Such marks apparently have no broader social significance beyond personal identification. They are casual creations made up by the individual, being more a matter of personal fancy than elaborate prescription.

Other types of marks, designated by Nelson as "totem marks," occur widely throughout Bering Sea Eskimo material culture. These include such representational forms as the raven's foot, the stylized wolf, and the bear claw—symbols that probably signify totem images of the raven, wolf, and bear clans. These clans, along with other corporate groups, are important in the social organization of this area. The marks do not identify individual ownership, but rather signify ownership by or affiliation with the clan itself. Such marks are found on many objects, including tobacco cutting boards and *qasgiq* (men's house) vent covers, that are used or owned communally by the members of the *qasgiq*, a structure that seems likely to have been clan-associated in the pre-Nelson era.

Similar totem marks are also found on a hunter's weapons. Here they probably symbolize a special relationship between the hunter, his intended game, and his clan's totem spirit, be it raven, wolf, bear, or otherwise. Due to the Eskimo's sensitivity at divulging clan secrets and Nelson's lack of interest or expertise in pursuing them, little is known of the meaning and relationships between totem signs and social institutions. Further work was done on this subject by the anthropologist and photographer Edward Curtis (1930) and the anthropologist Margaret Lantis (1946), but by this time information about such things had been largely lost.

Marks found on harpoon heads appear to be a more abstract variant of the symbolic system just discussed. These implements are not marked

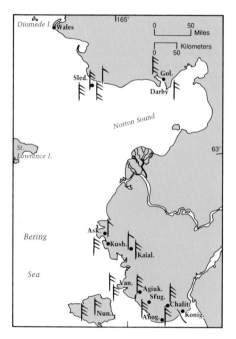

**67. Mark Types**

Marks are commonly found on harpoon heads used between Bering Strait and the Kuskokwim. Throughout this area only a few types of marks are noted, unlike the great variety seen on lance tips and arrows. In some cases all mark forms are found in a single village, as at Sledge Island. If these marks identify a person's clan or lineage, as reported by the anthropologist Margaret Lantis, this diversity might be explained by the presence of peoples gathered here from many villages during a time of famine to hunt and fish in the only spot where game remained.

## 68. Lance Point Marks

While some marks found on lances are similar to those found on harpoon points and may be lineage or clan related, their greater variety and elaboration suggest additional functions, perhaps for family or personal identification within clans. Nelson believed that some marks, such as the raven's foot and the wolf, had totemic functions, but he was not clear about their social meaning. South of the Yukon a greater variety of mark types is employed, and many of these occur in elaborated form. These social marks are often used in conjunction with family *inogos*, or inherited charm images such as the *palraiyuk*, and with painted bands, incised rings, and notches that probably signify individual ownership.

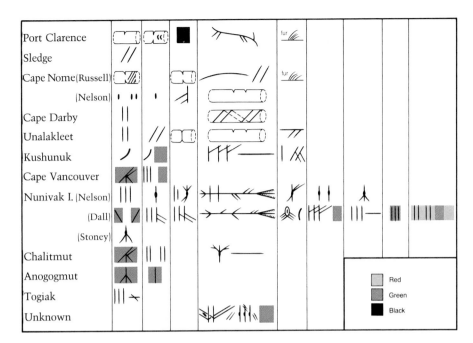

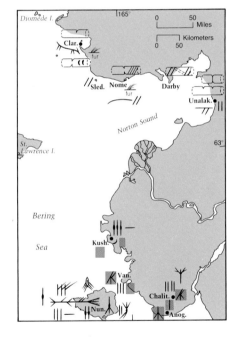

**69. Lance Markings**

with representational raven's foot or wolf motifs, which are found on lances and arrows, but with geometric marks usually positioned on the sides of the implement below the line hole. These marks are formed by appending one, two, three, or four equally spaced slashes or a double set of paired lines at slight angles to an incised baseline. These forms are few enough to represent the major clans in the region. Perhaps they equate, through some unknown key, to the representational marks.

Of the five mark forms found in this region, Nelson's collection of harpoon heads show that only one or two mark types are present in a given village. This pattern implies that these marks represent specific clans, for most Bering Sea villages contain only one or two dominant clans. Such a correlation would also lead to the conclusion, suggested by the predominance of three mark types, that most of the population of this region belonged to one of three major clans. The greater than normal diversity of harpoon head marks from Nelson's collections from Sledge Island is probably explained as the result of its being a spring camp occupied by groups from different villages in northern Norton Sound who had gathered here in search of better hunting during a time of famine.

The greatest elaboration seen in marked implements occurs on the lance tips found south of the Yukon mouth. Although the incised marks on these implements display considerable variation, most are found to be elaborations of simpler forms like the raven's foot and ring marks. The purpose of elaborating these forms seems to be to identify subclan groups, such as a family or sibling group within a particular clan that owned the basic mark (Lantis 1946:242). Incised marks are often used on the same lance in combination with painted bands of various colors and spacing, and family-inherited charm images, some of which resemble the *palraiyuk*.

# food from the waters

Edward Nelson, preparing to depart for four years on the Bering Sea coast, could not have imagined the extent to which his life would be dependent upon fish during his period of duty. Like others, then and today, he would have thought that Alaskan Eskimos subsisted largely on a diet of seal, walrus, and caribou meat, supplemented by smaller amounts of birds and fish. When Eskimo economy is quantified, however, one finds that fish provide the largest portion of the yearly food intake. Only in the most northern regions of Canada and Greenland and parts of northern Alaska does the stereotype of the Eskimo hunter ring true.

South of Bering Strait, the importance of fish increases dramatically, being greatest in the Yukon–Kuskokwim region and parts of eastern Norton Sound where in some villages more than eighty percent of the yearly food supply is derived from fish. Nelson found the majority of villages in the tundra lake country between the Yukon and Kuskokwim rivers subsisting on two freshwater species, whitefish and blackfish—the former being large, sometimes attaining 30–40 pounds, and the latter being under six inches long. The blackfish made up for its small size by its incredible abundance and year-round availability. These fish, and a few others, supported a population of nearly three thousand people living in many villages within a few hundred square miles. That this area was the most densely populated Eskimo region in Alaska was all the more surprising to Nelson because of the absence of driftwood and the small size of the houses.

Along the more luxurious banks of the Yukon and Kuskokwim, where driftwood is abundant or forest accessible, Nelson found many villages of 100–150 persons located only a few miles apart at productive salmon fishing stations. The economy of these villages was based almost exclusively on harvesting huge quantities of salmon and other saltwater fish that entered the river each summer and fall to spawn, or freshwater species that wintered in the main channels and spent their summers in the tundra lakes and ponds nearby. Both groups of migrants, in addition to other residents, were caught and dried or frozen for use in lean seasons when there was little else for people to eat. These river and river mouth villages were consistently larger than coastal villages visited by Nelson, which averaged between 50 to 100 people. The largest village, Rasboinsky, had a population of 151 living in twenty-five houses and two *qasgit*. Stories are told of the site of another Yukon River village, near Ikogmut, that was occupied some years earlier during the Malemut wars. People had counted thirty-five *qasgit* here, but only a few of these could have been used at one time. Both

**70. Salmon Bagfastener**
Several species of salmon ascend the rivers of the Bering Sea coast from June through October. Owing to their great numbers, the salmon constitute a large and relatively stable food and oil resource. In addition, salmon skin is sewn into clothing, bags, and other items. Other fish species are important, but salmon provides much that gives Bering Sea Eskimo culture its special flavor.

Nelson collected this simple yet elegant ivory carving from Nunivak Island, where it was used on a woman's work bag, known as a "housewife." Such pieces are often made by men as gifts for their wives or girlfriends. Its fine lustrous sheen bespeaks many years of use. Trading needles and beads for such trinkets earned Nelson his Eskimo nickname "the man who buys good-for-nothing things."
Nunivak Island 43694, 12 cm

### 71. Salmon's World *neqa*

Despite their economic importance fish do not figure strongly in ceremonial life and are rarely portrayed in masks. This fine Mage-mut piece reveals the *inua* of a salmon whose mouth, eyes, gills, pectoral fins, and tail are shown. Small salmon are attached near the tail, upon which rests a kayak that originally carried a hunter-fisherman. Beneath the salmon's head swims a white seal, and be-hind, along the sides of the fish, are a large incised toothy mouth and pair of eyes. A grinning, masked, semihuman *inua* is sculpted in relief on the fish's back, framed by a raised lip. Its mask, nostrils, mustache, and outlined border—the latter recalling symbolic parka ruffs and splint-wood hoops seen on other masks—are painted black, as are the salmon's eyes, the outline of the lower teeth and eyes, and the kayak's lines. Red paint is applied to the gills and mouth of the salmon, the teeth in the beasts' mouths, and the outline of the *inua's* mouth. The bands surrounding the salmon and the smaller fish are also red. Gull feathers originally pro-jected from the sides of the mask. This mask seems to portray the salmon in its real and spiritual element, preyed upon by seal from below and man from above. It is protected from man by the potent visage of its *inua* which, transformed and seen in profile on the fish's side, is about to attack the seal. The small fish symbolizes replenishment of the species.

South of Lower Yukon (Museum of Ameri-can Indian, Heye Foundation Collection 2/439) 33134, 31 cm

### 72. Lamprey Eel Netting *nemeryaq*

Lamprey eels can be caught through holes in the ice with dip nets when they ascend the rivers from the sea in wintertime. The eels move upriver in a single, compact, slow-moving mass for which Eskimos maintain a keen watch because the sun only lasts a few hours. During this brief interval huge num-bers can be caught, and piles of fish grow tall upon the river ice. The catch is greatly aug-mented by competitive, sporting, young men who, when the run begins to slack, race upriver to open new holes in front of the advancing school. The young men cease only when exhausted, or when they meet fish-ermen from the next village.

NAA 76–977

the large river villages and the densely populated regions of the tundra lake country owe their existence to the abundant and diverse fish resources that constitute a unique feature of this part of Alaska.

Fish are a principal food resource for men and dogs, and their skins are used for a variety of implements. In the interior of the Delta people without access to waterproof seal gut clothing make light foul-weather parkas and boots out of durable salmon and whitefish skin, and arrow quivers are frequently made of this material also. Fish fat is used for glue; fish eggs are an important ingredient in tanning hide; and some of the oily fish, especially whitefish and lamprey eels, are rendered for eating and lighting by people in the river villages. Many of these fish products are adequate substitutes for materials provided by large land and sea mammals in other regions, making life possible in areas where the large mammals are not available. However, in most cases the fish products must be supplemented by walrus ivory, caribou antler, and seal oil obtained by interior people trading with coastal or riverine groups. Trade networks link western Alaska Eskimos in a web of economic relationships that also include social and religious contacts.

## Netting Fish And Seals

Nets are a critical element of subsistence technology among Bering Sea Eskimos. Of the many varieties used, the most common and important is the gill net. This net has wide-open meshes that hang like a diaphanous curtain from the surface of the water, suspended from a head line buoyed by wood or bladder floats. Its foot line carries a number of stone or ivory sinkers that counter the action of the tide or current and keep the net hanging vertically. Gill nets are usually set perpendicular to the shore and sometimes have a dog-leg section angled in to catch fish that see the net and attempt to swim around it. They are set away from the bank into deeper water and frequently have large wooden floats carved in the shapes of birds supporting their outer ends, which are anchored with stones or stakes.

Gill nets have a fine-corded mesh large enough so that many fish attempt to swim through the holes, or fail to see the net at all until too late. As soon as the fish strike the line they turn, and in thrashing about become hopelessly entangled. Others pass part way through the netting before becoming firmly gripped when their fatter midsections fill the mesh space.

Although not strainers or barriers, gill nets are very efficient at catching fish that swim near the surface, as do salmon, trout, and grayling. However, a net must be tended regularly by the fisherman, who has to clear grass, weeds, and other debris that collect in its mesh, making it visible to the fish. He also must watch for driftwood and floating logs that can tear or rip the net from its moorings and carry it away downstream. Given the many hours it takes to acquire the materials and make a net, its loss, especially during the peak fishing period, is a serious setback that may have disastrous consequences for the fisherman's security and his ability to acquire capital for trading and exchanges.

Another type of net commonly used in the Yukon–Kuskokwim Delta is the dip net. This net usually has a very small mesh and is made in the shape of a bag. Attached to an oval wood frame on a long pole, dip nets are useful for capturing small fish like sticklebacks and blackfish found in tundra pools and lakes. In some cases dip nets are used to catch large fish running up the rivers in the summer. One technique used is to float with

**73. Whiskered "Nerpa"** *pugtaqutaq*
This delightful seal helps keep the net headline afloat. It illustrates the imagination used in manufacturing technological equipment and also the practice of using animal imagery in subsistence activities. Seals and birds, being especially fine "catchers," act as helping spirits on seal and fish nets. This fellow has the short snout of a young ring seal. Its water-blue eyes are made with a favorite type of trade bead, probably obtained from Russian traders before the U.S. purchase of Alaska. Its whiskers are of fine white fur. The placement of the net-fastening thong at the bottom of the head insures that the head will bob upright in the water.
Cape Nome 44142, 10 cm

### 74. Waterfowl and Seal Brethren Net Floats

Gill nets are set at right angles to the shore with one end fastened on land and the other anchored to a submerged rock. Waterfowl floats are often used to buoy the outer end of the net. According to Nelson, the abstract bird from Ikogmut is a brant. Its bottom and mouth are stained red from alder bark infusion, and it has a green back, unpainted wings, and a broad red groove around its border. The Sabotnisky float shows a loon sounding its call. It has a broad red groove from head to tail, and its mouth, wings, and back are colored like the brant's.

The "seal brethren" support the center of a seal net. They are made from weathered hardwood roots whose natural twists and knobs have been enhanced by the carver, who added nostrils, mouths, and eyes of ivory or bead. For fastening to the net the "seal brethren" are provided with ivory stirrups, sometimes ornamented with extra link-pieces formed into miniature seals and human faces. Clustered here, their individuality is expressed as much as it is when bobbing along the net in a light breeze, heads up and ivory links clinking.

Ikogmut 48699, 27 cm (base); Sabotnisky 48929, 21.5 cm (base); Point Hope 63776, 63777, 63778, 63779, 63780, 63783 (all ca. 12–16 cm)

the current holding the dip net with its opening facing downstream. Not seeing the net in the murky water, the fish enters and is captured when the fisherman feels the strike. Dip nets are also used for catching crabs and herring during the period when they swarm near the shore.

Seines are used in the coastal regions to capture schools of fish when they approach the shore. These nets have fine mesh and act more like strainers than gill nets. They are frequently operated by a number of men performing a variety of tasks. Some using a long pole or log extend the net into deep water; others with lines attached to the outboard end swing the net out and around toward shore again, using the log as a fulcrum, while others hold the inner end fast on the beach.

Nets similar to the gill nets used for salmon and other fish are also very helpful in catching seals and beluga. These nets are made of thick rawhide and have mesh as large as a man's head. Like fish, seals become entangled in the mesh where they are held under water by weights on the bottom of the net until they drown. Large numbers of seals are caught in this way in the open water season and also beneath the ice in winter.

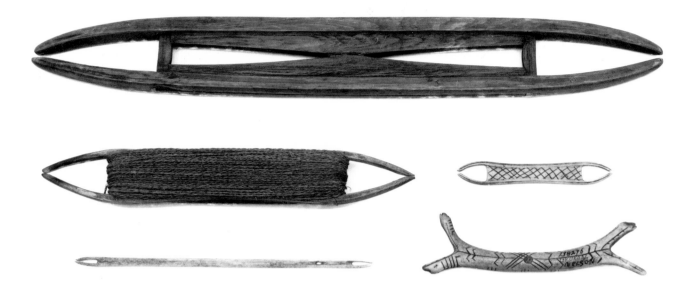

After the spring seal and bird hunts, coastal people prepare their nets for the herring runs that begin in early June. The nets are made from thin strands of caribou or beluga sinew stripped from the animal's back or from its legs, in the case of the caribou. Women break the sinew bundles down by shredding them with combs, splitting them into finer and finer strands, until they reach a suitable size for twisting pairs of strands together into cord. The cord is then wound on reels.

While the tedious preparation of sinew line is a task that falls to women, men generally have the equally tedious task of net making. Many thousands of knots must be tied to make a net that runs thirty or forty meters. The mesh must be tied just smaller than the girth of the fish to be caught, and all mesh must be made the same size. To do this the fisherman uses a small bone or ivory net gauge around which each mesh is tied. He also uses a line reel or netting needle to hold his line. These tools allow him to pass the line easily through the mesh and to tie the knots without snarls. Netting needles used for making large nets must be long enough to hold the large amounts of line, while those used for fine-meshed nets must be narrow enough to slip between the tiny meshes.

When the herring strike the coast, first in early June and again at later times in early summer, people flock to the shore to net and gather this rich oily fish. Long nets with wooden end-posts, frequently pictured in engraved drill bows, are used in the shallow water where this fish swarms to spawn, and great quantities are caught. Nelson observed several herring runs during his stay in St. Michael.

### 75. Net Shuttles and Mesh Gauges

The large spruce wood shuttle is for making large-mesh seal nets with baleen or sinew cord. A smaller birch shuttle for making salmon nets, obtained at Sabotnisky, is wound with two-ply cord of twisted willow bark. The pronged antler line reel is ornamented with beluga heads and heads of other fish-eating animals. Its shaft is marked with the skeletal or "X-ray" pattern showing the internal bones and has double- and triple-barred lines and possible tally marks. A small conical depression indicates the reel has also served as a make-shift drill cap. Very narrow shuttles are used to make fine-mesh nets for sticklebacks and minnows. The antler shuttle is used to make nets to catch young whitefish and has a net and raven's foot decoration.

Mesh gauges are used to insure all mesh squares are tied the same size. This is done by knotting the mesh loops around the gauge and slipping them off when beginning to tie another, as in knitting. The double-ended gauge from Sabotnisky may have been used for tying dip nets or blackfish nets. The larger gauge, also of antler, has a split handle and willow lashings. Its ridged blade ends in a spur used to untie knots and carries an identifying mark similar to ones found on hunting equipment.

Shuttles:Cape Vancouver 38672, 50 cm; Sabotnisky 48938, 29 cm; Chalitmut 36447, 23 cm; Lower Yukon 38286, 16.5 cm; Cape Vancouver 43525, 12 cm Gauges: Sabotnisky 49004, 17 cm; Lower Kuskokwim 176220, 24 cm

## 76. Fish Trap *taluyaq*

Great numbers of fish are caught in rivers, lakes, and sluggish streams with wood-splint traps. These traps have depressed cone-shaped openings with small holes to admit the fish at their inner ends. Their overall size and the space between the slats depend on the size of the fish to be caught.

Splint wood is made by splitting driftwood logs into increasingly finer units with stone or metal adzes. Intermediate work is done with hardwood wedges like the one from Ikogmut which has a short red-stained groove on each side that Nelson indicates represents the track of an otter in the snow and is the private mark of the owner. Reduction to pencil-thin splints is done with antler hand wedges like the one from the Lower Kuskokwim. Its gull's head effigy, incised collar, "Y" motif, and bordered crosshatching are often associated with representations of fish on items of fishing technology. Here the decorations seem to signify a fish predator, a stylized fishtail, and net motifs.

Lower Kuskokwim 36554, 33 cm; Ikogmut 48872, 13 cm; Andreievsky 38884, 43 cm

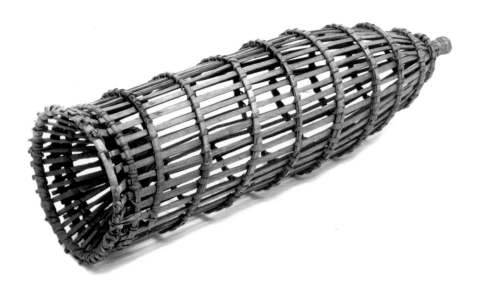

## 77. Trap Fishing *taluyarculviik*

Nelson took this photograph on the Lower Yukon where he found two men checking a splint trap set under the ice. A barricade of vertical stakes set through the ice into the river bottom channels fish into the trap's opening. Thinner sticks are used to raise and lower the trap.

NAA–6913

91

## Trap Fishing

In the rivers and lakes where currents and narrow constrictions in water passages make net fishing impractical, fish are caught with wicker traps made in the form of long, sleevelike cages with inverted conical openings. More durable than nets, they are set in places where river channels and sandbars concentrate the movement of fish and are often used in conjunction with stake or brush fences that converge toward the entrance of the trap. Some of the large trap systems used in prime locations require the efforts of several individuals to service and maintain them, especially those along the main courses of the Yukon and Kuskokwim rivers where the salmon runs are strongest. So important are some fishing sites that they are determining factors in village location and constitute a special communal resource integrated into the social and economic fabric of village life. In most cases the use of traps is a matter of individual or family concern, although families have traditional rights to use certain locations for their traps.

People living in both the river villages and the tundra lakes use these traps during winter and summer, but in different ways and for quite different purposes. During his travels on the Yukon, Nelson heard of traps being used during the summer for capturing salmon and other anadromous fish. The largest of these fish, King salmon, regularly reached weights of 60–70 pounds, and on occasion even 140 pounds. The sheer mass of these fish moving up the major rivers during peak runs was so large that these traps had to be continuously watched as they filled, for the traps would burst open under the strain when they reached their limit.

Similar traps are also used on the rivers during the winter, as illustrated by a photograph Nelson took at Ikogmut (fig. 77). Winter traps are set through the ice at the apex of coverging lines of fence poles oriented against the direction of fish movement. During this period, the catch consists of such species as whitefish, pickerel, pike, and other freshwater varieties that resort to the deeper waters of the main rivers during the seasons when

**78. Fish Spears** *kŭ-ki´-vit*

Large spears are used to catch fish attracted by jiggling antler lures suspended from boats or through holes in the ice. This spear has a central point of bone flanked by springy antler side-prongs with wedgelike tabs that close around the body of the fish once it has been impaled. Fish are also taken with detachable barbed harpoons fastened to hand lines and thrown with socketed shafts similar to those used in seal hunting. Once landed, fish are killed with clubs like this Sabotnisky example, which has a handle wrapped with willow bark and takes the form of an abstract fish with red-grooved mouth and midline.

St. Michael 33860, 179 cm; Sabotnisky 48998, 44 cm; Koyuk River, Norton Sound 44096, 26 cm; Ikogmut 48874, 18.5 cm

**79. Fish Club** *anautaq*

This club for killing fish is in the form of a seal, the chief predator of fish. Its ivory eyes are inlaid with dark wood plugs, and its whiskers and lashes are shown by finely incised lines and remnant stubs of inset fur.

Diomede Island 64218, 21 cm

**80. Thrusting Spear**

Slender spears with delicately barbed ivory prongs are used to spear small fish from the kayak in clear streams. The spear is held motionless under water until a fish swims within range. Sinew lashings and an ivory ferrule secure the prongs on the shaft. The type is found at Nunivak Island but is not common in this part of Alaska and may be a southern introduction.

Nunivak Island 48342, 14 cm (prong length)

### 81. Fish Arrows  *nuusaaq*

Different kinds of arrows are used to shoot fish and small game, especially muskrats and birds, in shallow ponds and streams. In addition to multipronged arrows, Nunivak Islanders use arrows with a barbed center prong flanked by a lateral spur. Double-pronged points with barbs are frequently found on the Lower Yukon and Kuskokwim. In areas where muskrats are plentiful, arrows with small detachable harpoons are used. This arrow acts like a sealing dart, the harpoon being attached by cord to the shaft to impede the escape of the muskrat, which is approached and killed with a club. Fish arrows, unlike those used for birds and larger game, are rarely marked with personal totems or insignia. This may be due to the fact that despite their importance economically, fish do not play a large role in spiritual and ceremonial life. Additionally, there is little reason to mark these weapons since fish do not travel far once struck.

These arrows have broad nocks for thick bowstrings, and their cross sections change from round at mid-shaft to a flattened oval at the nock end for better finger purchase and flight characteristics. The Rasboinsky arrow has a red-tailed hawk feather lashed with a split feather quill and twisted willow bark. The other arrows are fletched with cormorant feathers.

Kushunuk 36151, 78 cm; Nunivak Island 48340, 74 cm; Rasboinsky 49039, 84 cm

the smaller streams and lakes are frozen. Their exodus from the lakes and tributaries into the rivers in October and November allows large numbers to be caught in transit, and provides an additional and extremely important winter resource for those villages located along the larger rivers.

Most dramatic perhaps is the trap fishing that occurs in the tundra villages during the winter months, when little else remains in these regions but blackfish and men. In these locations their life histories are inextricably intertwined, and upon examination Nelson found the natural history of the blackfish and the life of the inland Delta Eskimos so remarkable that he gave this relationship immediate attention in short papers.

> Blackfish (*Dallia pectoralis*) occurs in such numbers in all the grass-grown, sluggish fresh-water streams and shallow lakes . . . that it forms a very important source of food supply to the natives within these limits. In the low country between the Lower Yukon and Kuskoquim Rivers these fish exist in greatest abundance, and here, also, is found the most dense Eskimo population in Alaska. In this region alone a population of nearly three thousand Eskimos rely upon this fish for one of their most abundant and certain sources of food supply. (Nelson 1884:466)

Blackfish, a species restricted to the Bering Strait area, have a number of characteristics that make them important to the inland tundra dwellers of this region. Among their unique capabilities is the ability to survive in the deeper pools of the shallow tundra lakes throughout the winter, after all other fish have been forced to retreat to the more protective environment of the larger rivers. Should the shallow ponds and streams inhabited by blackfish freeze to the bottom, their bodies become lifeless and bloated, but they can recover, provided the freeze does not persist for a long time. Eskimos living in the Big Lake country today also tell of blackfish surviving by finding small places where currents keep ice from forming. Here they rise to the surface and gulp air directly from the atmosphere. People encourage these efforts by chopping holes in the ice and placing a trap with its conical opening directly beneath the hole, thus capturing the blackfish as they breathe and then sink, euphoric, into the wicker trap below. In countless instances this individually insignificant fish sustains human survival in the otherwise barren tundra regions.

## Line Fishing

During the fall, soon after the sea freezes, the water around the mouths of the rivers is clear and fish can be speared through holes in the ice. Whitefish and pickerel are frequently caught in this way. The fisherman cuts a hole through the ice in a shallow channel, and then, jiggling a miniature lure while holding the leister poised a few inches away, waits for an overly curious or greedy fish to come within range. Smaller multipronged fish spears are used by fishermen in kayaks. Sometimes fish are also caught by shooting them with arrows in shallow water, or when they feed or bask near the surface. These arrows are made with diverging prongs or wedgelike points that are intended to keep the arrow in the body of the fish, thereby causing a drag to impede the fish's escape and to prevent its loss from sinking. Sometimes arrow darts similar to seal darts are used on fish, although they are designed primarily for hunting muskrats.

> The fishing season along the coast of Norton sound opens about the end of March or early in April of each year; at this time the spring tides begin to show along the shore, where the water forces its way up through the cracks in the ice. During this cold weather of winter the tomcod and the sculpin remain in deep water, but as spring approaches they begin to return to the vicinity of the shore, and holes in the ice are made through which they are caught by means of hook and line. During May, as the weather grows warmer, the tomcod become extremely numerous, and at this time the old men and women may be seen scattered about on the ice, a few hundred yards from the shore, where they fish during many hours of the day. (Nelson 1899:174)

> The species [tomcod] is abundant everywhere from Kotzebue Sound south along the coast to Bristol Bay. In fall, directly after the ice covers the sea along shore, they are extremely abundant, and with

**82. Tomcod Fishing** *iqsagcuun*

Tomcod fishing is a winter activity conducted in shallow water through holes in the ice. Holes are chopped with ivory or antler-tipped ice picks, and netted scoops are used to clear the holes of floating ice. This shuttlelike rod from Nome also serves as a reel and has a knotted baleen line tied to a sinker of fossil ivory. The sinker, which also serves as a lure, is decorated with a sinew tassle and red and white beads and has a composite hook of stone and ivory, itself ornamented with red beads and bits of horny sheath from the bills of crested auklets. Possibly these imbue the hook with the holding power of its mentor's talons.

Cape Nome 45440, 64 cm; SI–6384

**83. Tomcod Fishing Gear** *ceturnarcurcuutet*

Regional variation in style, materials, and ritual treatment is seen in these tomcod rigs. St. Lawrence Island forms utilize premade iron treble hooks obtained from Europeans. Baleen leaders, which have the property of never freezing or icing up, are fastened to the bottom and outer edges of square-sectioned ivory sinkers. Charms and decorative elements are absent. At Port Clarence, sinkers are often made of ground stone, and hooks are handmade from small iron or brass nails inserted into ivory shanks with sinew, feather quill, and baleen attachments. Decoration, fine workmanship, and ritual functions are plainly evident.

Southern hook technology differs in using large bone and antler gang hooks accompanied by small smelt hooks and fish-effigy sinkers. Ritually related materials are infrequent in Nelson's tomcod gear from this area because of the reduced economic importance of tomcod and the general lack of fish ceremonialism.

Cape Vancouver 36376, 12 cm ; Port Clarence 37648, 9 cm; St. Lawrence Island 63513, 11 cm

a single line the natives about Norton Sound take from 150 to 200 pounds per day and in spring, during the month of May, they are equally abundant. They ascend all tide creeks to the upper limit of brackish water, and about Cape Vancouver great numbers of them are taken in dipnets. They are packed away and frozen in grass bags and kept in great quantities for winter use by the Eskimo of the Eastern coast of Bering Sea, and are next to or perhaps equally important with the Dog-salmon in the position it occupies in the food supply list. It is particularly valuable from the fact that, except during the severe winter months, it is rare that a mess of these fish cannot be secured when all other food fails. (Nelson 1887:302)

Hook and line fishing is conducted throughout the region at all times of the year, but is especially important in late winter when, for those people living on the coast, it may make the difference between survival or starvation. Considerable care is given to the manufacture of bright, attractive lures made from short shanks of antler or ivory through which bits of metal have been inserted for barbs. Sinkers attached to the fishing lines a few inches above the hooks are often made from polished stone or fossil walrus ivory and decorated with incised eyes and other features of small fish. These sinkers serve both to sink the hook and line and act as lures to attract fish.

The hooks used by Bering Sea Eskimos vary greatly in form and decoration, and many, especially those made by peoples of northern Norton Sound and points farther north, are exquisite miniature works of art. Oddly enough, the smallest hooks, those used to catch the ugly sculpin, are the most carefully made and most beautiful of all. The bodies of these hooks are composed of tiny fragments of brightly colored ground stone or trade beads joined together with split bird quill lashings. They are fitted with small hooks and bits of orange puffin bill parts that lure sculpins by their resemblance to fish eggs.

95

Eskimos design different kinds of hooks to catch different kinds of fish. In general, hook technology is given greater attention by peoples of the Norton Sound region than by those living south of the Yukon. Despite the importance of fish in the economy of the southern people, their hooks are more plain, and one finds few indications of their being important in ritual or mythological life when compared to the recognition they accord to mammals and birds. Perhaps their reduced status in the spiritual and intellectual life results from their being less well known than other animals. Men cannot sit and study fish as they can other animals, for fish are hidden from view when in their natural habitat. They are less observed, and consequently also less susceptible to personification.

### 84. Sculpin, Grayling, and Herring Hooks

People in Norton Sound excel in making elaborate, small fishhooks in a variety of forms, each designated for catching different types of fish. The two composite hooks at the left are for the ignominious sculpin, whose horny head and spines make him the net-fisherman's bane. Perhaps to compensate for the sculpin's ugliness, sculpin hooks are elaborate and colorful. One sculpin hook from Cape Nome (176271) has a composite shank made of ground and fitted pieces of fossil ivory, glass bead, and quartz, which have been grooved and lashed together with feather quill and strips of bird foot skin. Attached to its body are small beads and orange auklet sheaths used as bait, suspended on quill or sinew line pegged into holes in the shank. Another hook (176137), used for grayling, has a shank of fossil ivory with unusual tan and white stripes. The second grayling hook (33720) resembles a fish and has an ivory shank inlaid with red and white beads and sections of an organic stem of some type commonly used to plug holes, to make eye inlays, and to secure lines. A herring hook has a shank filled with many of these inlays. This profusion of decorated and specialized miniature hooks from Norton Sound can be contrasted with the more simple, standardized hooks found south of the Yukon, where the forms resemble the smelt hooks attached to the Cape Vancouver tomcod rig previously illustrated.

Cape Nome 176271, 3.1 cm; 176272, 3.0 cm; Unalakleet 176137, 2.7 cm; 33720, 4.9 cm; 33731, 4.3 cm

### 85. Large Hooks *iqsiit*

Hooks for larger fish tend to be simpler and less variable than smaller hooks and are less decorated. This series includes a barbed hook cut from a single piece of walrus ivory, with a baleen leader remnant and lashings to attach a sinker to its bottom. It is used for catching wolf-fish and cod on St. Lawrence Island. Shown also are a graceful antler pickerel and whitefish hook with a notched, spatulate shank from Unalakleet, an antler whitefish hook from the Lower Yukon, and a cod hook from Nunivak Island of which the brown fossil ivory shank has a split feather quill wrapped around it for attaching to a smaller secondary hook, and a thick baleen leader loop lashed with sinew. The hook has been made to resemble a minnow by adding eyes and a mouth.

St. Lawrence Island 126938, 14 cm; Unalakleet 43852, 11.5 cm; Lower Yukon 38282, 13 cm; Nunivak Island 48296, 14.5 cm

## 86. Whitefish Hooks *manat*

Nelson describes these hooks as being used for catching whitefish and losh. One, similar to those previously shown, has a dark-stained antler shank altered into a smeltlike image with blue eye beads and an incised mouth. The method of attaching the leader through two holes in the upper shank and of supporting it in vertical position with sinew lashings can be seen. The other is a curious piece collected on the Lower Yukon. Its bent hardwood shank is fitted with a curved iron barb lashed with European cotton line wrapped in bark sheathing. A similar technique has been used to fasten a cotton twine leader protected by bark serving. This hook is clearly not a product of local Eskimo handiwork. It is a type of hook used for halibut fishing among cultures of the Northwest Coast, from which location it may have been introduced by trade with southern Indian or Eskimo groups or by transfer from European sailors having visited that region. If it were actually used as a whitefish hook, as Nelson suggests, it must have remained a curio of the outside world, for the idea did not spread, and it was the only one collected.

Koyuk River 44118, 13 cm; Starikwikhpak 38110, 13 cm (shank)

## 87. Bundle of Losh Hooks *qerrlurcat*

An extremely simple type of hook is sometimes used for catching losh, a large, slow-swimming bottom feeder in the cod family caught on the Lower Yukon and elsewhere. These hooks have short, tapered shanks whose bases are split to receive sharp-angled prongs of wood or antler tied by spruce root lashing. Rawhide leaders are attached in similar fashion to the tops of the shanks. These hooks are baited and set in large numbers on the river bottom. When taken into the fish's throat they cannot be dislodged even though their prongs are not barbed. When not in use they are stored with prongs inserted into bundles of grass.

Lower Yukon 38816, ca. 30 cm

# life on the tundra

## Chorus of Dogs

Eskimos in western Alaska have, over many centuries, developed extremely effective methods of traveling over land, ice, and snow. Their systems of land travel are no less ingenious than those of water transportation. Land travel is important not only for hunting caribou and fur trapping, for setting fish traps through the ice, and for hunting sea mammals at the ice edge, but also for reaching trading posts and other villages, visiting distant relatives, taking part in special festivals, and evacuating villages in the event of natural disaster, starvation, or war.

During the summer most travel is by umiak and kayak, but hunting, trapping, egging, and berry-picking frequently take people short distances away from watercourses. On such trips only minimal amounts of clothing and equipment are taken, and heavy loads of meat, skins, firewood, or other materials are carried back to the camp or the boat. Eskimos generally try to do as little overland walking as possible, especially during summer because so much of the country is marshy and covered with tussocks. The soft, lumpy ground makes walking difficult, even without a load, and people break their stride adopting a hopping gait when encountering soft ground.

**88. Harnessed Dog Toy** *qimagteruaq*

Nelson described this wooden carving as a toy polar bear wearing a dog harness. While its head slightly resembles a bear, its body is that of a dog. The discrepancy points out the ambivalent role of dogs in Eskimo society, where they function as important servants and protectors but also profane the spirits of wild food animals should they chew their bones. This belief, common in many cultures, may arise from the idea that dogs have lost their freedom in domestication. Perhaps for this reason they are rarely seen in the rich menagerie of Bering Sea Eskimo animal carvings.

Diomede Island 63644, 14 cm

## 89. Malemut Sled Model *u-ni´-ăt*

Despite its cold and frequently stormy weather, winter is a time when frozen marshes, lakes, and sea make cross-country traveling easiest, and long journeys are frequently made to hunt, trade, and visit relatives. Nelson himself made his collecting trips at this time, probably using a sled similar to this Malemut model. At full scale such sleds are 9–10 feet long and 19–24 inches wide and, with a team of seven dogs, can haul 300–400 pounds over great distances. The high bed permits travel through the soft snow often found in these regions, while the upper rail allows skin curtains or lashings to be tied between the rail and bed for protection, as in the accompanying photograph of a traveling Malemut family. Like other models collected by Nelson this one is superbly crafted. Crosspieces are tapered to reduce their weight to the structural minimum. Wooden parts are slotted or mortised and lashed or pegged into position.

SI–3845; Norton Bay 48104, 60 cm

Traveling over the tundra is more frequently done during the winter months when the surfaces are frozen and marshy ground becomes easier to traverse by direct—as the raven flies—routes. During this time of year movements are made with the aid of sleds, dogs, and snowshoes. Several different forms of sleds are used in this region. The varieties have been developed in response to ice and snow conditions occurring in different localities and the type of activity for which the sled is to be used. Eskimos traveling to the ice edge with kayaks use short hand-drawn sleds to transport their boats across pans of ice. Nelson came to understand the importance of sleds and dog teams to the Eskimo of this region from first-hand experience during his several long winter expeditions.

... Without dogs the larger portion of the great Eskimo family peopling the barren northern coast of America would find it impossible to exist in its chosen home.

In winter, the hunter is accompanied by his sledge and dogs on every important hunt. The dogs are invaluable aids in finding game in many cases, and are used to drag it homeward across the icy hummocks or snowy plains. They haul the sledges laden with household goods and children when a change of abode becomes necessary, and are ever at hand for the unstinted amount of work heaped upon them, spiced with a plentitude of kicks and blows. During the summer months they are forced to shift for themselves, unless put into harness to tow a large boat along the coast, or to accompany a hunter in the chase. ...

The moon has great influence over the dogs, and during full moon half the night is passed by them howling in chorus. During the entire winter at Saint Michaels we were invariably given a chorus every moonlight night, and the dogs of two neighboring villages joined in the serenade. Their howl is a long-drawn cry, rising and falling in somewhat regular cadence. The chorus of a hundred dogs, slightly softened by the distance, has a weird, wild harmony in keeping with the surroundings, and produces a strong and stirring effect upon the listener. (Nelson 1887:236)

## 90. Breast Yoke

People between Nunivak Island and the Kuskokwim River use breast yokes to assist them when carrying loads on their backs. A cord, permanently tied to one end of the yoke, is passed over the load, and its looped end is secured over a ridge at the other end. This yoke bears the charm image of a tattooed woman carved in relief between grooved and tapered channels bordered with inset caribou teeth, an image recalling beastly mouths on masks. Such yokes ease the burden of the load while protecting the traveler from harm on the journey.

Nunivak Island (W.H. Dall Collection) 16251, 51 cm

## A Winter Hunt

In a village on the Lower Yukon a man is preparing for a winter hunt. He gathers extra clothing and several caribou robes, used for shelter and bedding; collects his bow and arrows, other weapons, and fire-starting kit; his axe and crooked knife; lashing cord; animal snares and heavy-duty thong; a supply of dried meat; and a small bag containing fish or seal oil to be consumed with the meat. These he ties onto his sled, being sure to add a few arms-full of dried fish for dog food, and lashes everything down beneath a skin covering. He unties his dogs from their stakes and attaches them in pairs along the central trace, placing his trusted leader, a female, at the front. Then, with a wave to his family the hunter mushes out through the village, picking up the trail that has been beaten into the snow on the river by other hunters, and heads off toward the dark band to the east which marks the edge of the forest. There he plans to check his traps and, if he is lucky, hopes to find a bear's den, or a caribou.

The hunter travels at the rear of the sled, sometimes riding when the road is hard and smooth, but more often working with the dogs and using the handlelike projections of the side rails to maneuver the sled over bumps and through grassy or brush-clogged areas. Periodically he calls orders to the dogs to urge them on or turn them one way or the other, but they need little instruction here in the flat land. Hooked near his right hand is a whip with a short wooden handle, its supple thong tipped with a frayed sealskin tassel. This he uses more for psychological effect than punishment, satisfied with the result produced by the whip's crack over the dogs' heads to spur the entire team onward. Occasionally he allows the whip to bite, and the yelp of the laggard has a remarkable effect on the whole team.

Although it is a fine day, the hunter is wearing his snow goggles, which protect his eyes from blowing snow. More importantly, however, they prevent him from being blinded by the glare off the bright snow and ice. It is spring and the days are lengthening, making longer trips possible, but

**91. Snow Goggles** *i-gauk´*

Snow blindness, an occupational hazard of northern travelers, results when the retina becomes burned by excessive ultraviolet radiation reflected from snow-covered landscapes. Protection is afforded from this debilitating and painful condition by wearing goggles to cut down the amount of light entering the eye. This selection shows some of the styles found north and south of Norton Sound, carved and painted according to regional patterns and individual preferences. The three goggles on the left from Point Hope and northern Norton Sound illustrate the "graphic" spectacle and visor forms common here and in northern Alaska and Canada. South of the Yukon they are replaced by more "plastic" grooved and modeled forms, painted a variety of subtle colors and frequently having an animal or masklike appearance seen most clearly in the pair from Sabotnisky. The boundary of the graphic and plastic mask-form styles conforms to the Yupik–Inupiak language frontier.

Left, top to bottom: Point Hope 63825, 15 cm; Cape Darby 44256, 15 cm; Norton Sound 44329, 13 cm Right, top to bottom: Mission 38251, 15.5 cm; Lower Yukon 38658, 16 cm; Sabotnisky 48996, 16.5 cm

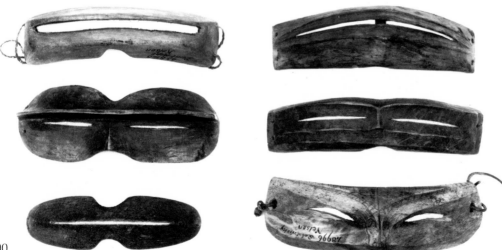

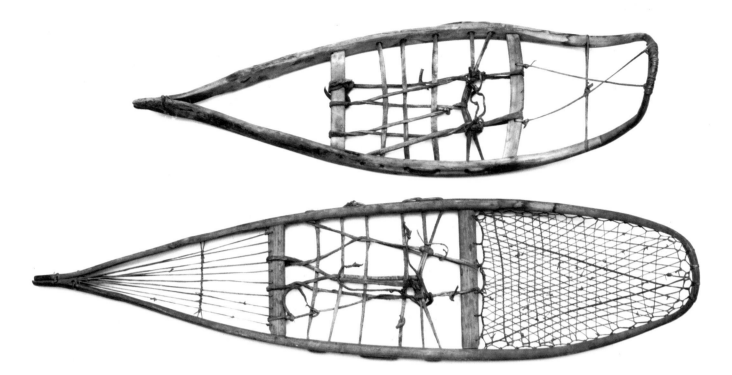

**92. Snowshoes** *tangluk*

Snowshoes of the lower type are used by the Eskimos in eastern Norton Sound and south along the coast to the Kuskokwim for traveling over land in areas where protected conditions result in the accumulation of soft, deep snow. Each is made with two wooden strips bent and joined at the front and back ends. Coarse thong netting fills the foot space between two crossbars, while fine rawhide netting is used for the front and back sections. The frames are bent up in front to facilitate their rising to the surface of the snow when walking. Ornamental grooves are found on the crossbars and sides of the frames.

These snowshoes are nearly identical to ones used by the Ingalik Indians east of Norton Sound and probably are modeled after the Indian form. Snowshoes used for travel over sea ice are shorter and have coarse mesh to withstand the ravages of jagged ice. Here, where deep snow does not collect, their purpose is to prevent the foot from falling into cracks in broken and hummocky ice, and to distribute a person's weight over a wider area when traversing new or weak ice. A specimen from Cape Darby illustrates this type, a smaller variant of which is also used on St. Lawrence Island and the Siberian mainland.

Malemut 45400, 112 cm; Cape Darby 48092, 88 cm

also bringing a greater danger of snow blindness. The affliction, caused by burns on the retina, can strike without warning if one is not wearing goggles, even on overcast days. Therefore he wears the goggles nearly continuously while traveling, pleased also that they carry the image of a protective animal to mask his own appearance and give him confidence in dealing with the unknown ahead.

At times, when encountering heavy snow, he breaks out his snowshoes to tramp a path ahead for the dogs, whose legs are not long enough to haul the sled through the deep soft snow. The snowshoes are old, and he has replaced the thong and sinew webbing many times since the wooden frames were made. With them he can easily work in the deep snow that accumulates along the forest edge and in the soft brushy landscape and tall grass tundra in marshy ground. When spring sealing on the hard snow of the sea ice, he uses a shorter, more sturdy pair, lacking the delicate sinew webbing of his fine sledging snowshoes. He has seen Indians using nearly identical snowshoes on the Upper Yukon, and supposes that, as in many other cases, they have borrowed this idea from the Eskimo. In his kit, he also carries antler ice creepers with small teeth on their bottoms, which he lashes to the soles of his boots for use on hard icy surfaces.

Before leaving the village the hunter performed certain rituals customary for one preparing to hunt the fierce grizzly or brown bear, known as *Ta-ku´-ka*. This knowledgeable and cunning creature lives in the surrounding country and hibernates during the winter months when it can be more safely hunted if one can find its den. He has been careful not to speak disrespectfully of bears, and has never mentioned to anyone that he intended to go bear hunting. He knows that bears are clairvoyant and would have been instantly aware of his intention, making the hunt more difficult and perhaps even leading to his death if a bear should lie in wait to attack him. The bear spirit is exceedingly powerful. Many stories are told about the origins of its wild and vengeful nature, and ceremonies are performed in the *qasgiq* on its behalf. As the hunter thinks of this, one of these stories comes to mind:

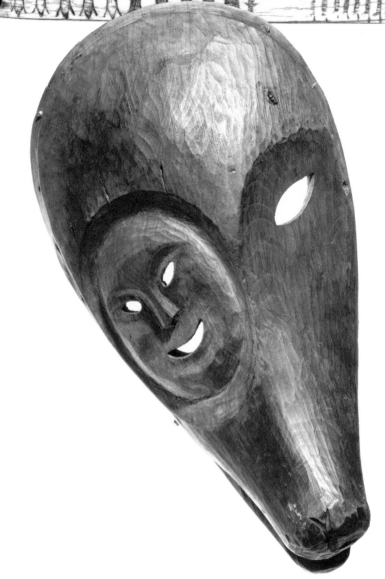

THE RED BEAR (TA-KU´-KA)

On the tundra, south of the Yukon mouth, there once lived an orphan boy with his aunt. They were quite alone, and one summer day the boy took his kaiak and traveled away to see where people lived on the Yukon, of whom he had heard. When he came to the river, he traveled up its course until he reached a large village. There he landed and the people ran down to the shore, seized him, broke his kaiak to pieces, tore his clothing from him, and beat him badly.

The boy was kept there until the end of summer, the subject of continual beating and ill treatment from the villagers. In the fall one of the men took pity on him, made him a kaiak, and started him homeward, where he arrived after a long absence. When he reached home he saw that a large village had grown up by his aunt's house. As soon as he landed, he went to this aunt's house and entered, frightening her very much, for he had been starved and beaten so long that he looked almost like a skeleton.

**93. Hunting Tallies** *pitat tavenrait*
The pelts of furbearing animals are important to people of western Alaska where the wide variety of animal furs has contributed to the development of elaborate clothing styles and decorative use of fur. Trade in pelts of different and prized species is important in local and regional exchange, and has become even more important with the onset of European trapping trade. This engraved ivory drill bow illustrates the custom of portraying different kinds of pelts on men's objects of this kind. This side shows thirty foxes, one otter, and ten wolves or wolverines. The reverse side has ten otters, ten wolves, and four walrus.
Probably north of Bering Strait T–16051, 40 cm

**94. Bear Inua Mask** *taqukaruaq*
This mask, representing the *inua* of the largest land mammal, comes from Starikwikhpak, a salmon fishing village on the Lower Yukon below Rasboinsky. The mask is described by Nelson as a red (grizzly) bear. Its face is painted red except for the smiling *inua* in the right eye, which is left in natural finish and resembles iconlike images prevalent in the region. Small pegs are set in a groove surrounding the edge of the mask to secure a strip of fur or feathers, now missing, but probably similar to that drawn by Nelson (1899) on a black bear mask from Sabotnisky (fig. 263). Three slits over the *inua* face contain remnants of hair which would have hung down concealing it from view except when revealed in dance. Above the left eye is a large peg, probably for an ear attachment. Smaller pegs are found at the corners of the mouth. The rear of the mask is slightly hollowed. Red paint, hidden from viewer and applied inside the animal's eye and in the eyes and mouth of the *inua*, is a common feature of religious symbolism in Yukon–Kuskokwim masks. Both red and black bears figure prominently in local mythology. This mask was probably used in dramatic performances relating to *Ta-kú-ka*, a vengeful wife who tricks her rivals and thrusts their faces under boiling oil. Then, turning into a red bear, she kills her husband and eats his unfaithful heart.
Starikwikhpak 38865, 30 cm

### 95. Braining Trap *naneryaq*

In northern Norton Sound and Bering Strait, and on St. Lawrence Island, foxes are caught with spring traps using heavy spiked clubs. These clubs are inserted through a sinew cord which passes down the inside of a hollow log or piece of whale bone. The ends of the cord are tied to a crosspiece of bone which, when twisted in opposite directions, develops great tension. When sufficiently tight, the braining lever is pulled back and secured to a trigger peg in a second arm rigidly fixed to the base. A bait line is tied to the trigger and runs out through a hole in the cylinder's base. The line's length is measured to insure that the fox's head will be precisely beneath the falling blow. The trap is buried in the ground with all but the lever and bait concealed. Larger versions are used to kill wolves and even polar bears. The limited distribution of such traps on the American mainland, where prototype trap technology of this kind is not used, suggests that they may have been introduced from Siberia.

Gambell, St. Lawrence Island (H.B. Collins Collection) 356917, 37 cm wide

### 96. "Wolf Killers"

In the early days many animals were captured by digging steep-sided pits and covering them over with grass mats on which bait was placed. Deadfalls were also constructed and continue in use today. Wary animals like wolves and wolverines are also taken with a simple but gruesome instrument made from sharpened strips of baleen. The strips are soaked until pliable, then are folded into an accordianlike bundle and tied with a cord. When dry, the cord is removed and the bundle is wrapped in an oil-soaked piece of fish skin and set out. Once in the warm belly, stomach juices cause it to unfold, piercing the organs and causing an agonizing death. The hunter, easily following the bloody trail, recovers the carcass whose pelt is important for parka ruffs and trade.

Anvik 38488; Point Barrow (P.H. Ray Collection) 89540, 32 cm

When his aunt recognized him, she received his story with words of pity, then words of anger at the cruel villagers. When he had finished telling her of his sufferings, she told him to bring her a piece of wood, which he did; this they worked into a small image of an animal with long teeth and long, sharp claws, painting it red upon the sides and white on the throat. Then they took the image to the edge of the creek and placed it in the water, the aunt telling it to go and destroy every one it could find at the village where her boy had been.

The image did not move, and the old woman took it out of the water and cried over it, letting her tears fall upon it, and then put it back in the water, saying, "Now, go and kill the bad people who beat my boy." At this the image floated across the creek and crawled up the other bank, where it began to grow, soon reaching a large size, when it became a red bear. It turned and looked at the old woman until she called out to it to go and spare none.

The bear then went away until he came to the village on the great river. It met a man just going for water and it quickly tore him to pieces; then the bear stayed near this village until he had killed more than half of the people, and the others were preparing to leave it in

order to escape destruction. He then swam across the Yukon and went over the tundra to the farther side of Kuskokwim river, killing every one he saw, for the least sign of life seemed to fill him with fury until it was destroyed. From the Kuskokwim the bear turned back, and one day it stood on the creek bank where it had become endowed with life. Seeing the people on the other bank he became filled with fury, tearing the ground with his claws and growling, and began to cross the creek. When the villagers saw this they were much frightened and ran about, saying "Here is the old woman's dog; we shall all be killed. Tell the old woman to stop her dog." And they sent her to meet the bear. The bear did not try to hurt her, but was passing by to get at the other people when she caught it by the hair on its neck, saying "Do not hurt these people who have been kind to me and have given me food when I was hungry."

After this she led the bear into her house and, sitting down, told him that he had done her bidding well and had pleased her, but that he must not injure people any more unless they tried to hurt or abuse him. When she had finished telling him this she led him to the door and sent him away over the tundra. Since this time there have always been red bears. (Nelson 1899:485–86)

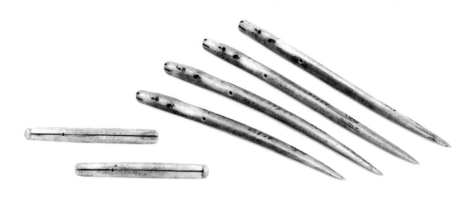

### 97. Bow Cable Twisters *qiputaq*

Cable twisters are used to tighten the sinew backing on a bow. They are made with one end slightly thicker than the other, each end having a low ridge on opposite sides. The sinew cable is spread with an ivory wedge until the thin end of a twister can be inserted. After levering a half-turn the twister is slipped back through the cable to the other side and given another half-turn, and so on. Sometimes two twisters are used simultaneously. When the desired tension is obtained, the twisted cable is fixed in position with sinew lashing.

The wedges, ornamented with caribou heads, are also used as throwing sticks in a gambling game. Each player first places a set of two stakes in the ground. He then withdraws one from his set and places his "stakes" in the form of furs or other property on the remaining one. The players withdraw a given distance, and each in turn makes his throw. The one whose thrown stake lodges closest to his placed stake wins the "stakes" of the other.

Sledge Island 44688 (set), twisters 10.5 cm long; stakes ca. 18–20 cm

### 98. Sinew-backed Bow

Hunters in the Yukon–Kuskokwim region make sinew-backed bows for hunting and war. These bows are among the finest native weapons produced in North America. In making this bow a Cape Vancouver hunter began with a flawless piece of seasoned spruce or larch. Using his crooked knife he carved the wood into shape, adding an ornamental groove. Then, after steaming it, he blocked in three bends, an in-curving one in the center and two out-curving ones in the elbows. After the bends had set, he fastened twenty lengths of braided sinew cord from end to end along its outside edge, drawing the bow into "recurved" position. Then he lashed the strands together into a single cable, leaving six openings. Through these he inserted his sinew twisters to tighten the cable still further, lashing each in sequence to the bow when tight. Then he carved an ivory stiffener to fit between the cable and the bow and lashed stiffener and cable to the bow. Finally, he made a sinew bowstring with looped ends and fitted it to the bow, which was now many times more powerful than an unreinforced wooden bow.

Cape Vancouver 36029, 141 cm

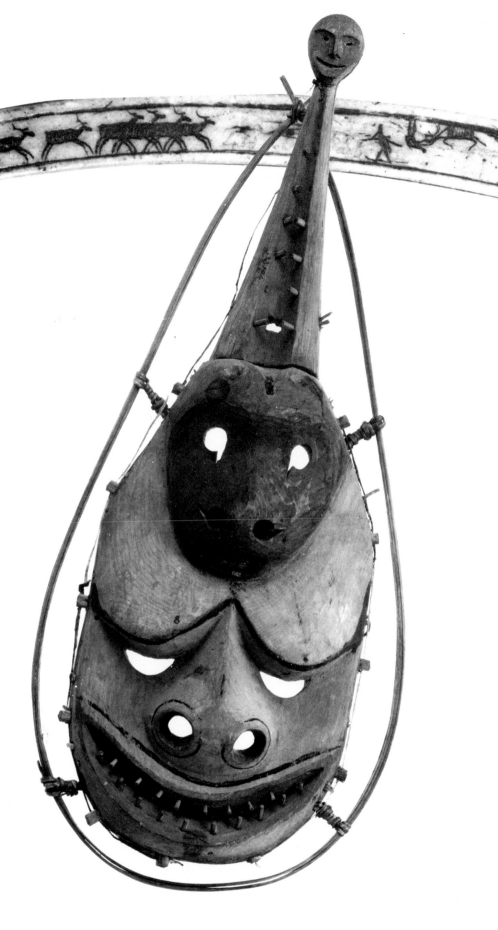

### 99. Caribou Inua Mask *tuntupiaruaq*

According to legend, Raven created the caribou next after man and mountain sheep, making the caribou ferocious and giving them sharp, wolflike teeth with which they sometimes attacked man. Later, after man tricked them into eating an *agoutak* of caribou fat and berries, their sharp teeth fell out and were replaced by small ones, and they became docile and harmless.

These mythological events are expressed symbolically in this *inua* mask from Cape Romanzof, the fierce, beastly image of which bears a benign caribou upon its lowering brow. The caribou's flat and harmless incisors are seen along with its distinctive eye slits and empty holes for its missing antlers. This is surmounted by a grooved, peg-toothed extension topped by a human face. The relationship between spirit, caribou, and man is continuously strengthened through ritual and ceremonial activity because caribou provide many materials—fur, hide, antler, sinew, food—critical to the maintenance of Bering Sea culture.

The periphery of the mask was once bordered by a delicate caribou fur ruff mounted in split pegs around the mask, and a similar fringe, parkalike, surrounded the human face. The mask also has an outer hoop of thin splints mounted to the body with split willow roots, a common feature of Yukon–Kuskokwim masks which probably signifies symbolic containment or "wholeness." The mouths of both beast and caribou are painted red, as is the pegged "mouth" groove above, indicating blood or life-substance. Nostrils, upper lip, and brows are outlined with black paint, while the caribou head is colored with a blue pigment often noted in Nelson's notes but which is rarely preserved on his artifacts due to its fugitive condition and lack of a strong bonding agent.

Cape Romanzof 33104, 79 cm tall

As the hunter travels he thinks also of other game he might find. Fur pelts are next in his mind, knowing that they will be useful for trading and for the new garments his wife plans to make for the next festival season. On a previous trip into the country he set traps for foxes, otters, and beavers, and hopes that they have not been discovered by wolverines.

> The Wolverine is one of the most detested animals found in all the fur country. Its life is a continual warfare against all living things, and every man's hand is against it. They invariably steal the bait from traps whenever they have the opportunity, and very rarely do they get caught. Should they find an animal in the trap they make short work of it, and in Northern Alaska, as elsewhere in the fur country, they sometimes take up a line of traps so persistently that the hunter is forced to abandon it and look for a new route. They frequently follow a sledge party in the interior for days, visiting every camp as soon as it is abandoned, in order to pick up the scraps left, and anything left in a tree for safe-keeping is sure to be destroyed if the Wolverine can get at it. (Nelson 1887:249)

Reaching the higher ground within the forest fringe the hunter pauses for a light meal consisting of strips of dried whitefish dipped in seal oil. Continuing on, he soon comes upon the tracks of a small group of caribou, the first such sign he has seen in this region for several years. Wolf tracks are also present. Many years ago caribou herds were common throughout the country, even in many of the low Delta regions, and during his younger years and those of his father's, had been hunted extensively for trade to

**100. Hunting and War Arrows** *khūt*

Arrows with stone tips were still being used in Nelson's day for hunting caribou and for war. Self-tipped antler points with barbs and conical tangs were most common. A large arrow for caribou and grizzly bear is marked with two red stripes on its shaft. One of the arrows from Nunivak Island, lacking its blade, has a V-shaped hafting splice and an unusual point style for this area. Most Nunivak Island arrows have triangular cross-sections and multiple barbs. This arrow has a wolf totem and was obtained from a Malemut group formerly residing in Norton Sound. Nelson's collection from Nunivak Island includes many artifacts indicating contacts or origins elsewhere, probably because it was a trading crossroads, and because its rich ecology included caribou and attracted foreigners whose homelands suffered economic privation or unrest.

Cape Romanzof 176124, 80 cm; Rasboinsky 49043, 99 cm; Nunivak Island (W.H. Dall Collection) 16418, 81 cm; Nunivak Island 43689, 73 cm

**101. Wrist Guards** *mal´-iñ-i´-ûk*

Wrist guards, part of the Eskimo bow hunting complex for at least two thousand years, are worn to protect the bow arm wrist from being injured by the string when the arrow is released. The smaller piece is made from a thin ivory sheet decorated with the chain or "tooth" pattern. The larger piece is made from fossil mammoth tusk, a material that can be found in various localities eroding from permafrost banks. Mammoth ivory is an important trade item. Its geological occurrence is explained in legends about *ko-gukh´-pûk*, a huge mythical beast who lives underground and is figured on a fine serving bowl collected by Nelson at Nulukhtulo-gumut (fig. 125).

Norton Sound 44080, 6.5 cm; Pikmiktalik 33615, 5 cm

## 102. Arrowshaft Straighteners *nalqigutek*

Wooden shafts intended for use as arrows are straightened by inserting them into wrench-like tools and applying pressure at points where kinks and bends occur. Found throughout western Alaska, those from north of the Yukon are often carved in the form of caribou. The Cape Nome specimen is made from walrus jawbone carved into a caribou head with a blue glass bead for one eye and a shiny blue-green rock crystal (jadeite?) for the other. The caribou's mouth is open and tongue outstretched as so often seen in Paleolithic art and in real life. The hoof amulet helps guide the arrow's flight, a useful device on a straightening tool. The masterful crouching caribou has protruding eyes, a skeletized windpipe incised on its throat, thin legs with detailed hooves, and a mark for its umbilical attachment. Rather than emphasizing hunting magic, these immature features suggest a young or fetal caribou amulet whose function is to insure the continued abundance of the species. Fetal caribou are frequently taken during the spring hunt before the females have dropped their calves. Their soft hide is prized for certain items of clothing.

Cape Nome 44415, 20 cm; Cape Denbigh 176245, 15 cm

## 103. Quiver Stiffener

This old, polished ivory quiver stiffener is lashed alongside a pliable fishskin arrow quiver to protect the arrows from damage. The image, which Nelson identifies as a wolf, may be a social insignia or clan affiliation or may have magical properties. The beast's eyes are set in raised ivory sockets and consist of polished blackened plugs of wood inset with small ivory beads. An unusual halterlike motif, perhaps representing a muzzle, crossing the jaw suggests "leashed power" on a container of weapons. This type of motif is not found on beasts portrayed on harpoons intended for direct action. The postcranial decoration—a bilateral spurred line with symmetrical limb appendages—recalls stories of fearsome multilegged mythological beasts and decoration on storyknives and Nunivak Island walrus harpoons.

St. Michael (L. Turner Collection) 24596, 54 cm

the Russians. Now caribou skins, antler, and sinew have to be obtained from other peoples to the north, where they are still common, in exchange for small mammal furs, such as those he is trapping.

The disappearance of the caribou has always seemed strange to the hunter and as he thought about it he recalled a portion of the Raven story:

> . . . After a time the old man began to wish to see the fine sky land again, but his people tried to induce him to stay with them. He told his children that they must not feel badly at his absence, and then, in company with Raven, he returned to the sky land. The dwarf people welcomed them, and they lived there for a long time, until the villagers on the earth had become very numerous and killed a great many animals. This angered Man and Raven so much that one night they took a long line and a grass basket with which they descended to the earth, Raven caught ten reindeer, which he put into the basket with the old man; then one end of the cord was fastened to the basket and Raven returned to the sky, drawing it up after him. The next evening they took the reindeer and went down close to Man's village; the deer were then told to break down the first house they came to and destroy the people, for men were becoming too numerous. The reindeer did as they were told and ate up the people with their sharp, wolf-like teeth, after which they returned to the sky; the next night they came back and destroyed another house with its people in the same manner. The villagers had now become much frightened and covered the third house with a mixture of deer fat and berries. When the reindeer tried to destroy this house they filled their mouths with the fat and sour berries, which caused them to run off shaking their heads so violently that all their long, sharp teeth fell out. Afterward small teeth, such as reindeer now have, grew in their places, and these animals became harmless.
>
> Man and Raven returned to the sky after the reindeer ran away, Man saying, "If something is not done to stop people from taking so many animals they will continue until they have killed everything you have made. It is better to take away the sun from them so that they will be in the dark and will die." (Nelson 1899:460)

These words had a strong effect on the men, who frequently discussed this story. Perhaps Raven and Man were right about the growing numbers of people and how they had killed too many caribou in the early days before they knew better. But, they argued, people then did not know how to properly treat the animal spirits, and were sometimes slanderous of them. This, too, could have caused the caribou's disappearance, as in recent times. For this reason, careful attention had since been given to caribou ritual in hopes that their numbers would increase again. Such treatment was also given to birds, but they seemed less sensitive to the ways of men. Only fish seemed totally oblivious to human treatment, and since their numbers do not diminish or fluctuate greatly, people feel less inclined to give them the special attention in stories and ceremonies called for in the case of land and sea mammals and birds.

Certainly the hunter recalled the many caribou that he and his father had killed in earlier years. Women still wear belts ornamented with hundreds of their teeth. In winter and summer men had set snares with strong loops of rawhide attached to trees, brush, or stakes set into the ground. They had also stalked caribou with bows and arrows, approaching them from downwind with their bodies close together, belly to back, imitating a four-legged caribou until they were within range. Hunters had participated in communal drives in valleys and at natural crossing places, using fences of wood, stone, and brush to channel the animals' movement toward pens and enclosures where they were killed. Pitfalls, sometimes combined with snares, were also dug into deep snowbanks in winter or into the permafrost in summer, and were covered with grass mats camouflaged with snow or earth. Some say that this method was widely used in the past and that many animals were taken this way. The depressions in the ground can still be seen in places where this type of hunting was practiced. This method could also be used to capture wolves, foxes, and other animals that could be tempted to venture out to take the bait placed in the center of a camouflaged grass mat covering.

When he is able to get close enough to this group of caribou, he will stalk them with his bow and arrow, circling around them to lie in wait downwind in their direction of movement. His dogs will have to be concealed some distance away, and he will need a good hiding place.

**104. Caribou Snare Cord**

Caribou snaring is practical in areas where brush or trees provide means for supporting the cords. One end of the snare is fastened to a limb or trunk, and the opened noose is supported by light lines or a stick. Caribou, who do not see very well, frequently become caught. In some areas pits used to be dug beneath the snares to help capture the animals.

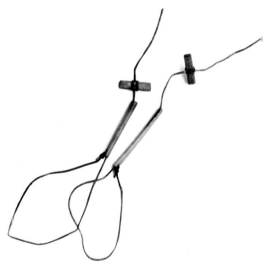

**105. Marmot Snares** *qanganarcuun negaq*

Parry's Marmot, a small ground squirrel whose fur is prized for light, colorful summer parkas, is caught with small noose snares. The loose end is tied to a bent sapling with the noose suspended over its habitual runways and held open with grass attachments. When the marmot touches the trigger stick the sapling lifts the animal off the ground. He cannot bite through the line because it is protected by a bird bone sheath.

Koyuk River, Norton Sound 44129, sheaths ca. 6 cm

## 106. Horned Puffin Eating Walrus *qaterpak*

A horned puffin (*Fratercula corn.*), a small bird with a large appetite, is shown in this Magemut dance mask swimming on the surface of the water with a walrus in its beak. The walrus's body is held firmly while its head, attached with a cloth neck, flops lifelessly when the mask-wearer dances.

The mask is surrounded by two hoops which are mounted on pegs and held apart by root fiber lashings. They once sported fancy feather plumes. Also missing is the caribou fur ruff which encircled the body of the bird. The bird's feet and one of its three wooden tail feathers are also missing. Its wings "flap" near its head, attached with flexible sections of spruce or willow root.

The symbolism of this mask is as complex as its design and execution. It embodies a powerful *inua* spirit-hunter acting, with his magical reddened parts, through the person of the horned puffin. The perforated hands signify the spirit's compassion for the animals he hunts, allowing some to successfully slip through his palms and return safely to their homes in the sea.

South of Lower Yukon 33107, 28 cm (between fingertips)

## 107. Duck and Goose Snare
*yaqulegcurcuutet negat*

Snares often are used to catch waterfowl that are too wary to be stalked. This type of snare is set just above the water's surface near the mouths of small streams or between clumps of grass and weeds in areas frequented by these birds. It consists of a 3.5-meter-long strip of baleen to which nearly thirty small slip nooses have been tied at 10-centimeter intervals.

Koyuk River, Norton Sound 44063, 3.5 m long

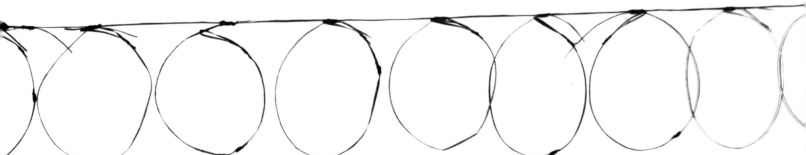

**108. Gull Snares** *naruyarcurcuutet negat*
Gulls are caught with bi-pointed antler gorges attached to a floating line. The gorges are slipped down the gullets of small bait fish. When the bird takes the bait and tries to fly away, the gorge toggles in its throat, capturing the "captor."
Northern Norton Sound 37651, ca. 8 cm

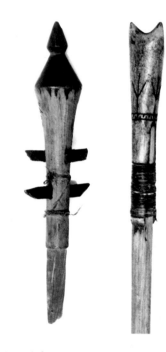

The only live animals along his route are ptarmigan, seen in flocks of up to one hundred birds feeding among the willow thickets and low brush. Several times he stops to shoot some with his blunt-tipped bird arrows. He is always amazed at the way they remain motionless as he approaches, apparently counting on their white winter plumage as a disguise.

> In the northern portion of their range these Grouse (willow ptarmigan) are summer residents; but in autumn, the last of August and during September, they unite in great flocks and migrate south to the sheltered banks of the Kuskokwim and Yukon Rivers and their numerous tributaries. In early spring, as the warmth of the returning sun begins to be felt, they troop back to their breeding grounds once more. During a large portion of the year these birds form one of the most characteristic accompaniments of the scenery in the northern portion of Alaska. They change their summer dress for the white of winter in autumn before they make their migration, and after they arrive at their winter destination they keep in immense flocks about the open glades and willow-grown country along the courses of various inland streams. . . .
>
> Among the Alaskan natives, both Eskimo and Indian, especially those in the northern two-thirds of the Territory, this bird is one of the most important sources of food supply, and through the entire winter it is snared and shot in great abundance, and many times it is the only defense they possess against the ever-recurring periods of scarcity and famine. . . . (Nelson 1887:132)

These birds provide a meal or two and are excellent roasted over the fire, but a steady diet of ptarmigan, like rabbits, is too low in fat to nourish a hunter for long in winter time. At other times of the year ptarmigan are netted in large numbers by hunters concealed along their customary flight paths. Men lie on the tundra at dusk with a long fishnet stretched between poles. When they hear the sound of an approaching flock they raise the net, flopping it back down again on top of the birds that strike it. After dispatching them, the hunters prepare for another flock. At other times,

**109. Bird Points**
Crosspieces have been passed through the body of this arrowpoint, which belonged to a Nunivak Island boy, so that it will lodge in the bird's flesh and feathers and not pass through. The saddle-shaped point is another common form, here decorated with tooth pattern and raven's foot engravings. It is fastened to the shaft with a V-scarf joint and lashed with sinew.
Nunivak Island 48259, 15.5 cm; Unalakleet 33824, 11 cm

### 110. Ivory Bird Bolas

While traveling in eastern Norton Sound, Nelson collected this bird bolas made with walrus ivory balls. The balls have rounded bottoms and taper to a point in faceted cuts marked with red-pigmented engravings of ravens' feet. Thongs tied through small inset holes join in a central knot together with a gull's feather, which helps guide the implement in flight. Red pigment is not often found on engraved ivory objects, black being more common. The significance of the color change is not known.

Shaktolik 38444, cords ca. 1 m, balls, 6 cm

### 111. Ptarmigan Snare Stick and Net
*qangqiircurcuutet*

In spring, stakes with noose snares ringed around a stuffed "challenger" decoy are placed on a hill within the territory of a pugnacious male ptarmigan. The hunter, concealed nearby, makes the answering call which almost invariably results in the defender dashing at the invading rival, and dinner for the Eskimo.

Ptarmigan are also caught during their spring "rut" with small nets of twisted sinew set in snow-free patches of tundra where birds search for wintered-over berries. Nelson describes traveling with an Eskimo friend who set one of these nets around a ptarmigan decoy made of snow, to which he added brown grass about the neck to simulate emerging spring plumage. Nearby males were then called in. Failing to notice the mesh, they became entangled and were captured. This net is made of extremely light filaments of two-ply caribou sinew tied in twelve-centimeter mesh. The mesh is fastened to heavier head and foot lines, with their ends secured to wooden stakes tipped with antler points. A third stake in the middle of the net forms the triangular enclosure around the decoy.

St. Michael 33812, 33.5 cm; 33820, ca. 50 cm tall

### 112. Bird Hunting Arrows

Bow hunting for birds is usually conducted with blunt-tipped arrows which stun or kill the prey without damaging its plumage or skin. Arrow tips made from antler, ivory, or wood occur in crenelated, conical, saddle, and dentate forms. Some have crossbars inserted through their shafts. Nelson collected a few quiver sets that contain different types of arrows for hunting different types of birds, each arrow carrying the same owner's mark. In these quivers an arrow with a different mark occasionally is seen, probably a loan from a friend or someone else's lost stray.

Materials for making bird arrows are selected for practical and spiritual reasons. The Nulato arrow, attributed by Nelson to Eskimos although collected in Indian territory, is fletched with gyrfalcon feathers. This formidable bird of prey hunts the same birds man does, striking them out of the air with deadly accuracy and speed. Used here, its feathers lend potency and help guide the arrow to its mark.

In addition to blunt-tipped arrows, barbed, multipronged points are sometimes used for waterfowl.

Nulato 33827, 71 cm; Yukon Delta 33857, 86 cm

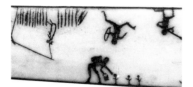

## 113. Bent-Wood Berry Bucket and Pestle
*qaltaq*

In late summer the countryside fills with stooping people carrying small wooden berry buckets like this one. Young or old, all gather sweet berries which they crush with pestles and mix with seal fat, fish liver, or other delectables to make a treat known as *agoutak*, sometimes called "Eskimo ice cream."

Buckets are made by men from thinned slabs of wood which they steam in the *qasgiq*, bend, and join in a broad scarf with glue made from seal blood and ocher, and spruce root stitching. The bottoms are carved separately and are snapped into the wall section in the final stage of construction. The oval shape is produced by leaving a thicker section of wall for the long sides of the oval and thinning the ends for bending tighter curves. The handle is steamed and then bent after crimping its inside with the teeth.

This bucket has a pale red wash and stronger red painting on its rim and outside joint. Shallow grooves trace its outside upper and lower wall and inside the rim. A raven's foot motif is found on the bucket's bottom enclosed by another groove. Like many Yukon–Kuskokwim containers the bottom has a small rectangular impression punched into the wood, perhaps formed when the bottom is snapped in place. However, similar marks are often found on food containers with painted or incised marks of social or religious significance.

Kigiktauik 33066, 10 cm; Mission 48844, 12 cm

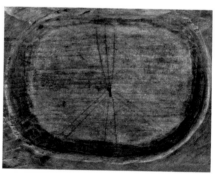

## 114. Root Pick *elautaq*

One of the favorite vegetable foods is the bulbous root of a cotton grass plant (*Eriophorum angustifolium*) occurring in the wet lowland delta country. Resembling small onions, the roots are peeled and eaten on the spot or cooked with other foods. Mice also like these roots and bring them into their nests in the tall grass. When the snow melts in spring people follow the mouse trails through the dead winter grass until they reach the nests, which they break open, and take the roots. Later, when the ground thaws, people leave the mice alone and dig for roots themselves with picks like this.

Kigiktauik 33081, 29 cm (pick)

**115. Driftwood at Russian Mission**

In the spring each year the Yukon, Kuskokwim, and other rivers bring down huge quantities of driftwood from the Alaskan interior. For villages like Mission, within the forest edge, driftwood is supplemented by a variety of forest trees and shrubs. For the tundra villages in the lower delta and those on the coast, driftwood forms the major supply of materials for houses, caches, boat frames, and other artifacts. Where driftwood is scarce it is carefully collected and conserved.

Large logs may be claimed and marked with the finder's insignia until the piece can be brought home. Seasoned driftwood is prized for making masks. Since different woods have different properties of strength, hardness, and flexibility, freshly cut woods with special characteristics are often traded far from their sources. Indians supplied some wood to Bering Sea Eskimos, whose artifacts sometimes make use of exotic species like Douglas fir and oak. These woods may have been obtained through trade from the south or from visiting European vessels or their wrecks.

SI–76–983

especially in spring when the ground begins to uncover, decoy birds are set up on knolls and are used together with nets or snares to capture male birds that attack the decoys in an effort to defend their turf. Other types of snares designed for different birds, including ducks, geese, and gulls, are set in the summer along the shores of lakes and streams.

These thoughts quickly bring to the hunter's mind the highlight of the summer season when people in the Delta gather in August on the lakes to conduct massive bird drives. These drives are planned to take place when the young are not yet able to fly and when the adults are still in the moult and can only swim or dive. Beginning at the end of a long narrow lake, people form a chain of kayaks across the water from shore to shore and sweep downwind banging the sides of their boats and making a general commotion to scare the birds to the supposed sanctuary at the other end. When the birds approach the far shore, they become more anxious and excited. People set long fishnets between poles across the line of boats, both in the air and under the water. As the birds try to fly or swim underwater through the line, they strike the net and are quickly gathered up by the boatmen. At its height, the drive takes on a scene of wild pandemonium—with birds dashing back and forth and diving, their heads popping up and down as they panic as the enclosure tightens, and all the while the squawks and calls of the distressed and dying mingle with the hunters' cries as they converge on the small remaining patch of bird-filled water.

These hunts result in boatloads of birds being taken, so that the hunters are able to fill their larders for the fall and winter months ahead, and will have plenty of skins and feathers for garments and ceremonial items.

*Where the first man lived there had now grown a large village, for the people did everything as Raven directed them, and as soon as a child was born it was rubbed with clay and so caused to grow to its full stature in three days. One day Raven came back and sat by Man, and they talked of many things. Man asked Raven about the land he had made in the sky. Raven said that he had made a fine land there, whereupon Man asked to be taken to see it. This was agreed to and they started toward the sky where they arrived in a short time. . . .*

*There man found himself in a beautiful country with a very much better climate than that on earth. The people living here wore handsomely made fur clothing, worked in ornamental patterns, such as people now wear on earth; for Man, on his return, showed his people how to make clothes in this manner, and the patterns have been retained ever since.*

Nelson 1899:457

around the lamp

# life in the village

## Approaching a Village

Long, flat marshy expanses, occasionally broken up by distant mountain ranges, are spotted with clusters of houses built along the coast and along the river banks in the interior of the Yukon–Kuskokwim region. Seen from a distance Bering Sea Eskimo villages rise from their wet grassy surroundings, a mixture of inhabited and abandoned structures—villages in this region being of unknown archeological age.

Bering Sea Eskimos have, through the ages, selected their habitation sites on the basis of various criteria. Proximity to hunting and fishing grounds is always a primary concern. When possible, villages are constructed on raised land, in order to escape annual flooding from ice-clogged rivers as well as from the high tides created by great storms in the shallow Bering Sea that sweep over the low Yukon and Kuskokwim land. People state that in pre-Russian times, when warfare was widespread, localities that were easily defended from aggressive neighbors also were considered desirable.

Each winter village is made up of numerous semisubterranean sod and wood houses and one or two *qasgit*, or men's houses. Summer houses are permanent wooden structures built above ground. In some cases, such as at the village of Rasboinsky, both winter and summer structures have been built at a single locale, but usually the winter and summer villages are built separately but close by. Tents and snow houses are commonly used by northern Eskimo groups, but are erected by Bering Sea people only when they travel.

In addition to houses and *qasgit* the landscape is cluttered with food and equipment storehouses, boat and sled racks, and stakes to which dogs are fastened. The food and equipment caches are raised above ground so that the village's perpetually hungry and ever-alert dogs, as well as bold foxes, cannot reach and devour meat and skins.

Adjoining or near each village is a cemetery which is an integral part of the village, for the deceased and their shades are considered to be part of the community and are cared for ceremonially. The cemetery consists of

**116. Winter Village** *nunat*
Western Alaska villages, such as the village of Hooper Bay illustrated on the previous page, consist of semisubterranean houses, *qasgit* or men's houses, meat and equipment caches, and graveyards. The villages appear to rise out of the marshy grasslands and are built on spots of relatively dry land.

The village shown on this drill bow is full of activity. During the day women prepare foods and skins in the houses, while men, working in the *qasgiq,* repair tools and tend to their caches, which are raised on stilts to keep the dogs from devouring the food supply.

**117. Summer Camp** *neqlilleq*
During the summer months people living in the northern regions of western Alaska inhabit skin tents or lodges, while southern groups live in more permanent wood structures erected at or near the winter village site. Many summer activities take place outdoors including cooking, drying strips of meat and split fish, making boats, and repairing fishing and sealing equipment.

## 118. Village of Rasboinsky

Rasboinsky is built on a bank above the Yukon approximately one hundred miles inland from the coast. At the time of Nelson's visit Rasboinsky was the largest village along the river, consisting of twenty-five houses, two *qasgit*, meat caches, boat and sled racks, and a graveyard. Nelson took this photograph during a winter visit. The log houses are summer structures facing a creek. People are standing next to and ducking into semi-subterranean winter structures, which appear as raised snow-covered mounds.

Nelson encountered problems when photographing people going about their business. Having set up his camera to take this picture, he let the village headman look in the camera. Seeing the villagers upside down in the ground glass, the headman shouted, "He has all your shades [spirits] in this box," whereupon people ran for cover into their houses.

SI–6371

## 119. St. Michael House *uksivik ena*

The house illustrated here (based on a Nelson drawing) is typical of dwellings constructed in the Yukon–Kuskokwim region. The rectangular, semisubterranean log structure is eight to nine feet high and is covered with earth. Sleeping platforms line three walls, and the house has a central fireplace under the window or smoke hole in the roof. During the summer the house is entered through an aboveground passage covered with a bearskin curtain. During the winter an underground passage is used in order to conserve heat.

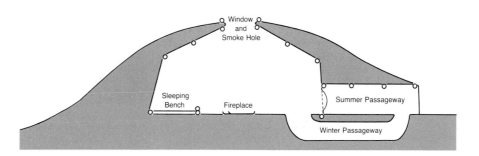

## 120. Rasboinsky Graveyard *qungu*

*People are like grass. The older ones die and others after them take their place.* (Henry 1981:97)

When a person dies he is placed in a sitting position with his legs drawn up to his chest, wrapped in grass mats and deer skins, placed in a wooden box, and taken to the village graveyard. A man is buried with his tobacco and snuff boxes, and his paddle showing his totemic affiliation is placed upright near his grave. A woman is buried with her wooden dishes and pots, her caribou tooth belt, and her fish knife. Her favorite wooden dish is placed on a post next to her grave.

SI–6340

**121. Clay Lamps** *kenurraq*
Saucer-shaped lamps similar to this toy are used in houses throughout the Yukon and Kuskokwim region. Every woman keeps a lamp next to her sleeping platform, where she can easily tend the burning oil-saturated wick while doing her household chores.

Lamps are made by mixing clay with grasses and a small amount of volcanic sand. The clay is shaped into the desired form by hand and incised with a stick.

Big Lake 38078, 11 cm (diameter)

decorated wooden coffins raised on stilts. Kayak paddles and stakes to which bent-wood bowls and other artifacts are attached stand in front of or next to graves and are in various stages of decay.

Women, girls, and preadolescent boys live in and around the houses, while men usually eat, work, and often sleep in the *qasgit*. Each winter house has a long semisubterranean entrance passage which leads up into a single rectangular-shaped room with raised platforms against three walls. The sunken entrance passage traps cold air, and the main room of the house, insulated by sod and snow cover, retains heat produced by people, the hearth, and lamps.

Each platform may be occupied by one family, separated from others by grass mats hung as room dividers. A woman's saucer-shaped lamp lights

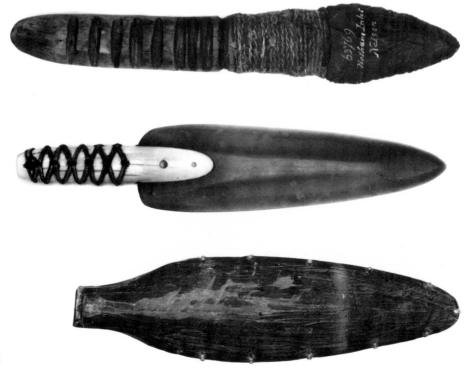

**122. Butchering and Skinning Knives**
During Nelson's four-year stay European knives were rapidly replacing the older forms, and he was able to collect some of the last stone-bladed knives still in active use in Alaska. The chipped stone knife illustrated here is for cleaning fish and has a grooved wooden handle for better hand purchase. Fish scales can still be seen lodged among the lashings. The ground nephrite knife and wooden sheath were not still in use, but had been kept as beautiful heirlooms by their owner. Nelson spent two years patiently grooming the owner before he agreed to sell them!

Hotham Inlet 63769, 25.5 cm; Nubviukh-chugaluk 176072, 29 cm; 176072, 26 cm

118

### 123. Semi-Lunar Knives *uluaq*

Women use hafted semi-lunar knives for skinning and cutting up fish and game. Ivory handles are often decorated with geometric designs—concentric circles and circles with spurred lines being common motifs. Ivory handles are also carved in the forms of real and mythological animals. The mythological creatures, like the beast carrying a walrus in its mouth, are often shown wearing goggles, paraphernalia associated with ceremonial masks as well.

Konigunugumut 36316, 7 cm; Sfugunugumut 37960, 12 cm; Starikwikhpak 38139, 10.5 cm; Agiukchugumut 37327, 8 cm

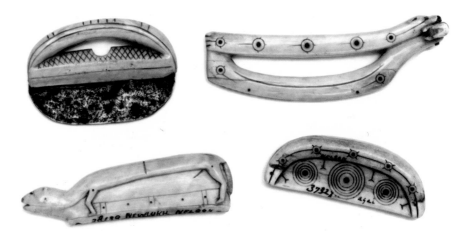

the family's platform and her wooden dishes as well as the family's bedding of reindeer skins and grass mats are stored in a corner of the room. The long entrance passage, the front of the house, and the roof also serve as storage space.

A fireplace or hearth, built out of stone slabs and resting on the floor, lies directly under the smokehole in the roof. Due to the abundance of driftwood in this region, Bering Sea people do not have to cook food and heat their houses with sea mammal oil as do more northern Alaskan groups and Canadian Inuit.

Since activities performed by husband and wife are complementary, the family under ideal circumstances functions as a self-sufficient unit. Men are the principal hunters and women are primarily responsible for the processing of meat and skins. Men work ivory, wood, and stone, while the women do all the grass weaving and skin work. Each individual should be equipped to survive alone should he or she be caught in an emergency situation, and in fact men and women may frequently perform one another's chores.

### 124. Stone-bladed Knives

Women's semi-lunar knives usually have ground slate blades, though chipped stone blades are sometimes used. Knives such as these are made by Eskimos throughout the western and eastern Arctic. Ground stone has the advantage of being quick and easy to resharpen with a whetstone, with little loss of stone material. Chipped stone blades must be resharpened by a skilled flint knapper, and a considerable amount of the rim edge is lost in the retouching process. Handles are a matter of personal preference and can be made out of ivory, wood, woven spruce, or willow root.

Askinuk 37569, 11 cm; Kushunuk 36304, 9 cm; Ikogmut 48831, 20 cm; Hotham Inlet 63765, 10.5 cm

119

### 125. Food Tray

Every woman has a set of wooden dishes stacked in the corner of her house ready to be used when serving food to family and house guests. The dishes, made by men, are often decorated with mythological and supernatural creatures, their ribs and entrails showing, and their mouths set in toothy grins. The decorations recall stories and help women identify their bowls.

This elegant tray has been dyed red and has a ridged rim fashioned out of two pieces of bent wood inlaid with white stone lozenges. The image of a mythological character, possibly *Ko-gukh´-pûk*, a mammoth-like creature, has been painted in black in the tray's interior. The black lines which encircle the beast are similar to those painted on a pair of kayak paddles, identified by Nelson as symbols of the female sex. They also echo the image of bent-wood hoops which often frame ceremonial masks.

Nulukhtulogumut 38642, 35.5 cm long

## Preparations for a Meal

When a man returns to the village after a fishing or hunting trip he may go to his house or storehouse where he unloads his sled. Working quickly, he and his wife will split fish down to the tail using sharp stone-bladed knives. Many of the drier fish, like flounder, sculpin, tomcod, and trout are hung on a raised rack and allowed to dry, and the dried bunches of fish are cached in the storehouse. Certain kinds of salmon are so oily that they are smoked to avoid spoilage. Fish caught during the winter are stored frozen in open-twined grass bags and must be separated from one another with the aid of wedges and mauls.

When a larger animal such as a seal is brought home, a decision is made regarding the intended use of the animal's skin and organs. Equipped with one of her handiest tools, the semi-lunar knife, a woman skins the animal, but carefully avoids making unnecessary holes in the animal's hide. She may put aside the seal's esophagus, intestines, and bladder for eventual use. The blubber too is saved, and after it is rendered the oil is stored in skin bags. While in the process of butchering the animal, the woman may drop a choice piece of meat, along with some blubber, into the hot water in her clay cooking pot. Preparation of a meal for her husband and children begins.

Seal meat, blubber, fish, birds, and small mammals, supplemented by caribou meat and bird's eggs, are the basic ingredients of a Bering Sea Eskimo family's diet. Foods are prepared in a variety of ways. Fish may be eaten boiled, roasted, frozen and raw, or dried. Flakes of dried King salmon dipped in whitefish oil are considered particularly good. Fresh seal meat and blood make a delicious rich stew. Dried seal meat is dipped in oil and eaten. During the summer months, particularly throughout the month of

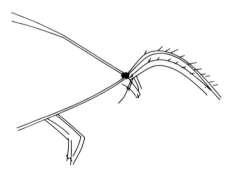

### 126. Food Tray Detail

The image of a caribou has been incised on the bottom and sides of the bent-wood tray. Nelson was unclear regarding the significance of such marks. They may identify the maker of the tray, the owner, or the owner's animal totem.

Nulukhtulogumut 38642

### 127. Food Bowls *qantat*

Food bowls and trays are often fashioned by steaming a thin, grooved slab of wood, intended to be the vessel wall, into the desired shape. Once formed, the ends are stitched together with willow or spruce root, or pegged with wood. The bottom of the tray is then carved to a slightly larger diameter and snapped into the groove by pushing with the heel of the hand or foot. Marks of various kinds, but frequently caribou heads, parallel stripes, or ravens' feet, are incised or painted on the bottoms of bowls and trays.

Red clay and charcoal mixed with seal blood are used to decorate trays, bowls, boxes, and masks. These pigments are fixed by the blood and do not come off in contact with wet and hot foods.

Tukchugamut 38680, 33 cm; Big Lake 38340, 30 cm

### 128. Bowl with Handles *aṅ-u´-chĭn-û-g'ŭk*

Food trays and bowls are constantly in use. Men may return to the house for their meals or may request that wooden dishes of food be brought to them in the *qasgiq*. Regardless of the hour, arriving guests are always fed. Dishes may contain strips of dried whitefish, seal meat, and blubber brought in from the coast, or a pasty delicacy of tomcod livers blended with berries.

This food tray was carved from a single block of wood. The entire vessel has been painted red, and a black, bird-headed quadruped has been painted in the bowl's interior. The masks on the two grimacing faces, which form bowl handles, have been painted black as well. White glass beads, rather than ivory, form eyes and rim decorations.

Big Lake 38677, 35 cm long

August, women and children equipped with root picks and carrying berry buckets and twined bags gather various kinds of berries and vegetable foods. These include blueberries, salmonberries, crowberries, a wild sorrel which is made into a relish, tender young willow leaves, and the succulent root of the cotton grass. On Nelson Island more than forty-two species of vascular plants are gathered and used as food, medicine, insulation, and weaving material (Ager and Ager 1980).

A woman is always prepared to feed her family and guests, it being the custom to present food to all visitors, who usually arrive unannounced. Her serving dishes, which often travel to the *qasgiq* laden with food for ceremonies or for her husband's and sons' meals, are wooden bowls and trays. They are made for her by her husband, or are acquired in trade with Indians living upriver. Sometimes a dish has been carved from a single piece of wood, but many have bent-wood rims with tightly fitted wooden bottoms and are decorated with figures encircled by black lines. The painted circles and grooved rims and bases of the containers suggest bent-wood hoops surrounding ceremonial masks and, as in the case of masks, may be symbolic of the heavens and the universe.

**129. Wooden Tub** *mervik*
Children are often sent out with bent-wood tubs such as this one to collect fresh or salt water needed in the house. Ladles and dippers are used to transfer the water into smaller containers. Tubs similar to this one are also used to store urine, which is an important component of bathing and vital to many hide processing and manufacturing procedures. The widespread use of urine was noted by the Russian explorer Lavrentii A. Zagoskin during his explorations in western Alaska in the 1840s, who referred obliquely to "that special fluid."
Ikogmut 45495, 37 cm high

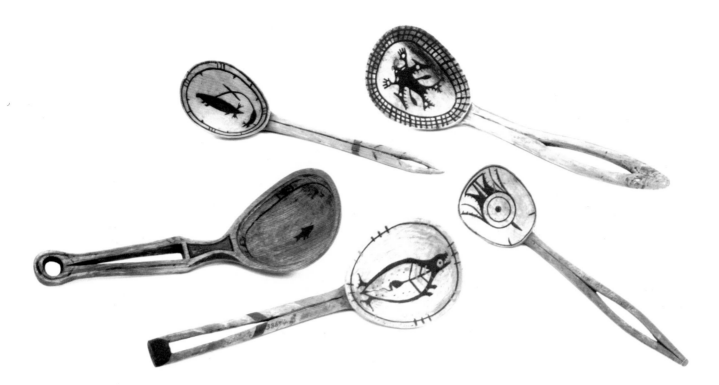

**130. Ladles** *ipuun*

Throughout Alaska foods are served and eaten with ladles made out of wood, antler, Dall sheep horn, and bone. Painted wooden ladles with carved handles are commonly used by Bering Strait people. Indian groups living in the interior and Eskimos living north of Norton Sound also make wooden ladles but rarely decorate them elaborately.

Mythological animals, often shown with pierced hands, are painted in the cup section of Bering Sea ladles and are framed by rings of black pigment suggesting the bent-wood hoops encircling ceremonial masks. The supernatural beasts are shown in "X-ray" view as well as split down the middle and splayed out. Scenes of animals, stationary or hunted, are also represented. The ladle from the Lower Kuskokwim has a harpooned walrus painted in its cup, with the harpoon shaft, line, and inflated sealskin float attached to him.

Sfugunugumut 38634, 28 cm; Paimut 38638, 26.5 cm; Lower Kuskokwim 38503, 27 cm; Chalitmut 38632, 32 cm; Cape Vancouver 43491, 27 cm

The implements' decorations serve many functions. The images on the bowls may be inherited family designs (Lantis 1960:55) which represent supernatural or mythological creatures known to families through stories and songs. These creatures, often resembling composites of real animals, are frequently depicted with prominent ribs and alimentary canals. Some of the creatures have pierced hands which, depending on the context, symbolically allow animals to reach the earth from the sky or let some animals escape capture by man so that they can propagate and return to be hunted in future years.

Creatures painted in the cupped sections of ladles sometimes appear as skins splayed out as if on drying racks, or they may have harpoons in their backs. In both cases the implication is that the animal has been caught. These paintings are related to the images appearing on the food bowls and trays and may serve as amulets. Also, they constantly remind people about the spirits and creatures inhabiting the world and of the need to practice caution when traveling about the countryside. They reinforce the idea that caches should be filled with food so that the serving dishes may be filled as well.

In addition to lamps, a large bent-wood tub used to store fresh water is found in every house. During the summer children are often sent to collect the water from streams. In the winter blocks of river and lake ice must be hauled up to the house and melted. Since the land is so low and the ocean tides often are quite strong and reach far upriver, finding truly fresh water is sometimes a difficult task, despite the number of rivers and streams crisscrossing the land.

Each family also has a large bent-wood urine tub. Urine is an important component of hide working and some bone working processes. It is also used for bathing and washing hair. The urine combines with body oils and acts like a soap and when it is rinsed off it leaves skin and hair clean.

## Discontented Grass Plants

In addition to food preparation, skin and grass working are major activities that take place around the house. Grass is important in both a practical and symbolic sense and is used in innumerable ways. Grass is woven into mats used to cover sleeping platforms and to partition house space; it is also used as seats in kayak manholes and as sails for large umiaks. The respirators used by men when they take sweat baths are woven out of grass. Hoops on bird snares are often held open with blades of grass. Grass is twisted, braided, and passed through fish gills to form strands of fish which can be hung to dry or easily stored. Grasses line subterranean storage pits preventing cached foods from freezing to the soil. Grass is stuffed into the bottoms of boots forming soft pads, creating a layer of insulation between the cold ground and the wearer's feet, and absorbing moisture from leaky boots or sweaty feet. Grass socks, worn inside sealskin boots, serve a similar function. Grass is used to make bags and baskets for food, clothing, and personal effects.

If a person has the misfortune of falling into icy water on a cold day and is far away from a camp or a village, his only chance of survival is to stuff his clothes full of grass. The grass acts as an insulator preserving his body heat while also keeping his clothes, which will freeze stiff as boards, from touching his body and chilling him further.

Grass is placed in the entrance passages of *qasgit* during certain ceremonies in order to keep the shades from entering the structures. Strands of grass are either scattered or burnt during certain ceremonies. Shamans often kneel on grass mats when performing rituals.

At one point in the Raven Myth, Raven teaches people to start a fire with a spark of tinder and a bunch of grass. When Raven gets angry with Man and carries the sun away, he puts the sun in a grass basket. Raven's son creates the brilliant morning star when he sticks a glowing brand of grass into the sky. Physically and symbolically grass seems to be associated

Pages 124–29 are the contribution of Linda Lichliter Eisenhart.

**131. Grass Fish Bag** *issran*
Open-twined grass bags are used as all-purpose containers capable of carrying up to one hundred pounds of clothing, skins, and fish. A quantity of fish can be placed in such a bag for transport to racks, where fish are split, gutted, and dried. During the winter, grass containers filled with frozen fish are stored in caches raised on stilts out of reach of hungry dogs.

**132. Grass Comb** *täl-ú-tīt*
Women use combs like this ivory-toothed piece when preparing dried marsh and beach grasses for weaving. Grasses are extremely important to Bering Sea Eskimos and are accorded special significance in their mythology. They are woven into storage containers, clothing, mats, and umiak sails, and when stuffed into the soaked clothes of those unfortunate enough to fall through the ice, provide one's only hope against freezing to death.
Lower Yukon 48877, 17 cm

### 133. Twined Grass Bag

Twined river and beach grasses produce surprisingly strong containers, made all the more durable by their flexibility. In the Yukon–Kuskokwim region, grass-work bags are simply but elegantly constructed of tight, even rows of open, two-strand twining.

The weaver who made the Norton Sound bag collected by Nelson began by laying her warp strands flat together, side by side, as if she were making a mat. Twining a row or two down the center, she then folded the warp in half along her line of weaving, adding additional warp in the side gaps. The attractive rim was made by simply catching and braiding groups of warp, and joining them in a horizontal braid at the top. Three rows of twining were then worked into the resulting open spaces.

Norton Sound 176077, 44 cm

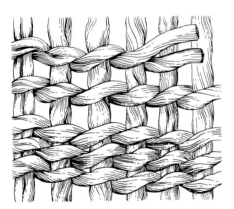

with light, and with warmth. In addition, its annual growth and death cycle has a dramatic effect on the landscape and marks the passing of the seasons. The use of grass to deter the shades suggests an association with life.

In addition to its many uses, grass even has a personality, as Nelson discovered in collecting tales from the people of this region:

### THE DISCONTENTED GRASS PLANT

Near the village of Pastolik, at the Yukon mouth, grows a tall, slender kind of grass. Every fall just before winter commences the women from the villages go out and gather great stores of it, pulling or cutting it off close to the ground, and making large bundles which they carry home on their backs. This grass is dried and used for braiding mats and baskets and for pads in the soles of skin boots.

One of these Grass-stalks that had been almost pulled out of the ground by a woman, began to think that it had been very unfortunate in not being something else, so it looked about. Almost at first glance it spied a bunch of herbs growing near by, looking so quiet and undisturbed that the Grass began to wish to be like them. As soon as this wish had been formed the Grass-stem became an Herb like those it had envied, and for a short time it remained in peace.

One day it saw the women coming back carrying sharp-pointed picks, with which they began to dig up these herbs and eat some of the roots, while others were put into baskets and carried home. The changeling was left when the women went home in the evening, and having seen the fate of its companions, it wished it had taken another form; so looking about it, it saw a small creeping plant which pleased it, being so tiny and obscure; without delay it wished and became one of them. . . . (Nelson 1899:505–6)

125

**134. Twined Baskets**

These two twined grass baskets illustrate what clever weavers can accomplish by varying their treatment of a basic stitch. The toy basket was made by combining open twining of the base with closed twining of the sides. The basket's pleasing texture was achieved by alternating three rows of two-strand twining with three rows of three-strand twining, alternating the slant of the stitches as well. The weaver also began her bag in an ingenious manner. She gathered her intended warp strands into three groups, braided them, and tied the braids together to form a base of radiating warp strands.

The basketmaker who wove the larger container also chose to have an open-twined base and closed-twined sides. To give the piece some added strength she included a single row of three-strand twining at the point where the warp was turned up to form the sides of the basket. She decorated the basket by weaving darkened strands of grass into the piece. The lower continuous bands consist of two dark strands twined together. The spotted effect of the upper band was achieved by twisting one dark strand together with a light strand.

Yukon 38204, 10 cm; Lower Yukon 38872, 12 cm

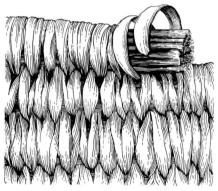

Rye grass is gathered in the fall after the first frost and again in the spring when the last year's grass is collected. Women carry home great bundles of grass which they hang on the sides and roofs of their houses and caches. When the grass has dried, it is combed and hatcheled. Rye grass is used to make mats and containers, as well as boot pads. A sedge is gathered in July and early August when it is fresh. Its stem and roots are eaten and its leaves are dried and used along with rye grass to make socks. Sedge has a nicer coloring than does rye grass and makes a more ornamental piece of work (Lantis 1946:180).

Women use two weaving techniques that are common throughout the world, twining and coiling. When twining a basket, a woman begins with a foundation of grass strands that radiate out from the center of the basket's intended bottom and travel vertically up to form the container's sides.

**135. Coiled Baskets** *mingqaaq*

These two baskets have been made by wrapping strands of grass around grass bundles, moving the coils in a counter-clockwise direction. The open-mouth work basket is covered with grease, suggesting that it was in use for quite a while before Nelson bought it. The lidded basket was once decorated with tufts of red wool which must have given it a festive appearance. The slightly convex lid is attached to the basket with hide hinges, and the bottom of the basket is made out of seal skin.

St. Michael 32977, 10 cm; Pastolik 38469, 17 cm

**136. Pastolik Bird Toe Basket**

This basket is made with bundle coils worked in a counter-clockwise direction. Tufts of purple and red wool have been tucked under the grass coils, strands of red and black wool have been coiled into the basket's sides, and horned puffin toes, strung on sinew, have been dangled from the coils. The basket's hinged lid is shut with birdskin and cotton ties.

Pastolik 37626, 23 cm (diameter)

**137. Innovative Weaving**

The woman who made this rare grass basket may have seen coiled work but not known how to do it. She experimented and came up with her own technique, which involved wrapping bundle coils with a "blanket stitch." After she made her coils the weaver sewed them onto a sealskin base and stitched them to one another, moving her tiny stitches and the coils in a counter-clockwise direction. Her basket proved to be sturdy and has a textured surface which cannot be achieved with the regular coiling method. This individual approach to basket weaving gives an excellent idea of the experimental nature of the art at the time of Nelson's visit.

Yukon River 36190, 11 cm high

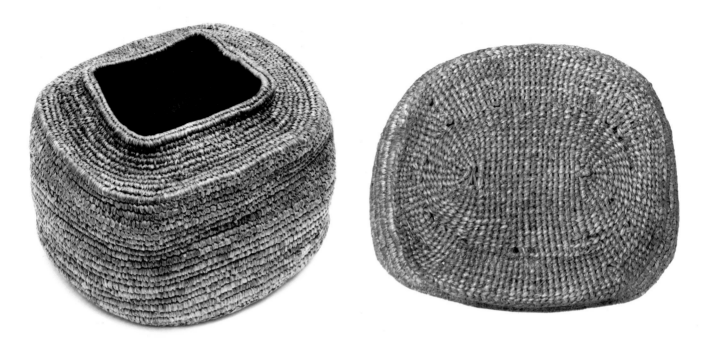

These strands are called the "warp" and are the foundation around which the weaving is done. To weave, a woman works two, or occasionally three, separate strands horizontally through the warp, twisting them front to back around each strand. These horizontal weaving strands are known as the "weft."

The weaving progresses around the basket in spiral fashion. Sometimes the weaver will leave space between each successive row, in which case she is doing "open-twined" work. If the rows are placed directly above one another so that the basket's warp strands are barely showing, the work is referred to as "closed-twined." When the tops of the warp strands are reached the rim is finished off in a variety of ways. The warp may be folded down and caught in the final row of weaving or braided together along the top.

Eskimo women also make baskets using a "coiling" technique. A weaver does not have to set up a vertical foundation of warp strands, since coiling carries its foundation around the basket. The weaver works with what is called a bundle foundation, composed of parallel grass stems. She turns the bundle in on itself, winding her grass thread around it as she goes, and stitching the wrapped bundle down to the lower coil. An awl is used to punch a hole in the existing coil and the grass thread is pushed through the hole. New grass stems are added to the bundle foundation as it begins to thin out by simply inserting them at intervals. In the finished basket the foundation stems are hidden by the horizontal rows of vertical stitches.

A number of coiled baskets collected by Nelson are made of materials other than grass. Spruce root and willow root have also been used to make coiled baskets. The finished container has a different appearance from one made out of rye grasses. Root baskets have a single "rod" foundation consisting of a solid root segment, and whole or split strands of root are coiled around the rod.

Both Indians and Bering Sea Eskimos are known to have made twined and coiled baskets during the time of Nelson's visit and there is some question concerning who actually made the baskets he collected, since baskets were one of the items Eskimos and Indians traded with one another and across Bering Strait to Siberia.

### 138. Coiled and Twined Basket

Many of the coiled baskets brought back by Nelson have wide circles of seal skin stitched into their bases. This eliminates the need to make a coiled start, often the most difficult part of weaving. The woman who wove this Kushunuk basket arrived at an alternative way of sidestepping the coiled start. She began her basket by twining a flat oval mat, which she finished with a braid. She used the mat as the base for her basket, stitching grass bundle coils to the mat's circumference, working up the sides of the basket in a clockwise direction. This unique construction provides a rare example of a basket combining both the twining and coiling weaving techniques.

Kushunuk 35962, 24 cm wide

**139. Spruce Root Baskets** *kevraarcinraat*
The Eskimo woman is limited in her choice of weaving materials. Along the Lower Yukon women have used spruce roots as well as grasses to weave containers. The three baskets illustrated here have been made by coiling spruce root over rods of the root. Coiling methods vary; sometimes the weaver will pierce the rods while coiling her stitches, as in the case of the square waterproof container, or she will encircle the lower coil completely, as in the case of the round open-mouth container.

Though Nelson collected these baskets from Eskimos, it is unclear whether Eskimo weavers made them or they were obtained in trade with Indians who also do this kind of weaving.

Yukon River 176078, 9 cm; Sledge Island 44234, 14 cm; Alaska 37926, 13 cm

The two techniques of twining and coiling produce quite different results. A twined basket of grass is very flexible; it can be crushed or rolled up. Coiling, on the other hand, makes a more rigid container, far less compact to pack and store, but more likely to protect items which might otherwise get damaged.

Twining is probably the older form of weaving used by Bering Sea Eskimos, whereas coiling appears to be a skill recently introduced among these people about the time of Nelson's visit. Coiling has the advantage of being a faster method of making a container. Nelson's collection of coiled baskets offers a glimpse of the art in its developmental stages in this culture.

Starting the tiny spirals in the base of the basket is the most difficult part of the coiling technique. Many of the baskets collected by Nelson show that the weavers eliminated this source of frustration by cutting round pieces of seal skin to which they sewed the first bundle coil rather than dealing with the tiny initial foundation spirals. An alternative solution to this problem was the twining of a flat base in the same manner one would go about twining a mat, followed by sewing the first coil around the sides of the mat.

One of the most interesting and innovative baskets Nelson collected is shown in figure 137. Its foundation coils were made first, using a wrapped blanket stitch. Each coil was then stitched to the blanket-stitched coil below it. The top of the blanket stitch and the individual stiches which join the coils make an intricately textured pattern. The individual technique suggests that the weaver may have seen coiled work but had never been taught the actual procedure, and through experimentation found a way to replicate it.

Baskets have been decorated in a variety of ways. Dyed seal gut strips, tufts of fur, wool, and cloth, as well as bird toes have been woven into or attached onto containers. In rare instances the actual grass has been dyed as well.

**140. Skills of a Seamstress** *arnam mingqellri*

A Bering Sea Eskimo family is dependent on a woman's knowledge and skill as a seamstress. Frocks, pants, undergarments, boots, gloves, and mittens are made from the skins of small furbearers, birds, fish, caribou, reindeer, and seals. Not only does a woman prepare skins and her sinew thread, she knows the different properties of skins and processes them in certain ways depending upon the type of garment she is making. The Kuskokwogmut couple in this photograph are handsomely dressed in clothing made from small furbearers in a style popular among peoples living in the interior of the Yukon–Kuskokwim region.

SI–6914

## Working with Skins

One of a woman's most important roles is that of seamstress. Well-made clothes keep her family warm and dry and are essential for survival in the harsh northern environment. These garments require specific knowledge concerning how to treat certain skins to give them desired properties, and well cut and sewn clothes are the work of patient and experienced women. It is not uncommon to give a little girl a miniature sewing kit so that she can play "house" and begin to acquire these important skills at an early age.

The garments made by a wife may be scrutinized by her husband's family and other women in the community who judge her worth on the basis of her handiness with semi-lunar knife, needle, and sinew thread. Women living north and south of Norton Sound also jealously inspect one another's work. Northerners use caribou, imported reindeer, seal, and polar bear skins to make their garments. Yukon–Kuskokwim people wear sealskin and

**141. Southern Skin Scrapers** *calugun*

Women living between the Lower Yukon and northern Norton Sound generally use long-handled stone-bladed scrapers when dressing and tanning skins. These two pieces have wooden handles shaped, grooved, and wrapped for maximum leverage and comfortable gripping.

Skins are scraped at various intervals in the hide-working process. When seal skins are fresh, they are first flensed. Then, to remove hair, the skins are dipped in urine, rolled up, and put away. When the hairs begin to fall out, the skins are unrolled, scraped clean, and stretched out to dry.

In order to process reindeer skins for clothing with hair intact, the fat is soaked out with hot water or urine, and the hides are stretched and dried. The brittle skins are then thoroughly scraped, rubbed with warm fish eggs, and then scraped again, at which point they become soft and pliable.

Sledge Island 44982, 19 cm; Lower Yukon 38252, 16 cm

**142. Northern Skin Scrapers** *ellumerun*

Northern scrapers, like these two from Point Hope, are made to fit a woman's hand. The handy mammoth-ivory scraper illustrated here has a groove on its side for the thumb. Two slight indentations on the top of the handle near the blade accommodate the first and second fingers, while the third and fourth fingers naturally wrap around the scraper and rest in the indentation on the underside of the tool.

The wooden scraper has been made for a woman with a small hand. Depressions along the top and sides of the handle are contoured for each finger. The high polish of the wood is a result of use and suggests that it was a favorite tool, used for a long time before it was traded to Nelson.

Point Hope 63850, 12.5 cm; 63848, 9.5 cm

reindeerskin garments, as well as frocks made out of the skins of small furbearing animals, birds, and fish. Northerners have nothing good to say about fishskin garments, calling them "poor-man's" clothes, though in fact fishskin clothing is sturdy, resistant to wind, and waterproof.

Though Bering Sea and Bering Strait seamstresses use essentially the same tools, the implements are stylistically distinct, and the methods by which the two groups store their sewing tools differ as well. Southern women keep their fragile bone needles in plugged needlecases made of bird bones, and store their awls, skin thimbles, semi-lunar knives, and long-handled scrapers in bags often made out of caribou ears. These containers are called "housewives." When traveling, a woman places her tools in the pouch of the housewife and rolls it up, securing it with an ivory rod called a "bagfastener."

Northern women do not use housewives. Their storage container is the needlecase which consists of an ivory tube with a strap of rawhide through it. Bone needles are placed in a section of the strap which is pulled inside the tube. When the needles are needed the top of the strap is pulled up, and the section of hide containing the needles is exposed. Awls, creasers, thimbles, and other handy tools are attached to the lower end of the needlecase strap along with charms and amulets.

**143. Scrapers** *urugun*

Aside from northern and southern styles, scrapers are made in many forms depending on the kind of skin being processed, its intended use, and the personal preferences of the skin worker. Caribou bone beamers are used for initial heavy scraping of large skins, a task performed by both men and women. Women find that scoop-shaped antler scrapers are handy tools with which to remove fat lying close to the skin. Small mammal and bird skins are scraped with the ivory knives which resemble storyknives (fig. 192). These scrapers are equipped with a series of small teeth on the butt end of the handle used to remove flesh and vellum and to clean the hairs and feathers of the skin being worked.

Cape Darby 44178, 25.5 cm; Lower Yukon 38490, 24 cm; Chalitmut 37967, 18 cm

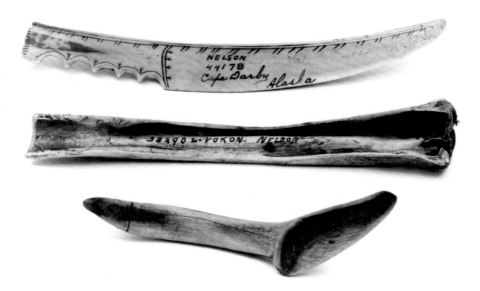

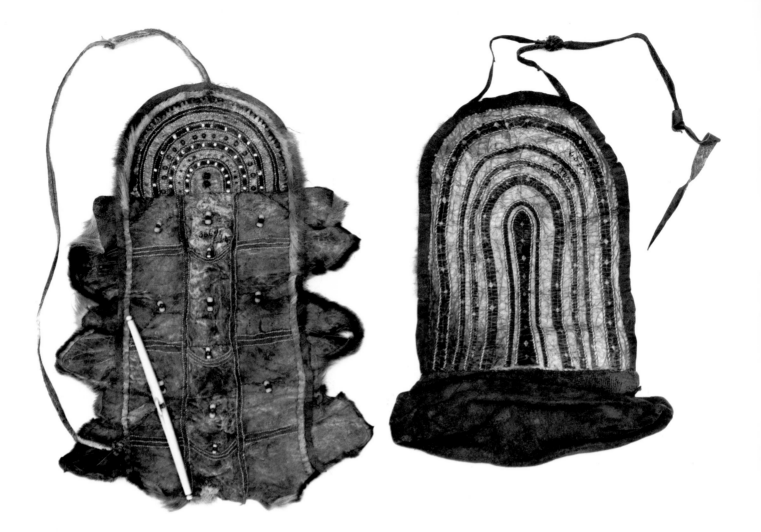

Sexual differences are expressed in clothing, most obviously in the cut of the lower part of men's and women's garments. A man's frock has a straight lower edge, while a woman's is U-shaped. Women's outer frocks are also cut full in the back in order to accommodate a child. These attributes of male and female clothing are evident in the Canadian Arctic, while Greenland Eskimo men once wore frocks with a U-shaped cut. Other images of maleness and femaleness have been identified in Canadian garments (Driscoll 1980) and may have been present on Alaskan garments as well. Since Nelson's time Alaskan clothing has undergone major changes as a result of contact with Europeans and Laplanders, who were sent to Alaska to teach the Eskimos how to herd domestic reindeer, and the woman's frock has lost its full back and U-shaped skirt.

Garments are also cut differently in the north and south. Women living north of Norton Sound wear outer frocks with long side slits and a deep U-shaped bottom cut. Kuskokwim women's frocks curve gently along the lower border. Caps are fashionable among inland dwelling southerners, while northerners always wear hoods attached to their frocks.

While women living in the Yukon–Kuskokwim region are excellent seamstresses, they do not embroider boots and gloves with fancy designs as do northern seamstresses and for this reason are not considered to be skilled with the needle. Yupik speakers are quick to point out that southern women are by far better dancers, however, and they know a tale which explains why this is so.

**144. Housewives** *kakivik*

A "housewife" is a small bag in which women living between Bristol Bay and Norton Sound store their needles, awls, bootsole creasers, and scrapers. When sewing implements are placed in the small pouch, the housewife is rolled up, and the cord is wound around the bag and fastened with an ivory crosspiece or "bagfastener." The Cape Nome housewife is made out of seal throat lining. Strips of dark wolf-fish (*Annarrichas lupus*) skin are sewn onto the seal parchment with decorative caribou hair and sinew. The housewife has a sealhair border and a pouch probably made of caribou nose skin.

The Big Lake housewife is missing its pouch. This piece is made out of strips of seal and caribou skin bordered by six caribou ears. The housewife has been sewn with sinew stitched around caribou hair. It is decorated with beads, and a red pigment has been applied to the stitching. The U-shaped motif forming the tops of the housewives is similar to the lower cut on women's frocks. This female-related motif is also embroidered on a pair of gloves (fig. 161).

Big Lake 38691, 35 cm; Cape Nome 45317, 32 cm

132

## 145. Symbolic Bagfasteners
*kakivik nagcessuuttii*

The bagfastener is a simple device used to keep the housewife rolled up. A small rod of bone would serve the purpose. Yet, throughout the Bering Sea area the bagfastener is an elaborately carved object revealing the artistic skills and rich imagination of the Bering Sea people.

This ivory bagfastener from Chalitmut depicts a smiling man wearing labrets and a tattooed woman who is frowning. Both are wearing fur-lined hoods and are flanked by collared seals tied to nets. The seals' back flippers take on the form of outstretched human hands with open palms. The portrayal of smiling men and frowning women can be followed through the collection, appearing on such diverse objects as kayak paddles, finger masks, dolls, and line fasteners.

Chalitmut 37319, 17 cm; Big Lake 38373, 18.5 cm; Lower Yukon River 48860, 15 cm; Yukon 48966, 16 cm; Big Lake 38402, 14.5 cm; Paimut 37189, 14.5 cm; Yukon River 48861, 17.5 cm; Lower Kuskokwim 36664, 15.5 cm; Big Lake 38387, 16 cm; Yukon 49001, 11 cm; Konigunugumut 36466, 11 cm; Sabotnisky 38017, 12 cm; Ukagamut 37457, 8 cm

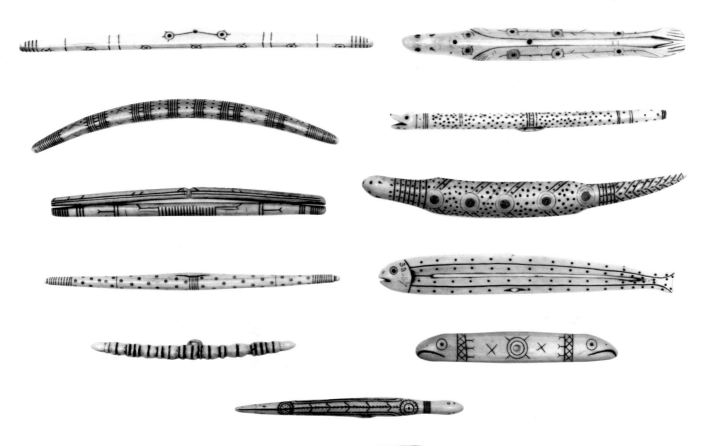

## THE LONE WOMAN

Very long ago there were many men living in the northland, but there was no woman living among them. Far away in the southland a single woman was known to live. At last one of the young men in the north started and traveled to the south until he came to the woman's house, where he stopped and in a short time he became her husband. One day he sat in the house thinking of his home and said, "Ah, I have a wife, while the son of the headman in the north has none." And he was much pleased in thinking of his good fortune.

Meanwhile the headman's son also had set out to journey toward the south, and while the husband was talking thus to himself the son stood in the entrance passage to the house listening to him. He waited there in the passage until the people inside were asleep. When he crept into the house and, seizing the woman by the shoulders, began dragging her away.

Just as he reached the doorway he was overtaken by the husband, who caught the woman by her feet. Then followed a struggle, which ended by pulling the woman in two, the thief carrying the upper half of the body away to his home in the northland, while the husband was left with the lower portion of his wife. Each man set to work to replace the missing parts from carved wood. After these were fitted on they became endowed with life, and so two women were made from the halves of one.

The woman in the south, however, was a poor needlewoman, owing to the clumsiness of her wooden fingers, but was a fine dancer. The woman in the north was very expert in needlework, but her wooden legs made her a very poor dancer. Each of these women gave to her daughters these characteristics, so that to the present time the same difference is noted between the women of the north and those of the south, thus showing that the tale is true. (Nelson 1899:479)

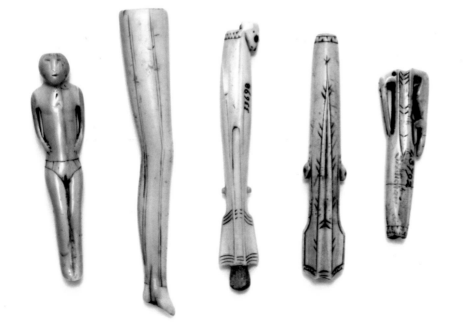

**146. Fish-shaped Needlecase** *mingqucivik*
Bone and metal needles have their own storage containers called needlecases. This needlecase takes the form of a blackfish, an important food resource for Bering Sea people. The fish has been made from a hollow goose or swan bone, plugged at either end with carved wooden stoppers, and has been ornamented with seal hair and red and black pigments.
Cape Vancouver 43505, 16.5 cm

**147. Needlecase with a Strap**
The needlecase form used by women living north of northern Norton Sound is an ivory tube through which a sealskin strap is passed. To store her needles, a woman pulls the upper section of the strap up and places her precious needles in the exposed seal skin. By pulling on the lower section of the strap, she draws the needles into the ivory tube, where they remain safe from breakage or loss. When she is ready to sew, the seamstress simply pulls up the sealskin strap, drawing the needles out of their protective case!
Kotzebue Sound 48568, 10.5 cm (needlecase only)

**148. Northern Needlecases** *uyamiutaq*
Men living in northern regions of western Alaska usually carve their wives' needlecases out of ivory, rather than bird bone.
Lower Yukon 48650, 12 cm; Pastolik 33214, 16.5 cm; 33698, 14 cm; Cape Nome 176230, 13 cm; St. Michael 43792, 9 cm

### 149. Southern Needlecases *mingqucivik*

Women living in the Bering Sea area store their needles in plugged and lidded needlecases. Traditionally made out of bird bone and ivory, they also include European materials. The Konigunugumut needlecase, for instance, is a traditional southern form, but the tube has been made out of spent rifle cartridge cases.

Needlecases, like bagfasteners, have decorations which carry much information about their owners. They portray important food and clothing resources: a fish caught in a net, a cormorant, a seal. Mythological and legendary creatures such as *kokogiak*, an eight-legged bear, are also represented.

Ukagamut 37492, 12 cm; Konigunugumut 37807, 14 cm; Lower Yukon 38128, 13 cm; Cape Vancouver 36478, 10 cm

Men make sewing tools for their wives and girlfriends and delight in carving serviceable but elegant forms. Scrapers are carefully shaped to a woman's hand, and ivory pieces are carved and incised with great care. Geometric motifs, particulary with circle-and-dot, and spurred and double-spurred lines, are popular throughout western Alaska. Here again Bering Sea and Bering Strait material culture differ. Yukon–Kuskokwim men carve mythological creatures, fish, birds, beluga, and seals on women's tools, while northerners are more apt to feature bowhead whales, seals, walrus, and polar bears, reflecting regional subsistence patterns and different religious ideas.

### 150. Thimbles and Thimble Guards *akngirnailitat*

Traditionally, women have used sealskin thimbles when sewing and mending clothing. With the advent of European contact they have begun to use European metal thimbles as well. Metal thimbles are not widely available, however. Therefore, enterprising avant-garde husbands have carved their wives exact copies in ivory.

A woman keeps track of her sealskin thimbles by slipping them onto thimble guards when they are not in use. Thimble guards take on various forms, from a slotted bird legbone to an ornate beast carrying a baby seal on its back. They are attached to the needlecase strap or stored with the needlecase in a housewife.

Kushunuk 36452, 9 cm; Kotzebue Sound 48570, 6 cm; Kushunuk 36453, 6 cm; Cape Darby 176227, 4 cm; St. Michael 48496, 8 cm; Konigunugumut 37666, 2 cm; Nunivak Island 43698, 9 cm

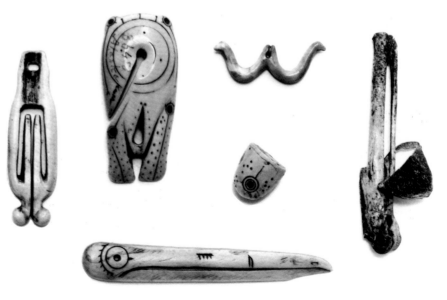

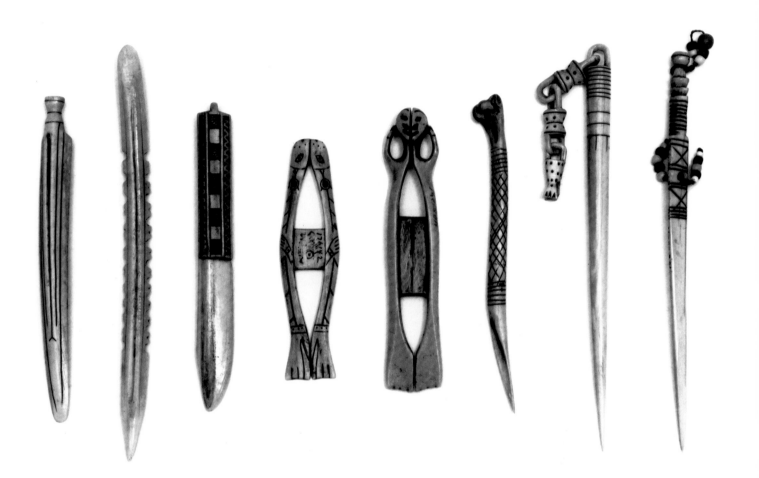

### 151. Bootsole Creasers *teguarcuun*

Bootsole creasers are ivory rods with flat, pointed ends. Every evening, after the family has finished its day's activities, clothing is inspected and repaired. Boots, which may be quite wet after a day's work, are dried and resoftened. In order to get into the corners of the heel and toe of the boot and keep the tiny pleats in order, a woman uses the thin flat end of this implement as a small scraper.

Bering Sea Eskimos are fond of designing tools for multiple functions. The Cape Vancouver piece is a bagfastener with one end shaped to function as a bootsole creaser. A Norton Sound piece is a bagfastener with one end shaped as a bootsole creaser, the other end designed as an awl.

Cape Vancouver 43663, 12.5 cm long; Norton Sound 33243, 16 cm long; Sledge Island 45140, 12 cm long

### 152. Thread Spools *nemrusvik*

Sinew from the legs or backs of caribou is a favorite thread. The sinew is dried, beaten, and cleaned. With small combs, women divide the sinew into strips which are then twisted or braided, depending upon their intended use. Prepared lengths of sinew are wrapped around spools or reels such as these and are stored in housewives with other sewing equipment.

The Cape Vancouver reel is in the form of a seal. Its cuffed flippers follow a style found on many wood and ivory carvings. The bisected Nunivak Island thread reel has the head and arms of a lady and the flippers of a walrus. Stories about mermaidlike creatures similar to this figurine were related to Nelson during his stay in Alaska.

Cape Vancouver 176142, 9.3 cm; Nunivak Island 43740, 11 cm

### 153. Awls *kaputaq*

When bone needles are used to sew thick hide, the holes for the stitches are made with bone, ivory, or metal awls. Using this procedure, a woman has complete control over the placement of her stitches and avoids the possibility of breaking her delicate needles. This simple and efficient tool can be traced back to Paleolithic times.

Awls, like bagfasteners and needlecases, are elaborately decorated by men and are among the women's treasured possessions. The bird bone awl is covered with a net mesh design; the knobbed form has geometric motifs and beaded tassels. The shaft of the Kuskokwim awl gives way to chain links which terminate in a seal's tail. It is a remarkable piece, having been carved from a single unbroken rod of ivory.

Askinuk 36630, 12 cm; Kuskokwim 36631, 22 cm; Cape Vancouver 37776, 12 cm

**154. Men's Fancy Boots** *kameksiik*

Men's boots usually come to just below the knee and are made with hard, oil-tanned sealskin soles and sealskin or reindeerskin uppers. The soles bend up around the foot, and are crimped at the toe and heel. Often a strip of tanned seal skin will be used to join the sole and the upper part of the boot. This beautiful pair of boots collected on King Island was probably used on ceremonial occasions. The boots have hard, tanned sealskin soles and white reindeerskin uppers. The boots are decorated with rectangles of russet-colored seal skin embroidered with long, white reindeer hair, red and blue thread, thin strips of yellow seal intestine, tufts of pup seal hair dyed chestnut brown, and strips of wolverine fur.

King Island 48132 (pair), 40 cm

**155. Grass Socks** *alliqsak*

Twined grass socks are worn inside skin boots. In addition to providing insulation, grass socks absorb water which might penetrate the outer boots, keeping the wearer's feet relatively dry. At night, wet grass socks are hung and dried and are ready to be worn the next morning.

Lower Kuskokwim 38814, 25 cm (heel to toe)

137

### 156. Women's Fur Frocks *atkuk*

Across the Arctic, Eskimo women's traditional outer frocks have U-shaped skirts and large hoods and back "pouches" designed to accommodate a baby. Nelson noted regional variations in the styles of women's garments, pointing out that northerner's frocks, like the one worn by the Kotzebue Sound figurine, have deep side slits and elongated U-shaped skirts, while frocks worn by Lower Kuskokwim women have short slits and gently curved hemlines. Many Alaskan women's garments are not designed to accommodate a child, and since the 1880s they have lost the U-shaped cut of the lower skirt.

The beautiful marmotskin (Arctic ground squirrel) frock illustrated here was collected from the head of Norton Sound. The white skirts and ornamented white strips of fur are made out of Siberian reindeer skins, as are the gores running down the front of the garment. The reindeer skins have been welted onto tanned, russet-colored sealskin strips. Skins from the crowns of marmots have been pieced together to form the back of the hood, not visible in the photograph. Hood rims and the lower edges of the skirts and sleeves are trimmed with wolverine and wolf fur, selected because water and breath condensation never freeze on these types of fur.

Kotzebue Sound 48582, 8.5 cm; Head of Norton Sound 176105 130 cm

**157. Man's Fur Frock** *atkuk*

During the milder months of the year Yukon and Kuskokwim men wear frocks made out of the skins of ground squirrels, mink, muskrats, and summer reindeer. Throughout the winter they wear two of these garments, or a coat made out of the warm skins of reindeer killed in the fall. The lower cut of a man's outer garment is straight rather than curved like a woman's. Coastal Eskimos wear coats with hoods, while interior peoples prefer to wear fur caps.

Alaska 176103, 130 cm

**158. Fishskin Frock** *amiraq*

Fishskin frocks are unique to the Bering Sea region, where people also make and use fishskin boots and mittens. When processed and sewn correctly, fishskin garments are waterproof and durable. Nelson repeatedly makes reference to this garment as a "poor-man's" frock, but this is probably a bias he picked up from northern Eskimos who did not use fishskin clothing. The frock illustrated here is made out of salmon skins sewn together with sinew. Gores along the shoulders are made out of fish skins dyed brown with alder bark. Thin strips of white seal throat lining and strips of dyed fish skins have been sewn along seamlines, giving the garment a simple but elegant line.

Mission 38817, 104 cm

**159. Gutskin Frock** *imarnin*

Throughout the Arctic strong waterproof garments are used by Eskimos and Aleuts, who make the frocks out of strips of seal intestines. Men in particular wear these garments when hunting in kayaks.

This beautiful gutskin garment has been sewn with sinew and decorated with cormorant feathers, red wool, and seal fur sewn onto tanned and dyed sealskin strips. Dyed sinew has been threaded around the exposed sinew stitching for additional decoration. The strips of gut skin have been joined in folds, and there are no stitches piercing through the entire thickness of the garment. The seams are thus reinforced, and the jacket retains the waterproof quality of the gut skin.

Golovnin Bay 43335, 84 cm

Bering Sea Eskimo implements are often incised with designs which have symbolic meaning. Animals may have defined skeletons and lifelines, and mythological creatures may be collared and cuffed as well. Fish are symbolically caught in nets, and cormorants, fish-eating birds, wear fishnet collars and have sinkers shaped like fishtails.

One bagfastener collected by Nelson when he was at Chalitmut is particularly rich in symbolism as well as being a magnificent piece of workmanship. The bagfastener (fig. 145) portrays smiling male and frowning female faces, images which may be guardian spirits and are often associated with kayak equipment. The spurred lines encircling the faces, meant to be the halolike wolverine trimming of a hooded frock, bring to mind framed *inua* images and the caribou fur fringes around many ceremonial masks. The seals flanking the faces are collared and attached to seal nets. They are double images, for their tails become thumbless hands attached to outstretched arms. Thumbless hands, like pierced hands, insure the continual presence of game on earth. All of these images find clear expression in ceremonies enacted by men in the *qasgiq*, but as an integral part of the Bering Sea Eskimo world view, they are appropriately expressed on utilitarian items.

**160. Mittens** *arilluuk*

When hunting at sea, men wear mittens which come up to the elbow and are secured with a drawstring or bracelet. Waterproof mittens are made out of salmon skin or seal skin, with the hair left on.

White dogskin mittens are used by men when they are hunting on the ice. The hunter, on his hands and knees, slowly creeps towards a seal. He knows that the seal will look up periodically, surveying for dangerous predators. As the seal raises its sleepy head, the hunter hides behind his large mittens, which blend in with the ice and snow. The seal, perceiving nothing dangerous on the landscape, puts down its head and the hunter continues his silent approach.

Sledge Island 45404, 50 cm

**161. Embroidered Gloves** *alimatet*

Regional styles of dress extend to gloves as well as parkas and boots. When making a glove, Diomede Island and Siberian women cut a single piece of hide for the back of the hand and four fingers. The palm section, including four fingers, is cut from another single piece. Three gores, each extending down the sides of two fingers, join the back and palm sections. The thumb and wrist pieces are sewn onto the glove separately. Gloves from Diomede Island, illustrated here, are made of skins dyed russet and chestnut brown. The gores are light tan. The intricate embroidery is done with caribou hair, sinew, and red wool. The motif on the back of the hand echoes the U-shaped cut of women's frocks and housewives, suggesting that these gloves may have belonged to a woman. This style of embroidery is popular on King and Diomede islands.

Diomede Island 38454 (pair), 18 cm

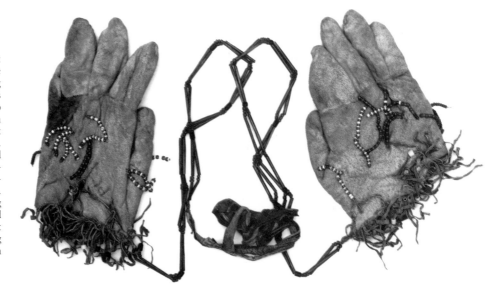

### 162. Gloves *alimatet*

Gloves worn by people living on the coast between the Yukon and Point Hope are made by piecing together each finger and sewing the fingers onto the body of the glove. Gloves are often joined by long straps, designed to go around a person's neck. In this way, when they are hurriedly removed, gloves will not get lost and will always be in easy reach. The pair illustrated here is made out of tanned reindeer skin, with the hair side turned inward. Each glove is decorated with russet-colored fringe and blue, red, and white beads. The two straps joining the gloves are strung with copper cylinders spaced with blue and black beads, except where the straps rest against the wearer's neck—this section being a wide, comfortable strip of soft skin which will not transmit cold.

Point Hope 64271 (pair), 20 cm

### 163. Snowbeaters *evcugcuutet*

Before entering the house, snow must be removed from fur garments or it will melt, wetting the clothes. A snowbeater enables a person to clean boots, cap, or the back of a parka with little trouble. Snowbeaters are made in a variety of shapes, some as straight rods similar to the snowbeater illustrated here. This piece is in the process of being decorated, and has a giant male caribou followed by two people incised along a baseline near the baleen lashings that hold the shaft and handle together. Dancing figures appear along a second baseline. S-curved snowbeaters made out of split antler are also popular forms. The shaft of the illustrated specimen is not decorated, but its handle terminates in a carving of a human face.

Lower Yukon 49175, 42 cm; Sledge Island 44998, 39 cm

Nelson bought many needlecases and bagfasteners from Bering Sea women. They readily parted with such items in exchange for beads, cloth, and metal. Beads have been sewn onto housewives, incorporated into jewelry, and used instead of ivory pegs to decorate boxes and bowls. Bits of cloth and yarn are used decoratively on baskets and frocks, and metal blades are hafted into semi-lunar knife handles in place of ground and chipped stone blades. Pieces of broken pottery have also been put to use, substituting for ivory on bracelets and boxes.

In addition to making clothing for her family, a woman will produce new sets of clothes for various ceremonial occasions. The most important is the Great Feast to the Dead, when the namesake of a deceased relative will be dressed in a new outfit. Presentation of the new garments and prepared foods is a way of symbolically clothing and feeding the shade of the dead person. During this important festival, feast givers will dress in new garments as well.

Maintaining skin garments is an important process, critical to their continued effectiveness. Every house has a snowbeater near the entryway so that an individual can knock or brush snow from his or her clothing before the snow melts and soaks the skins. Mittens, gloves, and inner and outer boots must be dried carefully, and boots in particular must be inspected for holes and resoftened with a bootsole creaser.

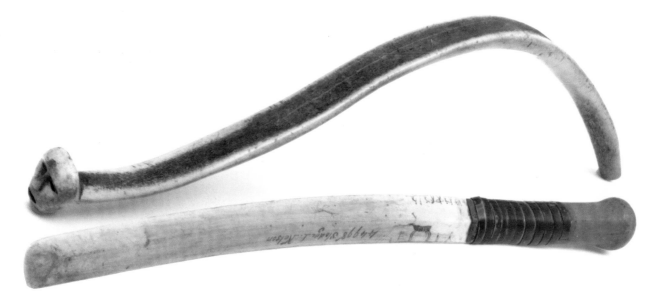

## Dressing Up

Eskimos living about Bering Strait can determine the homeland of an individual by noting the cut of his or her garments, the shape of his boat, as well as the kinds of ornaments he or she wears. Simple tattooed lines radiate from the lower lip and down the chin of a Yukon–Kuskokwim woman and she may wear a small sickle-shaped labret hung with beads in the center beneath her lower lip. As a small child her septum was pierced and beads were hung from her nose, but she no longer wears them, using the hole instead for holding her bone needles during a pause in her sewing. St. Lawrence Island and Siberian women have intricate tattooed designs covering their arms and faces and never wear labrets.

Men and boys cut their hair short except around the temples where it is slightly longer. A Siberian boy will attach a few beads to his hair, letting them dangle down his forehead. Women on both sides of Bering Strait delight in wearing fancy hair ornaments. Yukon–Kuskokwim women hang ivory goggled-face plaques from their braids which are also ornamented with great strands of multicolored beads.

Both men and women wear earrings hung from pierced earlobes. A man living in the vicinity of Bering Sea will wear flat rectangular-shaped earrings. None of the men's earrings collected by Nelson have realistic designs carved on them. Rather, the front of each earring is excavated and filled with spruce gum into which bits of glass, ivory, beads, and lead are stuck. The earrings are linked with one or two strands of multicolored beads which hang under the man's chin when the earrings are in place.

Earrings worn by Bering Sea Eskimo women are made by men and are quite imaginative. The main part of each earring is carved out of ivory and

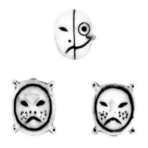

**164. Fashionable Earrings** *aqlitet*

Men living in the Bering Sea region often decorate women's earrings with concentric circles and dots. Each pair is slightly different either in the numbers of circles and their spacing, in the distribution of dots, or in the presence or absence of a bar along the bottom of each earring. The woman who received her traditionally shaped earrings fashioned out of copper rather than ivory must have been delighted.

Cape Vancouver 176175 (pair), 2 cm; Lower Yukon T–11974 (pair), 2 cm; Sfugunugumut 36003 (pair), 12 cm; SI–6394

**165. Women's Earrings**

Women living in the Yukon and Kuskokwim delight in wearing fancy earrings. *Tunghâk*, a powerful and potentially evil spirit, described in mythology and appearing on many ceremonial masks, is featured in a single ivory earring from Cape Vancouver. A pair of earrings representing the *inua* of a seal and another set representing two men wearing labrets are among the dozens of pairs traded to Nelson by western Alaska women.

Cape Vancouver 43670, 2 cm; Nunivak Island 43727 (pair), 2 cm

### 166. Comb and Hair Ornaments *nuyurun*

Women comb their hair with ivory and antler combs. They usually wear their hair in two braids, which they decorate with strings of beads, bits of fur, and ivory ornaments carved in the form of goggled, semihuman grimacing beasts. The iconography on combs can be complex, as in the case of the comb illustrated here. A two-headed creature appears at the top of the comb, and the entire piece is shaped to resemble a woman's frock.

Sledge Island 44765, 8 cm; Cape Vancouver 176233 (pair), 4 cm

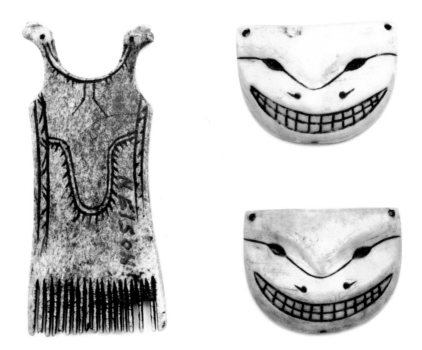

### 167. Men's Earrings *agluarutet*

Earrings worn by men are large tabular pieces of ivory with hooks on the back designed to slip through pierced earlobes. Men's earrings are attached to one another with strands of beads strung on sinew or rawhide cordage. When both earrings are in place the strand of multicolored beads hangs down under the wearer's chin. The earrings themselves are decorated with pieces of glass, fragments of beads, and chunks of lead.

Kaialigamut 37256 (pair), 3 cm long

### 168. Short-eared Owl Earrings

Household equipment, hunting tools, ceremonial masks, and, in this case, a pair of earrings portray personalities featured in stories. The story of *Mûn-kō-chē-wûk*, a little girl who turned into the short-eared owl, is a favorite among the Bering Sea Eskimo.

Kaialigamut 37261 (pair), 2 cm

has a hook on the back which fits through a woman's pierced earlobe. Strands of beads kept in rows with leather and ivory spacers are often hung from the ivory earrings. The front of each earring will be carved or incised with designs.

Earrings decorated with concentric circles were popular when Nelson was in the area, and he collected a number of pairs, including a rare set of copper earrings incised with this fashionable design. Images of mythological creatures are represented as are humanlike *inua* faces. Nelson collected a single earring said to represent a *tunghâk*, a potentially evil and extremely powerful spirit. Indeed it is sinister, half of its face is smiling, the other half frowning. Simple human and animal faces are also favorites for the Bering Sea carvers. The subject matter is sometimes associated with a story, as in the case of a charming pair of earrings representing a short-eared owl. Nelson reports:

> To account for the stupidity of this owl, and for its peculiarly-shaped head, the natives have a legend that *mûn-kō-chē-wûk* was a little girl living on the Lower Yukon with her parents; but for some cause she turned into a bird with a very long bill, very much like a curlew's, and when she started up with a wild confused way to get out of her village after the change, she flew plump into the side of a house, compressing her bill into a very short one, and flattening her face; and so it has remained to this day, as any one may see by examining the bird. (Nelson 1887:149)

When an Eskimo boy from North America reaches puberty, small thin stone or ivory labrets are inserted in holes made in his cheeks near the corners of his mouth. Each labret has a flat, flared end which rests against his lower gum and keeps the labret in place. As he gets older a man will wear bigger and fancier labrets, stretching his cheek holes to accommodate the larger pieces. He drills holes through the labrets he wore when he was young, and he might even decorate them before giving them to his wife, who hangs the labrets from her belt or needlecase strap.

Large labrets are made out of ivory, various kinds of stone including quartz and nephrite, and coal. There are regional labret styles which are

**169. Men Wearing Labrets** *angutet tuutalget*

Boys begin to wear labrets in the shape of small nails when they reach puberty. Holes are pierced on either side of the lower lip, through which tiny labrets are inserted. The slightly flared end of the labret is worn inside the lip and rests against the lower teeth.

Men wearing labrets resemble walrus, their tusks and labrets projecting from the corners of their mouths. The white gores sewn down the front of men's parkas reinforce the image of tusked men.

SI–3862–1

usually a variation on round, square, or oval shapes. Northern labrets are the exception. Some of them have been carved in the shape of whale flukes and probably function as whaling charms.

When a man is traveling long distances in cold weather, he removes his heavy labrets from his cheeks to avoid suffering frostbite, for their weight pulls down his lower lip, exposing it to the elements, and the labrets conduct cold as well. Upon approaching a community the labrets are reinserted, so that he makes his appearance as a well-dressed man.

Archeologists know that the ancestors of nineteenth-century Eskimos wore labrets. Prehistoric remains bear evidence of this in the form of ground surfaces where labrets have rested against a man's lower teeth. Why people began wearing them is not known, but their position and resemblance to emergent walrus tusks suggest a ritual significance.

Belts are also individualized pieces of apparel that reveal much about the wearer. The caribou mandible belt is particularly treasured, and is often inherited by a woman from her mother. Belts that have passed through several generations are regarded with great respect, for they acquire curative powers with age. A single belt may include the teeth of more than one hundred caribou. Therefore, a newly made belt is a great source of pride for the hunter and his family.

Along the north coast women's ceremonial belts sometimes are made from the claws and jaws of King crabs. People fish for King crabs only

**170. Facial Decoration** *tuutat, iyat*

Labrets are worn by men living north of the Kuskokwim River, but are uncommon among men living on the Asiatic coast or St. Lawrence Island.

The arms and faces of women living in Siberia, on St. Lawrence Island, and on the Bering Strait coast are covered with tattoos.

Lower Kuskokwim 36227, 5 cm; 36226, 5.5 cm

**171. Caribou Mandible Belt** *naqugun kavcakutarluni*

Women throughout western Alaska wear belts decorated with caribou incisors. The belts are made by men, who cut out the front lower jaw of the animal in such a manner as not to dislodge the teeth.

Belts used by many generations of women become heirlooms (*paituk*) and acquire curing powers. When a member of the family is in pain or is ill, the diseased area is struck with the end of the belt, with the expectation that healing will follow.

Norton Sound 176071, 127 cm

**172. Labret Styles** *tuutat ayuqucit*

The shapes of men's labrets vary with the age of the wearer and regional styles. Boys wear small labrets similar to the thin ground stone labret illustrated here. Hat-shaped labrets, made out of bone, ivory, coal, or ground stone, are popular among men living between the Kuskokwim River and Sledge Island. Large white quartz disc-shaped labrets ornamented with blue beads are worn by Point Hope and Point Barrow men.

Men remove large labrets from their cheeks when they travel long distances in cold weather to avoid frostbite conducted through the plug. They reinsert the labrets to appear as well-dressed guests when they enter the *qasgiq*.

Rasboinsky 48749, 4.5 cm long; Northern Norton Sound 37663, 2 cm long; Cape Nome 44544, 2.5 cm long; 44441, 1.3 cm long; Norton Sound 33510, 2 cm long; Sledge Island 44906, 2 cm long

**173. Male and Female Labrets** *tuutat*

Women living in the Yukon and Kuskokwim region sometimes wear small sickle-shaped labrets ornamented with pendants in holes just below the lower lip. These labrets look like a form of thimble holder. Labrets are rarely worn by Eskimo women living in other regions of Alaska.

Men's labret styles vary from region to region. This labret from King Island reflects the importance of whaling to the King Island community. A stone has been carved into the form of a right whale in a diving position, with only its flukes exposed.

Kulwoguwigumut 176069, 2 cm long; King Island 43757, 3 cm long

when they have depleted all other sources of food and are starving. When Nelson visited Sledge Island, people had resorted to fishing for crabs and were returning to the village with two-hundred-pound catches made in a single day. Crabs are not featured on masks or ornamentation, nor is there prominent reference to them in mythology. They have an ambiguous status, for they figure in people's lives usually when things have gone wrong. Their incorporation into a ceremonial item may be an oblique acknowledgment of their importance as a backup food.

Like their jewelry and sewing implements, women's belt buttons or fasteners contain a rich symbolism that makes reference to the spirits and forces filling the Bering Sea Eskimo's world. Belt fasteners take the forms of legendary beasts with ribs and lifelines defined, or of hunted animals and their *inuas*. These ivory objects, used to hook a person's belt closed, make respectful reference to the supernatural world, as well as being beautiful objects to see and feel.

Men wear various kinds of belts, but two kinds are highly prized by them. One is a wolverine or wolf belt, made from the tanned skin of one of these animals with its hair and claws left on. The skin of the animal's head, including its nose, is sewn to the back of the belt and the tail is fastened onto the fur as well. This belt is supposed to give a man strength and provide him with the wolf or wolverine's hunting skills. Belts which make reference to a man's or a boy's totem are also important. The mummified body of a little weasel may be attached to the front of such a belt, endowing the wearer with the weasel's prowess and cunningness.

There are a number of ways people can deal with, and to a certain extent manipulate, the Bering Sea world. Most people carry or wear tiny carvings they or a shaman have made which serve a variety of purposes. A tiny carving of a beast such as a worm-man may be worn by a woman who

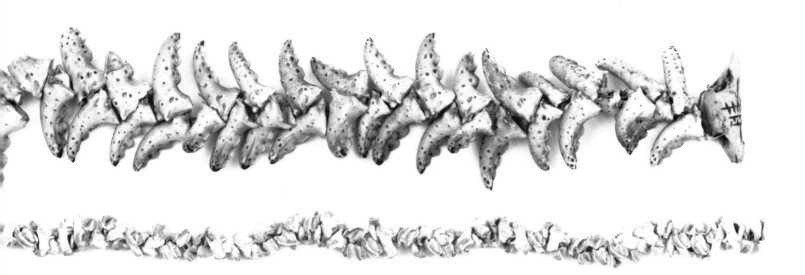

goes berry picking in the belief that the amulet will protect her from an attack by one of these creatures. Men often carry carvings of animals they are hunting, and women attach animal carvings to their clothing and implements. They believe in the clairvoyant powers of these amulets, which silently communicate to the wearer the location of distant game.

If a couple has been without child for a long time and desires a baby, the husband will carve an ivory or wooden doll-child which they will care for. This practice refers to a number of myths in which a childless couple makes a doll which is clothed and fed. The doll becomes a real child who in some myths goes on to do good, in others to do evil. Fertility figurines may be ivory carvings of women who may or may not be visibly pregnant. A variation on this is a little ivory doll collected by Nelson (fig. 179) with a womb incised on her abdomen.

There are people in Bering Sea society who practice witchcraft and they are feared, for they are trying to control the *inuas* of other people. However, the shaman is the individual who makes and owns the greatest variety of objects used to control the supernatural world for the benefit of his community. In addition to standard amulets and charms a truly powerful shaman may wear the mummified remains of an animal or even a human infant. Nelson recorded a story concerning the origin of the Doll Festival, and in the story a shaman has secured such a fetish, thereby gaining control over the *inuas* of many animals and becoming extremely powerful.

**174. Ceremonial Belts**

Large crabs, some of them measuring three feet from claw tip to claw tip, are eaten by people living between Golovnin Bay and Sledge Island. During the months of March and April people catch crabs by tying a dead fish on a line and sinking it through a hole in the ice. When there is a tug on the line, it is raised with care, and the crab is captured. Three or four lines fitted with indicator sticks may be tended by one person. When Nelson visited Sledge Island there was a food shortage and people were fishing for tomcod and crabs. He encountered a couple returning home, having caught two hundred pounds of crab in a single day. Crabs are not illustrated on pictographs or in carvings, probably because they are considered emergency food, improper to boast about. Their claws and jaws are strung on rawhide and made into belts worn by women on special ceremonial occasions.

St. Lawrence Island 63257, 55 cm long; Diomede Island 64221, 106 cm long

**175. Belt Fasteners** *nunguyun*

Belts are closed with ivory hooks or buttons. A fastening is sewn to one end of the belt, and a cord or loop is attached to the other end. To close the belt the cord is tied around or slipped over the fastening. A toothy fox and the circle-with-spurred-lines motif are featured on belt hooks from Kaialigamut and Cape Vancouver. The fox's lifeline extends down the center of the hook, and two pairs of legs are incised on either side of the piece. An ivory belt button from Konigunugumut is in the form of a seal *inua*, framed by pairs of seal flippers. Attachments at the top of the button are broken, and the entire piece is rounded and worn, suggesting that it was old when Nelson collected it. The button, like other heirloom items, may have been kept for its curative, ceremonial, or sentimental value.

Cape Vancouver 176144, 7.5 cm; Kaialigamut 37991, 5 cm; Konigunugumut 37763, 5 cm

### 176. Amulet *iinruq*

There are people in Bering Sea society who have the ability to make amulets endowed with supernatural powers. We know little about individual charms unless their significance was recorded when they were collected. According to Nelson, the tiny amulet illustrated here is an imaginary character with a froglike face, but he says nothing about its meaning or powers. However, the spots covering the figure's body also appear on ceremonial masks, suggesting that this motif has supernatural connotations. The amulet may be a shaman flying to the moon like a bird, or perhaps it is Big Belly, a shaman who lost a fight with another shaman when "traveling" under the ice, and who swallowed water and developed a huge belly.

Kushunuk 36880, 3.5 cm long

### 177. Amulets and Charms *iinrut*

Amulets and charms can be very old objects, broken tools, desiccated animals, animal tails and teeth, or special ivory carvings. A powerful shaman may even own a bundle containing the desiccated remains of an infant, whose *inua* gives him special powers over the invisible world. Women often attach charms to their clothing and needlecase straps. One woman's charms include small bird darts, an old worn carving of a seal, a broken pair of earrings, and a broken awl. Such charms may have the power to ward off evil spirits or cure disease. Tiny carvings of animals are worn or carried by hunters, who believe that the amulets have the power to hear the clicking of walking caribou or to see swimming geese and roaming polar bears that are far away. The amulets lead hunters to the animals or call the animals toward the hunters, and guide men's arrows, lances, and harpoons.

Unalakleet 43826, 10 cm; 33462, 4.5 cm; Lower Yukon Mouth 38571, 3 cm; 38572, 3 cm; Cape Nome 45252, 2 cm

In this village [Paimut] lived two young men who were relatives and were also noted shamans and fast friends. For a long time they remained unmarried, but at last one of them took a wife, and in the course of time had a daughter who grew to womanhood, was married, and to her was born a son. As soon as this child was born its grandfather killed it and carried the body out into the spruce forest and hung it to a tree, where it remained until it was dried and mummified. Then the old man took it down, placed it in a small bag, which he hung about his neck by a cord, and wore secretly under his clothing as an amulet, thus having the services of its *inua* to assist him in his ceremonies. His wife and daughter, however, knew what he had done with the child.

The unmarried shaman never took a wife, and after his friend began to wear the child about his neck, he frequently saw among the shades that came to do his bidding that of a small, new-born child. What it was or why it came he could not understand, as it did not come at his bidding. This was observed very often, and still he did not know that his friend had the body.

When one of these men was practicing his rites and found it difficult to obtain help from the shades, his friend would assist him to accomplish his object. One fine, warm day the unmarried shaman went up on the hillside back of the village and sat down. As night came on he fell asleep, and as he slept he saw the air filled with falling stars, and then that the sky was sinking toward him until finally it rested upon the hilltop so close that he had barely enough room to move about below it. Looking around, he saw that every star was in reality a round hole in the sky through which the light from above was shining. (Nelson 1899:494–95)

149

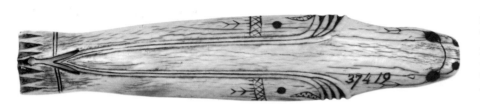

**178. Hat Ornament**
Much of the imagery found on Bering Sea Eskimo artifacts concerns the relationships between predators and their prey. Multiple relationships can be expressed in a single carving, as in the case of a flat ivory hat ornament stitched onto a visor worn by an Anogogmut seal hunter.
Anogogmut 37419, 16 cm

## Children's Life

Child rearing is the fourth major type of activity that takes place in and around the house. During the birth process mother and child are assisted by an older woman or, if there are complications, by a shaman. The new-born infant is wrapped in a diaper of soft seal skin lined with dried sphagnum moss, and a tiny eiderskin parka is made for him (Lantis 1946:223). The infant will go everywhere his mother goes, riding on her back and inside her frock, which has a large hood to accommodate him.

A childless couple may go to a shaman for help. The husband or the shaman will carve a wooden or ivory doll, perhaps representing a woman with her sexual features emphasized and her lifeline and womb defined. Or the doll may simply be a male or female figure which the couple cares for in hopes that the doll will come to life in the wife's womb.

Male infants are favored over females because as adults men have the capability of supporting their old parents. An unwanted infant is left outdoors to die in the snow, or may be adopted by another couple who will raise the child as their own.

A newborn may be named after the last person to die before the birth or after a deceased relative. According to Nelson a child may also be named after the first thing that catches his mother's eye following the birth. If named after a deceased individual, the child becomes the representative of that person. This relationship is most fully expressed during the Great Feast to the Dead when the namesake and by implication the shade of the dead person is fed and dressed in new clothes.

The first major event in a baby's life that is recognized by the community is when the baby is taken into the *qasgiq* for the first time. On Nunivak Island this usually occurs during the first Bladder Festival, a major hunting ceremony, after the baby's birth. The baby's parents present a number of gifts to the people assembled in the *qasgiq*, and the presents are divided amongst the older people (Lantis 1946:224).

On Nunivak Island and elsewhere in the Yukon–Kuskokwim region, the first time a little girl picks berries and takes them home and the first time she cuts grass for weaving are events recognized in the community. A

**179. Bracelets** *tallirat*
Bracelets made out of copper, brass, and iron are popular among Eskimo women. They like their shiny quality and the clinking sound of the bracelets as they knock against one another. This little ivory doll, collected by Nelson at Nubviukhchugaluk, represents a wealthy, well-dressed woman, if one considers the many metal bracelets she wears on her arms. She herself may be a fertility figurine, for a thin incised "lifeline" runs down her chest defining her stomach and womb.
Nubviukhchugaluk 43995, 6 cm

**180. Bracelets Worn by Men** *tallirat*
Ornamented sealskin bracelets, worn by men, serve both decorative and practical functions. When they are at sea hunting in their kayaks, the men secure the ends of the sleeves of their waterproof garments by folding the sleeves over and under the tight-fitting bracelets, thus preventing water from running up the sleeves. The owner of this particular bracelet was not impressed with the flowered European pottery available to him and preferred to display its white undecorated surface, which he passed off as a polished piece of ivory.
Nulukhtulogumut 38296, 7 cm across

**181. Women's Tool Boxes** *qungasviit*

Sewing implements, swatches of hide, and toys are among the items women store in their wooden work boxes. One of the finer examples of bent-wood technology is a circular box collected by Nelson when he was visiting Sledge Island. The sides of the box are a thinned spruce slab that has been bent and stitched with spruce root. The wooden bottom has been snapped into place, and the hinged lid has been fitted with leather fastenings. A personal or totem mark in the form of a red X has been painted on the bottom of the box.

A close examination of the beautiful rectangular work box from Cape Nome reveals that European materials and construction methods have found their way into local woodworking in the form of an oak panel, a blue bead, and dovetail joints. Despite the very different shapes of these two boxes, they are decorated in a similar and traditional manner. Grooves around their sides and on their lids are dyed black, and the box surfaces are rubbed with red pigment.

Sledge Island 45093, 25 cm (diameter); Cape Nome 45385, 36 cm long

small festival is held in the *qasgiq* and men are presented with food. The first time a little girl dances in the *qasgiq* is also recognized, and she is very excited by this event. She is given a fancy headdress and her father distributes gifts (Lantis 1946:224).

A little girl plays with miniature versions of the tools her mother uses including a tiny housewife with sewing equipment, a bent-wood box, a basket, and a root pick. By the age of thirteen or fourteen she should be able to make clothing and weave mats and baskets, for she has helped her mother around the house. She will soon be a wife herself, if she is not already married, and will be in a position of providing for rather than being cared for.

The first time a girl menstruates she must observe a number of taboos which range in duration from a few days to a year and which include eating restrictions and physical separation from the community. During the initial stage of her confinement an atmosphere is said to surround her, and if a hunter comes too close to her, this atmosphere will make him visible to animals he later tries to hunt.

The first bird a little boy manages to kill is skinned by his mother and presented in the *qasgiq* during the next Bladder Festival. The boy's father gives away many fine presents on this occasion. The little boy will continue to entertain himself around the village, setting traps for small animals and stalking song birds with a bow and arrow made for him by his father. Throughout his adolescence, every time a boy kills a new species of bird or mammal the captured animal is given special treatment. The killing of his first seal is an especially noteworthy occasion and is given recognition by its meat being distributed outside the family. Other important events

in a young boy's life include the first time he beats a drum in the *qasgiq* and the first time he sings a song he has composed.

On Nunivak Island when a young man has killed every kind of seal and finally brings home an adult bearded seal he is considered a man and eligible to marry. Before he marries however he is subject to a number of taboos similar to those a girl goes through when she reaches puberty (Lantis 1946:226–27).

On Nunivak Island a man teaches his children family songs and as a family they observe certain taboos and share totemic emblems. The man's daughters will learn this information but once they marry they will adopt the customs of their husbands' families. A man will teach his sons to hunt skillfully, also teaching them hunting magic and songs. If a couple separates, the children are in a potentially difficult situation, because their fathers may not be around to train them. In the case of boys this is particularly true. The boys' paternal uncles, their grandfathers, or stepfathers may take over this role (Lantis 1946). Boys in this situation sometimes become shamans' apprentices, seeking recognition and influence in social

**182. Steamer Trunk** *yaassigek qungasviik*
Nelson describes this red Kusilvak box as a container for small articles—and an ideal one it is, for it has four small compartments in which to store small knickknacks and a larger one for bigger objects. Each compartment is covered with a hinged wooden panel that can be opened by pulling on a thong passed through the lid. The box has been constructed out of many small pieces of wood, pegged together with wooden dowels cut flush with the box, and covered with red pigment. The hinges have been made by chain-stitching seal skin to wood with spruce or willow roots. The interiors of some of the compartment lids have red stripes painted on them which resemble marks found on the bottoms of bent-wood trays and bowls. The technology used to construct the box is traditional, but the form is not. Indeed, the piece resembles a European steamer trunk.
Kusilvak 49075, 38.5 cm

**183. Salmon-shaped Box**
According to an Eskimo legend, after Raven made Man he set to work making birds, fish, mosquitos, and other animals so that Man would not be lonely on earth. One day Raven flew to the sky and stayed away for four days. When he returned to earth he carried salmon with him, deposited them in rivers, and proceeded to explain to Man the many ways he could use this fish. Since then, Bering Sea Eskimo women dry and smoke salmon for food and sew salmon skins into bags, waterproof parkas, and mittens.
Sabotnisky 49015, 34.5 cm

### 184. Seal-shaped Box

Nelson states that this Ikogmut box represents a dead seal, its flippers tied up for better towing by the hunter. It also may be a seal swimming on its back, portrayed like Aleutian sea otters. A semihuman face, wearing labrets and framed by a red groove, stares out from the box lid and may be the seal's *inua*.

Rather crude figures have been painted in black on the interior lid of the box in a manner unlike the formal, public, narrative style found on drill bows. The lid surface has been split in half. On one side, floating without baselines, appear a caribou, a huge male toothy monster, a stomach, and a man wearing a hat, who is having an erection while carrying an animal in one hand and a club in the other. A smaller version of the toothy monster, a man holding scissors who appears to have cut someone in half, and a figure with upraised arms appear on the other half of the lid. The inner lids of men's tool-boxes contain similar paintings which have strong mythological and sexual overtones.

Ikogmut 43887, 30 cm long (box)

### 185. Ivory Inlaid Work Box

The bent-wood work box illustrated here is a showcase for the superb wood and ivory working skills and the fine sense of style of Bering Sea craftsmen. The bent-wood sides are pegged onto a truncated cone-shaped bottom. Six rods and eight circles carved out of ivory and incised with concentric circles have been set into and pegged onto the back and front of the box.

Sfugunugumut 36240, 23 cm

and religious activities rather than in the hunting arena (Lantis 1960:168).

Aside from ceremonial activities and subsistence endeavors, adults and children play games, sing songs, and listen to stories. Children spend many hours playing with toys similar to their parents' tools. They also play darts, jackstraws, and a number of games involving leather balls stuffed with caribou fur. They use braided grass jump ropes, wooden whistles, and bone buzzes. A favorite game involves a wooden top. The object of the game is to set the top spinning, race out of the house entrance passage, run around the house one time, and return to the top before it stops spinning.

Little girls play with an infinite variety of dolls. Some dolls are beautifully carved ivory figures with their hands sculpted close to their bodies to avoid breakage and to allow the girls to slip miniature versions of adult fur frocks on and off their little playmates. In some cases only the top portion of the doll is made out of a sturdy material, the body, arms, and legs being fur stuffed with down, lichen, or caribou fur.

**186. Toy Bird** *yaquleguaq*

The little blue bird illustrated here is fastened to a red-speckled platform by means of a bird quill. A string attached to the bird's beak runs through a hole in the platform. The bird's head is lowered when a child tugs on the string. When the string is released, the quill's tension causes the bird to spring upright. When the string is pulled and released repeatedly the bird appears to be pecking away at the red "food" on the "ground." Men carve toys such as this one in the shapes of birds and other animals for their own and their children's amusement.

St. Michael 33798, 15 cm

People gather in the *qasgiq* at night to listen to men tell stories. Many of the stories have been heard before but people enjoy hearing them again. Nelson reports that during his travels he frequently listened to young men learning and practicing songs and stories. The stories bring together the family and community. They also serve as vehicles of instruction, for in addition to myths and legends stories describe how hunters overcame predicaments and how individuals coped with certain situations. Nelson collected one story which he indicates was told by women. The story is interesting because it presents Raven as a fool rather than as a great teacher and provider.

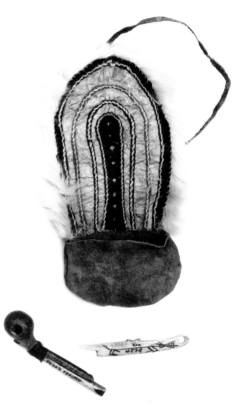

### THE RAVEN AND THE MARMOT

Once a Raven was flying over a reef near the seashore, when he was seen by some Sea-birds that were perched on the rocks, and they began to revile him, crying, "Oh, you offal eater! Oh, you carrion eater! Oh, you black one!" until the Raven turned and flew away crying, "*Gnak, gnak, gnak!* why do they revile me?" And he flew far away across the great water until he came to a mountain on the other side, where he stopped.

Looking about he saw just in front of him a marmot [ground squirrel] hole. The Raven stood by the hole watching, and very soon the Marmot came back bringing home some food. When the Marmot saw the Raven in front of his door he asked him to stand aside, but the Raven refused, saying "They called me carrion eater, and I will show that I am not, for I will eat you." To this the Marmot answered, "All right; but I have heard that you are a very fine dancer; now, if you will dance, I will sing, and then you can eat me, but I wish to see you dance before I die." This pleased the Raven so much that he agreed to dance, so the Marmot sang, "Oh, Raven, Raven, Raven, how well you dance! Oh, Raven, Raven, Raven, how well you dance!" Then they stopped to rest, and the Marmot said, "I am very much pleased with your dancing, and now I will sing once more, so shut your eyes and dance your best." The Raven closed his eyes and hopped clumsily about while the Marmot sang, "Oh, Raven, Raven, Raven, what a graceful dancer! Oh, Raven, Raven, Raven, what a fool you are!" Then the Marmot, with a quick run, darted between the Raven's legs and was safe in his hole. As soon as the Marmot was safe he put out the tip of his nose and laughed mockingly, saying, "*Chi-kik-kik, chi-kik-kik, chi-kik-kik!* you are the greatest fool I ever saw; what a comical figure you made while dancing; I could hardly keep from laughing; and just look at me; see how fat I am. Don't you wish you could eat me?" And he tormented the Raven until the latter flew far away in a rage. (Nelson 1899:514–15)

**187. Toys**

When not helping their grandparents, parents, or older brothers and sisters, children play games such as hide-and-seek, tag, jackstraws, and darts. They also entertain themselves with toys—wooden tops, bone and wood whistles, bone buzzes, skin balls filled with caribou fur or moss, and small versions of tools used by their parents. Little girls play house with tiny bent-wood dishes, grass mats, and skin bags; and little boys stalk birds with little bows and arrows, set traps for mice, and maneuver miniature sleds and kayaks. They spend many evenings in the *qasgiq* learning to make string figures and listening to stories told by their elders. Eskimo children have a great deal of fun while acquiring skills and knowledge they will use in their adult lives.

King Island 45391, 19 cm; Sledge Island 44707, 9 cm; Cape Nome 43629, 8.4 cm

**188. Doll Clothing** *atkuguaq*

A little girl usually owns a number of dolls made for her by her father. In addition to being equipped with miniature furnishings, some dolls have changeable suits of clothes, the garments being correct in every detail. This little Unalakleet doll can easily slip in and out of his frock because, like most Eskimo dolls, his arms are nonexistent or are held close to his body.

Unalakleet 38463, 14 cm

**189. Male and Female Dolls** *inuguat*

Often only the upper torso of a doll will be made out of hard material, the rest of the body consisting of soft skins, grasses, or down with clothes stitched on and around the soft body form. These little dolls, perhaps husband and wife or siblings, have skin bodies and bone heads. They are unusual because their heads have been hollowed out completely and holes define their eyes and mouths. He is elegantly dressed in a caribouskin outfit and wears beaded labrets on either side of his mouth. She represents the height of fashion, dressed in a frock made of European cloth trimmed with caribou fur. Her outfit is completed by a red wool scarf tied loosely around her neck.

Big Lake 38352, 15 cm; 38351, 17 cm

Perhaps the most interesting nonceremonial pastime is that spent by Bering Sea Eskimo girls who tell one another stories while illustrating them in the mud, or more rarely the snow, with the aid of storyknives. A storyknife is a knife-shaped implement usually made out of ivory, but sometimes fashioned out of antler or wood. The knife, made for a little girl by her father, has a handle carved in the form of a fish or a bird seen in profile. The creature's lifeline and ribs have been incised down the shaft of the handle on both faces of the knife. An extension of the upper incised line runs the length of the knife, and pairs of legs or spurs are often incised along this line. The flat top of the knife also has a series of horizontal and vertical lines incised into it, and their pattern and position suggest a backbone. In some cases a storyknife is decorated in this fashion but it is not possible to recognize it as an animal, for the image is so abstracted.

Little girls have favorite places where they gather to tell stories. These spots may be chosen because the mud is an unusual red or has lovely multicolored stripes running through it. Using the tip of her knife a little girl will draw an opening scene in the mud defining the space in which the story is taking place. She draws people, furniture, bushes, and mountains as they appear during the progress of the story. As she tells her story the narrator may decide that the scene is too cluttered or perhaps people have moved to another location. Using the blade of her knife she simply wipes the mud surface clean and continues with her tale, drawing as she talks.

Children in each village have a standard set of symbols that they use to illustrate buildings, people, and furniture, as well as action. These symbols vary from one village to the next. The stories a girl tells may be short versions of myths and tales she heard in the *qasgiq*. Her mother and older sisters may have taught her stories, and she makes up some of them herself.

### 190. Grouping of Dolls

While Nelson and his assistant spent time in the *qasgiq* on Sledge Island, two little girls came by to play. They had gathered together their dolls and proceeded to set them up in a semicircle facing the two men. The little girls took up positions behind the semicircle, letting their dolls get a good look at the strangers.

Nelson called many ivory and wood figurines dolls, but this is not necessarily the case, for human figures resembling dolls are carved for other purposes. When a couple has been without children for a long time and desires a baby, the husband may carve a doll which is fed and cared for. Figures are also carved to stand in for people away from the village during certain festivals, and a wooden image of a human is the center of attention during the Doll Festival, concerned with hunting and fishing conditions for the coming year. Whether toys, fertility figures, or ceremonial objects, the wood and ivory people are carefully carved, with great attention paid to the character of the face. Both male and female figures are made, their sex defined either by anatomical features or facial decorations.

Unalakleet 32931, 6 cm; Rasboinsky 48712, 17 cm; Kigiktauik 32916, 11 cm; Rasboinsky 48711, 9 cm; Sabotnisky 48907, 13 cm; Kushunuk 36225, 8.5 cm

**191. Brothers Rasboinsky and Their Cousins** *inuguat*

The two clay dolls illustrated here may have been the beloved companions of a little Rasboinsky girl, but even Nelson, who rarely passed value judgments, was moved to comment on the awkward and crude nature of these two pieces. They are extremely rare as well, being the only clay figures Nelson saw during his four-year stay in Alaska. The smaller figure has punctated eyes and mouth, and the larger figure's eyes and mouth are made out of quartz pebbles stuck into the gravel-tempered clay.

More commonly, dolls are made out of wood and ivory. The upper torsos of large dolls are carved out of wood, making them light and durable. Ivory and, more recently, glass beads are set into the wood to form eyes, mouths, and labrets. The Kushunuk doll has a beaded nose ring as well, making him an exceptionally well-dressed figure.

Rasboinsky 48735, 17.5 cm; 48734, 12 cm; Kaialigamut 37878, 20 cm; Kushunuk 37365, 23 cm

The stories cover a number of topics including myths, adventures, ghosts, and there is a class of stories that teach moral values. This last category is quite common, and usually features a child who disobeys her mother's or grandmother's instructions and brings misfortune to a relative. The strongest messages in these stories relate to how the disobedient child has risked her own life and has endangered the entire community because of her misdeeds.

Little girls living in the Yukon–Kuskokwim continue to tell one another knifestories, but since Nelson's time a little girl is lucky if her father makes her a storyknife. Today she uses a stick or a metal tableknife. Indeed, metal knives make very good storyknives, and mothers often complain that the silverware has disappeared and has been lost in the mud outdoors.

> One time there was a woman and her baby. She went to the tundra for berries. She left the baby on the ground to sleep. One time she looked up and saw the baby sitting up. She ran to him to hug him because he was so cute. The baby was so startled, and he flew up. The baby never came down. The mother tried to let the baby come down, but the baby didn't. She took a bunch of berries to show him, but when she looked up, the baby had turned into an ugly bird. She let down her long hair over her head, and ever since those birds have landed on those strange bumps on the tundra that look like a head of hair, and from then on those birds would have a place to land. (Lynn Ager 1980:99)

157

**192. Storyknives** *yaaruin*

Little girls gather around and tell each other stories based on myths, scarey experiences, or tales told to them by their older sisters and mothers. As a girl relates a story she illustrates the opening and succeeding scenes in a cleared area of mud or wet sand, using the tip of her storyknife, a wood or, more often, ivory knife made for her by her father.

Ivory storyknives, used in the Yukon and Kuskokwim, are carved and incised in a variety of styles, with the same decoration appearing on either side of the knife and incised lines running along the flattened top of the knife as well. A storyknife handle often is carved as a bird or fish head, the shaft decoration being an abstracted lifeline and skeletal motif.

Lower Kuskokwim 36595, 28 cm; Paimut 38359, 21.5 cm; Konigunugumut 37283, 30 cm; Nulukhtulogumut 36591, 30cm; 38120, 27.5 cm; Big Lake 37289, 23 cm; 38361, 28 cm

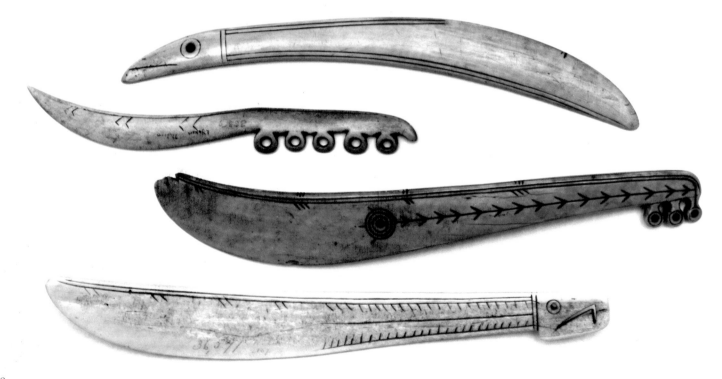

**193. Knifestory** *yaariluni qanemciq*

To the right is a knifestory told and illustrated by a little girl. Such stories introduce children to society's social values and traditions.

**194. Story Symbols** *yaariyaraq*

When telling a knifestory, a little girl will draw symbols representing the buildings, furniture, and people mentioned in the tale. Each girl draws the symbols in a slightly different way, but they are understood by all the children clustered around the scene.

man    woman    baby

house    qasgiq

sleeping in bed    tracks

trees    ptarmigan snare

## TRADITIONAL KNIFESTORY

There was an old lady in a house with only one son. She is a widow. She is very superstitious. There are trees outside. She told her son not to chop trees because they had some kind of supernatural powers. One day the boy was curious. His mother was sleeping. He went out and pulled up a tree, and afterwards he went in to see if anything happened. When he opened the door, there were trees crowding all over the house. He went over to his grandmother, and she was making a parka with her frill down over her face. When he called to her she looked up, and she was a skeleton. He was afraid and ran away, but the grandmother followed, and fire was coming out of her eyes. He ran out into space, and she followed. He became the sun, and she was the moon. (Lynn Ager 1980:226)

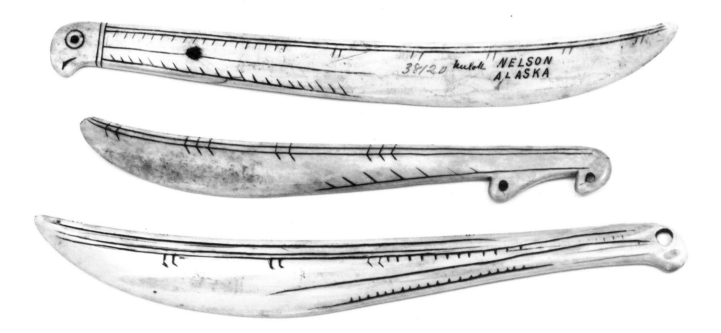

159

*I visited the* ԛasgimiut *("habitués of the* ԛasgiq"*) a number of times in the fall of 1978. On first descending through the front chamber and into the main room, I was struck by the scene: ten or so men sitting absolutely still on their haunches, almost birdlike, parkas pulled down over their knees so that only the tips of their sealskin boots protrude, arms folded, and the hoods of their parkas placed far forward over their heads, so that only the long bills of their caps stick out past the furry ruffs. From one emanated a deep, measured voice, in the midst of an account. After a time, he took a drum, and began singing while beating it; then he handed it to me, asking for a song, which I provided as well as I was able, remembering that Nelson had observed that this was a customary obligation of a visitor—however, in his case his hosts granted him a reprieve!*

Anthony C. Woodbury at Chevak, November 1978

with the spirits

# life in the qasgiq

Eskimo villages on the Alaskan side of the Bering Sea include among their houses large, square, semisubterranean structures known as *qasgit*. A *qasgiq* is similar in construction to family dwellings, but it is larger, and serves as both a men's house and as a place for community gatherings. In the larger villages there are several *qasgit*, and every man—and by extension, his family—is affiliated with one.

The *qasgiq**\* is a central place in the lives of the men. They eat, sleep, and make gear for hunting, fishing, and warfare here. They also take sweat baths, tell stories, and play games in the *qasgiq*. The structure itself has a single window with a removable gutskin covering at the top, and a large deep fire pit in the center of the floor that is kept covered when it is not in use. The entrance is through a passage door leading to an anteroom at the front wall in summer, but in winter that door is sealed off, and people enter and exit through a passage leading from the bottom of the fire pit, under the floor, to the anteroom. This passage serves to preserve warmth inside, and it also is necessary as a flue to ventilate fires in the fire pit. Along the side and back walls are platforms or benches, and each man has his own place. Elderly men of great status occupy the choice places beside the lamp in the back corner, while those of lesser standing are closer to the drafty entrance.

While the *qasgiq* is ordinarily the domain of men and boys, on special occasions it is a place for all in the community to gather. Many of the important ceremonies are held here, including the Great Feast to the Dead, and the Bladder Festival. These many-day-long celebrations involve varied and intricate sequences of dances, feasts, speeches, and other activities, and serve to honor the dead, give thanks to the spirits of animals taken in the hunt, and have many other purposes.

## 195. Qasgiq at St. Michael

Men living in the village of St. Michael spend most of the time in the *qasgiq*, or men's house. Found throughout western Alaska and also used by neighboring Indian groups, the *qasgiq* is the principal workplace and residence of the village men. The structure is built in similar fashion as family houses with a rectangular log framework dug partially into the ground. Over this is piled an insulating layer of earth reinforced by a log retaining wall. Entrance is gained through a long passageway that keeps out cold air. In this photograph of the *qasgiq* at St. Michael, a man stands beside the oval door in the planked facade of the entryway surveying both the surrounding scene and the photographer, whose activity with the black box may have caused him some concern. In front of him a large oval bent-wood container lies amid a pile of wood chips. A kayak rests on a rack erected above the *qasgiq* to keep it out of reach of dogs who would otherwise devour its skin covering. As shown in pictographs, much village activity, especially that of the children, takes place on the *qasgiq* roof. But at the time Nelson took his picture this vantage point was occupied only by a dog.
NAA–6908

---

\**Qasgiq* (plural *qasgit*) is the central Yupik name for this structure. "KUZZ-a-gick" is the closest one can get to its actual pronounciation using English sounds. In the literature, it has at times been called *kashim*; as E. W. Nelson recognized, this is simply a rendering of the possessive form, *qasgim*, and was perhaps the form that first impressed itself on early European visitors to Alaska.

Pages 160–63; 166–67 are the contribution of Anthony C. Woodbury.

## 196. Qasgiq Interior

Nelson's description and this diagram of the *qasgiq* at St. Michael illustrate the general form of *qasgit* from Norton Sound to the Kuskokwim River. Its main room is square and spacious, having a plank floor, several lamp stands, and low, side benches for sitting and sleeping. The log walls rise 7–8 feet before beginning to draw in, creating a pyramid-shaped roof with a central skylight and ventilator hole. In summer the *qasgiq* is entered through the ground-level passageway. In winter the inside door is sealed to prevent cold air from entering the house, and entry is gained through an underground passage emerging through a hole in the plank floor over the fire pit. The entire structure is insulated by covering it with a thick layer of earth, and even in winter it may be so warm inside, even without a fire, that clothes are frequently not worn.

When men prepare a sweat bath they take up the plank floor and build a large driftwood fire in the pit. As soon as the worst smoke has passed out they seal the ventilator hole and retain most of the heat for the bath, in which sweat and urine are the primary cleansers.

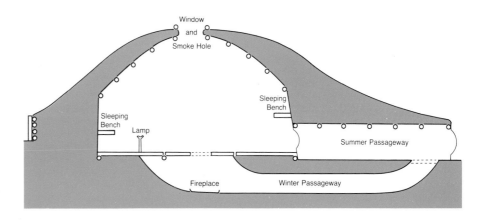

163

**197. Tobacco Pipes** *kuiniq*

Men pass many euphoric hours in the *qasgiq* getting high on tobacco obtained at great cost from Siberian or European traders. Their wide-rimmed pipes, which they make themselves, were introduced by Siberians before the Russians arrived and reflect their brief Asian ancestry. Yukon–Kuskokwim pipes are like this small one from the mouth of the Yukon. It has a two-piece wooden stem that can be opened to extract nicotine, the highly prized by-product of smoking used to good effect when mixed with chewing tobacco. It has a small lead bowl and an ivory mouthpiece with incised animal figures. A cleaning and tamping stick is attached with four strands of fine glass seed beads and a cloth strip. The beads are different from those in general use, reflecting a new, probably American, supply but are fitted with leather guide strips used in earrings and other jewelry.

During the time of Nelson's visit engraved ivory pipes were beginning to become popular around Bering Strait. Nelson obtained this one from St. Michael where it was intended to be traded to Europeans. Its well-worn stone bowl, used before copper and lead bowls became common, is fitted to a pristine polished ivory stem bearing graceless pictographs and lacking a nicotine trap. This is one of the few items Nelson collected showing an early development of handicrafts catering specifically to European tastes, and it foreshadows a major shift in the arts and economy of the region.

St. Michael 176286, 31 cm; Yukon Mouth 176169, 20 cm

## Smoking

In the *qasgiq* the men are frequently seen in their favorite resting position squatting on their haunches against the wall calmly smoking their pipes. No other pastime gives a man more hours of pleasure. Cradling his pipe in his hand with his arm resting on his knee and the pipestem in his mouth, he cogitates the events of the day, makes plans for the future, and engages in conversation with other men around him. Smoking, an expensive habit, is not only pleasurable personally, it marks a man's success and gives him status in the community. Well-established men can afford the cost of tobacco and the time taken out of subsistence efforts. Such men must have furs to trade and fish in their storehouses. They are also in a position to make small gifts of tobacco to other less provident persons who are poorer hunters and trappers. These gifts reflect favorably on the giver's social and economic position in the community.

Smoking is a relatively recent activity adopted by Bering Sea Eskimo men from their Siberian neighbors over the past few hundred years. Their long curved pipes with small out-flaring rims reflect the pipes' Asian ancestry and were probably copied by the Alaskans shortly after tobacco smoking was introduced to the Chukchi and Siberian Eskimos by traders from other Asian groups. Ultimately this chain stretches back through Europe to the Indians of Eastern North America. By the mid-1800s the Siberians were smoking with pipes that had bowls molded from lead. These pipes did not become common in Alaska until after 1880, when they were still considered very precious items, bringing a man who had obtained one considerable prestige. Once the technique of making the lead bowls with wooden molds was learned, they were more readily available; but many men continued using bowls made from polished stone in a style imitating

**198. Fungus and Fungus Ash Box** *kumakat, ararvik*

Fungus ash is an important component of chewing tobacco. The fungus is obtained by trade from the Yukon Indians, who collect it from dead birch trees. It is burned and mixed with finely shredded tobacco leaves, formerly originating through Siberian trade, and then is kneaded and rolled into rounded pellets or quids. At this point it is often given to a man's wife, who chews the mixture a bit to better incorporate the ashes with the tobacco. The processed quids are then packed in quid boxes ready for use. A man does not actually chew the quid, but holds it in his mouth, swallowing the juice. Nelson says if he wants to rest, eat, or drink, he takes it out, rolls it into a ball, and places it behind his right ear where it remains until it is needed.

This fungus ash box was made by bending an antler strip in the same way one bends the walls of wooden containers. It was probably soaked in urine and bent slowly, over a long period of time, then scarfed and pegged where the joint overlaps. The antler wall is decorated with the tooth or chain pattern and concentric circles with darkened center pegs. The top and bottom pieces are excavated from blocks of wood. A broad groove surrounds the conical-shaped bottom, while the top is decorated with polished sections of walrus teeth and tufts of seal hair.

St. Michael 43363, 15 cm; Yukon Mouth 38472, 9 cm (diameter)

**199. Tobacco Boxes** *iqmiutaat*

A blend of local and European ideas is seen in these tobacco boxes from the Kusko-kwim. While both show the skill and imagination men display in making articles for smoking, they reveal the introduction of new materials. The small quid box, identified by Nelson as a porcupine, has been sculptured from a solid wood block into an animal form with large reddened eyes, mouth, ears (or gills?), and neck, to which polished ivory eyeballs, studs for nostrils, and neck ornaments have been added. A lid opening through the throat reveals an excavated chamber in which tobacco plugs are stored.

A different design incorporating both old and new elements is seen in a bent-wood container with red and black grooves around its sides. The base is cut to fit the inside hoop and has an inner cloth covering to keep the tobacco dry and clean. Its bottom displays striations from cutting tobacco. The lid is ornamented with the face of a lady modeled in ivory, frowning, tattooed, and wearing labrets, surrounded by red and white glass beads and two halves of a white glass button—the epitomy of decorative fashion! A wafer-thin wood strip has been bent and glued around the edge of the rim, which is marked with notches to indicate the proper orientation for replacing the lid.

Kulwoguwigumut 36282, 9 cm; Ukagamut 36250, 9 cm

the hard-to-get metal bowls. After the coming of Russian traders and, more recently, American whalers, new sources of tobacco and pipes developed, and the influence of the Siberian tobacco monopoly began to diminish. Nevertheless, men continue to make fine tobacco, snuff, and quid boxes, and spend many hours making and ornamenting their pipes. To support their habit they must be successful trappers to supply themselves with the wherewithal for purchasing tobacco from the traders, and for trading with Indians or Eskimo middlemen for tree fungus, whose ashes form an important ingredient to a good smoke.

## Sweat Bath

It is the role of the eldest or most experienced man to preside over the doings in the *qasgiq*, and he, along with his peers, is the one who tells stories, composes songs, and determines the direction of events. The central activity of the day may be a sweat bath. An enormous, fast-burning fire is built of brittle driftwood in the central fire pit, and both the flue and the ceiling window are opened; when the fire is lit, the room rapidly attains excruciating temperatures and fills with smoke. The men breathe through smoke respirators they make of tightly bound wood shavings or tightly woven grass, and they roll on the floor, crying out from the intensity of the heat. As the fire burns down and everyone has washed himself, the group becomes very relaxed, and storytelling, singing, woodworking, and game playing begin.

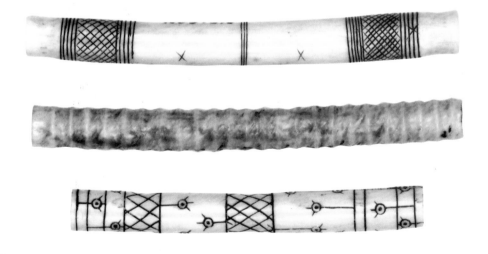

**200. Snuff Boxes** *meluskarvik*

Women rarely smoke tobacco, but they chew it and often take snuff, which is prepared by shredding tobacco leaves and pounding them into powder in goblet-shaped mortars. The powder is sifted through perforated gutskin strainers and stored in snuff boxes. These containers are often elaborately designed, as shown by this seal effigy box from the Lower Yukon. It is sculpted showing a small seal resting on the breast of a larger one. Perhaps they are mother and baby or, as suggested in Nelson's field notes, they are mates in a coupling position on the surface of the water. Stylized flippers are shown, and excavated portions of the body surfaces have been painted red, as are their mouths and the skeletal motif incised on the back of the larger seal. Bird symbolism, suggested by the split-feather quill collars, is also evident when the upper seal is viewed separately as a floating bird. In another visual twist the back of the upper seal can be seen as the head and beak of a large-eyed bird, possibly a raven.

Mission 48839, 10 cm; Anogogmut 37539, 8 cm (diameter)

**201. Snuff Tubes** *meluskarcuun*

Snuff tubes made from the hollow wing bones of geese and other waterfowl are inserted in a nostril while the other end is held inside the snuff box. Hefty snorts are taken with each nostril. These tubes, which are rarely seen north of the Yukon, are decorated in Yukon–Kuskokwim style.

Rasboinsky 49026, 10 cm; Sabotnisky 38042, 10 cm; Konigunugumut 37811, 8 cm

166

## 202. Powder Flasks and Cap Box

During Nelson's stay he noted the growing numbers of firearms, which had been present here since their introduction by Russian fur traders in the 1820s. In remote regions he found very early Russian rifle models used with the gun-crotch support, and collected one of the latter implements, locally made, with Eskimo decoration. Nelson also collected other articles associated with firearms use, such as this imaginative powder flask made from a block of wood that has been split, hollowed out, rejoined, and carved into the head of a horned puffin. Another flask departs from local style, its symmetrical spiral fluting and design imitating European metal flasks—rare prestige items. A masterwork, it is made from a single block of birch that has been excavated through its bottom and refitted with a pegged base. The small box, for storing gun caps, has a slotted lid. With its curved handle, it resembles a floating duck or goose. A remnant feather plume has been wedged in a small hole under the handle. This box has a red-painted encircling groove and a short groove segment on its base, similar to one found on wooden wedges from Ikogmut.

Typical of other items to be found in a "modern" hunter's kit is this ivory charging cup shaped into a cormorant head, used to measure out a single charge of powder. Bullet-starters, used to force the bullet into the barrel when loading, are needed because bullet sizes cannot be accurately controlled. Nelson noted the scarcity of European ammunition and found that bullets were frequently made with homemade molds, like this two-piece affair lined with a roughly fitting ground stone chamber.

Cape Vancouver 43490, 17 cm; Sledge Island 44966, 15 cm; 44961, 9.5 cm; Sfugunugumut 37234, 3.5 cm; Anogogmut 37433, 17 cm; Chalitmut 36323, 10.5 cm

Essentially the same scene was witnessed many times by Edward Nelson, who provides an elaboration of the aftermath of a typical sweat bath:

> . . . When the smoke has passed off and the wood is reduced to a bed of coals, a cover is put over the smoke hole in the roof and the men sit naked about the room until they are in profuse perspiration; they then bathe in the urine, which combines with the oil on their bodies and thus takes the place of soap, after which they go outside and pour water over their bodies until they become cool. While bathing they remain in the kashim with the temperature so high that their skin becomes shining red and appears to be almost at the point of blistering; then going outside they squat about in the snow perfectly nude, and seem to enjoy the contrasting temperature. On several occasions I saw them go from the sweat bath to holes in the ice on neighboring streams and, squatting there, pour ice water over their backs and shoulders with a wooden dipper, apparently experiencing the greatest pleasure from the operation. (Nelson 1899:287)

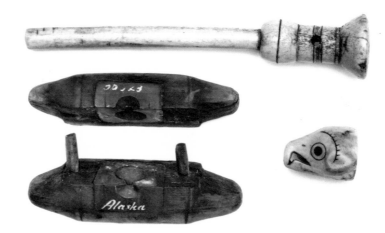

## Woodworking

Throughout the year men have gathered wood with careful attention to pieces ideally suited for making containers, hunting implements, boat and sled frames, and masks. Dishes and boxes may be carved from single blocks of wood. This task is made easier now that men have access to metal blades and axes. Metal tools do not often come ready-made. The men improvise and make crooked knife blades out of all manner of metal objects, sharpening them with grindstones, and then giving them a final honing with a beaver's incisor tooth whetstone. Beaver incisor teeth were used as crooked knives before metal became so plentiful. Stone adzes and bone and wooden wedges are used to rough out the basic forms of bowls, boxes, and masks, and to make wooden splints used in making fish traps.

Skillful craftsmen employ a number of woodworking techniques when making boxes and bowls. Bent-wood containers are made by first steaming long, thin strips of wood. The steaming and bending process is time consuming and tedious, and men do this work when they take sweat baths. Once the rim has been shaped into the desired form its beveled ends are sewn together with spruce or willow root, or are pegged. The wooden base is carved slightly larger than the circumference of the sides, and is forcefully snapped into place in the groove prepared for that purpose in the inside of the container.

The boxes may have detachable lids or lids which are hinged with strips of rawhide or braided sinew. The hinges are secured in place with knots and small wooden plugs.

A box may be constructed out of as many as five different pieces which are pegged together with long, thin, wooden pegs cut flush with the inner and outer surfaces of the box. Some men also join the box sections with dovetail joints, possibly adopted after an examination of wooden objects made by Europeans.

**203. Stone Tools, Flint Flaker, and Other "Useless Things"**

Among the items traded to Nelson were ground and chipped stone tools. Stone axes, points, and knives were still being used, not only in remote areas where iron was scarce but also in Bering Strait where religious beliefs prohibited its use for killing and butchering certain sea mammals. The axe from Sledge Island is made of nephrite, a jadelike stone whose principal source is on the Kobuk River. In early days nephrite and, to a lesser extent, chert (flint) were traded to Siberians and to Eskimos south of Bering Strait. Some points collected by Nelson came from old village sites he visited, while others were similarly obtained by Eskimos knowing that they could be traded to him for more useful things. This flint flaker, a northern tool type, is made from a Dall sheep horn and has an antler punch.

Sledge Island 45069, 23 cm; Kigiktauik 38517, 8 cm; Point Hope 63863, 8.5 cm; Big Lake 36292, 8.5 (scraper); Kotzebue 48556, 21 cm

**204. Polishers and Sharpeners** *ipegcaun*

The *qasgiq* is a workshop as well as a center for men's social and ceremonial activity. Many hours are spent here making and repairing objects used in everyday life. Among a man's tools will be found abraders of pumice, a "floating" stone obtained from local outcrops or found on beaches where it collects after volcanic eruptions. A fine polish can be given to ivory and wood artifacts by rubbing their surface vigorously with a smooth, hard stone like this striped pebble, chosen as much for its unusual appearance as for its physical properties. Nephrite whetstones are used to sharpen stone- and iron-bladed implements. Often made to be suspended from the belt or around the neck, they are especially prized possessions that may be handed down through several generations.

Alaska 63539, 5 cm; Norton Sound 33779, 4.5 cm; Unalakleet 43877, 13.5 cm

**205. Drill Kits** *igauquk*

Eskimo craftsmen make great use of drilled holes. North of the Yukon drill bows engraved with pictographic art are employed. To the south a strap replaces the bow, and drill caps are decorated with animal designs. This cap with a ground stone socket has a grizzly bear head carved on one end and a human face on the other. A projecting flange is used to hold the cap between the teeth. To use the tool, the craftsman presses down on the cap as the drill is turned with a strap with handles that are shaped as seals. The strap form is less efficient than the drill bow, which leaves one hand free to hold the work. The strap is probably the older style since drill bows have not been found in early archeological sites. Similar drills are used to make circles and dots on ivory and, with plain wood shafts, to make fire.

Kushunuk 36319, 130 cm (strap), 10 cm (handles); Mission 38084, 14 cm; Pastolik 33172, 25 cm

Men delight in woodworking and make containers for all sorts of articles, including their thin slate lance points, trinkets, pigments, tobacco, and snuff. They take great care when they carve and decorate tool boxes for themselves and their wives. Seal shapes are favorites because the animal's overall configuration is an ideal box shape, and men do the seal's *inua* honor when they feature this critical resource on a box. Some seal-shaped boxes are carved in standardized poses showing the animal with its head and flippers tied up, resembling the way seals are trussed by hunters before dragging them home over the ice—a pose also similar to that taken by live sea otters floating on their backs with food or young on their breast. A semihuman face, meant to represent the *inua* of a seal, appears on box lids. Craftsmen are careful to portray animals properly, and therefore often include the lifeline of the seal in their work. The lifeline may be a line painted red, but more commonly it is a red-pigmented groove running the length of the box. Boxes are usually encircled with grooves painted red or black. These features may relate to hoops and grooves around masks and to hoops used in ceremonies, and are said to represent the universe.

In a number of cases the general oval shape of the box and its fluted ends, indicating flippers, are all that identify a box as being seal shaped. The lifeline and the encircling grooves may also be present on this abstracted form.

Most of the ivory work also takes place in the *qasgiq*, and here again metal tools have made certain aspects of this work easier to do. Finely tipped metal incising tools are probably responsible for the engraving found on ivory implements, and metal-tipped drill bits have certainly proved more effective than nephrite bits.

**206. "Russian" Ivory Saw** *u-l'u-á-q'un*
Until recently ivory has always been worked with stone adzes and scrapers after being softened by soaking in urine. Now, in some areas, iron saws are made to imitate foreign models like this "Russian"-style buck saw. Its blade is tightened by twisting the rawhide thong against the fulcrum of the center strut. Dagger saws with short blades are used for working small pieces. Metal saws are not known prehistorically. They make work easier but have not caused major changes in production or style.
Cape Prince of Wales 48179, 30 cm

## Storytelling

Their bath finished, the men return to the *qasgiq* accompanied by a number of children and adolescents who, anticipating the evening's social activities, have gathered and followed the men inside. They watch the men put away their respirators, urine tubs, and loonskin caps, and as soon as this is done the children begin pestering the men with requests for their favorite games—darts, wrestling, making string figures, and others. Tonight the discussion is cut short by one of the respected elders who announces he will tell stories about the old days. For a few moments commotion reigns as the younger children are sent out to fetch their mothers from the houses, a fresh supply of oil is poured into the lamp, and the *qasgiq* is tidied up. Men bring out their work boxes and arrange themselves for a quiet evening with their families carving ivory or mending nets, while the women arrive with their sewing materials and bowls of salmon strips for snacks. When all is settled, a hush falls throughout the room, and to the small sounds of whittling and sewing and the questions of the children, the elder begins speaking in low but dramatic tones, recounting a tale about changes in the lives and customs of their ancestors long ago.

### THE DWARF PEOPLE

Very long ago, before we knew of the white men, there was a large village at Pikmiktalik. One winter day the people living there were very much surprised to see a little man and a little woman with a child coming down the river on the ice. The man was so small that he wore a coat made from a single white fox skin. The woman's coat was made from the skins of two white hares, and two muskrat skins clothed the child.

The old people were about two cubits high and the boy not over the length of one's forearm. Though he was so small, the man was dragging a sled much larger than those used by the villagers, and he had on it a heavy load of various articles. When they came to the village he easily drew his sled up the steep bank, and taking it by the rear end raised it on the sled frame, a feat that would have required the united strength of several villagers.

Then the couple entered one of the houses and were made welcome. This small family remained in the village for some time, the

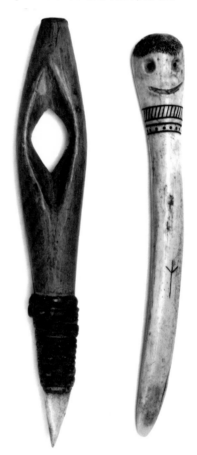

**207. Woodworking Tools**
South of Point Hope, in areas where driftwood is abundant, Eskimos excel at working wood. Tools used in this activity are few and simple: crooked knives, adzes, scrapers, wedges, and perforators. An antler-tipped perforator, shown here, has been used also as a drill cap, and the bone wedge for making splints is decorated with a raven's mark and a grotesque masklike collared face. Men living south of Bering Strait plane and shave wood with long-handled stone or iron scrapers with T-shaped or curved grips. Western Eskimo craftsmen, with a fine sense of design, have used this simple tool kit to create some of the most elegant pieces of ethnographic arts in North America.
Pastolik 33307, 20 cm; Ikogmut 43883, 19 cm; Big Lake 38838, 43.8 cm

### 208. Wolverine Head Tool Bag *terikaniaq*

A man at Cape Darby used to keep his tools in this bag made from the skins of four wolverine heads. It has a bottom of tanned seal skin with the hair side turned inward and a handle of walrus ivory depicting the pelts of thirty-four wolverine skins—a tally that may include some individuals used to make this fine, unusual work bag. The ends of the handle are carved into ornamental beasts. Wolverines are vicious and wily. They break into caches and steal food and often destroy the pelts of other animals caught in traps. This Cape Darby man must have been a fine, proud hunter to have made such a catch. One wonders if the wolverine was his totem animal, and why he parted with his bag.
Cape Darby 48089, 43 cm (handle)

man taking his place in the kashim with the other men. He was very fond of his little son, but one day as the latter was playing outside the house he was bitten so badly by a savage dog that he died. The father in his anger caught the dog up by the tail and struck it so hard against a post that the dog fell into halves. Then the father in great sorrow made a handsome grave box for his son, in which he placed the child with his toys, after which he returned into his house and for four days did no work. At the end of that time he took his sled and with his wife returned up the river on their old trail, while the villagers sorrowfully watched them go, for they had come to like the pair very much.

Before this time the villagers had always made a bed for their sleds from long strips of wood running lengthwise, but after they had seen the dwarf's sled with many crosspieces, they adopted this model.

Up to the time when they saw the dwarf people bury their son in a grave box with small articles placed about him, the villagers had always cast their dead out upon the tundra to be the prey of dogs and wild beasts. But thenceforth they buried their dead and observed four days of seclusion for mourning, as had been done by the dwarf.

Since that time the hunters claim that they sometimes see upon the tundra dwarf people who are said usually to carry bows and arrows, and when approached suddenly disappear into the ground, and deer hunters often see their tracks near Pikmiktalik mountains. No one has ever spoken to one of these dwarfs since the time they left the village. They are harmless people, never attempting to do any one an injury. (Nelson 1899:480–81)

### 209. Crooked Knives *mellgar*

No implement is more important to a man than his crooked knife. Its traditional form consists of a sharpened beaver or porcupine incisor tooth mounted in a wooden handle. The crooked knife, used with a drawing stroke, functions in every stage of woodworking, rough or fine. Its short, curved blade can make flat surfaces but will also produce hollow cuts needed for the interior of bowls, cups, boxes' finger grips, and other items. Its edge can be ground and shaped to desired specifications to make mortises and grooves.

The iron-bladed crooked knife, becoming popular in Nelson's time, follows earlier forms but is frequently elaborated to suit personal tastes. Seen here are two knives from St. Michael, one, with a composite wood and antler handle, has a simple elegance, while the other shows ships calling at the post as seen by its Eskimo owner. Even where iron is available, tooth knives continue in use for specialized functions. They also serve as sharpeners of iron knife blades, for the tooth's outer rind makes an excellent whetstone.
St. Michael 32882, 26 cm; 45488, 22 cm; Unalakleet 43859, 12.5 cm

## Box Lid Art

A man's tool box is one of his treasured possessions and there is little reason for someone other than himself to handle his box. Nelson bought a number of elegant tool boxes with hinged or detachable lids. The lids of a number of these boxes have paintings of animals, people, and mythological beasts covering their inner surfaces.

Compositionally the paintings suggest narratives, for characters and groups of characters may appear on a single lid, and the figures are generally arranged in a linear fashion. The fluted box lid illustrated in figure 215 has a central line down the center of its inner face. Comparison with the Nunivak Island wedge bearing a skeletized image of a mythological seal monster (fig. 219) and realistic seal-shaped boxes suggests that this line may represent a lifeline, which is lacking on the exterior of this particular box. Painted figures are oriented in relation to this lifeline. The black seal box lid painting (fig. 214) is organized in a similar fashion but without the painted lifeline. These boxes also resemble the Nunivak Island wedge in that the seal monster's body is filled with supernatural images as are the seals represented by the boxes.

### 210. Men's Tool Boxes *qungacivik*

Men make tool boxes for themselves and their wives by using bending, pegging, hollowing out, and mortising woodworking techniques. The smaller grooved Kigiktauik box, illustrated here, is carved from a single block of softwood, the bottom and sides being one piece.

The sides of the taller Kigiktauik box consist of two thinned and grooved pieces of wood bent to an oval shape and stitched together with baleen.

Kigiktauik 33008, 18 cm; 33009, 19.5 cm

### 212. Paint and Trinket Boxes

Men's boxes are often made in the form of realistic or stylized seals and may be carved from a single block of wood. Painted lid interiors contain mythological and sexual scenes, such as the whiskered creature on the Sfugunugumut box lid, and the male and female genitals, the wolflike beast, and the hunter on the Kaialigamut box lid.

Sfugunugumut 36242, 34 cm (two views); Kaialigamut 176083 (was 37863), 33.5 cm

### 211. Bent-Wood Technology

Using his crooked knife the craftsman thins and shapes a slab of wood and grooves the edge intended to be the inner and lower section of the box or bowl. Over a number of days he steams and bends the slab into the desired shape, the thicker parts of the rim helping him control the bends. He has beveled the ends of the slab so that when they meet they are flush with one another and the join is nearly invisible. He stitches the overlapping ends together with spruce or willow root, securing the ends of the root into tiny slits in the wood. With a great deal of force exerted by hand or foot, the bottom of the container, made slightly larger than the circumference of the rim, is snapped into place in the rim's prepared groove, creating a tight-fitting container.

Big Lake 38340, 30 cm

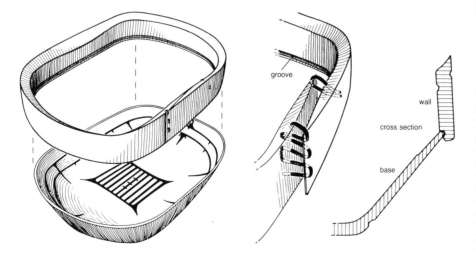

groove

wall

cross section

base

Mythology plays a prominent role in box lid paintings. Whereas bowls, ladles, drill bows, and hunting implements may feature a single image of a mythological creature, on box lids a section of the myth is narrated through illustrations. The clearest example can be seen on the inner face of the lid of the black seal box (fig. 214), where a thunderbird is shown carrying off a beluga and a seal in one instance, and a caribou and a man in a Norton-style kayak in another, while terrified caribou flee ahead of the bird, defecating in fear.

A wolflike beast is also prominent on box lids (figs. 212, 213). He may be *ăkh´-lut*, the killer whale who roams over the land having taken the shape of a wolf and kills both men and animals. Eskimos often see wolf-tracks leading out to and disappearing at the edge of the sea ice, marking the spot where the *ăkh´-lut* transformed itself back into a killer whale.

Hunting, with both traditional weapons and rifles, is also a major subject of box lid art. Major hunting sequences depict beluga being pursued by men in kayaks or already struck with bladder harpoons, and therefore symbolically caught. Featuring this particular animal suggests that the illustrations may function as hunting magic, for the beluga has an extremely powerful spirit and is the object of important taboos.

The black seal box lid (fig. 214) shows both beluga and caribou. This combination of animals may be a reference to the supernatural world and also to hunting magic. Nelson recorded a belief that beluga and caribou can interchange forms freely, therefore the artist may have considered them comparable images. Both animals are also major sources of sinew and other invaluable products needed by Bering Sea Eskimos.

Sex is the third major subject treated in box lid art. The painted seal box lid (fig. 212) has male and female genitals painted at opposite corners on the inner surface of the lid, framing a sexually active bow hunter together with a wolf and two walrus. The fluted box lid paintings (fig. 216) include men having erections, couples copulating, and figures involved in a variety

### 213. Storage Box

Comparison of this box with the preceding and following seal-shaped boxes suggests that this piece is an abstracted seal. The seals on all the boxes have been treated in a similar manner. Their lifelines run along their sides and backs in the form of reddened grooves, and scenes have been painted in the interior of their lids.

The central scene on the lid of this Askinuk box is painted in perspective, a technique rarely seen on Eskimo artifacts dating to this period. The scene consists of a red sled, steered by a red man, pulled by three red dogs or wolflike whiskered beasts, and ridden by a black man with a whip. In the top scene a male and a female caribou, both black, are being pursued by black and red toothy beasts. The lower figures include three red men in a red bidarka and a red man wearing a frock.

The figures may form a unit and portray scenes from a myth, or they may be individual scenes relating to legends or real and memorable events. The three-holed bidarka suggests the unusual, for this type of craft became common in the Yukon–Kuskokwim region only when Europeans like Nelson began traveling throughout the country. The symbolic meaning of the distinction between red and black figures is unknown, but the painting technique and superposition of the black figure and the red sled suggest that the figures were executed at one time by one person.

Askinuk 37561, 34 cm

### 214. Black Seal Box

This seal-shaped tool box is pegged together and has a detachable lid. The seal has ivory eyes and nostrils. Its front teeth are bone or ivory, its back teeth are wooden. Its mouth, the grooves along its back and sides, and grooves which define its flippers have been dyed red.

The interior of the box lid is covered with black figures, loosely organized in parallel scenes. Each scene is dominated by a thunderbird carrying off, in one instance, a caribou and a man in a Norton Sound-style kayak and, in another instance, a beluga and a seal. Running in front of the thunderbirds and defecating in fear are adult and young caribou. A man, connected to a two-headed creature, is figured between the lines of caribou. Behind the thunderbirds, beluga—animals given special ritual attention by Eskimos—are being hunted by a man in a Norton Sound-style kayak.

Whereas mythology and hunting are featured in the scenes painted in black, sexuality is implied in two red figures appearing on the lid. One is quite obviously a man wearing a European top hat and carrying a kettle and a bag. To the side and shown in profile is a pregnant woman with a tail.

Pastolik 36246, 41 cm

of sexual relationships. This lid appears to be a narrative and may represent a man's family life cycle in which scenes of copulation, pregnancy, birth, and grown children are linked by touching arms. It is likely that the same figures are shown in a number of scenes. In one, a woman is in a sexually receptive position between two men, one of whom is involved in traditional hunting. In the second scene she is wearing a European dress and holds a tea kettle toward an aroused male while the other male hunts with a firearm. These scenes may represent different social and economic stages in a family's career as it becomes more prosperous. They may also represent a hunter's fantasy world.

Another explicit form of male sexual imagery is seen on the lid of the painted seal box (fig. 184) showing a sexually active wolf presiding over a scene in which a European or American figure is depicted, judging from the figure's boots and hat. The figure holds an infant person or animal pelt in his left hand and a pipe in his right, and is engaged spewing semen over a detached womb. The other panel shows a figure, probably Eskimo, involved in sorcery with a pair of scissors, severing a human body in the presence of another wolf-beast. This is the only example of lid illustrations found on a woman's work box, but the old worn aspect of the object and the freshly painted lid interior suggest it was more recently used by a man, perhaps a shaman.

Paintings of European or American traders and their products—clothing, kettles, scissors, and firearms—are common. The bidarka, the three-man Aleutian boat often used by traders who hire native people to transport them about, may also belong to this class of motifs. Sleds, too, are featured prominently, and while not of foreign origin, they are the means by which trade and travel to other villages and trading posts is accomplished. These foreign materials and references are frequently used in connection with scenes involving hunting and sex.

The paintings appearing on the inner lids of men's tool boxes are quite different from the formal, public, incised pictographs found on drill bows. They are clearly meant to be private, and the exteriors of the boxes bear no hints of their presence. In contrast, drill bow pictographs are in plain view when men are drilling or making fires. The differences between the two narrative styles include organization as well as subject matter. Lid images are oriented to central lifelines, whereas drill bow engravings are oriented to baselines running along the edges of the bows.

The myth narrative is more developed on box lids than on drill bows, and, in fact, mythological creatures are more prominent in the paintings than in the incisings. Sex is a minor component of drill bow art, and whereas a variety of animals are shown being hunted or caught, these scenes function more like narratives of sequences of events than as hunting magic. Drill bows are full of houses, tents, qasgit, umiaks, communal hunts, games, and celebrations, none of which appear on the box lids. The latter display sleds and dog teams, kayaks, individual hunting efforts, mythological creatures, sexual and personal relationships—activities and objects that have a private stamp and which constitute a form of expression oriented toward personal sexual and spiritual power.

## A Trader Arrives

While men are occupied making and repairing tools and utensils, village life continues around them with children playing in and around the qasgiq, and people returning from hunting and fishing. Particularly during the winter months people travel long distances in order to visit relatives and to trade. En route they will stop in a village overnight and are always welcome whether they are personally known to individuals or not.

Men interested in trading will conduct their transactions in the qasgit, where local and exotic materials are exchanged. Materials also change hands during competitive and gambling games in which old and young men take part. Many an evening is spent watching these games while chewing or smoking tobacco and snuff which produce an altered state that the men find thoroughly enjoyable.

Trading goods within a village is only a small part of a much larger kind of economic contact that takes place between neighboring and distant villages in the Bering Sea and Bering Strait regions. Since the area around a village rarely provides all the necessities of life, people make arrangements to exchange commodities and services for everyone's benefit. People living in interior villages trade furs and forest products to coastal villagers. In return they get seal skins for boat covers and clothing, seal oil, and walrus ivory. In addition people regularly trade for exotic materials that may be available only in distant regions. Pigments, feathers, bent-wood containers, and skins of furbearing animals may be sent north by Delta people, who are seeking iron, Siberian reindeer skins, and cherts and nephrites.

The introduction of firearms, the increased supplies of iron, and the availability of hardwoods, cloth, beads, and tobacco supplied by European and American traders and whalers have opened up new possibilities for owning items that make life easier and are considered prestigious. The individual who is successful in acquiring these materials increases his status in his village and may establish himself as an important regional leader. Entrepreneurial skills and worldly ways are instilled in young men through their association with the village leaders in the qasgit, where they also become aware of the social roles available to them in future life.

### 215. Fluted Box

This elegant Pastolik tool box resembles a seal, its fluted ends more specifically recalling the lines of seal flippers. Like other men's tool boxes, this one has an inner lid covered with crudely painted figures enacting mythological, sexual, and subsistence activities which do not relate to the box exterior, suggesting that men's tool boxes have public and private aspects.

The box fluting is unusual, as is its unpainted surface. The container is made out of five separate pieces of wood, in addition to a lid. As Nelson noted, the two small end pieces have been mortised into the longer, slightly bowed side pieces, and wedges driven in the tenons insure that the end pieces stay firmly in the side slots. The fluted bottom has been pegged to the body of the box with evenly spaced wooden pegs. The lid is hinged with knotted rawhide and rests flush with the box rim when closed. Rawhide loops on the front of the box fit into V-shaped grooves and can be slipped over small bone pegs when the lid is to be securely closed.

Pastolik 38739, 48 cm

### 216. Painted Lid Interior

This Pastolik lid is the most complex example of this style of painting found in the Nelson Collection. Repetition of groups of red figures and their linear arrangement suggest that the illustrations form a narrative. Scenes include hunters in boats, caribou and sea mammals being pursued and struck with lances and harpoons, men with bows and arrows, and a man shooting a rifle.

The head of a toothy wolflike mythological creature appears on the ground, and two such creatures have intertwined and formed a womblike shape around a human figure. The scenes on the lid are sexually explicit and include copulating couples. Men are shown having erections, and males outnumber females on this and other box lids. The major characters appear to be two red-painted men and a woman, shown as a group on both halves of the lid. In one group the woman is wearing a European-style dress and is carrying a kettle. A man next to her is using a flintlock.

The European objects and the presence of a southern-style three-holed bidarka suggest foreigners. Whether these crude paintings relate to fertility or hunting rituals, stories, or activities associated with ceremonies is not known.

Pastolik 38739, 48 cm

**217. Seal-shaped Boxes**

Western Eskimo craftsmen have delighted in playing with box forms and have created pieces which show their skill and creativity. The Big Lake box, carved from a single block of wood, represents a seal on its back. The seal's *inua* appears on the detachable lid as a framed, reddened, humanlike face. The Konigunugumut seal-shaped box has grooved bent-wood sides, a pegged bottom, and a hinged lid. Glass buttons and beads have been used to define the animal's features.

Big Lake 35954, 19 cm; Konigunugumut 37562, 21 cm

It was getting dark. The people scattered. Two sleds appeared below, on the river; a few children, out of curiosity, remained on the bank to see those who were arriving. The visitors climbed quickly up to the village and stopped at one of the houses. It was a family consisting of a husband, wife, grown daughter, and half-grown boy. No one met them, but all the same they made themselves at home—they tied their dogs to the posts of the meat-cache, stored away in it the household utensils and trade goods, and lifted their sleds onto the rack. Then the women and the boy went into the house and the man proceeded to the kazhim [*qasgiq*].

When he warmed himself and sniffed or smoked some tobacco, the newcomer began to talk, without addressing himself to anyone in particular, about what was new in his part of the world, and what he had heard and seen in all the villages he had passed through. This was all done in the narrative style using the infinitive mood, or at other times allegorically as for example: "In such and such a village they say there are Kasyaks (Cossacks, i.e. Russians) going about giving presents of tobacco," which meant that he had seen some Russians and received a gift but he was not affirming definitely that the Russians gave gifts in other villages. . . .

The guest did not come to visit anyone in particular but hoped to find a buyer for his wares in exchange for the articles he needed. When he had satisfied himself and the others with his story, he brought into the kazhim everything he had brought with him to trade and explained that for such and such a thing he would like to have such and such in return. Everybody looked the things over and if anybody found a trade that would be advantageous or useful to him, then on his part without saying a word he would bring what was required so that all could see the worth and quality of the articles to be exchanged. If the price of the things which had been brought in was high, then some would silently leave while others would bargain. And at one point the visitor handed to one of the natives an article he had received from him in trade about a year before. "This," he said to him, "is of no use to me." And the other man looked the thing over, recognized it to be indeed his own, and returned that which he had received for it, and this without any comment. (Zagoskin, in Michael 1967:225)

**218. Diverse Box Forms** *yaassiiget*

Wooden boxes are made with particular storage requirements in mind. The long Sfugunugumut box represents a walrus swimming on its back, and is used to store medium-size objects. The elegant Cape Nome box is a slate endblade container, the baby seal riding its mother's back being a detachable lid. The unusual, featureless, unpainted birch container from Diomede Island is described as a trinket box. Its detachable lid has a square nail knob and the box opens into a deep cavity. Lumps of pigment are stored in the belly of the marvelous, fat, whiskered seal-shaped box from Norton Sound. The lid and its projecting handle are on the underside of the box, the storage container being the belly of the seal.

Sfugunugumut 36243, 34 cm; Cape Nome 33019, 29 cm; Norton Sound 33024, 13 cm; Diomede Island 64219, 24 cm

# Mythology

Mythology plays an important role in people's everyday lives and its cast of characters forms the basis for stories and dramatic presentations in the *qasgiq*. When used as illustrations or carvings, images of mythological characters serve both as decorative emblems and as mnemonic devices—keys to the characters and sequences of events that take place in a story or set of related stories—and give visual substance to oral traditions. The illustration of mythological characters and events seen on the inside covers of men's work boxes is more strongly and publicly affirmed through painted and incised drawings on ladles, wooden bowl bottoms, ivory wedges, boats, masks, and other artifacts. These illustrations generally identify the central character of the story and show him engaged in some activity or in some condition linking him to the myth or event: the worm-man as part man and part worm; the *palraiyuk* as a fierce multilegged and multistomached creature; and the thunderbird in the process of carrying off people, kayaks, or whales.

### *Tí-sīkh-pûk*, the Worm-Man

This creature, in the form of a huge worm or caterpillar, figures in numerous tales. It lived in the days when animals had the power to change their form at will into that of human beings, and in the tales may be presented either as a man or a worm. Eskimos sometimes make carvings of the *tí-sīkh-pûk* for use as amulets which also function as pendants or belt buttons, and illustrate their ivory pipes with its image (figs. 220, 221). The following tale from Kotzebue Sound recounts one of the many *tí-sīkh-pûk* stories:

> In very ancient days there lived a large Worm who was married to a woman, and they had a son who was also a Worm. When the son was fully grown the father told him to go to the middle of the earth plain and there in a small house he would find a wife. The son then used his magic powers and made himself small, so that he could travel faster, and journeyed away. When he came near the small house of which his father had told him, he felt the earth shake and tremble under his feet, and he feared that he would be killed. This happened several times, until finally he reached the house. Here he found that the cause of the shaking of the earth was the talk of an old woman who lived in the house with her daughter. These people received him hospitably, and finding that the girl was very beautiful, he married her. After he had lived there four years he remembered his parents and started to go back to visit them, but on the road he was killed by another Man-worm, who was a shaman. In a short time after this the father felt a strong desire to see his son, so he started to go to him. On the way he found the body of his son, and

**220. Tí-sīkh-pûk the Worm-Man**

Numerous tales are told about *tí-sīkh-pûk*, the huge, fearful class of beings combining human and worm or caterpillar features. One of these many-legged creatures has been depicted by a Norton Sound carver on an ivory pipe stem and is seen poised over the dead body of a seal. The image of a *tí-sīkh-pûk* is frequently carved on belt buckles, line fasteners, and other items. The carvings are decorative and also insure that the wearer will not be harmed by one of these creatures.

Norton Sound (M. M. Hazen Collection) 154075, (detail)

## 221. Living Mythology

Mythology pervades many aspects of Bering Sea Eskimo life. Although acquired through stories and legends, mythology directly affects people's lives. Actions are taken and events explained with reference to situations and norms supported by mythology. New mythology is constantly created by hunters, berry-pickers, and others perceiving mythological creatures, or their effects, in everyday life. The pervasiveness of living mythology is seen in the portrayal of events and personages in art and artifacts. Artisans—frequently shamans—give visual substance to visions and experience and interpret their meaning to others.

This bent-wood serving bowl has a painting of a segmented, spiny worm-man with a toothy grin, wolflike ears, and perforated hands. His dancing figure towers omnipotently over an entourage of walrus and seals.

*Ti-sĭkh-pûk* tales are told in dramatic presentations in the *qasgiq,* using masks which feature a spiny back and toothy grin. The mask illustrated shows a contented blood-stained face and red-painted mouth and toothed crest groove. Feathers and paddle-shaped appendages attached to split quills add motion and life to the mask as its wearer moves about.

Nulukhtulogumut 38685, 28 cm; Rasboinsky 38732, 48 cm tall (wood section)

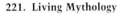

looking about saw a large village close at hand. He went to the spring where the villagers got their water, and making himself small, hid in it, where, by the use of magic, he killed nearly all the people in revenge for his son's death. When there were only a few people left, an old woman in the village, knowing that some magic was employed against them, worked a strong charm which caused the sea to rise and break the ice upon its surface and carried it over the land until the spring was covered; then the floating ice blocks were dashed together until the Man-worm was ground to pieces and destroyed, so that the people were freed from his magic. (Nelson 1899:516)

181

## 222. The End of the Palraiyuk

According to tradition, Magemut ancestors killed the last *palraiyuk* living in their country of shallow lakes and marshlands after it had devoured a woman fetching water from a pond. Formerly numerous, the memory of them lives on in stories and illustrations on darts, boats, and even on masks. A rare example of the latter appears on a red-painted mask showing a man wearing labrets whose anatomical features are rendered with a degree of realism unusual for this area. Its split pegs carried a bordering strip of fur that, according to Nelson, symbolized the winter parka ruff. A double-headed *palraiyuk* encircles the face, its tongues nearly touching under the chin.

South of Yukon Mouth 33131, 18.5 cm

## 223. Palraiyuk-Crocodile?

The *palraiyuk* depicted on a large *qantag*, or container, shows the animal's long tail, spiked back, three pairs of legs, and three stomachs. Its resemblance to crocodiles in physical form, behavior, and habitat was considered remarkable by Nelson, who noted these stories carefully. Further, Eskimos believe the *palraiyuk* was a relic of warmer climates when birds migrated north in February rather than in May, and that its numbers declined with today's colder climate. Nelson discounts European contact in the origin of these ideas, which are most prevalent in the more remote regions. He is undoubtedly correct, for *palraiyuk*-like images are known from two-thousand-year-old sites on St. Lawrence Island (fig. 295). However, perhaps an Oriental link is possible.

Mission 45494, 14.5 cm (diameter)

## Palraiyuk

The *palraiyuk* is a mythical monster that lived in lakes, marshes, and creeks in the region between the Yukon and the Kuskokwim rivers, where it killed men and animals for food. According to local tradition the climate in ancient times when the *palraiyuk* existed was very much warmer than at present and the winters were shorter. Waterfowl and other birds came back from the south in February, and the snow melted and ran into the houses through their sunken passageways at this time of year, rather than in April as it does today. In Raven's creation story he tells the first man about this beast as they travel together in the sky land, cautioning him not to drink from the lakes which they pass because in them are animals he made that will destroy anyone who ventures near. These are the *palraiyuk*. The *palraiyuk* was known to lie in wait among the grass in the lakes and marshes, to lunge forward to seize a person on the bank, or to attack kayaks crossing its haunts.

Drawings of the *palraiyuk* are commonly seen on kayaks and umiaks in the regions south of the Yukon and on Nunivak Island, on the insides of wooden dishes, and on masks (figs. 27, 223, 222). Similar creatures are found on ivory wedges and on Nunivak Island harpoon ice picks (figs. 224, 60). They are usually shown as having many sets of legs, a toothy wolflike mouth, and segmented stomachs containing human or animal legs, arms, or other body parts that signify their antisocial behavior.

### 224. Other Creatures

Other mythical beasts resembling the *palraiyuk* are known to Bering Sea hunters. An unnamed four-legged seal-beast, also on the Nunivak Island wedge, is shown on an ivory bodkin in magical "X-ray" form with multiple-spurred circles and dots and with its layer of blubber indicated. The hat ornament is decorated in a similar fashion resembling the "wolves" on dart socketpieces and quiver stiffeners. It may be *wǐ-lǔ-gho´-yǔk*, the sea shrew mouse who enters a hunter's clothing through a hole in his boot and devours him; or possibly *i-mǔkh´-pǐ-mǐ ǎ-klǎn´-kun*, the sea weasel who brings misfortune to lonely, inattentive hunters and was thought by Nelson to have been based on stories about real sea otters that disappeared from this area during the past century.

Cape Vancouver 43528, 19.5 cm; Sabotnisky 49014, 19 cm

Nelson comments on the curious likeness of this animal's form, behavior, and habitat to that of the alligator. "Nearly all of the umiaks in the country of the lower Yukon and to the southward have a picture of this animal drawn along the entire length on each side of the boat. . . . It appears to be a local myth and can scarcely have been brought to these people since the advent of the whites. The country where this myth is most prevalent is one of the least visited of any along the coast of the Bering Sea" (Nelson 1899:445). Implicit in Nelson's discussion is the idea that the *palraiyuk* might have had its origin from tales of an alligatorlike creature living in the Caribbean regions. A more likely possibility is that it may have come from tales of similar animals in southern Asia or from stories or images of dragons emanating from Chinese civilization over the course of thousands of years. That this idea may have a long history in Bering Sea Eskimo culture is suggested by images of similar beasts on archeological specimens from this region (fig. 304).

### Ko-gukh´-pûk, the Burrowing Mammoth

A tale commonly told throughout the region accounts for the existence of the bones of mammoths found eroding from stream beds and shorelines by Eskimos. These bones are said to belong to *ko-gukh´-pûk* (*kǐ-lûg-û-wûk*, north of Norton Sound), a huge animal living underground that burrows from place to place and emerges one night each year to roam the earth. At other times should it break through the surface and breathe air, it dies immediately. This accounts for the finds of its remains. The *ko-gukh´-pûk* is sometimes portrayed on artifacts such as in the interior of a fine serving bowl (fig. 125).

### 225. Ladle Beasts

Mythological creatures are often painted on ladles made in the Yukon–Kuskokwim region. The short-handled spoon is decorated with the head of a beast encircled by black and red bands and is covered with red dots, a treatment often given to ritual masks. Similarly, the cup of the long-handled ladle has a red and black border design resembling pegs and hoops on ceremonial masks. Within it, wolflike beasts with skeletized lifelines and pairs of animal and human legs devour a person's leg and pierced hand. Implements like these are used daily in connection with food consumption. Possibly intended for decoration and personal identification, these images constantly remind one of the ongoing relationship between mythology, religion, and life process.

Kaialigamut 38062, 13 cm long; Chalitmut 38068, 26 cm

## Tĭn-mi-ûk-pûk, the Thunderbird

In ancient times there lived many giant eagles or thunderbirds called the *tĭn-mi-ûk-pûk* by Yukon–Kuskokwim people, and the *mû-tûgh´-o-wĭk* by people living north of Norton Sound. These birds soared about in the sky, and when their shadows crossed over land animals and men, the earthlings feared for their lives, for thunderbirds carried off whales or caribou in the Bering Strait region, and in the south they preyed upon men and caribou. Many tales are told about these giant birds, which eventually were reduced to a single family whose nest was located in a volcanic cone near Sabotnisky. A vivid tale tells of how a heroic young hunter attacked this nest and drove the last bird from the land.

### THE LAST OF THE THUNDERBIRDS

In ancient times there were eagles of tremendous size frequenting the tops of the highest mountains in the interior and preying upon whales and full-grown reindeer, and even upon men. A volcanic crater of very regular outline, situated upon the summit of a mountain near the Lower Yukon, was ... the nest of the ancient *Mutughowik*. Around the rim of the crater are differently-colored stones, which, the natives claim, were gathered by these birds to ornament their nest. When the birds sat here, overlooking the Yukon on the one side and the sea far away to the horizon on the other, their screams could be heard for miles, and many luckless creatures were caught in their talons and carried swiftly to their eyrie, and there torn into fragments to be devoured. Year after year these birds remained, until men were afraid to go out on the broad bosom of the Yukon for fear of being caught by these evil guardians of the mountains overlooking the village. Each year the young were raised and flew away, none knew whither; so that never more than two old

### 226. Tĭn-mĭ-ûk-pûk, the Thunderbird

Stories about the *tĭn-mĭ-ûk-pûk* (thunderbird) are legion among the western Eskimo. Around Bering Strait it is described as a great eagle that carries off right whales and reindeer. A pair of these mythic birds is depicted on an ivory whaling harpoon rest from Cape Prince of Wales. On one side the birds are shown descending toward two spouting whales, while on the other they are climbing into the sky with the whales in their clutches. A blue Russian trade bead and two not-so-ferocious polar bears complete the design.

Cape Prince of Wales 48169, 13.5 cm wide

### 227. The Last of the Thunderbirds

In the Lower Yukon area the thunderbird (here known as *mû-tûgh´-o-wĭk*) preys on caribou and men, for large whales are not present here. This detail from the same pipe stem illustrating the worm-man shows a thunderbird attacking a caribou. A similar narrative is painted on a work box lid (fig. 214). Among the tales told in this area are ones describing the exploits of a courageous hunter who avenged his wife's death after she was carried off and fed to thunderbird young in their nest in the cone of an extinct volcano. This crater is known to Eskimos living nearby who believe implicitly that the human and animal bones, the kayak ribs, and colored stones they have seen strewn about the cone are the remains of the thunderbirds' last nest.

Norton Sound (M.M. Hazen Collection) 154075 (detail)

### 228. Animal Transformations

Animals have the ability to transform themselves into other animals. Despite the transformation, an animal's *inua* will not change. This concept of transformation is basic to western Eskimo thought and is described in stories as well as illustrated on implements. White whales undergoing metamorphosis into wolf-whale creatures are illustrated on this ladle from Chalitmut. An ivory drag handle takes the form of a dreaded half-polar bear, half-whale.

Sledge Island 176215, 17.5 cm; Chalitmut 37120, 25 cm

birds inhabited the mountains. One spring, after the birds, as usual, had hatched their young, a famous hunter of the village went out alone to attend to his fish-nets. While he was out one of these eagles soared high over the village, and seeing the hunter's wife outside of the house, swooped with a mighty rush of wings and carried her off to feed the nestlings. Ere long the hunter returned, and with wailing cries his friends told him of his loss. For a time he was inconsolable, but at length he seized his bow and examined it carefully, then he selected a quiver of his best arrows, and heedless of remonstrance began climbing toward the nest of the eagles. When he had nearly reached his goal he heard the whistling of great wings, and crouching behind a huge bowlder, with an arrow drawn to its head, he waited. In an instant the female bird was seen descending, her terrible eyes fired with rage; but just as she was about to grasp the hunter in her talons he buried an arrow under her wing and she fell far down the mountain. He then advanced, and in a short time reached the summit of the mountain, finding the young so large that they entirely filled the enormous nest. All about were strewn fragments of men and animals, among which were seen the frames of many kyaks. With vengeful heart he shot arrow after arrow until the last of the brood lay dead. He had scarcely finished, when a wild cry was heard close by, and he saw the male bird approaching. At the same instant the bird caught sight of its slain young and of the hunter. A still louder and more terrifying cry was heard, which made the villagers below shudder for their friend. The eagle darted at its enemy. With unshaken courage the hunter met each assault with a well-directed arrow until the bird, pierced with many wounds, turned, and, upon outspread wings, slowly glided away and vanished far off to the north. Since then none of its kind has ever been seen, and men have been able to hunt without fear. The villagers afterwards visited the nest with their deliverer and found many relics of friends who had perished, and it was only a few years ago that the remains of the kyaks were still to be seen about the nest. This story is implicitly believed by the natives of the Lower Yukon and adjacent seacoast, and the Bald Eagle is known by the name which they apply to the bird of their legend. (Nelson 1887:144–145)

### 229. Swimming Bear-Seal

These ivory drag handles were collected separately but appear to be the work of one man. They represent a swimming creature which has the head and front legs of a polar bear and the body and flippers of a seal. The creature's ribs stick out, suggesting that it is emaciated, despite the fact that its bear half is carrying a seal or fish in its mouth. The image of a starving bear-seal may relate to an event in a myth and may function as an amulet.

Cape Darby 44143, 8.5 cm; Sledge Island 176214, 9 cm

185

## Animal Transformations

The graphic representation of myths and beliefs on ladles, bowls, boats, ivory pieces, and other artifacts used in everyday life serves a number of purposes and is different from types of illustrations painted on box lids and incised on drill bows. The latter frequently utilize illustrations in a narrative form, often by associating sequential images with an organizing baseline or lifeline, or with other figures linked by line, by touch, or by directed action of some sort. Illustrations on ladles and other objects depict mythological and hunting subject matter in a more isolated and emblematic way. Here the purpose is not to tell a story, but to symbolize a widely known story or idea that the viewer can call to mind once provided with the visual key in the form of a chief character, or a recognizeable action, or event. The *palraiyuk* and mammoth images recall whole classes of

**230. Man-Walrus Transformation**

The concept of transformations—men into animals, animals into men, and animals into animals—permeates all aspects of life and is expressed on all kinds of objects. Man becomes Walrus in an engraving on a Norton Sound drill bow. The tusked prone figure develops the torso and back flippers of a walrus, though he retains, in an exaggerated form, the individual digits of the human hand and the flexibility of the human arm. A pair of finger masks worn by women during ceremonies represents a walrus-man or a humanlike image of a walrus's *inua*.

Norton Sound 33187 (detail); Lower Kuskokwim 38649, 13.5 cm; 37127, 13.5 cm

**231. Walrus-Man**

The walrus is an extremely important animal to the western Eskimo. Its meat, organs, bones, and tusks have been indispensable materials with which this late–nineteenth-century society has coped with the northern world. Man's dependency on the walrus is expressed as a close relationship in man-animal transformation beliefs conveyed every day in western Eskimo dress, particularly that of men. The labrets a man wears on either side of his lower lip give him a tusklike appearance. White gores, shaped like walrus tusks, decorate the front of his frock, also projecting the walrus-man image.

SI–3857

**232. Man-Seal Creatures**

Man-seals are creatures who live in the sea. If a hunter catches one of these animals in his net he is bound to suffer great misfortune. The wooden Kushunuk carving of a man-seal was made specifically for the purpose of telling such a story and has no other function, making it an unusual piece. The figure's face was once reddened, his human hands and arms are lightly incised into the sides of his body, and he carries a seal claw just below his arms. The ivory Sledge Island drag handle also has human arms, and the Nunivak Island belt fastener has line holes instead.

Nunivak Island 43717, 8 cm; Sledge Island 176211, 7 cm; Kushunuk 36336, 8 cm

**233. Man-Seal Box**

The man-seal is represented on a variety of objects, including this wooden box, used to store small things. The sides and base of the box, as well as the creature's head, are a single unbroken piece of wood, skillfully carved, grooved, and beveled.

The smiling man-seal has a blackened face, a red mouth, and white labrets fashioned out of European earthenware sherds. The hind flippers and tail are grooved and reddened. Like other boxes, this piece has a grooved lifeline running down the length of the man-seal's back.

Sfugunugumut 36244, 40.5 cm

stories and beliefs that are part of one's memory culture. Their use as decorations, sometimes as family ownership marks, constantly reinforces cultural values and traditions as these objects are used in everyday life.

Transformation stories are another category of oral tradition commonly illustrated in drawings and carvings. These include the stories previously related about killer whale-wolf and beluga-caribou transformations (fig. 228; Nelson 1899:444). The idea—that men can change into animals, animals into other animals, and animals into men—is a central part of western Eskimo religion, and a cornerstone of the Raven origin myth and the concept of *inua*.

The ability of men and animals to transform themselves into other beings, while always retaining their *inuas*, results in an unpredictable world in which one cannot be sure of the true identity of any given creature. A powerful, potentially evil spirit may take the form of a weasel or mouse to eavesdrop on men's intentions or to bring aid to a captured person. Sometimes small quirks of behavior give these disguises away, alerting a man to the possible deceptive appearance of another person or animal. Shamans make use of transformations in their performances and magic, and artists frequently depict the more commonly known transformation characters in their drawings and ivory work. A man becomes a walrus in an engraving on a drill bow from Norton Sound, while the same subject is treated on a set of finger masks and on a common parka style worn in northern regions (figs. 230, 231). These transformations may be the basis for the many "half-creatures" known in Bering Sea stories and mythology, which are also illustrated frequently in ivory carvings, especially on drag handles. Among them are the man-seal, the walrus-dog, and the seal-lamprey (figs. 232, 233). Today animals and men find it increasingly difficult to interchange forms at will as they could in early times. These transformational capabilities now lie within the domain of powerful spirits and shamans.

## Shaman

When a man observes something unusual, be it a seal that does not dive when approached or a strange cry in the darkness, he frequently goes to the shaman for an explanation. Such signs, after all, are common ways in which the spirits signal their feelings to men or convey information about food resources, weather, and sickness. The shaman is specially qualified to read these signs and is practiced in the art of ritual by which he attempts to influence or modify the course of events through intercession with the spirits that control these things. He is also counted on to foretell events, diagnose illness, and effect cures by exorcizing the evil spirits.

The shaman generally learns his trade by apprenticeship under an older shaman. In doing so, he may begin practicing secretly, without telling his tutor, fearful of being charged with sorcery or with responsibility for unforeseen disasters. He may be an orphan or a cripple who is unable to hunt or otherwise contribute to routine village life. He may be prone to fits or seizures, sure signs that spirits are at work within. Feeling different, or being perceived that way, he may seek the company of a shaman needing an assistant who can be trusted not to reveal the shaman's secret knowledge or the methods behind some of his more fantastic exploits.

Nelson encountered many shamans during his travels, for nearly every village has one or more practitioners. He found people reluctant to allow him to observe shamanistic performances and rites, especially powerful ones; but some rituals, like ones used to influence weather, were not barred:

> South of Cape Vancouver, at the village of Chichinagamut, we were overtaken by a severe storm and, in order to witness the rites, I paid a shaman to change the weather. After dark he knelt on a straw mat in the middle of the kashim and enveloped himself, with the exception of his face, in a large gut-skin shirt; then, resting his knees and elbows on the floor, he uttered a long speech at the top of his voice, when this was ended he concealed his face in the shirt and made a great variety of grunts, groans, and other noises. During this time two men stood on each side of him and over his back passed a double cord, extending lengthwise of his body, with a stick fastened to each end, which was held fast to the floor on each side of him. When the shaman finished making the noises mentioned a third man made a pantomime with his hands as if lifting some invisible substance from the shaman's back. This motion was repeated a number of times and then the two men raised the sticks to which the cords were tied and circled several times around the shaman, constantly turning their sticks end over end, and finally stopping in their former positions. The shaman then caused his voice to die away in the distance, after which he arose and said that we would have a change of weather in two days. (Nelson 1899:431)

**234. The Shaman** *angalkuq*

The shaman, or *tuṅghalīk*, has the ability to control supernatural beings as well as the shades of dead animals and people. He is a key figure in western Eskimo society, his advice being sought regarding hunting, curing, and ceremonial activities. He is also greatly feared, for he possesses the power to bring misfortune and death to an individual or a community.

Northern shamans, like the two depicted on the drill bow and belt fastener, fly to the land of the dead and to the moon. Southern shamans make their journeys under the ice and if they encounter other shamans during their travels, great battles ensue. Shamans make amulets, like the dance wristlet pictured on the opposite page, which are endowed with special powers. Ceremonial masks are often carved by these individuals and are interpretations of shamans' visions or dreams.

Kotzebue Sound 48522 (detail); Diomede Island 63887, 6 cm

**235. Spotted Shaman's Mask** *kegginaqaq*
A shaman from Pastolik made this mask to represent evil people seen only by him. The semihuman twisted features of the mask include a toothy mouth splattered with a brown pigment said to represent blood. Two legs, two arms, and tufts of swan feathers were once fastened to the mask by means of bird quills and swayed in a gruesome manner as the masked shaman moved about. White spots on the peak of the creature's head, like those painted on dancers' bodies during the Asking Festival, and red pigment rubbed on the back of the mask around the eyes and mouth have unknown ritual meanings.
Pastolik 33105, 32 cm

**236. White Fox Jaw Wristlet** *talliraq*
By virtue of having in his possession the jaw of a white fox, the owner of this dance wristlet has power over the shade of the animal.
Cape Nome 45336, 28 cm

**237. Caribou Spirit Link** *taqeq*

The link between a "real" animal and a spirit is sometimes depicted graphically by drawing lines between the two creatures. These connections are made at the throat near the origin of the lifeline. This image from the bottom of a bent-wood serving dish is surrounded with the usual black- and red-painted bands and carved grooves. The normal male caribou is linked to a spiritual likeness—perhaps its *inua* or an ancestor spirit—with a black band. In artistic portrayal, these spirits are identified by their spiked or spurred appendages which replace normal limbs. In myths and stories these connections are described as thin trails of fog.

Nulukhtulogumut 38644, 24 cm long

Shamans are often notorious figures who are both respected for their knowledge and feared for the powers they possess. They can obtain information from spirits and may, through devious means, take control of other people's *inuas*, using them to undertake nefarious tasks at the shaman's request. This power was made evident to Nelson once when he was photographing the village of Sabotnisky. A shaman approached and demanded to see what Nelson was doing under the black cloth. Upon viewing the ground glass screen with its inverted image of the village and its people, he cried out, "He has all of your shades in this box," whereupon a panic broke out among the people as they dove for the cover of their houses (Nelson 1899:422).

The shaman's powers are not won without risk, however. Just as a young shaman may be accused of sorcery, an old, powerful shaman may come on hard times if people lose faith in his abilities, as measured by frequent faulty predictions, ineffectual cures, or defeat at the hands of enemy shamans. Under these circumstances shamans have been put to death by communal consent, as may also happen to a shaman who abuses his powers for personal gain. However, as much as shamans mold their own destiny, they serve largely as agents for the community which supports their position as an intermediary between the village and the spirit world. An account of the shaman known as "Big Belly" from the Lower Kuskokwim illustrates this aspect of their role.

In this story, a shaman who frequently traveled under the water was preparing for a trip one winter day when he stopped his going-under-the-ice ritual, sensing that a shaman from another village was traveling at the same time. Despite the shaman's reluctance to continue, the men of the *qasgiq* insisted that the trip not be put off, and in due time they put him through a hole in the river ice. Traveling out to sea the Kuskokwim shaman encountered a shaman from Nelson Island, and after exchanging taunts the two began to fight. In a short while, the Nelson Island shaman, though smaller, trounced the Kuskokwim man, breaking his back and leaving him for dead on the bottom of the sea. As the victor departed the defeated

**238. Symbols of Darkness and Light** *tanqik, tan'geq*

Shaman artists and others also make symbolic use of color to communicate beliefs. One of these beliefs relates to light and darkness, ideas that are prominent in the Raven myths and which refer to both physical and spiritual conditions. Linked also to warmth and cold, life and death, colors are sometimes used symbolically on masks and everyday apparel. A St. Michael man wore this hunting visor shaped as a whiskered pike-beast with its red-painted mouth studded with caribou incisors. The balance of elemental forces is symbolized by a dark half having a fiendish red eye made from a faceted glass bead, and a light half with a natural animal eye of amber glass.

Nelson specifically noted these concepts on a Magemut mask showing a birdlike beast eating a walrus. Two red-mouthed wolves, one light and one dark, flank its brow. The dark wolf and other dark features on the mask have large white spots suggesting a magical or spiritual aspect to this color code. Symbolism of light and dark is also featured on an unusual graphic mask showing a woman's face decorated with a septum ornament and a pendant labret, surrounded by an array of swan's feathers.

St. Michael 33136, 35.5 cm; South of Yukon Mouth 33126, 37 cm wide; Lower Kuskokwim 64242, 29.5 cm tall

190

shaman cast a glance in the victor's direction. Feeling the glance on his back, the Nelson Island shaman realized the other was still alive and returned to beat him even more severely. This time the Kuskokwim man did not glance in the other's direction, and after some time crawled back home, arriving at his *qasgiq* with his back bent double and his belly distended. He instructed men to beat him upon his back and belly in the four corners of the *qasgiq*. This relieved his back condition, but though he vomited much sea water his belly remained large like a frog's. Thereafter he became known as "Big Belly." He never dared travel under the water again (Tennant and Bitar 1981:183–89).

Shamans also are accustomed to making dangerous trips to the moon. Their purpose may be to entreat the powerful manlike spirit who dwells there to release game that has become scarce in the shaman's district or to learn the cause of and the cure for the disease that has struck the village. In some areas, the shaman flies up to the moon and in others he may climb.

### THE SHAMAN IN THE MOON

A Malemut shaman from Kotzebue sound near Selawik lake told me that a great chief lives in the moon who is visited now and then by shamans, who always go to him two at a time, as one man is ashamed to go alone. In the moon live all kinds of animals that are on the earth, and when any animal becomes scarce here the shamans go up to the chief in the moon and, if he is pleased with the offerings that have been made to him, he gives them one of the animals that they wish for, and they bring it down to the earth and turn it loose, after which its kind becomes numerous again.

The shaman who told me the foregoing said he had never been to the moon himself, but he knew a shaman who had been there. He had been up only as high as the sky, and went up that high by flying like a bird and found that the sky was a land like the earth, only that the grass grew hanging downward and was filled with snow. When the wind blows up there it rustles the grass stems, loosening particles of snow which fall down to the earth as a snowstorm.

When he was up near the sky he saw a great many small, round lakes in the grass, and these shine at night to make the stars. The Malemut of Kotzebue sound also say that the north wind is the breath of a giant, and when the snow falls it is because he is building himself a snow house and the particles are flying from his snow shovel. The south wind is the breath of a woman living in the warm southland. (Nelson 1899:515)

**239. Male and Female Imagery** *angun, arnaq*

A Rasboinsky carver has made images on both sides of this set of finger masks. On one he has carved identical birds with red eyes and mouths, white faces, and green heads. A red-painted groove had been cut around the rim and fitted with places for seven pegs to clamp plumes and feathers. On the reverse he has carved two different images, one a white-faced smiling man and the other a red-faced frowning woman. While the sex identification is not evident on these carvings, it can be determined on many other pieces by their male or female styles of labrets or tattoos. This is seen on an ivory doll's head from Kaialigamut where the frowning face is decorated with female chin tattoos. Men's faces can frequently be identified by labrets below the corners of their mouths. The common occurrence of these two images, portrayed often in contexts that suggest they serve as charms, indicates there may be two guardian spirits, male and female, in Bering Sea Eskimo cosmology.

Rasboinsky 38852 (pair), 10, 10.5 cm high; Kaialigamut 37132, 3 cm wide (face)

## 240. Ultima Inua

When Raven alights in front of the First Man he pushes up his beak, revealing his human *inua*. This image of a bird *inua*, seen frequently on masks, is shown in these sculpted and engraved ivory spear guard carvings from Kaialigamut. On one side they show identical glowering faces of semihuman *inuas* revealed between borders being parted by cuffed and pierced hands. Their opposite sides have an image of the toothy smiling *inua* of a bird beneath its raised beak, and the masked face of a goggled grimacing beast whose cheekbones become pierced hands that grasp the *inua* border on its reverse side. A seal's body and face are seen in side and end views on the goggled piece, encircled by the arms. The other piece has a beluga, similarly grasped. Its tail overlaps a seal in end view. More serious than the typical "visual pun" these pieces demonstrate the exceptional creativity of some Bering Sea craftsmen in using intricate design and iconography to give visual substance to religious beliefs.

Kaialigamut 176086 (pair), 4.5 cm

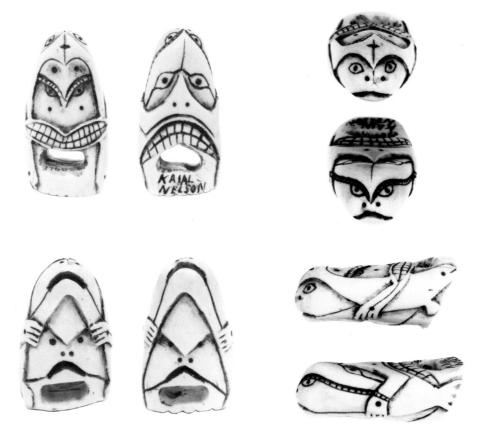

## 241. Goggled Belt Ornament

Artisans often paint or incise goggles on their carvings and masks. Although creating the appearance of snow goggles, this convention is a symbolic shorthand to indicate that the figure is masked and that its true identity is hidden from view. *Inuas*, for instance, are frequently shown as goggled beasts. This simple technique provides the maker with an easy way to spiritualize objects. Its use on everyday things like this belt ornament emphasizes the pervasiveness of these ideas of transformational reality in Bering Sea Eskimo culture.

Nunivak Island 43719, 3.5 cm high

South of the Yukon, a shaman sometimes goes to the moon by putting a slip noose around his neck and having someone drag him around the *qasgiq* until he is dead. Nelson was told that two noted shamans once did this, telling the people they would return during the next berry season. However, they did not return at the appointed time. It was said, some time later, that one started to come back, appearing partially out of the ground looking like a doll, very small and weak, but since there was no one outside the houses to feed and tend him except children, he was overlooked and went away.

> Nearly all epidemic diseases are supposed to come from the moon, but occasionally they descend from the sun. An eclipse of the moon is said to foretell an epidemic, and the shamans immediately proceed to learn the cause in order to appease the being living there and, by diverting his anger, save the people. Among the inhabitants along the lower Yukon it is believed that a subtle essence or unclean influence descends to the earth during an eclipse, and if any of it is caught in utensils of any kind it will produce sickness. As a result, immediately on the commencement of an eclipse, every woman turns bottom side up all her pots, wooden buckets, and dishes.
>
> After an eclipse at St Michael the Unalit said that the sun had died and come to life again. The length of duration of an eclipse is said to indicate the severity of the visitation to follow. In the village of Paimut, on the lower Yukon, in December, 1880, I overheard people talking about a recent eclipse of the moon and all agreed that it foreboded either an epidemic or war. Some thought that it meant a raid of the Tinné, living higher up the river, as revenge upon the Eskimo for having killed some moose the year before, the Eskimo evidently thinking that the moose belonged to the people in the region where they are usually found. (Nelson 1899:431)

193

**242. Toothy Beasts** *taruyamaarutet*

Finger masks are carved by men for women to use when they dance in the *qasgiq*. Inserting their fingers through the holes in the projections, the women dance with a slow swaying motion while the men accompany them with drumming and song. Feather plumes and fur fringes around the maskettes add to their motion and enhance the drama of the dance. Their use is restricted to the Yukon–Kuskokwim region where, according to a tale from St. Michael, women are fine dancers but poor seamstresses. These finger masks portray a common image of an eared beast in eager anticipation of a meal. They are carved in low relief, have traces of white paint, and, like larger masks, are surrounded by a ruff of caribou fur.

Lower Kuskokwim 37129 (pair), 8 cm (diameter)

## Shaman's Mask

One of the most important activities of the shaman is to plan and preside over major festivals and religious ceremonies. Some of these, like the Bladder Festival, are regular yearly events, while others, like the Feast to the Dead, are held at intervals of several years. These festivals take place over many days and require careful planning and direction. Songs and speeches are composed and memorized; drummers are instructed; dances are learned; the audience is trained to take part in sections of the performances. The men develop these plans with the shaman, who adds secret and dramatic touches of his own. A good festival must not only please the spirits; it must also be long remembered so as to guide the future actions and thoughts of individuals.

The theatrical aspects of Bering Sea Eskimo ceremonialism are greatly enhanced by dramatic use of carved masks, figures, staffs, and emblems. Masks, which represent the spirits themselves, are carefully made with attention to proper materials and symbolism. Sometimes these masks are made by other men. But if masks represent powerful spirits, or contain symbolic images and special materials, the shaman himself does the work. Often he works late at night or at times when women and children are not permitted in the *qasgiq*. At other times the masks are hidden away. Most masks are used only for a single festival or performance, after which they are burned or buried in the ground. Sometimes they will simply be dumped outside the *qasgiq* without further ado, their spiritual powers having been exhausted. Only rarely are masks hung up or kept in sight within the *qasgiq*. They are not idols to be worshiped or fixtures whose continued presence is required for religious reasons; nor are they used for decorative, aesthetic purposes. Rather they have limited lifespans, being created with impulse and inspiration, to be consumed in a burst of ceremonial energy associated with spirits and man in the larger train of events in a festival.

**243. Goggled, Toothy Masks**

Goggles appear on other types of objects, especially on men's masks used in religious or dramatic presentations in the *qasgiq*. The common form is seen on a Magemut mask showing a man wearing large labrets and (formerly) caribou fur ear ornaments. His tan-painted face sports a beard, mustache, and eyebrows. Three appendages once were fitted to the sides and top of his brow, and a caribou fur ruff once nested in the groove surrounding his face. Mouth outlines, nostril interiors, and ears are painted red.

A variation of the goggle motif is seen in an unusual mask from Askinuk used in the Feast to the Dead ceremony. This is one of the few masks that Nelson attributes to a specific religious event. A black flange rising from a red mouthlike trough bordered with wooden peg teeth divides the face. Raised nostrils and eye orbits have black interiors and outlining rings of the same color. Five feather appendages formerly adorned the mask, and large empty peg holes imply a hoop.

Many of these features are found on a handsome Magemut piece, the central element of which resembles the bird *inua* design of the Kaialigamut spear guards. Above a beast's toothy lower face, mustache, and nostrils are seen two sets of goggled eyes and arms with thumbless hands framed by beaklike forehead projections painted red and bordered with peg teeth. A similar "mouth" feature divides the forehead. Limb extremities and mouth outlines are red. The pose of this figure, with legs and arms outstretched, resembles a frequent stance used by male dancers in the *qasgiq*.

South of Lower Yukon 33133, 20 cm high; Askinuk 48701, 25 cm high; South of Lower Yukon 33135, 31 cm (toe-to-toe)

194

Masks used south of Bering Strait are marked by their extreme diversity of style and form. Despite a number of unifying features, discussed later, they include representations of humans, animals, spirits and other beings, physical objects, plants, and celestial bodies. Human faces may be portrayed in a realistic fashion, with carefully modeled features, including teeth, hair, labrets, tattoos, and other details; or, they may be abstracted so that if the viewer is not acquainted with the iconography, he will not know a human face is represented. Styles range from bold, roughhewn carving or painting to meticulous work with fine surface finish and textural detail. Some exude moods—they are comic, sad, fierce, or supportive; others are expressionless, opaque, and inscrutable. Seen in isolation they provide few clues to their meaning, since they are designed to be used within larger compositions involving dance, song, and testimony. Without knowledge of this larger context, very little of their true meaning and symbolism can be understood, especially by those who never witnessed the ceremonies and did not grow up as Bering Sea Eskimos in Nelson's day. Clues are provided in descriptions of masks and ceremonies left by Nelson, Zagoskin, and others (Ray 1967:65–71), but much remains unknown. Information from Eskimos themselves is no longer available due to the rapid replacement of traditional religion with Christian beliefs in the 1880s and 1890s.

**244. Distorted Faces**

Characters in the Eskimo pantheon of spirits are often endowed with exaggerated, distorted, or unusual humanlike features. The Nubviukhchugaluk belt fastener, shaped like an owl, has extremely puffy cheeks and a great toothy grimace. The belt fastener from Nunivak Island is in the shape of an animal with a long twisted snout. The creature represented on the Agiukchugumut belt button has lost an eye and is sticking its tongue out between its teeth, a very unusual attitude. Finally, the line fastener from Nunivak Island depicts a double-mouthed person.

These humanlike creatures may be identified as characters in Eskimo stories. Nelson indicated that this is the case with the twisted face mask from Big Lake. Unfortunately, he did not record the story that inspired the work.

Nubviukhchugaluk 43982, 6 cm; Agiukchugumut 37043, 5 cm; Nunivak Island 48628, 6 cm; Nunivak Island (W.H. Dall Collection) 16189, 5 cm; Big Lake 38646, 25 cm

**245. Twisted Faces** *taruyamaarutet*

The twisted faces depicted on this pair of Lower Kuskokwim finger masks represent evil spirits known as *tunghät*. The contorted faces suggest muscular distortions possibly resulting from seizures. Each maskette has an eye which projects forward on a peg, while the other eye remains half-closed. The reddened half-closed eyes and grotesque mouths of the *tunghät* once jumped out from white faces framed in red. As a woman dances the two ghouls, their caribou fur and feather ruffs swaying from side to side, appear to leer out at the audience.

Lower Kuskokwim 37895, 11 cm (wood only); 37130, 11.5 cm (wood only)

Analysis and reconstruction of the original meaning and context are even more difficult given the lack of standardization of mask forms and symbolism and the fact that Bering Sea Eskimo religion involved a world full of animals and spirits seen and interpreted differently by many Eskimo carvers, each of whom was encouraged to be individualistic and innovative in his artistic expression. The acceptability of widely varying personal styles, a rich artistic and mythological tradition, an unrestricted subject matter, and a theatrical presentation format are the essential features that contribute to the unusual strength and diversity of Bering Sea Eskimo mask ceremonialism.

As a mask maker, the shaman has at his fingertips the special motifs and forms that are used to communicate information to the human and spiritual audience about the subject of his performance. This is done through using standard motifs understood by others in the same way that illustrations on ladles symbolize myths. Among the more common forms used for this purpose are black spectaclelike goggles placed over the eyes of masks; single red eyes; white, red, or orange spots; crescentic eyes; twisted mouths; "male" and "female" mouths; peg teeth; red-painted grooves; pierced hands; thumbless hands; spirit "whiskers" and "spikes"; cuffed and collared images; encircling hoops; appendages; spirit-links; lifelines; feathers; red-painted eyes, nostrils and eye holes; blood splotches; darkness and light; and other forms of imagery. Most of these are employed on masks of the Yukon and Kuskokwim region and are infrequently found outside this area.

197

Many of these features are seen on a shaman's mask from Pastolik (fig. 235) representing a powerful *tunghât* spirit, the being of supreme power who controls the availability of animals on earth and is potentially harmful to man if not carefully treated. The Pastolik shaman who made this mask chose to represent this being in a tear-drop-shaped mask that opposes light and dark painted aspects, probably symbolizing the two domains, day and night. The face of the powerful spirit is gruesome, his toothy mouth spattered with blood from a recent meal, perhaps a human one as evidenced by the human legs attached to one side of his face, or possibly a bird, as shown by the winglike appendages on the other side. His nostrils are shown vertically rather than horizontally, and his grinning twisted mouth and offset crescent eye swirl about his other eye, which is round and calm. His entire visage looks like a full moon, his eyes and mouth its craters or phases. He is surmounted by a dark skylike crest with spots—perhaps stars or other types of symbols referring to celestial bodies or magical conditions of darkness—and feathers and downy plumes, which in certain ceremonies symbolize the stars and snowflakes (Nelson 1899:496). The inside surfaces of the eyes and mouth, seen only by the shaman, are reddened, giving power and life force to the mask. Together these features present a strong lunar aspect that suggests the Pastolik shaman believed that this *tunghât* dwelt in the moon, surrounded by heavens, and had just finished a meal of men and birds. When using this mask he may have been engaged in a trip to the moon to seek relief from disease or disaster that struck his village, which took as victims those whose limbs are attached to the mask, and expected to see the scene portrayed here on his approach.

## Symbols and Art

When making masks, ivory float plugs, dolls, ladles, bowls, and other items, a craftsman utilizes a variety of standard visual forms to symbolize religious and other concepts known to the people who regularly view these objects. A man is typically shown with an upturned mouth or with labrets under the corners of his mouth; a woman with a down-turned, frowning mouth, and perhaps with a central lower lip labret and radiating chin tattoos. Other sex indicators include various methods of portraying genitalia, including lenticular-spurred vulvae, oval views of phalli ends with central slits, and spike phalli on male sea mammals. Masked visages and transformed characters are signaled by the use of black spectacle goggles, by black circles around the eyes, or by sections of goggle frames. Peg teeth border red-painted "mouth" features which are frequently shown as shallow red grooves. Sometimes mouths are surrounded by brown or red blood splatters indicating beastly appetites and the aftermath of a meal. Pierced and thumbless hands signify a controlling spirit's willingness to allow animal spirits to pass through his grasp as they travel from the sky land to earth to repopulate the land with game animals. Wrist cuffs and neck collars are comparable to the use of net motifs used on fish, symbolizing restraining devices or leashes on tamed or captive animal spirits. Sometimes spirits are connected to their real bodies by external lifelines or linkage bonds, the limbs of spirit creatures are shown as abstract forms fringed with spiky thorns or teeth, and the snouts of such creatures frequently have very whiskery snouts. Analogy to lunar phases is suggested by round and crescentic eyes and twisted mouths. Magical treatment or indications of spiritness are also shown by using red, white, or orange spots, or by eyes in the middle of red-painted ovals. However, the specific meaning of many of these remains unclear.

198

### 246. Red-eyed Tunghät

Red eyes and spots are common motifs used on ceremonial masks. Unfortunately, Nelson never described the symbolic meaning of these attributes though he noted that if such inquiries were soon initiated, a symbolic study would be possible.

The Pastolik mask represents a *tunghâk* featured in a story. The spirit's half-closed eye is surrounded by a red oval spotted with blue pigment. The rest of the mask is white, save for a red border which terminates two-thirds of the way down the mask. The piece has lost its three feathers. Caribou fur, attached inside the mask, once flowed out of the spirit's mouth, suggesting that the *tunghâk* just finished a meal of caribou.

The interior and exterior of the Rasboinsky mask are equally powerful. Covered with red and green dots, the outer face is framed by a reddened groove. Caribou fur once hung from the mouth of the piece as well. The face of rough cut marks and great red splotches on the other side of the mask suggests that the mask is wearing a mask.

A *tunghâk* may be represented as the twisted red-eyed face on the Kuskokwim mask. Framed by wooden hoops, feathers, and the remains of a caribou fur ruff, he is either chewing or sucking on a wooden tube.

Pastolik 43779, 21 cm; Kuskokwim 64236, 18 cm (wood only); Rasboinsky 38809, 25.5 cm

199

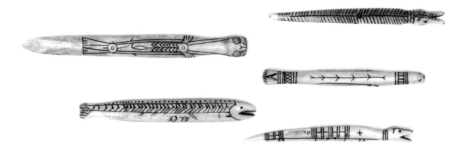

**247. Skeletal Patterns**
When Yukon–Kuskokwim artisans choose to elaborate their carved or painted images of animals, they frequently do so by portraying a simplified view of the skeleton and alimentary ("lifeline") tract. Attempts to make a surface rendering of their bodies are rarely done. The skeleton, or "X-ray" view, is especially common on ivory bagfasteners, bodkins, and small wedges. Here the technique is shown on bagfasteners depicting a salmon, a pike, a seal (cuffed and collared), and a mink, on which the animal's four feet are also marked. On an elegant ivory wedge appears a bristly nosed male walrus with inlaid eyes and joints. His skeletized torso is extended into a lifeline that includes his stomach and intestines.

More abstract skeletized diagrams are found on ivory storyknives from these same areas. In addition to showing the backbone and ribs, they sometimes depict sets of legs attached to a backbone that has been transferred to the blunt edge of the implement, along with corresponding notches that seem to signify limb girdles of many-legged creatures. These knives and others from Konigunugumut have curiously notched tips.

Nunivak Island 43738, 16 cm (walrus); Big Lake 36465, 12.5 cm (salmon); Rasboinsky 48769, 12.5 cm (pike); Nulukhtulogumut 38241, 11.5 cm (seal); Big Lake 38376, 12 cm (mink); Konigunugumut 36576, 36.5 cm; 37285, 26.5 cm; 37288, 25.5 cm

In addition to using different motifs to designate specific concepts of a rather detailed sort, Bering Sea Eskimos use more general visual devices to symbolize broader attitudes and philosophical concepts. These ideas are found in many types of art and visual expression and occur on many kinds of religious and everyday items. They are typically expressed in three kinds of symbol systems: lifelines, skeletal motifs, and a related set of images created by encircling hoops, grooves, radiating lines, pegs, and feathers. These devices do not qualify an object or image. Rather they impart an aspect—part decorative, part symbolic or religious—that conveys the image's condition or state of being with respect to biological life, human relationships, and its individualism or status as a discrete entity in the world.

Skeletal or "X-ray" depiction usually shows only the upper backbone and ribs, and only rarely the bones of the pelvis and limbs. Sometimes the skeleton merges with the lifeline motif, which begins at the mouth or throat and follows the alimentary system to the anus. The heart, lungs, and other vital organs may also be shown. These two internal views complement each other, one depicting the body's rigid frame and the other its soft organs, both of which are important to Eskimos who use bones and organs to make implements and clothing.

Lifelines and skeletal motifs are found on many kinds of implements. Both motifs are often shown combined on depictions of animals illustrated on serving bowls and ladles (figs. 128, 225), and on incised ivory wedges

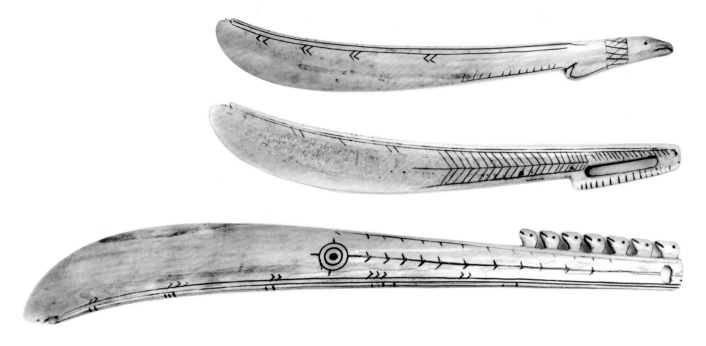

### 248. Lifeline Motifs

Bering Sea Eskimos believe that the lifeline is the central spiritual and biological channel of an organism. The lifeline is usually depicted as starting at the mouth, throat, or sometimes the eye, and from there it proceeds separately or via the backbone to the stomach. It may end here or be traced to the anus. Lifelines are painted on bowls and ladles, are carved on ivory animals, and are sometimes engraved on totemic animals carved on throwing boards. This practice is seen on a throwing board from Sabotnisky that has a sandhill crane, the totemic animal of its owner, carved into its fingergrip. An abstracted lifeline is seen on a board from Cape Nome embellished with a large blue glass bead.

Sabotnisky 49001, 46.5 cm; Cape Nome 44391, 44.5 cm

### 249. "Biologized" Seal Spirit

Lifelines and skeletal motifs portray Bering Sea Eskimo views of the biology and spiritual life of organisms. External forms are depicted in aspects essential for the artist's purpose, generally showing teeth, eyes, claws, sex, and other key features. Internal structure is limited to the upper spinal column and thoracic frame. The alimentary system, including the mouth, throat, stomach, and intestines, bladder, and occasionally other organs, is also shown. Lungs, heart, brain, and other systems are not illustrated. These representations are used for decoration and amusement, for identification of a person's property, and also for spiritual and religious reasons. They remind people of proper beliefs and acceptable practices, and are used to propitiate animal spirits. These ideas are combined in a ladle bowl showing a "biologized" seal spirit encircled with arms whose pierced hands permit his escape from capture so that he may continue to propagate and insure future abundance of seals for man.

Sfugunugumut 38637, 21.5 cm

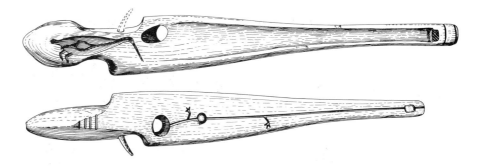

(figs. 219, 224). In one case, a lifeline has been incised on the torso of a female doll of ivory (fig. 179). Lifelines are also found abstracted on the tops, inner lids, and bottoms of boxes that have been carved as realistic or abstracted seals (figs. 213, 215, 218). Nelson did not obtain information on the meanings or reasons for using these motifs. Their widespread occurrence and the belief that the bladders of dead animals contain the animals' *inuas* suggest that these motifs represent important concepts in Bering Sea Eskimo religion and world view.

A particularly important type of visual symbolism is expressed in the use of hoops, pegs, and feathers on ceremonial masks. In this context their meaning appears to be similar to that recorded by Nelson for constructions erected inside the *qasgiq* at the time of the Doll Festival. For this, large hoops mounted with sticks and feathers just under the vent hole are said to represent the heavens and starry firmament (Nelson 1899:496). Similar hoops and feather arrangements are often mounted on *inua* face masks. Hoops are also used on flat plaque masks, which frequently carry one or more shallow painted grooves around the border of the plaque. These encircling grooves may also be present when hoops are not used, but in these cases they appear to represent the same or closely related idea expressed by the hoops, while also serving as decoration.

Hoops and encircling grooves are portrayed on nonceremonial objects as well. They ornament the rims and bases of wooden serving bowls (figs. 127, 128); run around the margins of ladles (figs. 130, 225); appear as incised grooves surrounding face images on float plugs and on earrings (figs. 62,

165); ornament the wooden planks used on dog sleds, and appear on many other items. The form and position of these grooves suggest that they serve both decorative and symbolic purposes, similar to that of hoops and grooves on masks, linking both ceremonial and secular materials in a unified spiritual context.

The probable meaning of pervasive hoop and groove iconography may be inferred from Nelson's documentation about the meaning of the hoops and feathers in the Doll Festival, together with information on the use of hoops and grooves on different kinds of artifacts. It is especially important that these motifs are present on utilitarian objects. Whether placed around a mask, around a bowl, or around a hunting spear, the encircling motif, echoing a person's fur parka ruff, defines the physical edge of the object, while also relating it to the world around it by framing it within a symbolic representation of its "heavens." In this way the wholeness and spiritual integrity of the object is established formally, in consonance with the religious view that all things—living or not—possess a unique spirit or *inua* which is an established entity.

One of the last things an artist will do upon completing an object he is making is to mount its hoops or carve or paint its encircling grooves or lines. By doing so he endows the piece with spiritual life, permitting it to take its place among the other things of the world. It is also significant, given the fact that the spirits of all things could, in the past, take on human form at will, that the symbolic key used is analogous to the human face shown within its furry parka ruff. Encircling hoops, grooves, and other decorative motifs symbolically portray the dominant beliefs that underlie Bering Sea Eskimo religion and philosophy. They constitute a visual expression of man's relationships with objects and the physical world around him and are his link to the spirit world that governs all.

## 250. Pierced and Thumbless Hands

Artifacts and drawings of *tunghät* are often shown with pierced and thumbless hands. These motifs are used to indicate the spirits' willingness to allow, by impairing their grasp, many animals to slip through their fingers, thus insuring the continued abundance of animals on earth. Here pierced hands are seen on a seal scratcher on whose hand gleams a bright blue glass bead, on an air bladder net float ornamented with a thumbless, black-spotted palm, and on a trinket box showing two toothy beasts, the left one red and the right one, on a red panel, black. Between them, apparently contested, is a black figure of a spiked or male beluga. Both beasts have spiked arms with elbow and palm perforations. The red figure is cuffed and collared in black and has a black spike added to its arm and "teeth" in its perforations. These designs recall spiked and channeled "mouths" on the outstretched arms and crests of masks. This piece may represent a story of friendly and unfriendly beasts contesting the descent of a beluga spirit to earth.

Konigunugumut 36241, 35 cm long; Big Lake 38867, 25 cm; Lower Yukon 49174, 27.5 cm

### 251. Friendly Tunghâk Amid Starry Heavens

Pierced, thumbless, red-painted hands are prominent features of this large mask showing a *tunghâk* adorned with two green fish heads on a shield above the face and two red seal heads below. The face, raised in relief above the shield, is white and has a bright green pigmented border. The mouth, painted red on the interior, as are the nostrils and eyes, is studded with animal teeth. The black mustache identifies the *tunghâk* as a male spirit.

The use of white feathers of swans, gulls, and emperor geese for mask borders seems to symbolize the surrounding heavens and stars. Feathers of birds of prey, commonly found as helping spirits on hunting arrows and darts, are not found on masks.

Lower Kuskokwim 64241, 73 cm (between finger tips)

### 252. Spear Guard Amulets

In addition to occurring on items used for ice hunting, fishing, household effects, and ceremonial masks, pierced-hand symbolism is found on equipment associated with kayak hunting. A set of ivory spear guards from a man's kayak displays pierced hands into which tufts of seal hair have been plugged to strengthen the effectiveness of the charm imagery.

Cape Vancouver 43538, 3 cm high

## Dancing

In addition to dances performed during the various festivals and religious ceremonies, others are performed at various times for entertainment and pastime. Some of these are performed simply for the pleasure of the dancers and others present, and consist of graceful flowing movements; others may illustrate a myth or story through use of gestures and pantomime. The dancers are usually accompanied by one or more male drummers, who also sing as a chorus. Some of the dances may be quite grotesque, with young men dancing nude or wearing a pair of ornamental caribouskin shorts, gesticulating with their arms and legs and contorting their bodies in every conceivable manner. Often two young men dance against each other in friendly rivalry, until one or the other drops from sheer exhaustion. Those dances are sources of great amusement to the viewers.

Both men and women take part in dances, each having a characteristic kind of movement and style. Women dance clothed, with the feet solidly fixed on the ground while their upper bodies sway with an undulating motion and their hands gesticulate in time with the music. They often use long dance wands made of eagle feathers tipped with downy plumes. Small circular finger masks are also worn, especially in religious dances. The finger masks, ornamented with feather plumes, often show *inua* face masks surrounded with a halolike ring of caribou or wolverine fur, symbolizing the fur ruff of a person's parka. Similar ruffs are used on masks, which are frequently worn in dances also.

Men often dance nude, moving their arms and hands vigorously. They may occasionally crouch and leap about, sometimes crying out periodically in time with the music. In other dances the object is to show their lightness, agility, and speed, and in these they may be flanked by women dancers whose smooth swaying movements contrast strongly with the men's. Men also dance singly, wearing animal masks, and act out stories that they have experienced or imagined.

It is customary for a stranger entering a *qasgiq* to make a small gift of tobacco or other material to the headman. The stranger then steps out onto the floor and performs a short dance in which he sings a song expressing his friendship with the people there, or some other sentiment that serves as his introduction to the group. With his introduction complete the stranger retires to smoke, awaiting the beginning of the dance.

> The people sit on all three tiers of benches and on the floor except for the front side, which is left free for the performers. The men occupy the benches; some are without their parkas, some altogether naked. It is hot and stifling. Two oil lamps on the "proscenium," that is, in the corners of the front side of the fire pit, and four additional ones in different parts of the kazhim throw a dim light on the motley crowd of spectators. There are grass mats hanging from the front edge of the lowest benches and they separate the actors' dressing-room. Four shamans are sitting on this bench holding drums 2½ feet in diameter in their teeth. Two old men in tattered

### 253. Tunghâk, Keeper of the Game

Among the most powerful, potentially malevolent spirits are the *tunghät*. Different from *inuas*, the spirits of animate and inanimate objects, *tunghät* are the central deities which control the supply of game. They are represented on many objects, even on earrings (fig. 165), and take a prominent position in ceremonial activities in the *qasgiq*.

This huge *tunghâk* representation is suspended at head-level by cords from the roof of a Magemut *qasgiq*. During ceremonies shamans dance behind it and sometimes utilize its powers as a tutelary spirit in their efforts to gain advantages needed by their village. *Tunghät* are believed to live on the moon (fig. 235), and shamans may occasionally travel there with offerings to enlist support in bringing game into their village district should hunting prove unsuccessful for a period.

*Tunghâk*'s form embodies many of the visual devices used to symbolize Bering Sea Eskimo religious concepts. He wears large, spotted male labrets and has upon his brow five seals and two caribou, signifying some of the game he controls. His red, toothy mouth extends across the forearms nearly to the palms, which are perforated and outlined in white. The hands are red and covered with magical white spots. (*Qasgiq* dancers paint similar spots on their bodies.) Side panels are also represented as toothed mouths. His masked face hides his true identity, making people mindful of their need to observe strictly ritual behavior toward him and animal spirits in the face of his omniscient presence.

South of the Lower Yukon 33118, 93 cm (between fingertips)

parkas and with smeared faces appear on the stage from time to time, tease each other and make fun of the spectators, saying that the latter in vain have come together hoping to see the new dance which they themselves, the old men, stole from the man who made it up. This is in place of an overture.

But now the skylight opens, and quickly, in a flash, a dancer slides down a strap and with a quick leap is on the stage; two pairs of women take their places beside him. He is wearing a mask representing a fantastic raven's head, and there he goes jumping about on the stage, calling like a raven; the drums sound their rhythmic beat, the singers strike up a song. The dancer at one time represents a raven perching and hopping like a bird; in another time he represents the familiar actions of a man who is unsuccessful in everything. The content of the dance is explained in the words of the song and may briefly be described as follows. A shaman is living in his trail camp. He is hungry, and he notices that wherever he goes a raven goes with him and gets in his way. If the game he is pursuing is a deer, the raven from some place or other caws, startles the deer, and makes it impossible to creep up within a bow-shot of it. If the man sets a noose for hare or partridge, the raven tangles it or runs off with it. If he sets a fish-trap for imagnat, there too the raven finds a way to do him harm. "Who are you?" cries the shaman at last. The spirit in the form of the raven smiles and answers: "Your evil fate." Thus in this dance are combined the mimicking of a deer hunt, the catching of hares, or partridges, and of fish, and a conversation between the shaman and the raven. (Zagoskin, in Michael 1967:226–27)

## Bladder Festival

Hanging from the roof and gliding up and down was a fantastic bird-shaped image, said to represent a sea gull. Its body was covered with the skin and feathers of a small Canada goose. Behind the bird and at the back of the *qasgiq* stood a ten-foot-long pole bound with a bundle of wild celery stalks. The pole was banded along its entire length with red and white paint. On the left side of the room and hung horizontally was a large sheaf of seal and walrus harpoons. Other harpoons and darts were arranged about the room. Attached to the harpoon sheath were several hundred seal and walrus bladders spotted and blotched with grayish-white paint. Hanging about the room, singly and in bunches, were a number of caribou bladders, but none of these were hung with bladders of sea mammals. Under the wild celery stalks and beneath the weapons and bladders was a pile of thirty or forty wooden hunting hats and visors, some ornamented with carved ivory images, others painted with female sexual symbols.

This was the fourth day of the Bladder Festival. Bladders were supposed to contain the shades of *inuas* of animals slain by hunters. Throughout the year each man had preserved the bladders of his game and when the time for the long festival approached he sang a song, inflated each bladder, and hung it in the *qasgiq*. The festival amused and pleased the shades of the animals, and the bladders were returned to the sea through a hole in the ice. The shades of the animals swam far out to sea where they entered the bodies of unborn animals of their kind. They thus became reincarnated, rendering game plentiful the following year. If the shades were pleased with the manner in which they had been treated by a hunter, they would not be afraid when they met him again, and they would permit him to approach and kill them without any trouble.

The festival began after the men cleaned the *qasgiq* and its fire pit. At night men, women, and children gathered on the roof of the *qasgiq* where they sang songs to the wild celery (*Angelica lucida*) which grew throughout the area. The following day bundles of this plant were gathered and dried, and a giant sheaf of wild celery now hung under the bladders. The celery would be used throughout the ceremony marking episodes and purifying the *qasgiq* before or after certain events took place.

The bladders of seals, beluga, and walrus were now marked with spots of paint and with charcoal and smoke from the celery torches. The spots were similar to those ornamenting masks worn by the shaman. Young men participating in the Asking Festival covered their bodies with similar kinds of spots, but few people understood their symbolic significance.

Men marched around the hunting hats, a walrus skull, a folded grass mat, and two wooden tubs full of water which had been placed close to the hole in the floor. People knew not to leave the *qasgiq* at this time, for the hole became a seal's breathing hole which led to the sea under the ice.

**254. Inua of a Sandhill Crane** *qucillagaq*
The shaman who made this wooden mask once saw a sandhill crane (*Grus canadensis*) standing on the tundra. As he approached the bird the feathers on the bird's breast parted and revealed the humanlike face of the bird's *inua*. This mask may have been worn or hung in the *qasgiq* with a small lamp resting in the top of the crane's excavated head, its light shining through the crane's eyes. His beak, once complete, was pegged with wooden teeth. Both the crane and his *inua* had red features, and the sides of the crane's long neck were also painted this color.
Rasboinsky 49020, 75 cm

### 255. Festival Accoutrements

Supporting props are used with festivals and ceremonies. Among those the functions of which are recorded are Asking Festival wands and Bladder Feast staffs. Little is known, however, about the uses of flying bird effigies made to hang in the *qasgiq*. A Kuskokwim carving of a mythical bird-man has reddened human legs attached through a bulbous collar to the head of a bird of prey shown with white eyes, hooked bill, and red mouth. His wings and other appendages are missing. Another wooden bird described as an idol has a toothy red beak and eyes fitted to the skin of an emperor goose. Perhaps the bird effigies illustrate a story of a shaman's flight aided by a powerful bird spirit. Similar ideas seem to be expressed by dancers who remove the heads and skins from certain birds and wear them as fillets with the bills projecting over and partially hiding their faces when they dance, recalling Raven's appearance and *inua* concepts.

Kuskokwim 63609, 67 cm; Kushunuk 63301, 53 cm

Men took up drums and began to beat loudly while a young man imitated the notes of the eider duck. The headman chanted, the drums beat, and men, women, and boys took turns singing one of the refrains. A young man began to imitate the motions of a loon, another those of a murre. Suddenly the room, once full of seated people, was filled with birds which were diving, swimming under water, and pecking for food. Beavers too were present cutting trees and building dams.

The dancing ended and a man entered the *qasgiq* with a bent-wood tray of food held high over his head. He circled the *qasgiq* offering food to the shades of the bladders and to the *tunghät*, the keepers of the game.

Late that night people were awakened by strange gutteral sounds uttered first from the smoke hole, then from the floor hole. Four men, wearing hunting hats and carrying painted paddles, entered the *qasgiq* and, going to the four corners of the room, touched the bladders and knocked the harpoons and darts to the floor. People removed the points from the fallen weapons and gathered the now harmless shafts in the back of the room. The four men removed their hunting hats and tied onto each a ring of grass (fig. 29). Small downy gull feathers were attached to the rings, which reminded some people of the ring of grass representing seaweed on the floor. Others thought of their starry universe.

The next morning youngsters were cautioned not to stamp their feet in the *qasgiq* for the shades of the animals would be scared by loud noises. During the course of the day the celery stalks were burnt and waved toward the four cardinal points. The smoke hole opened and four hunting hats attached to a sealskin bag were lowered into the room and were hung on a stake. Later the seal skin was inflated and the wing feathers of the glaucous gull were attached to its hind flippers. That evening the walrus

skull and grass mat were again placed near the hole in the floor. Four dishes laden with food were brought into the *qasgiq* and were ceremonially offered to the shades of the bladders. They responded with an approving shudder, accepting their food.

The four men who previously had entered the *qasgiq* with paddles now entered accompanied by a young girl. They performed a dance in which they imitated seals and walrus. When they tired three other sets of four men and a girl replaced them in turn. The dance consisted of short hops sideways and long jumps forward and was performed in perfect step to the beating of the drums. The individual sets of dancers were related, and their totemic marks were displayed on the four paddles standing in the corners of the room.

With the dances over, wisps of grass were distributed to the hunters, who made funny speeches which amused everyone, including the shades. Each wisp of grass was then broken and a wild celery torch with the lethal points of darts and harpoons attached was passed around each wisp. Then each hunter loudly stated, "When they sit down they are sleepy and fall down," at which point he fell and rolled over onto the grass on the floor. Symbolically the seals and walrus were thus caught by the weapons attached to the torch.

### 256. Drums and Drumming *cauyaq*

People dance and sing in the *qasgiq* accompanied by the resonant, repetitious beat of drum music. Drums are held in the left hand and are beaten with thin wood rods held in the right. They are played by men in measured time with two strokes in rapid succession followed by a pause and then two strokes again. The rod strikes the rim at the same time it hits the membrane, producing a sharp rap that mingles with the more sonorous tone of the skin. Drums vary in size and tonality, some very large ones being used in the Yukon–Kuskokwim region, where this large handle ornamented with the head of a horned puffin originates. The drum from Sledge Island has a sea mammal bladder membrane stretched across a grooved rim of bent spruce. Music is also produced by striking resonant logs or box drums with ivory mallets. A mallet from Port Clarence has a grass-cushioned handle wound with braided sinew and shows a right whale spouting water symbolized by bits of down pegged in its blowhole.

Sledge Island 45401, 50 cm (diameter); Cape Vancouver 38840, 66 cm

## 257. Dance Regalia

In addition to masks, carvings, and music, *qasgiq* ceremonies are enriched by specially prepared personal regalia which have ritualistic connotations. Dancers wear ornamental fillets of caribou, wolf, ermine, or bird skin, wristlets and armbands, caribou teeth or crab joint belts and bracelets, and special pants. Nelson collected many of these items from people in northern Norton Sound. Men from this area, who never dance with bare hands, wear large mittens made of seal skin. To these are attached, on short cords, the bills of horned puffins which rattle in time with the dancers' motions. Women do not use large gloves. In the south they dance with finger masks and, throughout the region, on special occasions use wands made of eagle quill feathers tipped with downy eagle plumes, a probable reference to thunderbird mythology and his star-filled dominion.

Cape Nome 45452 (pair), 66 cm long; 45446, ca. 75 cm

At midnight the shaman extinguished all lamps, stood on the roof, and made a speech to the bladders. After the speech people heard walrus and seals blowing above the *qasgiq*, and a little later they heard a pup seal squeak.

Wild celery torches purified the room and offerings of food followed. Then the shaman took a young boy and lay him over the entrance hole, making noises and gestures like a murre as he moved about. A man began to sing and all joined in. When the song ended the hunters rushed to their bladders, each man taking down his set and attaching it to the harmless spearshafts. The shaman stood on the roof, and bladders, celery stalks, and shafts were passed up to him through the smoke hole. The hunters departed through the entrance passage, gathered up their bladders, and following the shaman, who held a huge torch of burning celery stalks, ran toward the water.

The night was cold, calm, and very dark, so that the flame of the torch rose ten or twelve feet, casting a red glare over the snow-covered plain and lighting up the fur-covered figures streaming behind it. The crowd reached a hole the men had made in the ice. The hunters, each in turn, took a

harpoon head and ripped open their bladders. With bladders in one hand and kayak paddles in the other, they marched around the hole, wetting both paddles and bladders. Each bladder was then thrust below the water and, with their rising bubbles marking the path of the disappearing bladders, the shades began their journey out to the sea.

> It was good for us to hear the admonitions of those in the *qasgiq* who did the speaking there, though we did not always think so. Poor me! Sometimes I thought they could see right into me, into my life, when they spoke. It was chilling, I tingled all over. How could they know me so well. . .They wished for a better future for us. . .Their instructions on how to live have come up again and again. . .It is true, the *qasgiq* is a place of instruction, the only place where the necessary instructions can be given in full. (Joseph Friday of Chevak, 1978, as told to Anthony C. Woodbury)

### 258. Rasboinsky Face Masks

Nelson collected a number of masks from the village of Rasboinsky, which he visited during an observance of the Feast to the Dead. This important festival is held at ten-year intervals to honor the departed dead. Despite these masks originating from a single village and, possibly, from a single festival, they show wide variation in stylistic treatment. One red-faced mask, similar to the portrait style of masks carved in Bering Strait and further north, is fitted with a shock of caribou hair and teeth of the same animal. Its eyes and mouth are reddened from the inside, and its ears, brows, and nose are realistically modeled. At the other end of the spectrum is an abstract *tunghâk* mask composed of concentric grooves around a central mouth and slanting eyes.

Rasboinsky 38856, 22 cm; 38862, 18.5 cm high (incorrectly cited by Nelson as being from Sabotnisky)

**259. Animal Spirit Masks**

These masks may represent the *inuas* of a short-eared owl, a caribou, and a fox or wolf as they appeared to shamans. Masks such as these are important in the enactment of myths, stories, and in ceremonial presentations.

Sabotnisky 48989, 14.5 cm; 48984, 11 cm wide; Kuskokwim 64255, 12 cm wide

211

**260. Grizzly Bear Spirit's World** *taqukaq*

This mask represents the partially masked face of a grizzly bear spirit confronting his principal food, a fish which hangs in front of his mouth on a sinew cord. His nose has whiskers made from stripped feather quills. His nostrils and lower jaw are painted brownish-red, and the same color forms a border around his white face. Three duck feathers tipped with downy plumes are set into his brow. He is encircled with three asymmetric, conjoined splints the position of which is maintained by split-root lash- ings. The inner and outer hoops are red and have white feathers mounted in them. The central hoop is painted black. Hoops used in this context in the Doll Festival were represented to Nelson as being symbolic of the universe, with feathers and downy plumes being stars and snowflakes. It seems likely that this mask represents the bear spirit's realm, the hoops and plumes marking the boundaries of his existence.

Rasboinsky 38734, 36 cm (lateral diameter of hoops)

**261. Rasboinsky Plaque Mask** *kegginaquq*

A mask possibly used in the Rasboinsky Feast to the Dead during Nelson's visit displays the customary smiling charm or deity image. The forehead and nose are painted black and have the remnants of four duck feathers inserted in holes around the edge. The rest of the face is white, with inset teeth and a reddened mouth. A shallow groove extends across the upper lip and face. The face is surrounded by a red-painted groove, seen also around the margin of the tan-colored plaque of which it is a part. The insides of the four holes in the plaque, as well as the eyes and mouth, are painted red. Swan feathers inserted through holes in the rim are bent over and fastened with a rawhide thong. Similar examples of this type of mask, sometimes used for song-dances are known from the Lower Kuskokwim, Cape Vancouver, and Anvik.

Rasboinsky 38812, 27.5 cm (maximum width of plaque)

A shaman from a tundra village near Cape Romanzof may have been hunting one day at sea when he killed a horned puffin whose abnormal behavior troubled him. He could not put the incident out of his mind. Later, in a dream, he imagined he had seen the creature's *inua* through the puffin's open beak in the instant before his spear struck. Over successive days, in preparation for the forthcoming festival, he labored with his crooked knife to create this vision in physical form and planned his performance. He kept the work hidden from view until the last moment, and then, accompanied by drums, he slowly danced and sang the song of the animal whose spirit he had glimpsed.

To the assembled villagers the altered voice and body motions imitating a horned puffin skittering along the surface and diving for food were not those of the shaman but of his puffin ally. His head was a huge representation of the bird, through whose opened mandibles and red mouth bordered with peg teeth was seen a large, beastly face with almond-shaped eyes, bristled, red-pigmented nostrils, and down-turned mouth. The light face of the *inua* was framed by the red mouth and dark blue, white-spotted face enclosed by a single hoop, a caribou fur ruff, and long feather plumes. The visual effect in the darkened *qasgiq* was striking and, together with the music, song, and dance, had a powerful effect on the people, who were thankful to have such a powerful shaman in their village.

**262. Horned Puffin Inua**
Cape Romanzof 33108, 56 cm high

In the forested regions near Sabotnisky, far from the coastal tundra, another shaman may have surprised a huge black bear in the act of raiding his fish trap one winter day. The shaman released his dogs, who immediately surrounded the animal while he retrieved his bow from the sled. Suddenly the dogs' barking ceased, and as the shaman whirled about he thought he glimpsed a humanlike face partly concealed behind the bear's dark hair and in the area of the animal's right eye. Before he could aim, the dogs, still strangely silent, parted and allowed the bear to escape into the forest.

Returning to the village the shaman pondered this unusual experience. That same evening he began working feverishly to capture that fleeting view in wood, his bright knife flashing in the lamp's flame. He sang softly to himself as the form took shape in his hands. Strange words came, and these, too, he incorporated into his song. Later, when the work was done, he held secret rehearsals to instruct the rest of the men in their roles.

The performance was given before the village on a cold January day. Assisted by the others, the shaman reenacted the encounter, culminating in his appearance before the people as the bear at the instant his humanlike *inua* was revealed to the shaman. Following the revelation he danced, part man, part bear-spirit, and sang his song to the booming of the drums and the howling of the wind outside.

The image the shaman had created was meant to be destroyed after the performance, for shamans never allowed other villagers to view their masks, or to wear them. This time, however, there was a white man present, a man who made a habit of collecting old, useless things. The shaman decided he would sell his bear mask for a new piece of iron for his knife. The white man promised to hide the mask and to take it away from the village the next day. Concluding the exchange, the shaman took a block of fresh wood, equivalent in size to the one he had used for the bear mask, and threw it into the fire in place of the mask, along with other accoutrements he had used in the ceremony. He watched nervously as the smoke passed through the *qasgiq* smoke hole and vanished into the dark night sky.

**263. Black Bear Inua**
Sabotnisky 48986, 23 cm high

*The Chukchi generally start out on their trading voyages in May, traveling along the shore with dog sleds, hauling on them their umiaks, which are folded until they reach open water, when the sleds are left at some point and the umiaks set up; then, taking the dogs and goods on board, they coast along the shore of Bering sound and over to the American side. Some of them even visit the Russian fair at Ghigaga, near Anadyr river, during the winter to dispose of the furs they have gathered on their summer trading voyages.*

Nelson 1899:230

*distant lands, other times*

# distant lands

The Bering Sea Eskimos were bypassed by American and European whalers who hunted in waters north and west of the shallow Bering Sea coast. Although buffered from extensive contacts with these foreigners, the Bering Sea Eskimos were not isolated from nor ignorant about the larger world around them. Their knowledge of distant peoples and places resulted from both hostile and cordial relations with various groups frequenting the Bering Sea and Bering Strait regions. The umiak can be seen as the symbol of interregional relationships, for it was the means by which groups moved goods and people along coastal waters and across the often treacherous Bering Strait.

Early in the nineteenth century people on either side of the Strait had been at war with one another. Diomede and St. Lawrence Islanders were in league with the Eskimos of the Siberian coast, while people from King Island and Sledge Island were Alaskan allies. The Siberians were the more aggressive people. Fleets of umiaks loaded with war parties would cross the Bering Strait and attack Alaskan villages. The Siberian warriors were equipped with bows and arrows, and wore vests of armor which were made of bone or ivory slats fastened together with hide or baleen lashings. The slats overlapped one another slightly, creating a surface that an arrow could not penetrate. Armor slats have been found in archeological sites on St. Lawrence Island and on both sides of Bering Strait, and figures depicted on

**264. Bering Strait**

Yukon and Kuskokwim Eskimos have interacted with peoples living north and south of them, on islands off the coast, with Indians living upriver, and with Siberians. During Nelson's time North American Eskimos, Siberian Eskimos, and Chukchi, Siberians living west of Bering Strait, were involved in extensive trade networks. The Siberian traders exchanged white reindeer skins, highly valued for clothing, to the North Americans in return for more decorative skins of Alaskan furbearers and wooden implements. Large umiaks, similar to this gutskin model were used by Siberians who made the dangerous voyage across the Bering Strait. Nelson visited the Chukchi while on the *Corwin* and convinced a group of Reindeer Chukchi from Cape North to pose for the picture which appears on the opposite page. Cape Tchaplin 49144, 60 cm; SI–3844

### 265. Wars *inglukesteput*

Western Eskimos have waged wars against one another and have been in conflict with Siberian and Indian groups as well. Previous to Nelson's visit, the mainland Siberians were allied with the St. Lawrence and Diomede Islanders, the North Americans were in league with the King and Sledge Islanders, and the two groups would attack one another on sight. Siberians wore armor consisting of walrus bone slats strung on seal or walrus thong. The tight fitting and overlapping slats form a vest which stone- and metal-tipped arrows cannot penetrate. Pieces of bone-slat armor have been found in prehistoric archeological sites on St. Lawrence Island, and the armor suggests Asian connections and influences. Nelson was unable to buy a complete suit of bone-slat armor and paid handsomely for the few strips he managed to acquire.

Bering Strait (Collector unknown) CL–596, 39 cm tall

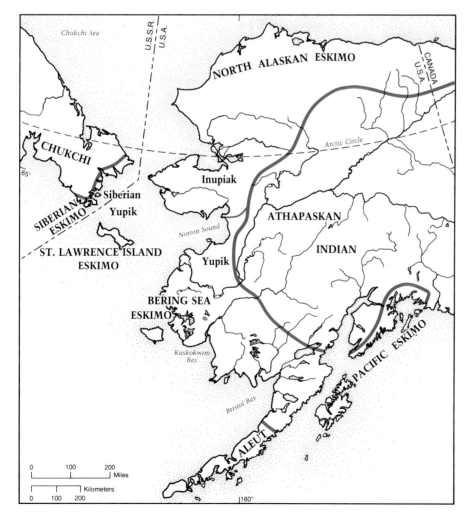

a drill bow collected by Captain Cook are wearing bone-slat armor, suggesting that hostilities between Bering Strait groups have historic depth. The idea of slat armor probably originated in Asia and was introduced long before the Russians began frequenting the coast.

The Bering Sea Eskimos had conflicts with their northern Alaskan neighbors as well. Inupiak speakers had been expanding their territory southward along the shores of Norton Sound, and the southernmost Inupiak group, the Malemut, were particularly aggressive. They usually attacked their Yupik-speaking enemies during the night, shooting volleys of arrows at their victims. If the raiders were victorious, they killed all the men and boys in the village and carried off the women and children as slaves.

Wars between the Bering Sea Eskimos and their southern neighbors were equally lethal. Nelson heard tales describing how the southerners decapitated their slain enemies, placing human heads with arrows stuck through their noses on stakes for display.

### 266. Yupik and Inupiak Speakers

Yupik and Inupiak speakers share some cultural traditions, but can be considered distinct groups. The people living around the Alaskan Bering Sea coast use housewives, bagfasteners, storyknives, ceremonial masks having multiple appendages and fantastic faces, bent-wood trays, strap drills, bladder darts, and detachable point lances. They exploit rich fish, bird, and seal resources and have access to wood and furbearing animals as well. Unplugged needlecases, drill bows, walrus and whaling harpoons, water buckets, short handle scrapers, baleen containers, snow knives, and portraitlike masks are used by Alaskan Inupiak speakers who live around Bering Strait. Alaskan Inupiak speakers have close affinities with central and eastern Arctic groups historically and ecologically, and have been in intensive contact with European whalers. These northern groups rely on high Arctic species such as the bowhead whale, walrus, and several species of seals, and must contend with polar bears. They have lesser quantities of birds, fish, and small furbearing animals.

## 267. High Arctic Hunters

Northern Eskimos' reliance on high Arctic species is reflected in their tools and ceremonial life. The water bag handle from Diomede Island is carved to represent a common scene in northern latitudes—polar bears attacking seals lying close to their breathing holes. Polar bears are also portrayed on a Diomede Island umiak whaling harpoon and lance rest which has been carved out of walrus jawbone. The walrus-man ceremonial mask from Ooglamie, near Point Barrow, and the man-bear soapstone carving, possibly a charm, from Point Barrow, reflect Northerners' ritual treatment of game.

Point Barrow (P. H. Ray Collection) 89567, 6 cm; Ooglamie (P. H. Ray Collection) 89813, 20 cm; Diomede Island 63878, 16 cm (nose-to-nose); 63789, 22 cm

The groups just discussed also maintained economic relations with one another. People would routinely embark on long distance voyages during the summer and winter months, visiting and trading at villages. They also gathered together for a great trade festival during the summer. In addition to tobacco, snuff, firearms, ammunition, metal, beads, cloth, and other European goods, people exchanged jadeite—only available inland from Kotzebue Sound and on Kaviak Peninsula—green, blue, red, and white pigments, chert, baleen, ivory, caribou skins, reindeer skins, Dall sheep horns, bird skins, small furbearing animal pelts, seal oil, and dried fish. Finished products, such as baskets and bent-wood bowls, some of them made by Yukon Indians, were also sought in trade.

In 1880 Captain C. L. Hooper found twelve hundred people camped at Cape Blossom, in Kotzebue Sound, where they had gathered for the annual summer trade festival. A European schooner was also present, and Hooper noted that it was surrounded by umiaks, three and four boats deep. In July 1881 the crew of the *Corwin* observed a camp of 150 conical tents strewn along a beach in Hotham Inlet. Along the coast the crew encountered umiaks filled with people and goods, the Hotham Inlet camp being their destination.

> This camp was arranged with almost military precision; along the beach, above the high-water mark, with their sterns to the sea, were ranged between sixty and seventy umiaks, turned with the bottom upward and toward the prevailing wind.... Seventy-five yards back from the umiaks, in a line parallel to the beach, were ranged over two hundred kaiaks, supported about three feet from the ground on low trestles made of branching stakes. (Nelson 1899:261)

## Northern Neighbors

Local subsistence patterns and geography were factors which contributed to the diversity of lifeways in the Bering Sea and Bering Strait regions. The Inupiak speakers inhabiting northern Alaska lived in a high Arctic environment and depended heavily on sea mammals for food and clothing. They also hunted caribou, fished, and caught birds. Yupik and Inupiak speakers shared a belief in hunting magic, and in the ability of men to become animals, and animals to become men. However, since these two groups relied heavily on different animals, their artistic and ceremonial traditions took on different forms.

The polar bear has always been the object of special treatment by northern peoples, probably because it stands on its hind feet and resembles man physically. It frequents the same territory as man, often hunting the same animals, and is an intelligent, cunning hunter. Images of the polar bear endowed hunting equipment with its skills, and stories of man-bear transformations were the subject of small man-bear carvings.

The walrus was a source of invaluable ivory for implements, hide for lines and boat covers, and meat and blubber for food. The walrus-man was a prominent northern character, appearing on masks, on drill bows, and as figurines. He was symbolically portrayed daily by Eskimos who took on this image when they wore parkas that had tusklike gores flanking their hoods.

The most important animal to northerners was the bowhead whale, a major source of meat, oil, and baleen. The northerners took great care in how they decorated and treated materials throughout the whaling season, so as not to offend the spirits of the whales and in order to insure success of the hunt. Women carried water buckets with ivory handles ornamented with swimming and diving whales. Small ivory carvings of these huge animals, and intricate chains with whale heads and tails at either end were attached to the sides of pails. Even needlecases and labrets were shaped in the forms of whales or their tails.

Implements associated with the hunt were treated in certain ways. Hunters stored their slate points, which tipped the large whaling harpoon heads, in boxes carved in the forms of bowhead whales with the whales' flukes clipped as a symbol of their capture. Each umiak had a number of whaling charms fastened to it, and once a whale was killed the first line to secure the whale to the umiaks was weighted with a whale carved out of graphite.

**268. Northern Hunting Magic and Ritual**

Hunting magic and ritual insure that whaling will be productive and that the animals will return in future years. Bowhead whales, in a variety of animated attitudes, are depicted on bag handles. Blades for whaling harpoon heads and lances are stored in wooden boxes, symbolically shaped like captured whales, their flukes having been clipped. Graphite whale-shaped sinkers are attached to the first lines drawn around freshly killed whales, making them fast to the umiaks, and insuring the propitiation of their spirits.

Point Hope 63801, 25 cm; Cape Darby 48137, 16.5 cm; Sledge Island 44690, 26.5 cm; Diomede Island 64220, 33 cm; Sledge Island 48384, 29 cm

**269. Whale Images** *arveruaq*

Images of bowhead whales, such as this ivory water bucket decoration from Diomede Island, appear on everyday items. The traditional northern needlecase, also found in prehistoric contexts, is shaped like a whale, its front flippers having been reduced to nubbins. The flasklike needlecase has polar bears and a whale on its neck, reflects European influences, and foreshadows a style of raised relief carving which became popular after Nelson's departure from Alaska.

Diomede Island 63699, 8 cm; Pikmiktalik 33700, 11 cm; Kotzebue Sound 48560, 13 cm

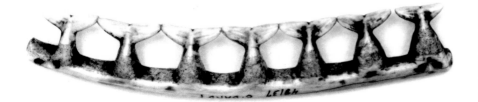

An old man from the Diomede islands told me that it was believed among his people that the first human beings who came to Big Diomede island were a man and a woman who came down from the sky and lived on the island a long time, but had no children. At last the man took some walrus ivory and carved five images of people. Then he took some wood and made five more images from it and put all of them to one side. The next morning the ten dolls had become transformed into ten people. Those coming from the ivory dolls were men, being hardy and brave, and those from the wood were women and were soft and timid. From these ten people came the inhabitants of the islands. (Nelson 1899:517)

### 270. Diomede and King Islanders
*imukhlimut, ukivagmut*

The Diomede and King Islanders have maintained relations with groups living on both the Siberian and North American mainland. Masks collected by Nelson are representative of the Islands' local styles, which bear affinities to the portrait style of Point Hope and Point Barrow masks. A wooden doll from Diomede Island has carefully defined musculature and suggests Siberian rather than North American influences, as does an ivory needlecase from King Island, possibly depicting four men involved in a singing contest.

Diomede Island 64216, 25.5 cm; King Island 64227, 19.5 cm; 44137, 11 cm; Diomede Island 63645, 15.5 cm

**271. King Island** *ukivagmut enait*

Nelson described King Island as "a rugged mass of granite rising sheer from the water for hundreds of feet." In this improbable setting the King Islanders have made their home, living in winter houses built out of and amongst loose rock. Their summer houses, shown in this photograph, are elevated wooden frames covered with walrus hide. Each house is constructed on two main poles, and their bases are wedged in rocks. A crosspiece runs between the two poles. Plank floors are supported by the crosspiece in the front and rest against the face of the hill in the back. The entire structure is given additional support by walrus hide thongs which secure it to the nearby rocks.

NAA–150827

People living on St. Lawrence, King, and Diomede islands lived a more precarious existence than did mainlanders, because if the islanders ran out of food during the winter or spring, they ran the risk of being trapped on the island with no means of escape and no alternate food resources. On the mainland people had access to terrestrial animals and fish and could turn to their neighbors for help if necessary.

The islands required other adaptations as well. King Islanders, for instance, had built their houses against the steep cliffs that make up the island. The houses were built on stilts wedged into and lashed onto rocks. Ropes hung down from the houses and were a means by which people could climb up to them.

The waters surrounding King Island's settlement were swift and rough and teeming with animals. The King Island men hunted in short, light, but strong kayaks that were well suited to the marine conditions and the tricky launching from King Island's "shore."

### 272. St. Lawrence Island Devastation

At the time of Nelson's visit to St. Lawrence Island the Island's population had been devastated by famine and disease, and hundreds of people had died. *Corwin* personnel found people lying dead, wrapped in their blankets, while others were found unburied or at graveyards.

Captain Hooper collected this mask from the Island. It is an unusual piece, having a wrinkled or tattooed forehead and a T-shaped groove under the chin. The mask's sunken eyes and cheeks, and white coloring project the image of an emaciated individual, and may relate to periodic famines experienced on the Island.

St. Lawrence Island (C. L. Hooper Collection) 45722, 21 cm

### 273. Siberian Lead Inlaid Pipe *kuingiq*

Previous to the disaster, St. Lawrence Islanders traded with Siberians and North American mainlanders, as well as with European whalers. They were eagerly acquiring exotic goods reaching the Bering Strait shores by way of the Chukchi, and pipes and tobacco were among the most sought after items. The pipe illustrated here was collected from St. Lawrence Island by Nelson and is probably a Chukchi trade piece. The pipe stem is solid lead and the bowl is wood and lead inlay.

Nowhere is there a record of the effects of smoking these lead pipes, but the St. Lawrence Islanders may have suffered the ill effects of lead poisoning, in addition to those caused by alcohol, European diseases, and hunting disasters to which their decline has been attributed.

St. Lawrence Island 63511, 23 cm

**274. Whale Bone Structures**

St. Lawrence Islanders lived in winter houses similar to those used on the North American mainland, though their structures had baleen and whale bones rather than driftwood supports. Their summer houses resembled those used by Siberians and consisted of upright whale ribs placed in an oval, the ribs arching inward and resting on a whale jawbone support. Since the ends of the bones were planted in shallow ground, a hundred-pound rock was hung from the jawbone to stabilize the structure. The frame was then covered with walrus skins which were weighed down with stone, bone, and driftwood.

**275. St. Lawrence Island Subsistence**

Previous to the 1879–80 famine in which two-thirds of the population of St. Lawrence Island died, hunting was productive—sea mammals being plentiful enough in the open waters surrounding the Island's ice edge to support six large villages, each inhabited by two hundred to three hundred people. Traveling in umiaks, St. Lawrence Islanders hunted bowhead whales, various kinds of seals, and large walrus herds which came by the Island on a seasonal basis. Small sleds like this one were used to transport meat, skins, baleen, blubber, bone, and ivory from the edge of the ice to the villages where they were processed and stored in raised caches. St. Lawrence Island 63587, 37.5 cm (runners)

# St. Lawrence Island

St. Lawrence Island was a wonderful place to live when hunting went well. The island, supporting a population of more than one thousand people, was visited by large herds of walrus, its waters abounded with seals, and bowhead whales passed close to the island on their annual migrations. In addition, St. Lawrence Islanders were in an excellent position to take advantage of the increased interest in and demand for European goods. Through their close social and economic relationships with Siberians they had access to metals, tobacco, and cloth which reached the Siberians prior to direct contact with Russians. Later in the nineteenth century whalers would make port calls at St. Lawrence Island, and Eskimos, and Europeans or Americans would engage in trade. Thus, the St. Lawrence Islanders had a wealth of tobacco, metal, pipes, beads, cloth, rifles, and ammunition that they used or exchanged for Alaskan goods. However, during 1878–79 St. Lawrence Islanders learned about the disadvantages of living on an island and coming into contact with Europeans.

The *Corwin* was dispatched to St. Lawrence Island during the summer of 1881 because of reports of massive deaths on the island. Sadly, Captain Hooper and Nelson had to report the rumors true, for most of the once-flourishing population of St. Lawrence was found dead.

> In July I landed at a place on the northern shore where two houses were standing, in which, wrapped in their fur blankets on the sleeping platforms, lay about 25 dead bodies of adults, and upon the ground and outside were a few others. Some miles to the eastward, along the coast, was another village, where there were 200 dead people. In a large house were found 15 bodies placed one upon another like cordwood at one end of the room, while as many others lay dead in their blankets on the platforms. (Nelson 1899:269)

Initially, it was suggested that alcohol, illegally supplied by whaling ships, may have accounted for the disaster. Nelson and Hooper saw the situation in a more realistic light. Having examined the villages and talked with a few survivors and others familiar with conditions around St. Lawrence Island during the 1878–1879 winter, Nelson and Hooper suggested that a combination of an epidemic and a famine caused the deaths. The

**276. The Hearth**

St. Lawrence Islanders used ceramic and soapstone lamps for heating and cooking. The lamps were similar to those used by other peoples on both sides of the Bering Strait, but quite different from the Bering Sea saucer-shaped lamps. Tray-shaped lamps like the one illustrated here have one or two raised ridges that form a ledge above the rendered oil. Lamp wicks rest on this ledge and drape over the rim. By adjusting the tilt of the lamp a woman controlled the amount of oil reaching the wick, thereby adjusting her flame size. A tall ceramic container with a slightly flared and depressed rim supported the lamp and caught the melted blubber that dripped down its front. For cooking purposes a rectangular ceramic pot was suspended above a lamp which had several wick stands.

St. Lawrence Island 63568, 25.5 cm long; 63544, 21.5 cm long; 63566, 14 cm

**277. Baleen and Wooden Dishes** *qantat*

*In the houses all the wooden and clay food vessels were found turned upward and put away in one corner—mute evidences of the famine. Scattered about the houses on the outside were various tools and implements, clay pots, wooden dishes, trays, guns, knives, axes, ammunition, and empty bottles; among these articles were the skulls of walrus and of many dogs. The bodies of the people were found everywhere in the village as well as scattered along in a line toward the grave-yard for half a mile inland. (Nelson 1899:269)*

The dishes used by the St. Lawrence Islanders during happier times and now put away were made out of strips of bent baleen rather than wood. The baleen containers had wooden bottoms and baleen stitching. They acquired bent-wood bowls and boxes from the North American mainland, and made similar pieces using baleen rather than spruce root lashings.

St. Lawrence Island 63249, 19 cm long; 63240, 19 cm long

epidemic could easily have been introduced by one of the many schooners stopping at the island and would have killed some people immediately, while incapacitating others. Nelson and Hooper found that some effort had been made initially to bury the dead. But the last to survive died in their homes.

> The first to die had been taken farthest away, and usually placed at full length beside the sled that had carried the bodies. Scattered about such bodies lay tools and implements belonging to the dead. In one instance a body lay outstretched upon a sled, while behind it, prone upon his face, with arms outstretched and almost touching the sled runners, lay the body of a man who had died while pushing the sled bearing the body of his friend or relative. (Nelson 1899:269)

Fast ice forms along the shores of St. Lawrence Island during the winter, and hunters used to load their umiaks onto their short sleds and carry the boats to the ice edge where they would be launched. Beyond the ice edge the waters were full of ice, and hunters risked having their boats crushed by thick ice moved by currents and winds. Every winter St. Lawrence Island hunters experienced anxious moments when hunting crews had to cope with the moving pack ice closing in on them. Some people told Hooper that the 1878–1879 winter was the worst winter experienced in Bering Strait in years. The weather was stormy and the ice was thick. The winter would have been troublesome for a healthy St. Lawrence Island population. However, with people dead and dying hunting efforts were minimal. The difficulties of getting to the game and the reduced population of hunters must have caused widespread food shortages. Those who were weak and may have otherwise recovered, died. The bad traveling conditions curtailed normal traffic to and from the island, isolating the islanders from outside help.

Nelson encountered two families on St. Lawrence Island. He noted that the adults seemed quite resigned to the fact that they too would die. He

was about to take a photograph of the women and little girls when the husband of one of the women asked Nelson if they would all die after Nelson took the picture. "He evidently took it for granted that my camera was a conjuring box, which would complete the work of the famine, yet he seemed perfectly indifferent to the consequences" (Nelson 1899:270).

Later, Hooper wrote his report on the *Corwin*'s 1881 voyage and described the villages of the dead. He knew that the St. Lawrence Island villages had been large and prosperous and that the island had been inhabited for a long time. In his summary of the disaster Hooper commented:

> At one deserted settlement I saw eight or nine bodies, probably an entire family, dead in a summer-house, showing that they must have survived the winter, as they would not put up the summer-house until the weather was warm enough to melt the snow and ice, thus making the winter-houses wet and uncomfortable. It appears strange that, after surviving the winter, and with strength enough remaining to put up and move into their summer-houses, they should be unable to supply themselves with food and regain their health and strength. By the time they could occupy their summer-houses the ice must have been broken so as to render seal hunting possible. It is probable that this family, having seen so many die, made no effort to save their own lives. Believing they were doomed, they submitted quietly to what to them appeared inevitable, and daily growing weaker, stretched upon the ground and covering themselves with furs, waited for the end. In this position we found them lying as if asleep, their guns, bows, arrows, spears, and traps lying strewn on the ground. I could not learn that any cannibalism had been practiced among them, and do not believe such to have been the case. On the contrary, I saw no indication of any struggle of existence. In many places I saw things untouched which have been eaten by white men and which have sustained life, such as the skin of seals, deer, and other animals. But one circumstance pointed to the possibility of cannibalism. (Hooper 1884:100–101)

> It is difficult to understand why a people who have lived and flourished for so many generations should be so suddenly and almost entirely swept away in one winter. (Hooper 1884:101)

**278. European Commodities and Influences**

St. Lawrence Island was visited frequently by European whalers who brought metal, guns, ammunition, liquor, beads, cloth, and tobacco to trade for baleen, fox and seal skins, and ivory. St. Lawrence Islanders were particularly eager for metal which they used to tip their arrows and harpoons, and which they hafted into knife handles instead of ground slate blades. The unusually large piece of copper used as a wrist guard speaks of their wealth in metal. The Islanders were also quick to copy pieces of European technology which might be useful to them. Some of their umiaks were equipped with European-style oar locks, and they obviously liked the design of the whalers' net shuttles, which they copied and made out of baleen.

St. Lawrence Island 63584, 71 cm; 63583, 76 cm; 127012, 21 cm (handle); 126913, 7 cm; 63308, 15 cm; 126988, 14 cm; 63279, 9.5 cm

232

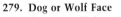

**279. Dog or Wolf Face**

This dog or wolf face, stretched over and pegged onto a wooden frame, may have been used during a Wolf Dance, a winter festival linked with trading and socializing and celebrated by Bering Strait people. Perhaps it was a fetish used by a shaman who desperately tried but failed to save his people from disease and starvation.

St. Lawrence Island 64286, 22 cm

**280. Death's Presence**

Nelson called this stern dark figurine a doll, though it seems more appropriate as a grave marker than as a child's toy. Its brooding image reminds one of the St. Lawrence Islanders' precarious existence and of Death's looming presence.

St. Lawrence Island 63244, 43 cm

## Indirect Contacts

Bering Sea Eskimos were surrounded by neighbors who spoke languages different from theirs, followed different subsistence patterns, and adapted to particular geographic and environmental conditions of their homelands. Each group had available to it resources desired by others, with the result that both hostile and cordial interregional relationships linked Bering Strait and Bering Sea people in a broad network. Influences were not felt solely through direct contacts however. As Dall (1870) noted, bent-wood bowls made by Yukon Indians and traded to Eskimos would continue to change hands, and would end up being used by Siberians who had never encountered the Indian craftsmen. Influences filtered through Siberia in the same manner. The East Asian shamans, who wore metal chains, were never seen on the Bering Strait shores. However, the intricate ivory chains used decoratively on Alaskan pails, toggles, and awls probably had their origins in the East Asian shaman complex. Indeed, archeologists (Larsen and Rainey 1948; Collins 1973) have suggested that Bering Strait cultures were influenced prehistorically by Scytho-Siberian art forms and shamanism.

**281. Distant Influences**

East Asian shamans wore garments covered with metal chains. Knowledge of chains, which were undoubtedly the subject of fantastic tales, must have spread far and wide. Ivory chains predating European contact have been found in archeological sites in western Alaska. During Nelson's time ivory chains, carved from unbroken sections of tusks, were used as decorations on awls and bag handles and as whaling charms on water buckets. Chains, like bone-slat armor, metal, and possibly the dragonlike *palraiyuk*, suggest influences from Asia filtered through Siberia.

Nelson described this belt attachment as a "plummet-like object," not realizing that he was looking at an ivory copy of a small metal bell! The concept of bells, like that of chains, may have been introduced to Bering Strait people by way of Siberia. Bells also may have come with the first Russian traders. Their status as prestige items would have prompted the nonfunctional ivory copy.

Sledge Island 44691, 32 cm (entire length); Chalitmut 37981, 16 cm; Cape Prince of Wales 48217, 34 cm; Chalitmut 37209, 4 cm

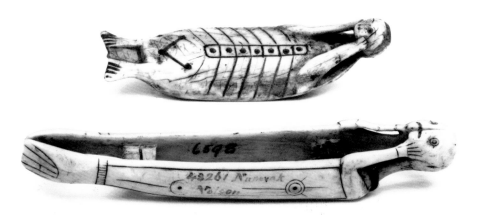

### 282. Aleutian Influences

Aleuts attached ivory carvings of male and female sea otters inside their kayaks, much the same way Yukon–Kuskokwim hunters used male and female face plaques. The sea otters were often carved in their characteristic feeding posture, on their backs with hands raised to their mouths. This figurine is very similar to eastern Aleutian forms and suggests that the Aglimut Yupik-speakers of Bristol Bay were in direct contact with Aleuts.

The Nunivak Island shuttle's shape is a modification of the sea otter theme, as are wooden boxes shaped like seals lying on their backs. This image, the concentric circle-and-dot motif, as well as the skeletal motif, are found in the Aleutians, Bristol Bay, and the Yukon–Kuskokwim region.

Bristol Bay (McKay Collection) 168626, 9.5 cm; Nunivak Island 48261, 14 cm

### 283. Southern Contacts

While ethnic boundaries were maintained, people living between the Aleutian Islands and Bering Strait were in direct contact with or knew of one another. Their social contacts are evident in shared artistic conventions present on artifacts. These two figurines from Nunivak Island appear to be Aleutian carvings of a woman wearing a typical Aleut cap and a man in an Aleut bentwood hat. The Nunivak Island shuttle and the female figurine have ears defined by small semilunar incisions on either side of the head, a motif uncharacteristic of Eskimo ivory work. The bent-wood hat, with local stylistic variation, is used by both Aleutian and Eskimo groups.

Nunivak Island 43713, 14 cm; 43715, 6 cm

## Southern Neighbors

Geographically, Nunivak Island, a rocky island off the Bering Sea coast, lies between the Aleutian Islands and the Yukon–Kuskokwim Delta. The island has a number of resources of particular interest to outsiders: walrus, caribou herds, and red, blue, and white pigments. The pigments were traded widely, for people applied them to masks and dishes. Even today Nunivak Island pigments are sought by artists. Walrus ivory too would have been traded from Nunivak Island into the interior, where ivory was used to make a variety of implements.

Nelson never visited Nunivak Island, but he met people who lived there and through them he caught glimmers of the island's complex history. Nunivak Island seemed to be a crossroads of cultures from the north and south. Among the people with whom Nelson talked and traded were a group of Norton Sound Malemut who had decimated their caribou herd and had taken up residence on Nunivak Island because of its caribou resources. Among the artifacts procured from Nunivak Island were carvings of Aleuts as well as images resembling the Aleut sea otter. Artifacts from Bristol Bay also reflect Aleutian influences and suggest contacts between Nunivak Islanders and their southern neighbors. Nelson commented that the dialects spoken on Nunivak Island and neighboring Cape Vancouver were distinct from those of surrounding areas. Margaret Lantis (1946) suggests that the language spoken here has relationships with the south as well.

The cultural boundaries which existed between groups in the Bering Sea and Bering Strait regions were constantly changing. Sometimes changes were gradual, at other times they were swift and dramatic. The large size of the Bering Sea Eskimo population and the complex network of small settlements in the huge Yukon–Kuskokwim Delta insured that the Bering Sea Eskimo culture would survive despite wars, migrations, and new lifeways which came to its borders.

## Neighbors in the Interior

In 1880 Nelson took a sledge trip up the Lower and Middle Yukon and encountered interior-dwelling Ingalik Indians who subsisted on fish, caribou, birds, and forest-dwelling furbearing animals. Both Indians and Eskimos told Nelson that they used to fight with one another and that relationships between the Malemut and the Ingalik were particularly bad because both groups hunted caribou in the same area.

Nelson, and William H. Dall (1870) before him, noted that an ongoing trade existed between Indian and Eskimo groups. Eskimos would actually travel to Anvik for the purpose of trading with Indians living there, and Indians would periodically travel to the coast. Eskimos sought bent-wood containers, wooden ladles, woven baskets, as well as a tree fungus which they mixed with their tobacco. Indians wanted seal skins, seal oil, and, occasionally, umiaks from their coastal neighbors (VanStone 1978:72).

Despite the history of uneasy relations, the Indians whom Nelson visited had much in common with their Eskimo neighbors. Many of the implements found in Indian camps Nelson had seen in use among the Bering Sea Eskimos. These included wooden containers, woven grass and spruce root baskets, crooked knives, fish traps, and wedges with incised and pigmented designs such as double-spurred lines and the raven's foot. Nelson observed a number of Ingalik festivals at Anvik that differed from festivals celebrated by Bering Sea Eskimos only in details, having the same overall structure and concepts behind them. These included the important

**284. Indian Mask from Anvik**

Visiting Indian villages on the Lower Yukon in the winter of 1880, Nelson became aware of many features shared with Eskimo culture downstream. Most surprising was their observance of many "Eskimo" religious events like the Bladder Festival, the Feast to the Dead, the Doll Festival, and the Messenger Feast. These ceremonies not only closely followed their Eskimo counterparts, but also employed similar artifacts. This shield mask from Anvik has a low-relief carving depicting a frowning face with female chin tattoos and lip ornaments. It is framed by a border of red and green painted grooves surrounded by feathers. The iconography and design resemble Eskimo masks such as that shown on the facing page. Elements that are rare or absent in Eskimo masks include red cheek spots, ears, raised wooden plugs, and centrally parted hair styles.

Anvik 45502, 36.5 cm wide

**285. Eskimo Mask from Sabotnisky**

This Eskimo mask from Sabotnisky, a village only a short distance down the Yukon from Anvik, has a toothed mouth and a fluted upper lip that extends across the entire face. It formerly had mouth and ear decorations and feathers in its forehead. Although this mask is similar to some Indian masks, its organization and many minor details point to Eskimo authorship.

Sabotnisky 48982, 42.5 cm wide

Bladder Festival, the Festival to the Dead, and the Messenger Festival. Bladders of game were treated by Indians in the same manner as they were treated by Eskimos, and during many of the ceremonies Indians wore full face masks and finger masks resembling those used by their neighbors.

Nelson also had occasion to collect a number of myths while he was among the Ingalik. Details of material culture, customs, and the prominent roles of small forest-dwelling animals identify them as Indian myths, but the stories are the same ones told by Bering Sea Eskimos. In a section of the Raven Myth collected from Indians living in Anvik, Raven prepared to take a wife:

> Soon after this, the Raven, who had been in the sweat house disguised by the dogskins, came out and crossed the river in his canoe. Then he took the canoes of the sisters and towed them across the river to the village and left them. After doing this Raven went back and cut a spruce root and began making wooden dishes and ladles (the custom of a lower Yukon Indian lover) and worked at this the rest of the day. Toward evening the oldest sisters came down to the river bank and, their canoes being gone, Raven took them across in his and the two women went home without thinking anything wrong. The Raven went back and took the youngest sister in his canoe, but when he pushed out into the river he turned up the stream and paddled away from the village with great swiftness. (Nelson, in VanStone 1978:48)

### 286. Indian Fancy Dress *ingqiliq*

By the time Nelson arrived at St. Michael, trading posts had been operating on the Yukon River for many years. Despite the presence of these facilities, Indians sometimes traveled to St. Michael to trade. These visits were eagerly anticipated, and while at the post Indians dressed in fancy clothes and enjoyed the pleasures of town.

This photograph was probably taken by Nelson at St. Michael during one such visit by an Ingalik Indian, here seen posing with his newly purchased rifle and in an ornate suit of clothes. Unlike Eskimo clothing, which is decorated by fine needlework and appliqué, his heavily fringed garments employ a mixture of native and European designs. The beaded pouch is a European floral design first introduced into Indian cultures in northeastern North America, later carried west through Indian contacts in conjunction with missionary and trading activity. This Indian's cheeks are painted red, as are the cheeks on Indian masks from Anvik.

SI–6362

### 287. Indian and Eskimo Contacts

Nelson noted that the Indians living on lands adjoining Eskimo territory on the Lower Yukon specialized in making bent-wood containers and ladles. They decorated them with red and black bands, grooves, and often painted figures inside the bowls. On the bottoms they frequently inscribed or painted their totem marks. These items were traded on a regular basis to the Eskimos who, in turn, traded them to other Eskimo groups. In addition, Eskimos also made similar artifacts themselves, and may have painted their own designs on pieces obtained from Indians. This food tray, painted with the face of a stylized animal and collected at the Eskimo village of Kigiktauik, was attributed by Nelson to Ingalik manufacture.

For some reason birchbark containers, which were also made in large numbers by Indians, were not traded to Eskimos, perhaps because the Eskimos found their grass, root, and wooden containers sufficient. However, Nelson collected a barking knife from Indians at Nulato with raven's foot and tooth pattern decorations common on Eskimo artifacts from northern Norton Sound. This piece may have been obtained by Indians trading at the coast, or it may be a copy of an Eskimo tool.

Kigiktauik (bowl) 33060, 49 cm wide; Anvik 43893, 34 cm; 49166, 19.5 cm wide; Nulato 33026, 31 cm

### 288. Lady with Goggles and Labret

Anvik Indians carved this fine mask of a lady by using many features typically found on Eskimo masks. They include not only symbols of female gender, such as the downturned mouth, female labret, and diagonal chin tattoos, but also the common Eskimo goggle motif and use of multiple hoops, both representing religious concepts. Indian features include the use of large red spots on the cheeks, here seen faintly, and the hairstyle. Although the mask is a close copy of Eskimo masks, the use of goggles on a female face is rarely seen in Eskimo pieces, as are the use of single-piece hoop splints. Eskimo mask hoops usually have conjoined splints and employ different fastening methods and materials.

Anvik 45503, 43 cm wide

# other times

When Edward Nelson arrived at Kushunuk on the fifteenth of December, 1878, the entire village was celebrating its annual Bladder Festival.

> Kushunuk is a large village of between 100–200 people, and consists of a cluster of the usual underground huts built on a mound some 8 or 10 feet above the level of the surrounding country. This mound has been formed by the constant accumulation formed during the great length of time this spot has been occupied, and its artificial character becomes evident upon examination.
>
> On entering the *kazgha* we found a hunting festival in full progress, and as, during this feast, no visitor or any one else must leave the village on a journey or do any ordinary work, we found ourselves compelled to rest here a few days. (Nelson 1882:7)

The village consisted of two *qasgit,* each of which was the focal point of its festival proceedings, and about twenty houses built in a haphazard way on a slightly raised piece of circular ground less than a quarter mile long. Perched beside the *qasgit* and houses were a number of elevated storehouses and raised frames for boats and sleds. Nelson was welcomed into the smaller of the two *qasgit* where, sitting beneath a "fantastic bird-shaped image" (fig. 255), he took notes on the activities of the festival, described the construction of the building, and over several days was able to purchase a large collection of ethnographic specimens.

Nelson was also told of the existence, some distance away, of even older villages where the ancestors of the Kushunuk people had once lived. These villages had been abandoned, one after the other, as a result of progressively worsening winter and spring floods that destroyed the villages and houses. A few days after leaving Kushunuk, Nelson personally experienced a violent winter storm and noted its dire effects on land, life, and property.

**289. Aerial View of Kushunuk Mound**

While in Kushunuk Nelson noted the artificial nature of the mound on which the village stood. Centuries of human occupation had caused the natural eminence on which the village was built to reach a height eight to ten feet above the surrounding marshy grassland. At the time of Nelson's visit Kushunuk had two *qasgit,* about twenty houses, a number of elevated storage sheds and racks, and a population of 125 (Nelson, in Petroff 1884:11). The village survived another sixty years after Nelson's departure, being abandoned in the wake of severe floods that struck during winter gales and spring river breakup in the late 1940s. Today the descendants of Kushunuk people live in Chevak, ten miles to the north of the old site.

Modern aerial and ground surveys have helped archeologists locate old village sites. This view of Kushunuk, taken in the summer of 1981, shows the outlines of the main mound and three satellite mounds. Several of the larger depressions are *qasgit* foundations, while most of the forty-five-odd smaller pits represent houses, many of which were occupied during the early 1900s when the village reached its maximum size.

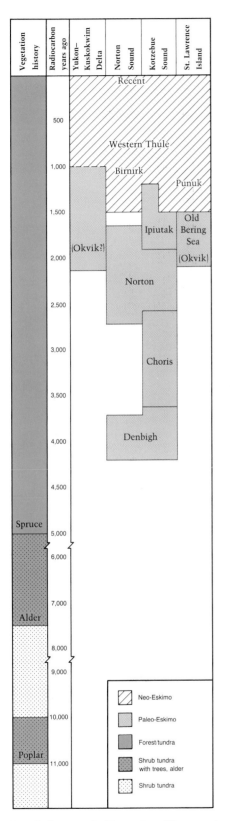

**290. Culture and Vegetation History of Western Alaska** (modified from Anderson 1978; Ager, this volume)

Today Kushunuk, too, is an abandoned village, having succumbed to the rising waters in the late 1940s. At that time it had been the largest winter settlement in the area. The village was moved to a new site at Old Chevak for a few years, but once again, floods struck and caused it to be abandoned in favor of the present village of Chevak. Chevak now carries the traditions of the old people whose ancestors have for ages survived the onslaughts of nature and war, leaving their villages behind to start new lives in new places. These traditions are still passed on from the elders to the younger members of the community through practiced advice, old stories, and lore of ancient times.

Among the accounts (*qanemcit*) that tell of real people and historical events, including the period of Eskimo wars that preceded the Russian period, are stories about volcanic ashfalls, floods, and the disappearance of animals that formerly lived in the region. Others from the more remote past explain the origin of the land and Eskimo peoples (p. 39) in an almost scientific manner, noting the arrival of man from across the frozen ocean during an ice age and the subsequent retreat of the ice and carving of the landscape by turbulent meltwater rivers. Others, like those in the Raven Myth, take a more allegorical position. That these tales contradict each other matters little to the Bering Sea people, who delight in hearing different stories and permit many points of view to be expressed. This rich oral tradition is a great repository of literary and factual information about the past, and many thoughts expressed in them have been verified by modern historical, archeological, and paleontological studies.

Among his other accomplishments, Edward Nelson initiated archeological studies in western Alaska. His collections include artifacts acquired from Eskimos who had found them at old village sites or while digging foundations for new houses at established villages. In a number of cases Nelson himself excavated in house ruins in abandoned villages, several of which were located around St. Michael.

> Near St. Michael, on the top of an elevated islet close to the coast, is the site of an ancient village which had been surprised and destroyed by this last-named people [Malemut] long before the arrival of the Russians in that region. Digging in some of the pits marking the places once occupied by houses, I found charred fragments of wood and various small articles belonging to the former inhabitants. (Nelson 1899:328)

In his field list of artifacts is the handwritten note: "All these specimens were dug up on the site of two old villages on St. Michael's Is. and show among the skinning knives a greater variety of shapes than is seen in those in use here at present." The entry of twenty pieces includes stone knives, an ivory doll, an ivory snow (story) knife, parts of ivory pail or bucket handles, a point for a three-pronged bird spear, a stone skin scraper, flint axheads, raw material for making drill points, and a small seal harpoon head (fig. 291). Despite changes in tool forms during the 50–100 years that had elapsed since the site had been destroyed, the artifacts were easily recognized as having belonged to the ancestors of the Unalit people.

In several other instances Nelson purchased items that had been passed down as family heirlooms or that had been found by Eskimos and were being kept as curiosities. Among the former is a fine jade knife (fig. 122) that for more than two years Nelson wooed from a man at Nubviukhchugaluk in northern Norton Sound. Nelson also purchased an old ivory boat hook prong (fig. 293) from a man at Cape Nome, noting in his log, "This specimen has been dug up on an ancient village site and since then has

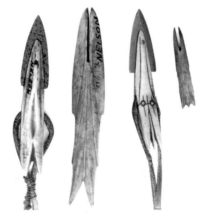

**291. Present-day Bering Sea Harpoon Heads**
A variety of harpoon head types were used along the Bering Sea coast in Nelson's day. In contrast with the simple undecorated forms used in Bering Strait, southern forms were artfully decorated with multiple-spurred bases, incised lines, ivory inlays, and circle-dots, demonstrating care in the production of these hunting weapons. Ethnographic evidence from the Yukon–Kuskokwim region, where harpoon points are finely made, indicates that harpoon head decoration is associated with hunting magic, for sea mammals are displeased when attacked with ugly weapons. While multiple spurs and circle-dot features ceased to be used in the north after the beginning of Western Thule culture, their presence in nineteenth-century Bering Sea Eskimo culture suggests that these forms were also used by prehistoric cultures living south of the Bering Strait as part of a ritually based hunting complex.
Cape Darby 44252, 10 cm; Unalakleet 33632, 12.2 cm; St. Michael 43448, 5 cm; Lower Kuskokwim 176173, 8.8 cm

been in possession of its owner two generations when I bought it.'' The prong is ornamented with engraved figures illustrated in two separate panels. One is a realistic scene depicting umiak hunters attacking whales and a walrus, while the other depicts the myth of the killer whale-wolf transformation. In style, content, and organization, the engraving is indistinguishable from illustrations on drill bows used by Bering Strait people between 1877 and 1881. Nelson's documentation, however, suggests that it was engraved earlier than 1830, making the piece comparable in age to the engraved pieces collected from the Bering Strait by Otto von Kotzebue's expedition of 1816 and Frederick William Beechey's expedition of 1826–27.

The addition of this engraved prong to the meager evidence relating to the origins of the distinctive but geographically-restricted pictorial art style reinforces the view that such engraving was not introduced by European explorers and whalers. Further, the presence of rudimentary pictographic engravings from prehistoric Western Thule and Thule/Punuk sites at Cape Krusenstern (Giddings 1967:91) and Cape Prince of Wales has led to the suggestion, formulated by Henry Collins (1973), that western Eskimo pictographic art developed independently as an elaboration of geometric baseline art in the Bering Strait region between A.D. 1000 and 1500.

The development of pictographic art is only one of many questions in the larger study of the origins and development of Eskimo culture in general. Nelson's collections and observations about archeological sites, together with similar observations by his contemporaries William H. Dall in the Aleutians and P.H. Ray and John Murdoch at Point Barrow, led to the foundation of later archeological studies of Eskimo origins. Today, however—a century later—there is still no concensus on the Eskimo origin problem. Among the several contending theories are three that offer rad-

**292. Bering Strait Culture Change**
These four harpoon heads illustrate stylistic changes that archeologists have identified in the two-thousand-year Bering Strait Eskimo sequence. Harpoons used by Old Bering Sea hunters, the earliest inhabitants yet discovered here, are also the most elegant. Their harpoon heads are decorated with flowing curvilinear designs that swirl around raised bosses and have basal spurs and angled surface planes made to imitate tucked bird plumage. The art may have functioned primarily as hunting magic to please the spirits of seals and walrus, and only secondarily as formal decoration.

An intrusion of Birnirk culture, centered in northwestern Alaska, brought multiple-spurred and linear design styles into the Bering Strait for a brief period about A.D. 800. Birnirk influences were followed by Punuk cultural influences. Art and harpoon styles developed from earlier Old Bering Sea forms, but Punuk geometric patterns were simpler and more mechanically applied, usually without zoomorphic roots. Modern harpoon heads of this region are even simpler in form, often entirely lacking in decoration. They have lost all artistic and ritual connections while retaining basic functional features.

The changes seen in harpoon head styles and decoration reflect a steady reduction in the role of art in hunting magic through time. Stylistic simplification and reduction to elemental functional features occurred during a time when Bering Strait people were being brought into closer economic contacts with Siberians, who supplied them with iron and prestige items—eventually with tobacco—in exchange for Alaskan products desired by Siberian traders elsewhere.
Little Diomede Island 347940, 11.5 cm; Cape Prince of Wales 395076, 10 cm; St. Lawrence Island 371933, 8 cm; Cape Nome 44485, 10.5 cm

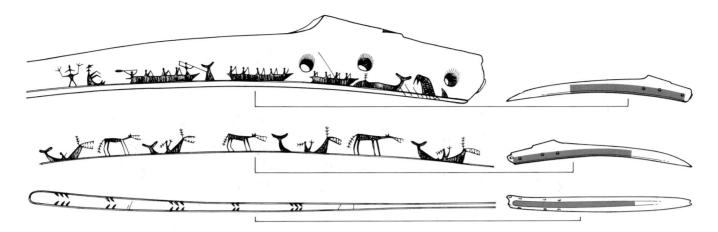

## 293. Pictographic Prong

Nelson purchased this boat hook prong from an Eskimo at Cape Nome who told him the artifact had been kept as a curiosity in his family for two generations after having been dug up at an old village site. Pictographs, which are not common on late nineteenth-century prongs, are seen on two panels. One shows umiak hunters attacking whales, a walrus, a man, and a cariboulike creature seated on his rump. The second shows alternating figures of standing wolves and spouting sea mammal monsters ridden by humans with spiked hands and headdresses. This scene depicts the killer whale-wolf transformation myth. Similar to late nineteenth-century engraving, this specimen suggests that the technique must have preceded 1830 and therefore probably was not introduced by European explorers or whalers.

Cape Nome 44405, 37.5 cm

## 294. Origins of Pictographic Art

Artifacts with pictographs similar to those on Nelson's drill bows were collected as early as Captain James Cook's expedition of 1778. Numerous theories have been advanced to explain the origin of this engraving style. Evidence suggesting a local prehistoric development exists in a series of engraved pieces from Kurigitavik, an archeological site excavated by Henry B. Collins at Cape Prince of Wales. These pieces show a stylistic development from simple baseline and freestanding geometric motifs into organized pictographs showing men and animals engaged in activities similar to those illustrated in later pictographic art (Collins 1973). A few of the Thule/Punuk artifacts figuring in this sequence include brow bands with rudimentary baseline forms, a wrist guard with two free-standing men, and a detail of a caribou hunting scene on an antler adze handle.

Cape Prince of Wales 392832, 5.8 cm; 393685, 7 cm; 393678, 5.3 cm; 393714, 31.5 cm

ically different hypotheses. One holds that Eskimo culture developed from a common Eskimo-Aleut base along the southern edge of the Bering Land Bridge at the end of the last continental glaciation about ten thousand years ago, with proto-Eskimo peoples moving north along the Bering Sea coast as the land bridge became inundated under rising sea levels (Laughlin 1963). Another theory proposes a movement of interior Alaskan people to the coast where their distinctive adaptations were developed more than four thousand years ago (Anderson 1978). A third idea links Eskimo developments to an eastern migration or strong influences from Siberian neolithic peoples (Irving 1968).

The course of Eskimo developments in western Alaska becomes clearer since 4,500 B.P. Coastal sites are found which contain small, finely made chipped stone tools that are the hallmark of the *Arctic Small Tool* tradition. These sites are distributed along the coast of the Bering Sea, in Norton and Kotzebue sounds, and across the north coast of Alaska into the Canadian Arctic and Greenland. These people are generally called *Paleo-Eskimos*. They are known to have had a variety of different regional cultures, and hunted caribou, small sea mammals, birds, and fish, but they lacked the highly developed and specialized large sea mammal hunting technology—such as efficient harpoons and float gear—necessary for intensive exploitation of marine resources.

Between 500 B.C. and A.D. 500 several distinct Paleo-Eskimo cultures existed in the coastal regions of western Alaska, including *Ipiutak* in the region north of the Seward Peninsula and *Old Bering Sea* in the Bering

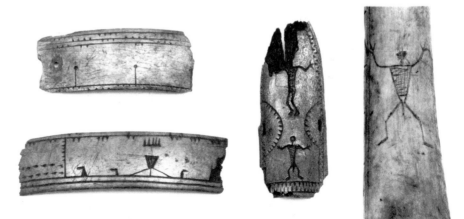

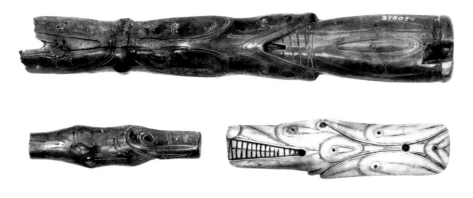

Strait (fig. 295). Each of these cultures had different subsistence economies and distinctive artifact styles (Larsen and Rainey 1948; Collins 1937; Rainey 1941). In addition, both had strong artistic traditions in which incised and sculptured art was applied to hunting weapons, household utensils, and mortuary objects. Both linear and curvilinear styles were used, and implements were often carved into the form of realistic or abstract animals. Hunting magic and shamanistic overtones pervade the subject matter and context of this art and, in the case of Ipiutak, links with mortuary art of Shang China and Scytho-Siberian animal form styles have been suggested (Larsen and Rainey 1948; Collins 1971).

Ipiutak and Old Bering Sea cultures are not found south of Bering Strait, where the local early Paleo-Eskimo culture developed into a different culture known as *Norton* (Giddings 1964; Bockstoce 1979). Also considered a Paleo-Eskimo culture, Norton developed a highly successful adaptation to coastal life along the Bering Sea coast. In northern Norton Sound, Norton subsistence was based on caribou, fish (taken with hooks and nets), birds, and small sea mammals. The latter were hunted with harpoons that lacked float technology. Norton people lived in square houses in relatively large villages that were occupied throughout much of the year. Storable fish—primarily salmon—probably contributed greatly to the stability of Norton village life, as did the presence of abundant wood for fires and construction of houses and artifacts. Little is known of Norton material culture, art, or ceremonialism because organic preservation at these sites is usually poor. For this reason Norton culture is often dismissed as a poor relation when consideration is given to the spectacular finds from Ipiutak and Old Bering Sea cultures of the same time period.

Another factor in our knowledge of Norton culture relates to the nature of the Bering Sea coast. Between Norton Sound and Bristol Bay the coastline

### 295. Ancient Hunting Magic and Art

Hunters of the Old Bering Sea culture in Bering Strait decorated their equipment with elegant carvings that are among the finest art ever produced by hunting peoples. The small dart socket from Little Diomede Island is carved in the form of an abstract animal head in the Okvik style, an early Old Bering Sea art style dating to about two-thousand years ago. A more developed style is seen on an ivory piece from St. Lawrence Island which may have been an ornament worn on a hunting visor, showing a toothy animal representing a polar bear or a mythical beast. A similar beast or bear is found on a harpoon socketpiece whose elegant design and artistry befits the most highly developed and latest style of Old Bering Sea art. Here the animal form is clearly defined with raised eyes and ears, and a prominent snout with nostrils and sharp teeth (Collins 1962).

The use of beast images as decorative and symbolic charms on sea hunting weapons is a tradition that survived into nineteenth-century Bering Sea Eskimo culture (fig. 41) despite the passage of fifteen hundred years, and is one of the closest links between the Yukon–Kuskokwim Eskimos and their Paleo-Eskimo ancestors.

Little Diomede Island (H. B. Collins, collector) 344674, 7 cm; St. Lawrence Island (H. B. Collins, collector) 371978, 9 cm, 378054, 19 cm

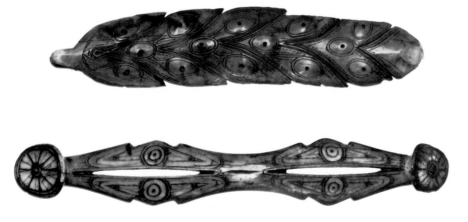

### 296. Decorated Handles

Pail or bag handles have been decorated for more than two-thousand years by Eskimos living in the Bering Strait and Bering Sea regions. Early examples include these two specimens executed in the delicate curvilinear Old Bering Sea style. In each case the artist approached the function, form, and decorative elements as an integrated unit. In the succeeding Punuk period artistic attitudes emphasized decorative features applied to an object rather than being an inherent part of the whole. The changes seen from Old Bering Sea to Punuk may reflect a shift away from cultural influences dominated by Asian curvilinear styles to a resurgence of Okvik-related linear styles dominant on the Alaskan mainland.

Little Diomede Island or St. Lawrence Island (H. B. Collins, collector) 377352, 17 cm; St. Lawrence Island (H. B. Collins, collector) 353765, 15 cm

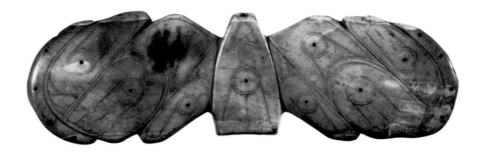

### 297. Winged Object

Eskimos of the Old Bering Sea and Punuk cultures used winged objects on the butt ends of their dart shafts to act as counterbalances and stabilizers when the darts were being thrown. Each winged object has a recessed notch to engage the hook at the end of the throwing stick, used to propel the dart. Winged objects—their functional and stylistic changes through time having been identified by Henry Collins (1962)—often are elaborately decorated, as shown on this specimen from Point Hope which is carved in a late Old Bering Sea style dating to about A.D. 500. Winged objects ceased to be used after Punuk times. Large numbers of superbly engraved winged objects and other Old Bering Sea style artifacts have been recovered from cemeteries at sites on the Siberian coast of the Bering Strait.

Point Hope 42927 (W.H. Dall Collection), 20.5 cm

### 298. Ivory Ulu Handles—Two-Thousand Years Ago and Today

Many types of implements utilized by people of the Old Bering Sea culture continued in use in Nelson's day. The Okvik designs on the knife handle with an animal head effigy on one end, from St. Lawrence Island, are different from the incised lines and circle-dots on the handle from Chalitmut, but betray a related history. Eskimo artifacts from south of the Yukon are frequently decorated with motifs strongly reminiscent of Old Bering Sea, Punuk, and Ipiutak Paleo-Eskimo motifs, with skeletal patterns, radiating lines, and animal effigies being notable, especially on tool handles.

Bering Strait 345466, 14 cm; St. Lawrence Island 353540, 7 cm; Chalitmut 37460, 11.8 cm

presents an archeological landscape of almost unrelieved obscurity by comparison with the better known coastal regions to the north and south. No other area of Alaska—and perhaps of North America—is so poorly known and explored. To a large degree this is the result of its lowland geography, which makes archeological survey difficult. The real problem, however, is the dynamic geology of the Yukon-Kuskokwim Delta. Shallow coastal waters, rapid sedimentation, dramatic changes in river channels, erosion of stream banks, ice scouring, and subsidence or marine inundation are among the principal physical impediments. Only in a few areas where highlands approach the sea has the dismal prospect for archeological reconnaissance been mitigated.

Surveys in several of these locations, especially on Nunivak Island, at Tanunak on Nelson Island, and at Hooper Bay, have provided a preliminary view of cultural development in this region. The results of this work have demonstrated that the immediate proto-historic and historic ancestors (ca. A.D. 1600–1850) of the Yukon-Kuskokwim people lived a life nearly identical to that observed by Nelson (Collins 1928; Oswalt 1952). Most of the artifacts recovered from these studies are comparable to those in Nelson's Bering Sea Eskimo collections, and they include similar types of art and religious symbolism. This archeological culture seems likely to have developed as a direct outgrowth of prehistoric *Western Thule* culture, evidence of which has been found at a number of sites on Nunivak Island (VanStone 1957; Nowak 1970).

The period between A.D. 600–1200 was a time of great culture change in western Alaska. During this time new techniques of sea mammal hunting, primarily the invention of bladder and sealskin float apparatus, developed and spread widely throughout Eskimo cultures in Alaska. Accompanying these changes were intensification of large sea mammal exploitation, including the hunting of large whales, spread of ground slate technology, and increasing availability of Siberian trade goods, especially iron. These changes brought about a more specialized and efficient *Neo-Eskimo* way of life which replaced the older Paleo-Eskimo traditions in most areas. It is thought that these developments took place first in the Bering Strait

and northwest Alaska regions and from there spread rapidly south and north, sometimes by population movements as was the case in Canada, but mostly through the spread of ideas. Neo-Eskimo patterns then became the basis for the widespread Western Thule culture that continued until the historic period in most Eskimo areas, including on Nunivak Island and other coastal regions of the Yukon-Kuskokwim Delta. Few of these ideas, however, seem to have penetrated inland.

At a considerably earlier period, about two thousand years ago, there is evidence of Norton culture at several sites on Nunivak Island. Like most Norton sites in Norton Sound, organic remains have not been found. This in not the case, however, at one of the few interior Delta sites known, located on the Manokinak River in the Lower Yukon. Here several cultural levels have been found to contain Norton-related implements of wood, bone, ivory, and other perishables, as well as the more commonly encountered inorganic remains. Some of the wood and bone materials are decorated with incised and sculpted human face masks and animal forms, and bear traces of red ocher paint and inset fur tufts (Robert Shaw, personal communication). Providing a rare glimpse into the kinds of perishable materials that might be expected in other Norton sites under circumstances of ideal preservation, the ornamented objects from this site strongly foreshadow the styles, materials, and symbolic nature of later Bering Sea Eskimo art and religion. Although influenced by Western Thule ideas, Norton culture seems likely to have persisted in its essential features in the Yukon-Kuskokwim region for at least the past thousand years.

Another important clue to the prehistory of this area is found in a single unusual artifact that Nelson bought from an Eskimo in Chalitmut (fig. 304). Nelson's field list indicates that the piece was considered to be very old; so old, in fact, that no one in the village knew what it had been made for. Formed from dark, polished, and partially fossilized bone, the piece has a sculptured beast head at one end, and its sides are decorated with a variety of geometric motifs. The artifact has since been identified as being a quiver stiffener (cf. fig. 103), a type of implement that is not used in the Bering Strait region. Nevertheless, the style of ornamentation is Okvik, which would suggest connections with northern cultures approximately two thousand years ago (Collins 1959). This would make the piece the oldest artifact identified to date from the Yukon-Kuskokwim Delta.

### 299. Ivory Birds

Eskimos have made carvings of small animals for thousands of years. Often these carvings show only minor changes in form through time. The two darker birds are decorated in the Old Bering Sea culture style and are about fifteen hundred years old. The puffin once had inlaid eyes and wing plugs. The smaller bird has the head of a wolf or some other toothy monster, and its body is decorated with an early style of Old Bering Sea engraving. Both have grooves on their bases for lashing to another surface, suggesting that they were spear guards or charms fastened to kayaks. Like many Neo-Eskimo birds, the two nineteenth-century geese from St. Michael are more simply made, have no surface decoration, and served as gaming pieces. They are made from beluga or walrus teeth.

St. Lawrence Island 352700, 3.5 cm; 352722a, 3.2 cm; St. Michael 49189 (three), 3.0; 2.7; 2.4 cm

### 300. Ornamented Mouthpiece

Four human faces have been carved on both sides of this prehistoric ivory bow drill mouthpiece. Rudimentary images of faces are sometimes found in Bering Sea Eskimo ivory work (fig. 219), but are more common in early archeological cultures in Alaska, Canada, and Greenland, where they are frequently executed as clusters of faces on single objects, resembling faces in a crowd. The simple yet powerful faces on this undated specimen from Little Diomede Island closely resemble faces seen in Dorset culture art of the eastern Arctic (fig. 310; Meldgaard 1959: pl. 25).

Little Diomede Island 347943a, 3.7 cm

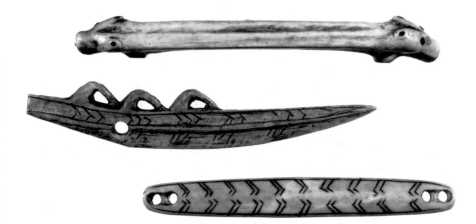

### 301. Effigy and "Bent Leg" Decoration

Modern animal effigy and incised "bent leg" decoration has developed from older Paleo-Eskimo art traditions in western Alaska. The practice of carving beastly or realistic animal heads on the ends of handles and other tools began at least as early as Old Bering Sea and Ipiutak times. These effigy traditions are strongest today south of Norton Sound, but are also found in northern regions, as seen by the effigy handle from Diomede Island. Leg patterns are found throughout western Alaska. They appear to have developed from the full skeletal pattern in which the central spine-baseline has been split onto one or two separate baselines carrying the appendages of multiple-legged beasts. These designs seem to represent old ideas. Myths tell of monsters, like the *kokogiak*, that lie on their backs waving many sets of their long legs in the air. This image may be related to the practice of nineteenth-century Eskimo warriors who showed derision for their enemies by flopping down on their backs in the heat of battle and flailing their legs in the air.

Diomede Island 63662, 14.3 cm; 63665, 13.7 cm; Sledge Island 45153, 12.3 cm

Meager though it is, this archeological evidence suggests that the Delta region has been occupied by people whose culture has developed from Norton and perhaps even Okvik Paleo-Eskimo roots during the past two thousand years. It can be expected that the coastal areas were occupied first, probably thousands of years earlier, and that people soon learned how to live among the lower courses of the Yukon and Kuskokwim rivers, taking advantage of the huge fish runs and other game, and, soon after, moving into the tundra lake country as well. Moving into the interior would have enabled the small coastal population to expand dramatically, offering protection against fluctuations in climate or poor hunting conditions on the coast or aggression from outside groups, while adding diversity to the ecological base of the population as a whole. Once established, this large population would have been a strong buffering force to cultural change, dependent as it was, at least in part, upon fish and other small game. For this reason one may expect considerable continuity in the cultural life of the Yukon–Kuskokwim people.

Judging from the Chalitmut quiver stiffener, the early Delta dwellers of about two thousand years ago had a well-developed artistic tradition which included use of geometric Okvik-related designs and sculptured animal forms with strong mythological symbolism, reminiscent of Ipiutak art. This comparison is strengthened, though indirectly, by a number of features of Bering Sea Eskimo culture which probably originated from early Paleo-Eskimo culture roots. These features include the widespread importance of shamanism, the use of ceremonial masks and fetishes, prom-

### 302. Needlecase Decoration

Tubular bird bone needlecases, used by Bering Sea Eskimo women living south of the Yukon mouth, are decorated in a variety of geometric patterns. Cross-hatching, rings, crosses, spurred lines, and skeletal patterns are commonly employed. These patterns are not applied as border designs, as are most of the designs on Thule culture artifacts and those of historic northern Eskimos, but are commonly seen on Dorset culture implements.

Rasboinsky 48807, 10.2 cm; Big Lake 36759, 14.5 cm (with plugs); Paimut 37154, 16.5 cm (with plugs)

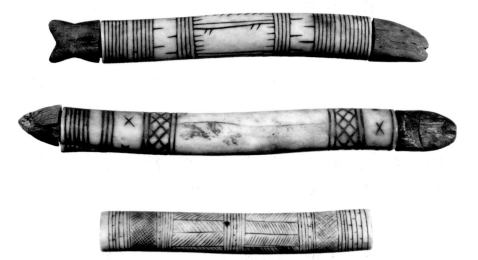

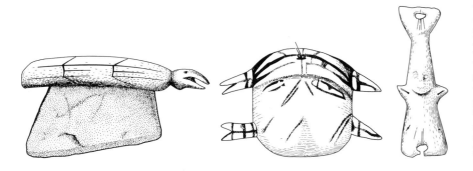

## 304. Chalitmut Quiver Stiffener

Nelson purchased this unusual engraved bone artifact from an Eskimo in Chalitmut. He was told it was very old, so old that the people "knew not what it was made for." Being of unknown origin and function, Nelson did not describe it and the artifact was overlooked until rediscovered by Henry Collins, who made it the subject of a short report (Collins 1959).

The object is a flat fragment of dark, polished bone, one end of which has been carved into the head and face of a beast with raised nostrils and eyes. The face is decorated with incised lines which form pointed ovoids around the eyes. Behind the head, both sides of the bone are incised with geometric patterns. The "stomach" side has paired sets of diagonal lines ornamented with small sets of ticks or spurs divided into panels by ladderlike motifs. The "back" side of the beast has a skeletal or lifeline motif of bolder design, with radiating lines in positions

suggestive of beastly legs or joint attachments. The design of the piece is clearly zoomorphic and is very similar to the beast design on an ethnographic quiver stiffener collected by Lucien M. Turner from St. Michael (fig. 103).

Both pieces appear to illustrate a many-legged mythological beast, possibly a *pal-raiyuk*. However, the Chalitmut piece is decorated in the Okvik style which flourished in Bering Strait more than two-thousand years ago. The presence of this art on a type of implement not known to occur north of Norton Sound in historic times raises interesting questions about the distribution of Okvik art and the ancient roots of Bering Sea Eskimo culture. At present the Chalitmut piece is the oldest known Eskimo artifact originating from the Yukon–Kuskokwim Delta region.

Chalitmut 36396, 28 cm

## 303. Prehistoric Art from the Lower Yukon

Several ornamented objects recently recovered from an archeological site in the Yukon Delta provide a rare glimpse of prehistoric art in wood and bone from A.D. 1000. The stone-bladed ulu has a bone handle carved into the shape of an animal's head and body, which has been engraved with a skeletonlike pattern. Chronologically and stylistically, the ulu decoration is transitional between incised and animal effigy ulu handles of the Old Bering Sea culture and those of modern Bering Sea Eskimos.

A small, partially eroded wooden plaque ornament has downward slanting eyes, ocher-painted lines, a tuft of hair inserted into a slit in the forehead, and projecting spurs. The image may depict a tattooed human face or be a miniature rendition of a face mask with ornamental projections, possibly representing fish (cf. Blodgett 1979:fig. 129). The piece is made to be mounted on a flat surface.

A bone fish or whale-shaped object, perhaps used as a hat ornament, has holes for mounting it to another surface and is decorated with punctures for fur or feather inserts. A smiling face carved into the middle of the zoomorphic figure is in a style reminiscent of Bering Sea Eskimo charm images. Its context and form suggest that it represents the animal's *inua*. These carvings may represent the early roots of traditions seen in later Bering Sea Eskimo culture and provide the closest prehistoric prototypes for their distinctive style of art.

Manokinak River Site 49–Mar–007 (Collection of U.S. Fish and Wildlife Service, on loan to Washington State University), 8.2 cm (ulu); 7 cm wide (plaque); 6.3 cm (whale/fish)

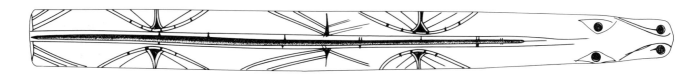

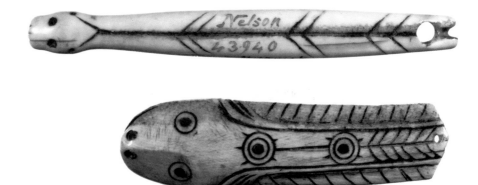

## 305. Skeletized Animals

One of the most characteristic devices of the Bering Sea Eskimo art is the use of the skeleton motif on animal carvings, seen here on a box handle and a fragment of a belt ornament. Skeletized engraving is also found on Paleo-Eskimo artifacts from Alaska and is a dominant feature of Dorset decorative art in Arctic Canada. The "bent leg" motif, common in Punuk art, in the Bering Strait region appears to have developed as a variation of earlier forms of skeleton patterns, The skeletal motif is common on artifacts collected from regions south of Norton Sound. In other regions of Alaska and Canada the skeleton pattern dropped out of use after the spread of Thule culture.

Nubviukhchugaluk 43940, 10.6 cm; Nunivak Island 43735, 8.1 cm

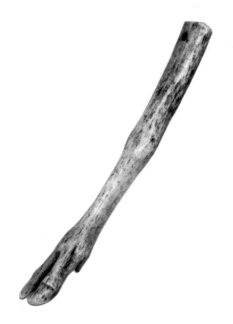

## 306. Caribou Leg Carving

Pendants of many types are used by Bering Sea Eskimos as amulets with magical or spiritual powers. This specimen was not perforated when Nelson obtained it, and it may have been carried in a pouch. Similar caribou leg carvings were made by prehistoric Dorset Eskimos in the Canadian Arctic, who also appear to have used them as amulets.

Historic-period Canadian Eskimos had religious prohibitions against using products of the land, especially materials like caribou antler and bone, for making harpoons used for hunting seals and other sea creatures. Likewise, the caribou spirits would be offended if walrus ivory were used for arrowheads to kill caribou. This spiritual division between the worlds of land and sea seems not to have been as important to Bering Sea Eskimos, who regularly made seal harpoon heads out of caribou antler, while caribou-shaped amulets were made of ivory (fig. 177).

Unalakleet 33511, 10 cm

inent animal symbolism in many kinds of material culture, and extensive use of lifeline and skeletal motifs as decorative and religious insignia. For these reasons, and because Bering Sea Eskimo society is suffused with spiritual and religious ideology, archeological research in this area can be expected to produce important new information on the early Eskimo artistic development in western Alaska.

The absence of archeological evidence—particularly that of organic remains—from the Yukon-Kuskokwim Delta is especially frustrating given the strong parallels that exist between the ethnographic culture of the Bering Sea people and prehistoric *Dorset* culture (800 B.C.–A.D.1400) of the Canadian Arctic and Greenland. For many years archeologists have been aware of similarities in stone tool technology between the two contemporaneous prehistoric cultures, Norton and Dorset, both of which are part of the broader Paleo-Eskimo cultural tradition. More detailed comparisons, however, have been hampered primarily by the lack of organic preservation in Norton sites.

It is interesting to note, therefore, the many striking parallels between the material culture and art of Bering Sea Eskimo culture—a Norton descendant—and Dorset art and symbolism. The strongest of these parallels relate to the shamanistic and mythological components of these cultures, as expressed in their carvings and methods and forms of decoration. Masking and art are important in their shamanistic religions, and myths are often portrayed through the use of carved figurines. Both cultures make frequent use of small animal carvings, decorating them with lifelines, skeletal, and sometimes windpipe patterns. Skull renditions and "trick" images utilizing the "visual pun" (Carpenter 1973) are common, as are a variety of small amulets including caribou leg and hoof forms. Spatulate-shaped "marrow spoons" are found in both cultures, as are perforated faces and small stylized human face masks engraved on bone or ivory, and widespread use of crosses, hatched and diagonal line decoration (cf. Canadian Eskimo Arts Council 1971; Meldgaard 1959).

In addition to sharing stylistic similarities, Dorset and Bering Sea Eskimo art forms include the narration or illustration of myth as an important element in their content. Both cultures utilize images of what appear to be flying or swimming shamans, employ similar forms of animal effigies for amulets and hunting charms, and appear to relate mythology and religious beliefs with similar artistic conventions. Study of the art of both cultures suggests similarities in their spiritual and religious beliefs, seen most clearly in attitudes toward shamanism, the use of amulets and hunting magic, masking, and elements of mythology. If these impressions are

correct, the similarities between these two cultures—one persisting today and the other having been extinct for at least six hundred years—may indicate deeply rooted historical connections.

These correspondences in art, and potentially in religion and mythology, have not been noted previously. This subject needs further investigation by more detailed studies of Nelson's and other Bering Sea Eskimo collections, and of regional and chronological variants of Dorset art, whose later expressions—from A.D. 500–1200—are most similar to ethnographic Alaskan forms. These studies should take Ipiutak and Old Bering Sea cultures into account and seek to understand the relationships between these ancient and modern art forms and the social and religious systems in which they functioned.

It is particularly significant that the nineteenth–century Bering Sea Eskimo culture has a type of spiritually based art and religion that differs greatly from the art and religion of other historically known Eskimo cultures in the Arctic. The only possible exception may be the Angmassalik of East Greenland, a geographically isolated people whose culture is thought to have some Dorset roots, and whose language, interestingly, has certain similarities with Yupik Eskimo, the language of the Bering Sea Eskimo. For these and other reasons, Bering Sea Eskimo culture is the most appropriate ethnographic model for interpreting archeological remains of the extinct Dorset culture and of other extinct Paleo-Eskimo cultures of the North American and Siberian Arctic.

Although separated greatly in time and space, these similarities suggest that Dorset and Bering Sea Eskimo trails may have crossed or diverged in the ancestral days of the early Alaskan Paleo-Eskimos, and that certain aspects of traditional Bering Sea Eskimo culture—especially those related to shamanism, world view, mythology, and art—may be the closest examples of that spiritually and artistically rich, ancient way of life. Although the details of this connection remain more than unclear at present, it is most reasonable, in seeking an explanation, to direct attention to the stable, conservative way of life that the Yukon–Kuskokwim Delta offers by being able to support a large interior-based population in relative isolation from the many crosscurrents and unpredictable events associated with life in other Eskimo-occupied regions of Alaska.

### 307. Polar Bear Skull and Animal Carvings

Small, lifelike animal carvings are a common subject of western Alaskan ivory carvers, just as they were for prehistoric Dorset carvers in the eastern Arctic. Both cultures took pleasure in making carvings of animals with hidden surprises, sometimes called "visual puns" (cf. Carpenter 1973). This tradition was established in the Dorset period in the eastern Arctic but diminished in the later Thule and recent period. In Alaska, these traditions continued from Old Bering Sea and Punuk times (puffin) into the recent period. The polar bear skull from Point Hope is one of several carvings from the recent period that strongly recall Dorset skull renditions and skeletized art.

Little Diomede Island 347943, 3.7 cm; Point Hope 63835, 4.0 cm; Sledge Island 44523, 5.2 cm

### 308. Marked Polar Bear

This handle for a large sealskin float is ornamented with polar bear heads whose jaws are marked on each side with crosses. Polar bear effigies found in Dorset culture sites in the eastern Canadian Arctic sometimes have the same kind of ornamentation. Cross marks are not as common in Bering Sea Eskimo art as they are in Dorset art, however. The meaning of this motif is not known and the motif may relate to a mythological theme held in common by both cultures. Sometimes crosses or circles appear to coincide with major body joints, in this case, with the mandible joint. Although Bering Sea Eskimos place marks on joints occasionally, they do not make regular use of this symbolic technique as has been suggested by Carl Schuster (1952).

St. Michael 33620, 12.6 cm

### 309. Dorset Polar Bear Amulet

An ivory polar bear head excavated from a Dorset site at Avayalik Island in northern Labrador has the same markings on its jaw seen in the Bering Sea Eskimo carving from St. Michael. The Dorset bear head also has a grooved throat canal and is perforated for use as a pendant amulet. It probably protected its wearer from his competitor, or it may have helped provide him with the bear's cunningness as a hunter.

Avayalik Island, Labrador, Canada JaDb–10:3558 (Collection, Newfoundland Museum), 3.0 cm

## 310. Dorset Plaque Mask

Dorset art from the eastern Arctic is both simple and powerful and is infused with spiritual, mythological, and shamanistic ideas. Human beings are often shown as well as modeled figurines wearing high collars rather than parka hoods of Neo-Eskimo style. Life-sized face masks, small maskettes, and face plaques must have been used in shamanistic ceremonies, for they are rarely of benevolent countenance. Judging from its rough finish, this fifteen-hundred-year-old wooden plaque mask from Avayalik Island in northern Labrador, Canada, was made and used quickly, perhaps serving for a single ceremony or purpose, before being thrown out with the rest of the house trash. Its back is gouged, possibly symbolizing spiritual violence, although the cuts may have served other purposes such as releasing the spirit from the image when its work was done. Gouge marks are common on Dorset human figurines and masks.

While many differences exist between Dorset art and the art of Bering Sea Eskimos and their Paleo-Eskimo ancestors in Alaska, these cultures' artifacts suggest that the people shared common attitudes toward the importance of shamanistic and animistic religion and expressed these ideas strongly in their art and iconography.

Avayalik Island, Labrador, Canada, JaDb–10:2998 (Collection, Newfoundland Museum) 11.5 cm high

art in transformation

# reflections in ivory

Dorothy Jean Ray

Some people, even the Eskimos themselves, call them etchings (although properly speaking this refers to an acid process), and others call them pictographs, or picture writing. By whatever name the tiny engravings on ivory and bone are known, they are unique in Eskimo culture, combining unusual technique and artistry to portray, in miniature, scenes from a vast and stark environment.

The engraving of representational subjects on hard surfaces was practiced mainly by Eskimos living north of Norton Sound in Alaska. (South of the Sound the Eskimos painted such subjects in a different style on wooden utensils and on stretched sea mammal membranes.) Although almost all Eskimos of northern Alaska engraved one or two simple pictographs on various objects, those living in the Bering Strait area between Norton Sound and Kotzebue Sound raised the engraving art to its heights of the nineteenth century, pouring dozens of ideas onto objects, especially the drill bow handle, an implement that was found in every man's tool kit.[1]

A drill bow handle is one part of a bow drill, which is used to make holes or to create a combustible level of heat. The two principal parts of the bow drill are: a wooden shaft with a metal point on one end and a mouthpiece on the other; and a bow made by stretching a thong between the ends of a slightly curved, slender handle, twelve to eighteen inches long. When in use, the thong is wrapped once around the shaft, the mouthpiece is held in the operator's mouth, and the bow is moved from side to side to revolve the shaft and drive the point into a surface.

Except in the Bering Strait area, almost all drill bow handles (called drill bows hereafter) were made of undecorated wood or bone, and as yet the origin of ivory bows with engraved pictography is not known. The drill bow seems to be an unlikely vehicle for an important art style because of its limited size. An engraved subject is rarely more than a centimeter high across the width of the bow, and even smaller when both edges are engraved. Utility was also sacrificed to art because ivory is considered to be inferior to bone for a drill bow, but the first man to use this medium (no woman was an engraver) obviously saw the possibilities of recording the adventures of a lifetime on several surfaces—on three- and four-sided handles—and of bringing his white-on-white incisions dramatically to life by applying graphite or ashes mixed with oil.

Probably no ethnic art is as varied, yet so distinctly identifiable, as the art of the Eskimos. Throughout time and space the works of art that ranged from these small pictures and equally small ivory sculptures to huge wooden masks and mortuary monuments of southwest Alaska always presented an unmistakable "Eskimoness." This unique stamp with its variations

**311. Bow Drill**

The principal components of a bow drill are a wooden shaft with a metal or nephrite drill bit, a wooden mouthpiece with a tooth grip and a shallow stone socket, and a bow made out of wood, bone, or, more commonly, ivory with pliable rawhide stretched between the bow's ends.

To drill a hole the bow's thong is wrapped around the shaft. The drill bit is positioned on the object about to be drilled. The other end of the shaft is placed in the socket of the mouthpiece which is gripped in the craftsman's mouth. When the craftsman moves the bow from side to side the shaft rotates and drives its tip into the surface of the object being drilled. The man controls the speed of the work and the depth of the hole by varying the amount of pressure being exerted by the drill point.

Bow drills are used by people living north of Norton Sound. People living to the south of this area rotate the drill shaft using a hide strap with handles on either end rather than a drill bow. The bow drill setup has the advantage of freeing one of the craftsman's hands so he can maneuver his work.

NAA–44826–B

255

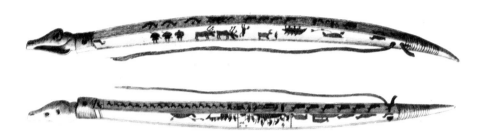

**312. Cook Drill Bow**
The first drill bow collected by a European was obtained in 1778 by James Cook's expedition and illustrated by John Pennant in 1784. The images appearing on this piece are quite similar to those on later drill bows. The origins of this form of narrative engraving are not yet known.

expressed the duality of all Alaskan Eskimo culture—a conservatism and a willingness (sometimes an eagerness) to change. The ability to adapt and incorporate ideas from outside sources so that they appear to be "Eskimo" has apparently characterized Eskimo art throughout its "known" two-thousand-year existence. The most familiar and best-documented examples are, of course, the souvenir objects of the past century—heavily decorated ivory pipes, cribbage boards, cane handles, and billikens—untraditional objects that readily became known as "Eskimo art" (Collins 1973; Smith 1980; Ray 1981). But there were also borrowings in distant times. The unusual abstract sculpture and curvilinear engraved designs of the Ipiutak period of about a thousand years ago are said to resemble certain elements of the Scytho–Siberian style of art, and ivory chains, also dating from Ipiutak and before, were undoubtedly copied from metal chains in Siberia (Larsen and Rainey 1948: 131,145).

The engraving of pictorial subjects on ivory exemplifies both this conservatism (in materials and subject matter drawn from the environment) and change (a decidedly new approach to art), yet its mysterious and unknown roots leave us debating whether this unusual art was borrowed from European sources or was indeed an Eskimo invention. Until archeological work of the 1920s and 1930s in both Alaska and Canada turned up engraved artifacts—mostly small objects like combs and wrist guards of bone with single subjects—dating from the Thule period (A. D.1200–1800), the consensus was that Alaskan pictorial art had been inspired by Russians from eastern Siberian trading posts dating back to the 1640s, or possibly through even earlier nonnative contacts in Canada. If objects found in Alaska turn out to be as old as the earliest Thule dates, the pictographic

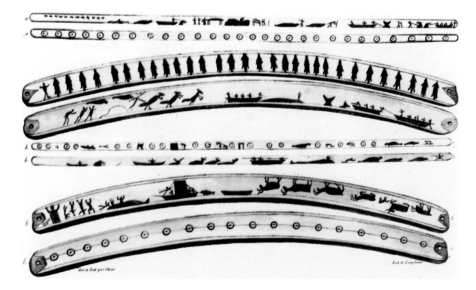

**313. Choris Drill Bows**
Ludovik Choris, an artist on Otto von Kotzebue's 1816 expedition to Alaska, illustrated his account of the voyage. Among his drawings are sketches of the four sides of two drill bows from Alaska. They resemble drill bows collected seventy years later by Nelson—depicting hunting scenes, village life, and the supernatural world. The row of pelts probably represents the red fox, a medium of exchange in the early Siberian–Alaskan fur trade at Bering Strait.

idea could not have come from a European source. There still remains, however, the puzzle of how both style and subject matter can be so similar between objects separated by a hiatus of five or six hundred years.

Almost all traditional objects with pictorial engravings made during the nineteenth century were collected by Europeans before the 1890s, most of them during the busy collecting decades of the 1870s and 1880s, just over a century after the first drill bow of historical times was obtained by James Cook's expedition of 1778.[2] This drill bow was illustrated by Thomas Pennant in *Arctic Zoology* with the caption, "The place it came from is uncertain; but doubtlessly from the part of the western coast of *America* frequented by the WALRUS" (Pennant 1792: caption to pl. VI).[3] All but one of the subjects—three Siberians in slat armor—are found on nineteenth-century bows. These men are not found on any other specimen to my knowledge, and might represent Chukchi traders or a party of real or imagined Siberian raiders to Alaska.

Next to come to public attention were two bows collected at Kotzebue Sound by Otto von Kotzebue's expedition of 1816 and illustrated by Ludovik Choris, artist of the expedition (1822: pl. IV). All subjects are found on later bows, especially such popular ones as mythological animals, men pulling seals, two men wrestling in a standing position, a sailing umiak, caribou hunted by kayak, and animal pelts.

Ten years later, in 1826 and 1827, members of Federick William Beechey's expedition collected a number of engraved objects, most of them also with the provenience of Kotzebue Sound. So far, nine drill bows, two bag handles, and two ivory snow knives have been illustrated. Several drill bows were obtained by those searching for Sir John Franklin in northwest Alaska between 1848 and 1854. One bow from Port Clarence shows European subjects for the first time, probably the crew of the *Rattlesnake,* a ship that wintered at Port Clarence in 1854. The subjects are depicted standing around and working at a forge.[4]

The largest and best-documented collection of engraved art in any museum was obtained from northwest Alaska villages for the Smithsonian Institution by Edward William Nelson when he was stationed at St. Michael as U. S. Signal Corps officer between 1877 and 1881. Lucien M. Turner, Nelson's predecessor, also collected a number of objects from the Norton Sound area between 1873 and 1877 for the Smithsonian Institution, as did John Murdoch and Patrick H. Ray from the extreme north of Alaska when they were stationed at Point Barrow as members of the International Polar Expedition between 1881 and 1883. The only other documented collection of engraved art made before the 1890s was obtained by Johan Adrian Jacobsen, employed by the Royal Berlin Museum, during 1882 and 1883 from villages on Seward Peninsula not visited by Nelson.[5]

Although most of the objects collected before the 1890s had specific provenience, the place of collection was not always the place of origin. The two most common proveniences—Kotzebue Sound and Norton Sound— are too general to mean much for a detailed study of style and subject

**314. Baselines**

Drill bow engravings are oriented to baselines, straight lines drawn along the edges of the bows. Due to the configuration of drill bows, one side may have two baselines, with the result that one set of figures is always going to be seen upside down.

Sledge Island 45022 (detail)

matter because the many villages around these bodies of water had different subsistence patterns and material culture. Furthermore, there were two separate languages on Norton Sound, Inupiak (northern Eskimo) and Yupik (southern Eskimo). The objects tagged "Norton Sound" were probably made in that huge area (perhaps at one of Nelson's other provenences located on the Sound: Cape Nome, Cape Darby, Golovnin Bay, Nuviachuk, Shaktoolik, or Unalakleet),[6] but many of the objects collected at Kotzebue Sound were undoubtedly obtained from visiting Eskimos who had come for summer fishing or the annual international trade fair.

The trade fair at Kotzebue Sound drew people for miles around after Chukchi traders had begun to bring Russian wares across the Bering Strait to trade for Alaskan furs toward the end of the eighteenth century. Some of the Beechey drill bows collected at Kotzebue Sound were no doubt made by Wales and Port Clarence people whom Beechey visited on Chamisso Island and Choris Peninsula, and the Choris bows of 1816 came from the Cape Espenberg–Goodhope Bay area on the northern shore of Seward Peninsula (Beechey 1831, 1:287–93; Kotzebue 1821, 1:203–5, 225–36).

"Kotzebue Sound" drill bows also originated elsewhere on the basis of subject matter, for both walrus and black whale hunting figure prominently on many of the bows, yet Kotzebue Sound people hunted neither the walrus nor the black whale.

Several early collectors have reported that drill bows were engraved over a period of months or years, then handed down in the family; but despite this custom, the Eskimos readily parted with them. In 1879, every man at Cape Nome must have sold Nelson a bow because he obtained fifteen from a total population of sixty, including men, women, and children. From Sledge Island, with a total population of about fifty, he obtained eight (Petroff 1884:11; Porter 1893:8). Strange though it seems, about fifty-five percent of all bows collected by Nelson are unfinished. Although the trade goods in exchange obviously more than compensated for their loss, it may be that the supposed attitudes toward the value of the bows as prized possessions were exaggerated.

During my research with the ivory carvers of Bering Strait in the 1950s, I learned that pictorial engraving had not been a popular art form since the influenza epidemic of 1918 when many of the master engravers of Nome and St. Michael died. A few men still engraved cribbage boards, paper knives, and vases with simple subjects. But, for the most part, the work was uninspired, and the carvers found sculpture more to their liking. The consensus was that engraving was "hard to do," was "too slow" (to make money), and took a lot of practice. If a carver tried it once and it "didn't turn out right," he would not likely try again.

The carvers also agreed that a person had to have "excellent tools" and "good eyesight" for the best work. Andrew Tingook, one of the few contemporary artists skilled in the delicate engraving of the nineteenth century, used a magnifying glass for his work, which, of course, the drill bow engravers did not have. There are some poor engravings in the nineteenth-century collections, to be sure, but the majority are so good that one wonders where the practice pieces went, and how much stock we can put in Lucien Turner's statement that "sharp edges of fragments of flints" were used for the incising (Hoffman 1897:775). Although Turner may have seen someone using flint at one time (just as a Nome carver told me that he had once watched a man engraving ivory with jade) I think that further examination will show that most, if not all, nineteenth-century work was done with metal points, for the Eskimos had been acquainted with metal for almost two thousand years (Ray 1977:6), and all of the gravers that Nelson collected had metal points. A comparison of the best objects collected in the early nineteenth century with later ones shows that there is little difference in engraving skill. Individual talent, not age of the artifacts, accounted for the better specimens.

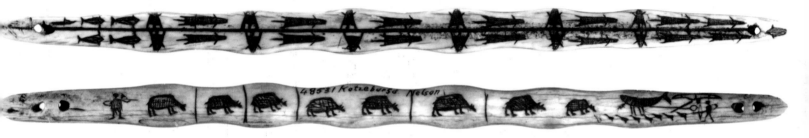

### 317. Bag Handle

This broadly scalloped ivory bag handle shows, in symmetrical design, a tally of stretched pelts and five beluga (white whales) or black whales. A man in a kayak appears to be pursuing the whales. The reverse side of the handle is carved with an unusual rendition of eight bears, all facing right. This side of the handle has been divided into six sections, each containing one or two bears. A man standing to the left of the bears appears to be shooting at them with a flintlock. To the right of the bears a man is hunting geese with a bow and blunt arrow, and a man in a kayak has thrown his harpoon, attached to a float, into a whale.

Kotzebue Sound 48531, 37.5 cm (two views)

There are two kinds of drill bows on the basis of subject matter. One is a record or tally of animals killed or boats made during a certain time period—day, season, or lifetime. The other is a visual narrative of Eskimo activities. The most usual tallies recorded foxes, otters, wolverines, beavers, ermine, bears, and whales (as entire animals or flukes)—with a single engraving probably representing one animal. Except for whales and bears, the animals were usually portrayed as pelts, sometimes with a man at one end. One side of a Choris bow of 1816 has a row of thirty red fox pelts, a pelt being the medium of exchange in the Bering Strait fur trade. Tallies were more often engraved on bag handles than on drill bows, and sometimes on only a bone or ivory slab. This practice was more common—and with cruder drawings—at Point Barrow than farther south.

The other kind of drill bow—more numerous by far than the tally bow—had all-encompassing subject matter, from bears to mosquitoes, from hunters to lovers, and from the most commonplace domestic chores to mythological scenes. Almost everything was recorded and endowed with tremendous vitality. Whales spouted; people danced, hunted, shot, wrestled, ran, fished, cooked, and loved. The caribou was portrayed in every imaginable position. Even winter dwellings were not permitted to be mere shells—smoke issued from the smoke hole, and people gestured, waved, and jumped about on the roofs.

The pictorial engravings represented specific personal experiences, but the meanings of these events are lost forever because collectors rarely obtained the stories at the time of collecting.[7] W. J. Hoffman, in *The Graphic Art of the Eskimos*, described and attempted to interpret the ac-

tivities on some of Nelson's bows with the aid of a Kodiak Eskimo–Russian man, Vladimir Naomoff, who was employed by the Alaska Commercial Company in San Francisco in the 1880s. Hoffman himself had never been to Alaska, and Naomoff's explanations cannot be accepted because he was interpreting activities and an art style of a culture quite foreign to him. In the 1950s I learned that it was too late to interpret specific events, because the Eskimos could no longer "read" the engravings—although there is no evidence that the symbols were intended for communication. One man, however, told me that his brother and sister could "guess" them. "A good guesser can guess exactly," he said.

Even if we cannot "guess exactly" the stories behind the engravings, we can gather a wealth of ethnographic information about Bering Strait life of the nineteenth century. Almost every bow has a hunting scene—caribou, whales, walrus, seals, or bears. The favorite animal, the caribou, is found on fifty-eight percent of all drill bows examined, yet this percentage, compared to an equally impressive fifty-five percent of bows with seals or fifty percent with whales, does not reveal the almost obsessive use of caribou on many of the bows.[8] A bow might have on it only one whaling scene or a tiny seal, but it would have an entire side—sometimes more—devoted to the caribou in many poses: standing, running, lying down, grazing, nursing a fawn, swimming, and migrating. The caribou might also be portrayed in a "cluster herd" (a long body with individual legs and heads). It might be shown crippled by a shot, or dead (lying upside down). The inordinate amount of space devoted to this animal cannot be explained by its economic importance, because the seal was more important, or by the challenge of the hunt, because whaling and sea mammal hunting were more dangerous. The reason for its popularity, I am sure, is that the caribou simply appealed to the artists as an exciting subject. What else could they do with a whale but let it spout, or a seal but let it lie there like a fat sausage?

Nevertheless, the artist did sometimes attempt to make a seal more interesting than it looks in real life by portraying men straining mightily, pulling home a seal or an *ugruk* (bearded seal) with a rope, or by portraying a conventionalized birdlike creature that represents the head and shoulders of a swimming seal. Both of these motifs appear on the very earliest drill bows.

### 318. Caribou and Reindeer

Caribou and reindeer are illustrated in a variety of poses and appear to be favorite subjects for drill bow art. A herd is often shown as one long body with a mass of heads and legs, while individual animals are often shown in animated poses. The scene presented here includes three animals being ridden by men. The animals are Siberian reindeer herded by Chukchi and Siberian Eskimos. Domestic caribou herds did not exist in Alaska until 1892, when they were introduced from Siberia. Prior to this Alaskan Eskimos acquired reindeer skins in trade with Siberians, and hunted wild caribou that roamed their lands.

The second face of this three-sided bow presents activities which take place in and around houses, as well as showing an umiak being launched. A Siberian-style sled, with bent-back front runners, appears between the last structure and the first boat scene. The sled and the reindeer on the first face to be described suggest that the carver was well acquainted with his Asian neighbors.

The third face portrays people and animals being tormented by mosquitos—insects that in legendary times only ate meat. Man, discovering his major food source being threatened by an abundance of voracious mosquitos, instructed that henceforth they must bite people and not eat meat.

Alaska (Collector unknown) T–1077, 34.5 cm (three views)

### 319. Mundane Activities

Few aspects of daily life have escaped being figured on drill bows. In this detail of a finely engraved drill bow from Sledge Island, two figures are fishing through the ice. To the right of them men are hauling home seals. The leading figure has a line passing around his shoulders, suggesting that he is hauling with a pack line tied around his chest.

Sledge Island 45016 (detail)

The whale was shown either in hunting scenes or as a single subject (a whole whale or flukes). Some of the whales on drill bows collected at Cape Darby and Norton Sound, where there was no black whale hunting, are probably beluga (white whales), but several bows also have the classic scene of umiak and spouting black whale. One side of a Cape Darby bow (fig. 316) depicts an unusual scene of an entire village hauling and cutting up a drifted whale—a tremendous bonanza for people who did not normally hunt the black whale.

The walrus, which supplied ivory for most of the engraved art, is represented on about forty-five percent of the bows, but is shown in active hunting on only one-third of them. This animal, which is more animated than the whale or the seal, is depicted in a number of characteristic poses: swimming (often represented only by head and shoulders), resting on its mother's back, and lying on an ice floe being attacked by men in umiaks and kayaks. Bears (polar bears and land bears) are found on only eight of the seventy-one bows collected by Nelson. Only two show active hunting with a spear or bow and arrow, reflecting either the rarity of this dangerous undertaking or a skewing of the sample. Nelson obtained few bows from the leading polar bear hunting villages, including King Island, which strangely enough is not represented by a single bow in the Smithsonian Institution collection, or any other collection prior to 1890.

### 320. Hunting the Animals

Bering Strait people hunt caribou on land and herd them into the water where they dispatch the caribou from kayaks. The men also are excellent walrus and whale hunters. A carver has presented all of these activities on a single face of a four-sided drill bow. Moving from left to right: a man sneaks up on a caribou from behind a bush; caribou are pursued through the water; men and walrus, which are in the water and on an ice pan, clash; and umiak crews, with harpoons poised to strike, approach whales and walrus. At the extreme left are figured a tent and drying rack, a dog-drawn sled, and a domed structure housing two people, with two human figures attached to its exterior. The significance of the last image is not known. The incised scenes are rubbed with red pigment making this bow a rather unusual specimen.

Cape Prince of Wales 43360, 44 cm

Although the hunting scenes and animals are artistic gems, the people in their everyday and festival activities provide the greatest variety and spice. At every get-together the Eskimos indulged in dancing and athletic contests, shown most often on the bows as taking place outdoors at a summer camp. Occasionally, winter festival activities, which took place indoors, are presented in a cross-section view of a dwelling or a *kazgi* (*qasgiq*), the ceremonial house. Some of the agile movements of the athletes cannot be identified, but a pair of men wrestling on their feet is recognizable on bows as early as 1816. This sport must have been a very popular form of competition during the nineteenth century because it is found on bows from all areas and was one of the subjects transferred onto engraved souvenir pipes and tusks, which came into being almost simultaneously with the demise of drill bow engraving.

Another feat—and a very difficult one—is the still-popular "Eskimo high kick" (fig. 321). The purpose of the game is to see how high off the ground a person can touch a suspended ball with both feet. One of the figures is unusual in that the object held in the hand of a man on the opposite edge serves as the ball that the kicker has touched. The "tail" that this athlete wears is just that: a wolf or fox tail tied to the back of his belt—the height of fashion for all smartly dressed young men on Seward Peninsula as late as the 1890s. The scenes probably represent one of the winter festivals when an entire village traveled to a host village. Here are shown the winter village, the visitors who have stopped their dogteams to observe the proper protocol before meeting their hosts, and the happy participants with gifts in their hands. The activities in the middle of the bow are not taking place as the guests arrive, but represent events that took place later in the *kazgi*. 261

Human bodies were made with the strictest economy of movement of the graving tool, as an oval, square, triangle, or merely a line, but the arms and the legs and the inclination of the body were so deftly engineered that one is not often left in doubt as to what is transpiring. Because clothing or sexual characteristics are rarely indicated, men and women are usually recognized by their actions. An exception is a male figure with exaggerated genitalia, in various postures, especially holding a bow and arrow—a subject also found on prehistoric objects. Whenever special identification was needed, the artist added distinguishing characteristics. For example, a white man was provided with a line across his head for a hat, which the Eskimos did not wear, and if standing, his legs were drawn slightly apart and his arms placed on his hips—the typical Yankee! (The English sailors on the 1854 bow, already mentioned, were not identified in this way; they appear to be hatless, and of the four standing men, only two have arms akimbo.)

Dancers, sometimes shamans or even mythological beings, are usually identified by headgear or a facial protuberance—an eagle, a raven, a caribou, and, on some early bows, whale flukes. Shaggy arms on dancers represent dancing gauntlets adorned with dozens of puffin beaks that became percussion instruments during the dance.

Shamanistic performances and mythological beings are as difficult to explain or identify as are the personal adventures. In the old days, it was believed that a multitude of mythological creatures inhabited Eskimo terrain, each village visualizing them differently. The *tirisuk*, the *kokogiak*, the giant who could hold a whale aloft in each hand, and the half-caribou–half-man were among the creatures put on drill bows. The *tirisuk* and the *kokogiak* were greatly feared, but the other two were benign beings regarded with awe. In one area of Seward Peninsula, the *tirisuk*, six to twelve feet long, looked like a big cumbersome beast with two scissorlike teeth that could cut a man in half (fig. 325 is possibly a rendition of this being). But elsewhere the *tirisuk* looked like a "caterpillar-dragon," which plucked umiaks out of the water with its long teeth or "feelers." The *kokogiak* was as large as a polar bear, but propelled itself over the ice on its back

**321. Winter Festival**

This delicately carved drill bow represents a winter festival, when one village plays host to another. The guests have arrived in their sleds. Some people have already unhitched their dogs and are contentedly smoking their pipes. Groups of men, wearing fashionable wolf tails, are dancing and playing "high kick," a game in which a person tries to touch a suspended ball with both his feet. Back in the village people are tending their caches and men and dogs are standing on house roofs. People are also on top of the *qasgiq*, which appears as the largest building in the scene. Charms, shaped like a bird and a caribou, cap poles that have been erected next to this structure.

Alaska (L.M. Turner Collection) 24541, 32 cm

**322. Umiak Travel**

Travel by umiak is the subject of this drill bow engraving. Four umiaks are pictured sailing between two villages. The checkered pattern on the umiaks results from their skin covers being pieced together from walrus hides that have been split in half to thin them. The light panels show the split inner surface, and the dark, the natural brown of the outer surface of the skin.

Sledge Island 45107 (detail)

**323. Shamanistic Performances**

Shamans have fantastic powers, flying and swimming to distant places or, as in this case, sending a spirit helper to other lands. Shamans are also key figures in ceremonies, where they perform dances, seeming to become the animals featured on masks they wear. Lively, solemn, and tense moods are created by the beating of the ever-present drums.

Kotzebue Sound 48522 (detail)

## 324. Kokogiak

*Kokogiak* is an eight- or ten-legged being the size of a polar bear. It travels over the ice on its back, moving itself along with its elbows. When the beast wants to eat, it waves its legs in the air and cries *"ko-ko-ko"* in order to look and sound like hunters in distress. The creature eats those who venture close when they try to come to its aid.

Alaska T–1076 (detail)

## 325. Tirisuk

Animals featured in myths are also presented on drill bows. Here, a creature has grasped a man in its mouth. Perhaps this is the greatly feared *tirisuk*, a beast that can cut a man in half with its two scissorlike teeth, and is known to pluck umiaks out of the water.

Norton Sound 33187 (detail)

with its eight or ten elbows. When hungry, it waved its legs to look like hunters in distress, crying *ko-ko-ko* to lure people to the rescue (fig. 324).

Northwest Alaska folklore is full of stories of surprise attacks by Indians, Siberians, and even other Eskimos. These stories, which are treated as both fact and myth by anthropologists, do not appear on a single drill bow. Likewise, there are few episodes of personal physical struggles (though Johan Adrian Jacobsen described a rare scene on a drill bow from Kauwerak—about 45 miles east of Teller—as a man killing his unfaithful wife's seducer). The artists, it seems, preferred to memorialize the rigors and excitement of hunting and festivals rather than the more painful realities of life.

More than one-fifth of the drill bows collected by Nelson have nonnative subjects—ships, people, and buildings. The first documented bow with European subjects is the one previously discussed that was obtained at Port Clarence in 1854. None of the Beechey bows have European motifs, not even ships, which are the most prominent nonnative subjects on Nelson's bows, yet at least ten European vessels had preceded Beechey to northwest Alaska by 1826.[9] The drill bow artists portrayed ships in faithful detail—showing their rigging, trading with Eskimos in their umiaks, discharging sailors in tenders, engaging in whaling, and, in one instance, hunting walrus.

Before 1880 the number of nonnative structures north of the Russian fort at St. Michael could be counted on one hand, so it is not surprising that only four bows collected by Nelson depict buildings, all but one in rather sketchy outline. But that one (fig. 326), collected at Kotzebue Sound, is unusual in that it shows a group of buildings similar to those illustrated on two bows collected by Jacobsen from Kauwerak in 1882. This cluster of buildings undoubtedly represents "Libbysville," a little village built on the northern spit between Port Clarence and Grantley Harbor by the Western Union Telegraph Expedition and named after Daniel B. Libby, leader of the northern contingent. (Jacobsen's bows are illustrated in *Amerika's Nordwest-Küste*, pls. IX–16, X–7.)

The Western Union Telegraph Expedition from 1865 to 1867 was attempting to connect Europe with the United States by telegraph via a route through British Columbia, Alaska, and Siberia. At St. Michael and Unalakleet, two of its three Alaskan headquarters, the men lived mainly in Russian-American Company buildings, but at Port Clarence, where the Russians were not situated, they constructed their own buildings—these they named Tower Cottage, Main Building, Smithsonian "Institute," and the West End Hotel, a hostelry for visiting Eskimos (Ray 1975:164–68). A more elegant style of engraving on a bow and a little ivory slab (figs. 328, 329) appear to be episodes of this Expedition at either St. Michael or Unalakleet, if the vessel on the bow proves to be one of the Expedition's supply ships.[10] These two objects are of special interest because they were apparently engraved by the same person, but were collected at different places (St. Michael and Golovnin Bay) and at different times (between 1873 and 1881).

Changes in Eskimo life that were created by the white man are also brought out in ways more subtle than the bold engravings of ships or

buildings. For example, the figures of Eskimo men smoking pipes reveal more than just a pleasant pastime; they reveal possession of a rare and highly sought-after commodity that became an important agent of change. Tobacco, brought by native traders from Siberia to Alaska sometime in the eighteenth century before the first white explorer had arrived, equaled, if not surpassed, metal knives as the preferred trade item, and was used by the Eskimos to achieve a reaction resembling intoxication. Until the introduction of liquor after the 1850s, the pipe smoker induced a short-lived but debilitating "drunk" by swallowing the smoke from a tiny bowl of tobacco. The three men in figure 321 are smoking their pipes in peaceful reflection, as do all such individuals of the 1880s. But a bow collected by Frederick William Beechey at Kotzebue Sound has an astonishing scene of four men, each in a progressive state of euphoria from smoking—two are sitting with head on knees, and a third is reeling backward (Bockstoce 1977: fig. 63A). Nelson and Jacobsen collected seven bows with people smoking, all from a limited area on southern Seward Peninsula—Kauwerak, Cape Darby, and "Norton Sound"—one of which (Cape Darby, USNM 48116) has many motifs in common with the Beechey bow.

Firearms, which Nelson said had already driven caribou away from Norton Sound by 1879, are found on twenty-one percent of the drill bows, but men using bows and arrows are on only fourteen percent. Unfortunately, age of objects cannot be ascertained by the absence or presence of these implements because guns reached villages of northwest Alaska at different times, and were used simultaneously with bows and arrows. Several bows from Norton Sound, Cape Nome, and Sledge Island have both guns and bows and arrows, usually in connection with caribou hunting scenes.

### 326. Western Union Telegraph Expedition Headquarters

The buildings illustrated on one side of this drill bow were probably modeled after the 1866–67 Western Union Telegraph Expedition headquarters, "Libbysville," at Port Clarence. In addition to the building cluster the artist engraved images of European schooners seen from head on and side views. Johan Adrian Jacobsen, an ethnographer who traveled in Alaska in 1882, collected two drill bows bearing similar scenes.

Kotzebue Sound 48519 (detail)

### 327. European Man and Woman

An unfinished drill bow from Cape Nome illustrates a nonnative man and woman. This presentation of a nonnative woman—or at least a woman dressed in European clothes—is the only such depiction seen on a pre-1879 drill bow. The engraving may represent the wife of a whaling captain or of a St. Michael trader. European or American men are shown wearing brimmed hats and standing with their hands on their hips.

Cape Nome 45332 (detail)

The engraved art of the drill bows is representational and literal, but not realistic. Photographic realism was not associated with pictorial art until a man named Happy Jack (Angokwazhuk) incised portraits and scenes from printed illustrations on cribbage boards, gavels, and tusks from the 1890s until his death in 1918. The early artist had a knack of depicting realistic *impression* through essential lines—an understated minimum for maximum effect—and human figures go through their paces without the slightest attempt at realistic faces or apparel. But the artist did try to be literal, and through his literalness, probably thought he was realistic, as did the Eskimo artist of the 1950s. For example, the engraver depicted alternate white and black panels on the sides of umiaks, showing three, four, or five to indicate the umiak's size. The color of these panels represented the inside and outside of the split walrus hides that made up the boat's skin covering. The engraver had the crew performing specific duties, and he sometimes hung a charm on the bow of the boat. But, for artistic effect,

### 328. European Camp

The St. Michael or Unalakleet 1865–67 camp of the Western Union Telegraph Expedition may be the subject of this beautiful engraving. In addition to portraying details of Western clothes, boats, tents, and mannerisms, the engraver placed the scene alongside a more familiar traditional Eskimo camp, creating a contrast.

The other two faces of this remarkable drill bow illustrate dancing and wrestling scenes, a whale hunting tally, and butchering, ice hole hunting, and whaling activities.

Golovnin Bay 176172, 34.5 cm

### 329. Engraved Plaque

This small slab of ivory, collected by Lucien M. Turner between 1873 and 1877, apparently was engraved by the same man who illustrated the Golovnin Bay drill bow (fig. 328) collected by Nelson between 1877 and 1881. Europeans, probably members of the Telegraph Expedition, are involved in various activities. A man is in a European-style tent leaning over a trunk, another man is carrying a bucket, and a third individual is rolling a barrel toward a boat. Alongside the Europeans, Eskimos are cooking and drying fish in front of their northern-style tent. On the same plaque face, but oriented to a different baseline, a dog-drawn sled is approaching a village.

Scenes have been drawn along two baselines on the reverse side of the plaque as well. Along one baseline men are performing in a *qasgiq* while two people look on through the smoke hole and three men collect and chop wood outdoors. Along the second baseline a whale hunt is in progress.

St. Michael (L.M. Turner Collection) 129287, 11 cm (two views)

he departed even from the literal by putting only four or five rowers in the umiak instead of the usual complement of nine or ten, and by having them row on only one side—away from the viewer—so as not to detract from the umiak design. His dogteams, too, were apparently scaled down to only one or two dogs, although five or six often made up a team at mid-nineteenth century.

If the artist wanted to show that the permanent dwelling was occupied, or perhaps to indicate that it was wintertime, smoke issues from the smoke hole in the roof. The smoke looks like a big feather, a motif that was also used for campfire smoke, for whale spouts, and for trees, especially one that was invariably placed between a hunter and a caribou. The engraver also conventionalized the animals on his tallies, compressing them into symbols like the stretched pelts or the seals that look like swimming birds.

### 330. Souvenir Pipe

Eskimo engravers quickly realized that Europeans were eager to own engraved ivories. Around Bering Strait and to the north, an ivory carving industry developed, and many of the engraved scenes found on bag handles and drill bows were transferred onto non-functional ivory pipes similar to this one from St. Lawrence Island. Unlike drill bows, the figures on this pipe are oriented to a single baseline, but traditional hunting, ceremonial, and architectural engravings decorate the piece.

St. Lawrence Island (R.D. Moore Collection) 280599, 38 cm

These engravings constitute one of the most unusual legacies of ethnography left by a nonliterate people. They were unique in Eskimo culture, too, because they were not made for religious or ceremonial purposes, except possibly on a few pieces of sculpture—arrowshaft straighteners or harpoon foreshafts—used directly in hunting. That is why the drill bow style of engraving could be shifted with impunity, and intact—except for size—onto the souvenir objects made only for sale by some of the drill bow artists themselves. The drill bow engravings, with faint roots in prehistory, thus forged a bold and positive link, both artistically and economically, with the future.

**331. Ivory Earring**

This is an engraving on a tiny ivory earring engraved in Nome by Andrew Tingook of Shishmaref in 1955. Tingook was one of the few contemporary artists whose engravings compared favorably with those of artists of the nineteenth century. Unlike them, however, he used a magnifying glass while incising.

Andrew Tingook (b. 1898, Shishmaref, Alaska) (Collection of D.J. Ray), 1.8 cm

### Notes

1. I inspected more than 170 engraved objects, all collected before 1890, at the Smithsonian Institution for this article. My conclusions, however, are based not only on these objects but many others that I have seen in other museums, photographs, and drawings. The Smithsonian Institution objects are as follows: 71 drill bows with provenience collected by E. W. Nelson between 1877 and 1881; 8 drill bows from St. Michael, and 14 drill bows without provenience collected by Lucien M. Turner between 1873 and 1877; 22 bag handles and bodkins with provenience collected by Nelson; 40 miscellaneous objects, not including ivory pipes, all with provenience, collected by Turner, Nelson, John Murdoch, and Patrick H. Ray; and more than 15 miscellaneous objects without provenience, collected by various persons. Not included in this count are a number of drill bows without ornamentation, or only with geometric designs. The 71 drill bows may not be a firm number because several that are called bows might have been used as bag handles, and some of the bag handles could be drill bows. It is sometimes difficult to differentiate them, and even Nelson and W. J. Hoffman interchanged identification of several of these objects in their respective books.

2. After 1890 the Eskimos engraved a few drill bows, and collectors found a few of the older bows to buy here and there. One of the most ambitious collectors of the 1890s, Miner W. Bruce obtained only 3 engraved objects among 866 artifacts from Kotzebue Sound and only 6 engraved objects (5 of them souvenir pipes) among 425 artifacts from Port Clarence, all of which are now in the Field Museum of Natural History, Chicago. There is not one drill bow with pictorial engraving (VanStone 1976; 1980).

3. The Cook drill bow has been reproduced in a more accessible publication by Jonathan King (1981:pl. 6). James Cook, who seemed to take little interest in the artifacts of northern Alaska, did not mention engraved art in his report, but the surgeon of the expedition, Thomas Samwell, said that on 10 August 1778, "We bought some curious Articles of [the inhabitants of Saint Lawrence Bay, Siberia, almost directly west of Cape Prince of Wales], among which were small pieces of Ivory with Images of Dogs & rein Deer drawing Sledges & very ingeniously executed" (Beaglehole 1967, 3:1133). The "small pieces" were probably imports from Alaska because Vladimir Bogoras, the foremost ethnographer of the Chukchi, wrote in 1907 that "etchings are scarce in Asia, and those that I had an opportunity to observe are comparatively poor specimens of art" (Bogoras 1907:295). Later, the Chukchi developed a spectacular souvenir art of engraving on tusks under the auspices of the Soviet art councils.

4. Engraved artifacts collected by Beechey and Edward Belcher are illustrated and discussed in Bockstoce 1977:79–87, and those collected by George Peard, also of the Beechey expedition, are illustrated in Pearce 1975:36–37, 43. The bow collected by Mr. Spark of the *Rattlesnake* crew is illustrated in D. Ray 1977:fig. 238.

5. Nelson's collection is illustrated and discussed in Hoffman 1897 and Nelson 1899. Many items of Murdoch and Ray's collection are noted in Murdoch 1892, and all are listed in P. H. Ray 1885. Jacobsen's thirty-four engraved objects are illustrated, front and back, with extensive captions, in plates VI–X in *Amerika's Nordwest-Küste*. Illustrations of other drill bows collected after the 1850s and before the 1890s are found in Fagg 1972; *The Far North* 1973; Mason 1927; and Ray 1969 and 1977.

**332. Portrait of William Henry Milleman**

By the early twentieth century Eskimo artisans were producing engraved ivories for Europeans. This portrait is part of an ivory gavel made and engraved by Happy Jack, and given to William Henry Milleman whose portrait Happy Jack engraved on one face of the piece. In 1903 Milleman was manager of the Standard Oil Company in Nome.

Happy Jack (Diomede Island, Alaska) (Carrie M. McLain Memorial Museum, Nome), 5.5 cm (height of face)

6. Nelson's provenience of "Cape Nome" is the village of Ayasayuk; "Golovnin Bay" could be either the village of Atnuk or Chinik (now Golovin); Cape Darby is probably the village of Atnuk, which is on Norton Sound, only a few miles from Golovnin Bay.

7. Jacobsen supplied explanations for several scenes in the captions to the illustrations in *Amerika's Nordwest-Küste*. In 1905 "at the mouth of the Yukon River," G. B. Gordon purchased a drill bow from a man who identified several mythological animals for him, although he said that it was eleven generations old. The seller's ancestor did not make the bow, which is obviously a traded piece because it is in the style of northern Norton Sound. The bow is now in the University Museum, Philadelphia (NA 461), but is given the provenience of Cape Prince of Wales in an article about Eskimo pictorial art in the museum by J. Alden Mason (Gordon 1917:232–33, 245–47; Mason 1927:278, 281).

8. Whale hunting is engraved on four of the thirty-odd Thule objects uncovered so far, but these are from Canada, not Alaska. The caribou was an equal favorite of both the Alaskan and Canadian Thule artists, but there are no walrus or seals on Thule pieces.

9. These expeditions are those of James Cook and Charles Clerke in the *Discovery* and the *Resolution*, as far north as Icy Cape in 1778; Joseph Billings in the *Glory of Russia*, which sailed to the Nome area from Siberia, 1791; Otto von Kotzebue in the *Rurik*, as far north as Kotzebue Sound, 1816; Frederick William Beechey in the *Blossom*, as far north as Point Barrow, 1826 and 1827; Gleb S. Shishmarev and Mikhail N. Vasiliev in the *Discovery* and the *Good Intent*, as far north as Icy Cape in 1821, and as far north as Cape Mulgrave in 1822; and Vasilii S. Khromchenko in the *Golovin* to Golovnin Bay in 1821 and 1822. In 1819 an unnamed trading vessel under the command of a Captain Gray was reported at Bering Strait, and in 1820 the *Pedler*, a brig owned by John Jacob Astor, traded at Kotzebue Sound. It is possible there were even more trading vessels there before 1826 (Ray 1975).

10. When I first saw the bow in 1967, I thought that it depicted the Omilak miners, a group of men who had begun a lead mining enterprise in 1881 at Golovnin Bay, where this object supposedly was collected. The vessel does not fit any of the Western Union Telegraph Expedition's boats, yet the little slab, with its identical style of engraving and subject matter, was collected before the Omilak venture. The brimmed hats and stance do not necessarily indicate military men, and the first military district was not organized in this area until 1897 at St. Michael.

I wish to thank John Bockstoce, Ernest S. Burch, Jr., and Melvin Olanna for their helpful conversations concerning these pieces and other historical and ethnographical mysteries on the drill bows. I am grateful, also, to Jonathan C. H. King and Yvonne Neverson of the British Museum for supplying copies of the Jacobsen illustrations.

### 333. Nunivak Island Cribbage Board

With increased frequency Alaskan Eskimos and American and European travelers and traders came into contact with one another in the late nineteenth and early twentieth century. Eskimo carvers began to manufacture pieces for the outside market, and cribbage boards were among the items popular at the time. Made from a single piece of tusk, cribbage boards might have intricate scenes etched onto them, or be interlaced with sculpted animals.

Nunivak Island 396171, 49 cm

# roots in the past

Saradell Ard Frederick

Today's Eskimo is the product of many influences—the deeply rooted traditions of his own culture, the new techniques and aesthetic standards of Western civilization, and the pressures of the twentieth century to develop a highly personal form of self-expression. Eskimo art, therefore, ranges from repetition of historic styles to highly creative work in new media. Some artists are old and self-taught; others are young and formally schooled.

## Deeply Rooted Traditions

Living in one of the most difficult climates in the world, with limited raw materials available, the Eskimos have become famous for their ingenious use of materials and practical adaptations to the environment. A strong belief in animism with the attendant need to placate the spirits was the basis for festivals and ceremonies which required the production of elaborate masks and dance accessories (Nelson 1899:393–95; Ray 1967:9–10; Blodgett 1979:47–50). These beliefs even dictated decoration of hunting tools and weapons because it was thought animals preferred to be killed with a beautiful weapon. Therefore, Eskimos became skilled craftsmen capable of transforming bone, ivory, driftwood, and skins into richly ornamented utensils and ceremonial objects. Cunning amulets to ward off evil spirits and ritual objects for the shaman's use (Blodgett 1979:203) exhibit not only technical skill but a high level of creativity.

While the incentive for prehistoric decoration seems to have had a spiritual connotation, in historic times the motivation quickly changed to an economic one as soon as there were possibilities for trade. The skills remained but the need for quantity often resulted in less quality.

The Eskimo culture, which has successfully adapted to change for thousands of years, has been subjected to massive outside influences in the last two centuries. Although there are remote villages still comparatively untouched, Western civilization has influenced the lives of most Eskimos in Alaska.

## Effects of Western Civilization

By 1914 every village of more than one hundred inhabitants had a school and a white schoolteacher (Hughes 1965:29). World War II brought increased contact, military service, and a change from a fishing and hunting economy to a cash economy (Hughes 1965:29). Explorers, missionaries, sailors, teachers, gold miners, and ubiquitous tourists have all influenced Eskimos and their art. The ivory carver has made what the visitors will buy. Thousands of small ivory figurines are still carved by the older men—and a few younger ones—for the tourist trade. Mass production of stereo-

**334. Loon**

Masks such as this have evolved from nineteenth-century prototypes. In earlier times each appendage carried a symbolic meaning. The food in the mouth of an animal may have symbolized a wish for abundant game or careful attention to and feeding of an animal's *inua* by a hunter; the concentric hoops and grooves may have represented the stars and the heavens; and the smaller image of a semihuman face or other animal may have represented the *inua* of the mask.

Edward Kiokan has included all these ingredients in a mask never intended to be worn but rather to be hung on a wall. His choice of appendages reflects the swimming and flying capabilities of the loon as well as its source of food.

Edward Kiokan (Nunivak Island, Alaska). *Loon Mask*. Wood and pigment (Collection, Alaska State Museum, Juneau, II A 1457), 72 cm long

269

**335. Dance**

Kivetoruk Moses is Alaska's equivalent to Grandma Moses for he is a genuine primitive who takes great pains with minor details—often microscopic ones such as single guard hairs in a piece of fur. Most of his subjects are based on real life happenings that he remembers. Here he records a special performance for the entertainment of white visitors from the sailing vessel in the background.

The drums, gloves, and wolf mask featured in his drawing have their counterparts in the Nelson Collection. The juxtaposition of traditional and European activities and people, and the components of the scene—the dance, the tent, a European wearing a top hat with a hand on his hip, and the schooner—were subjects incised onto drill bows by late-nineteenth-century artists. Moses works in a new medium and presents a full three-dimensional perspective.

Kivetoruk Moses (b. 1901, near Cape Espenberg, Alaska). *The Wolf Dance*, 1970. Drawing, india ink, watercolor, and photographic pencils on poster board (Collection, United States Department of the Interior, Indian Arts and Crafts Board, Washington, D.C.), 25.4 cm × 40.6 cm

typed seals, walrus, bears, and humans has provided a livelihood for the older generation. Several thriving firms produce commercial imitations of "genuine Eskimo carvings" with an electrical planographic device that even inscribes an Eskimo signature. Some "Eskimo" items in curio shops even have a stamp on the bottom that says "Made in Japan." In addition, nonnative sculptors fashion items similar enough to fool naive buyers. Such inartistic products do not deserve to be classified as art. Thus, critics have coined distinguishing phrases such as "airport art," "market art," or "souvenir art."

Efforts to offset this deplorable situation have included workshops, training courses, conferences, and competitions for Eskimo craftsmen. Good design, quality workmanship, and new techniques and materials have been emphasized. However, programs have been irregular; funds have been limited; results have been uneven. The projects sponsored by the Indian Arts and Crafts Board, the University of Alaska Extension Center for Arts and Crafts, and the Visual Arts Center of Alaska have been more successful than others, but there has been no breakthrough comparable to the renaissance in Canadian Eskimo sculpture or in their flood of prints of the last three decades.

**336. Shaman and Devil**

This shaman, whom Kivetoruk Moses remembers from his youth, has been the subject of a number of Moses's drawings. The shaman is wearing labrets and a traditional hairstyle. Great care has been taken to describe the shaman's personal possessions, which include a Devil mask, a bent-wood box with ivory inlays, a bow and a quiver full of arrows, a lance, a lamp, a pipe, and of course a drum. The Devil is a concept introduced by Christian missionaries, and has replaced Bering Sea spirits and mythological creatures as a personality with whom the shaman must deal.

Kivetoruk Moses (b. 1901, near Cape Espenberg, Alaska). *Shaman Exorcising Devil*, 1963–65. Drawing, india ink, colored pencil, and watercolor on paper (Collection, Anchorage Historical and Fine Arts Museum, Mrs. Edith R. Bullock Collection), 19 cm × 42 cm

**337. Caribou**

Bernard Katexac's work reflects his formal training at the University of Alaska, Fairbanks, where he received an Associate of Arts degree in 1967. The composition of the work and the engraving technique employed indicate Western influences. The caribou herd has been a favorite topic for nineteenth- and twentieth-century Alaskan artists, and many of the caribou portrayed here are similar to those engraved on late–nineteenth-century drill bows.

Bernard Katexac (b. 1922, King Island, Alaska). *Tutut (caribou)*, 1964. Engraving (Collection, Dorothy Jean Ray), 44.6 cm × 29.8 cm

**338. Four Seasons**

Like the nineteenth-century ivory engravers, Bernard Katexac has produced an extended description of the many activities of Eskimo life. Whereas the nineteenth-century engravers used different baselines or faces for their various scenes, Katexac uses different canvases. He also employs color and perspective extensively.

Bernard Katexac (b. 1922, King Island, Alaska). *Seasons of the Arctic*, 1978. Woodcuts (Collection, Anchorage Historical and Fine Arts Museum, 78.6.1–4), 62.86 cm × 52.7 cm

## Emergence of Individual Artists

Fortunately, through efforts of the Alaska projects a small group of talented artists has emerged. Most of the younger ones, through scholarships and grants, have received professional training in art. Higher education and travel have exposed these Eskimos to international art movements and styles of the twentieth century. Their creative work has been included in exhibitions nationwide; at least one artist, Ronald Senungetuk, has achieved international recognition. Several artists have expressed resentment at being categorized as "Eskimo" artists. Rather, they maintain they are artists who happen to be Eskimos and prefer to have their work judged by international standards of artistic worth.

## Sculpture

A few well-trained and talented artists are producing original sculpture ranging from minute, realistic ivory figures to sizable stone abstractions. They have experimented with a variety of imported materials—marble, alabaster, African wonderstone, hardwoods, metal, glass, and even "found objects." Forms may be deliberately rough and archaic or purposely stream-

### 339. New Resources

This print is one of the few examples of protest art produced by an Eskimo artist. Joseph Senungetuk contrasts a small image of the old way of life with the current image of the ever-present oil derrick shown towering over and penetrating into the land.

Joseph Senungetuk (b. 1940, Wales, Alaska). *Emergence of Resource*, 1969. Woodblock (Courtesy of Indian Historian Press, San Francisco, Collection, Anchorage Historical and Fine Arts Museum), 59 cm × 29.2 cm

### 340. Sea Inhabitants

Joseph Senungetuk's *The Silent Sea* contains images indicating his familiarity with nineteenth-century Bering Sea Eskimo visual symbolism. Animals that inhabit the sea are shown with lifelines and skeletons defined, and the standing man has legs which terminate in seal flippers. Senungetuk's choice of black and red colors may also have been influenced by an examination of nineteenth-century painted trays and ladles.

Joseph Senungetuk (b. 1940, Wales, Alaska). *The Silent Sea*, 1967. Woodblock (Private Collection), 29.2 cm × 38.1 cm

### 341. Old and New

Joseph Senungetuk has juxtaposed in this print traditional and modern life scenes that he has experienced during his lifetime. A shaman sits cross-legged playing a drum, with deathlike images, possibly shades, behind him. A seal shown in skeletal view swims up one side of the print. A young man holds a small ivory carving of a seal in one hand and a toggling harpoon head and foreshaft in the other, while he looks toward a jet soaring above the skyline of San Francisco.

Joseph Senungetuk (b. 1940, Wales, Alaska). *Whither Goest Thou, Oh Shaman!*, 1970. Lithograph (Collection, United States Department of the Interior, Indian Arts and Crafts Board, Washington, D.C.), 36.2 cm × 36.2 cm

### 342. Portrait

This print speaks eloquently of the power of Eskimo traditions, the changing life pattern, the political and economic pressures of today, and the current need on the part of all Eskimos for self-identity and recognition. The subject matter dealt with in this piece, and the technique by which it was produced make this color lithograph one of the most important Eskimo prints of the twentieth century.

Joseph Senungetuk (b. 1940, Wales, Alaska). *Self Portrait*, 1970. Color lithograph (Courtesy Indian Historian Press, San Francisco, Collection, Anchorage Historical and Fine Arts Museum), 48.18 cm × 35.56 cm lined and sophisticated. Subject matter still focuses on hunting, fishing, and—sometimes—nostalgic scenes of Eskimo dances or home life.

The spectacular masks of the nineteenth century have become a source of inspiration for sculpture of the last decade. Though devoid of their previous magical or spiritual connotation, these masks provide a vast repertory of highly dramatic and aesthetic compositions. Several of the strongest contemporary sculptures are derived from historical masks.

Two recent workshops at the University of Alaska, Fairbanks campus, have been designed to encourage a revival in mask making. Masks carved included reinterpretations of old themes and highly personal, autobiographic themes revealing a great amount of imagination. These creations—and the best of contemporary sculpture—demonstrate a high level of technical skill which results from both training and the use of modern tools.

A multiplicity of sculptural forms, some reflecting international artistic styles, characterizes the work of the leading Eskimo artists today. Aesthetically pleasing and highly individualistic, these creations represent the unique blending of cultures.

## Drawings and Prints

The graphic arts of the Alaskan Eskimos have a long history. In his archeological research Henry B. Collins has identified what he considers the beginnings of pictographic scenes on objects excavated at Cape Prince of Wales and dated A.D. 600 to 800 (Collins 1975:59–61). Collins has identified small deviations from the long-established geometric border designs incised on earlier prehistoric ivory implements. These deliberate changes produced simple "stick figure" humans and animals. Somewhat more elaborate scenes have been excavated in Alaska by J. Louis Giddings and Douglas Anderson of Brown University; the artifacts on which these scenes are incised have been radiocarbon-dated at A.D. 1000 and 1200 (Giddings 1967:90–92; Anderson, personal communication, 1969). More advanced engraved scenes decorated the first bow drills collected by a European, Otto von Kotzebue, in 1816 (Choris 1822:pl. IV). These scattered findings indicate an indigenous graphic tradition.

In the accounts of early explorers, there are numerous references to the innate ability of Eskimos to draw accurate maps and to reproduce pictorial images from newspapers as soon as paper and pencil became available (Murdoch 1892:389–410; Beechey 1831:298; Nelson 1899:197–98). Twentieth-century researchers have found Eskimo children consistently superior in culture-free drawing tests (Harris 1963:130). It is theorized that centuries of selective breeding have intensified an ability to observe and reproduce minute details. Survival itself was often dependent upon this keen eye, and it was the survivor who lived to breed children (Kleinfeld 1970:5, 7).

One would expect this lengthy graphic tradition in Alaska to manifest itself in drawings and prints in quantities comparable to the Canadian Eskimo output of the last twenty years (Goetz 1977:260). Such has not been the case. Only a handful of older Eskimos have concentrated on drawings; few younger Eskimos have produced prints.

A type of genre art, clearly derived from nineteenth-century scenes on ivory, has been popularized by two men, George Ahgupuk and Robert Mayokok; their ink drawings on bleached seal skin or paper depict traditional Eskimo methods of hunting, fishing, and dancing. These romanticized portrayals of bygone days have a great appeal for tourists who prefer to think of Alaska in these terms. Perhaps because carving and engraving have long been considered the province of males, only one woman, Florence

### 343. Wolf

The wolf and other terrestrial creatures were popular mask subjects in the nineteenth century, when the animals were often shown with great snouts and tongues. The wolf received a more modern treatment by Richard Seeganna, who created this curved mask using driftwood, acrylic paint, and horsehair.

Richard Seeganna (b. 1949, King Island, Alaska). *Wolf Mask*, 1978. Driftwood, acrylic paint, linseed oil, and horsehair (Collection, Alaska Contemporary Art Bank, Alaska State Council on the Arts, Anchorage, 78.59), 31.75 cm × 12.7 cm

### 344. Mask of the Crow

Nelson collected a number of stories about Raven—referred to here as Crow—and his creation of the earth and man. Versions of these stories are still told to children and are a source of wonderment and amusement. Sam Fox stated about this mask: "I always used to hear stories about the crow and the fox and this is based on them. . . . I usually don't draw before carving masks, only when doing relief carving and then on the wood itself, not on paper. On this mask I wasn't able to get raven feathers, so some are mallard and some are spruce hen. The lower beak moves. I don't know why they used to do it that way. Most of the Eskimo artists get ideas from the materials they use. I used dots for decoration on the sides because you usually see dots with rings around them in Eskimo designs" (Sam Fox, in Miller 1978:16).

Sam Fox (b. 1935, Goodnews Bay, Alaska). *Crow Mask*, 1978. Driftwood, cherry stain, india ink, paint, and feathers (Private Collection), 26.67 cm × 13.33 cm

### 345. Bear-Man Transformation

Implicit in the nineteenth-century Bering Sea Eskimo world view was the belief that humans could transform themselves into animals, animals could become people, and spirits could appear as animals or humans. This belief was communicated in the multi-image treatment of objects. In a twentieth-century context Earl Mayac returns to the theme of transformations in his ivory carving of a bear and hunter.

Earl Mayac (b. 1938, King Island, Alaska). *Bear-man*, 1977. Ivory (Collection, Anchorage Historical and Fine Arts Museum, 77.82.1), 3.81 cm × 8.83 cm

### 346. Hunter with Seal

Because Peter Seeganna's pieces are often quite small and the forms are streamlined, the strong sculptural qualities of his figures are often overlooked. Here a hunter is shown pulling a seal onto the shore.

Peter Seeganna (b. 1938, King Island, Alaska). *Seal Hunter*, 1973. Ivory and rock base (Collection, Anchorage Historical and Fine Arts Museum, 73.51.1), 7.92 cm × 8.89 cm × 7.23 cm

### 347. Miniature Loon

This loon, realistically carved with painstakingly engraved feathers, is a twentieth-century descendant of ivory amulets worn by nineteenth-century Eskimo hunters and of tiny figurines collected by whalers and explorers. The artist, Peter Mayac—once he arrived at a satisfactory likeness—carved dozens of versions of this miniature loon.

Peter Mayac (b. 1913, Cape Nome, Alaska). *Loon*, 1970. Ivory (Collection, Anchorage Historical and Fine Arts Museum, 71.50.10), 3.81 cm × 2.84 cm × 7.62 cm

Nupok Malewotkuk, has displayed exceptional ability in drawing. Her delicately shaded ice floes, walrus, and hunters have been reproduced by the thousands by a commercial firm with, unfortunately, little financial reward to her (Bauman 1972:D–8). Another well-known traditionalist is Kivetoruk Moses, whose tinted drawings have become collector's items. Like another primitive, Grandma Moses, he produces painstaking drawings in india ink which are enlivened with watercolor or colored pencils. Moses is a visual storyteller; most of his scenes describe events that actually occurred. Frequently a verbal account is inscribed on the back of the drawing. These four Eskimos, all self-taught, might be termed the "rear guard." Though their personal lives have been changed by twentieth-century invention, their art has retained close ties with nineteenth-century graphic styles.

One of the workshops prepared by the Indian Arts and Crafts Board and funded by the Manpower Development and Training Assistance program in 1964 sought to upgrade native arts through classes in metalwork; stone, wood, and ivory carving; and printmaking. With an emphasis on good design, new techniques, and efficient power tools, the program, managed by George Fedoroff, the board's field representative, and supervised by Ronald Senungetuk, a professor at the University of Alaska, seemed to be most successful. Most of thirty-two graduates were Eskimos from northwestern Alaska; their works and their training gave promise of a new level of excellence in Eskimo art (Indian Arts and Crafts Board 1966:12–17). Unfortunately, the majority have turned to other pursuits. Several of the older craftsmen no longer produce; at least two are now dead. Less than a half dozen have become full-time, innovative artists. Two or three have continued study at the University of Alaska, Fairbanks campus. One, Bernard Katexac, received an Associate of Arts degree upon completion of two years of courses there (Ray 1969:71).

Prints made during the Manpower workshop could hardly be considered great art; they look like student work. However, several artists who continued to study printmaking at various schools have emerged as today's leading Eskimo printmakers. Interestingly, these artists also excel at sculpting, and two have become good painters as a result of their training.

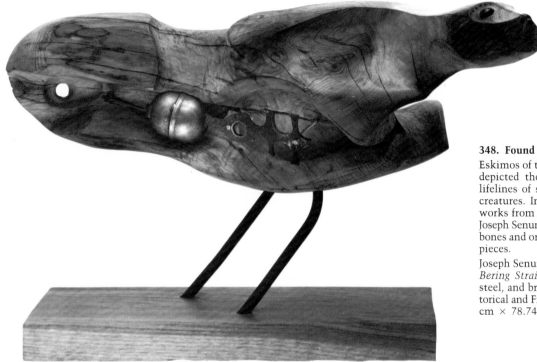

### 348. Found Objects

Eskimos of the nineteenth century carefully depicted the skeletal outline, organs, and lifelines of seals, people, and mythological creatures. In one of the few contemporary works from Alaska to utilize found objects, Joseph Senungetuk has cleverly suggested the bones and organs of a seal by means of metal pieces.

Joseph Senungetuk (b. 1940, Wales, Alaska). *Bering Strait Soul on Ice*, 1971–76. Wood, steel, and brass (Collection, Anchorage Historical and Fine Arts Museum, 76.11.1), 51.43 cm × 78.74 cm × 27.94 cm

### 349. Polar Bear Sculpture

The polar bear has been portrayed in realistic and abstract ways by many northern Eskimo peoples. The use of laminated wood and the streamlined contours of the polar bear seen here are indicative of Peter Seeganna's use of twentieth-century design and materials.

Prior to his untimely death in 1974, Seeganna voiced his hope that his work would be judged on the basis of its artistic worth rather than as "Eskimo" art.

Peter Seeganna (b. 1938, King Island, Alaska). *Polar Bear*, 1966. Alder (Collection, United States Department of the Interior, Indian Arts and Crafts Board, Washington, D.C., W 69.33.21), 12.7 cm × 17.78 cm

### 350. Seal on Its Back

The image of a seal lying on its back is commonly found in nineteenth-century Bering Sea Eskimo objects. The seal was commonly trussed in this manner after it had been killed. The image was also similar to the eating sea otter of the Aleutian Islands. Wilfred Olanna has enlarged the size of the animal represented in his contemporary treatment of this subject. Rather than driftwood used by earlier carvers, Olanna uses teak, walnut, and even ebony in many of his carvings.

Wilfred Olanna (b. 1933, Shishmaref, Alaska). Untitled, 1971. Wood (Collection, Anchorage Historical and Fine Arts Museum, 71.96.11), 13 cm × 33.02 cm × 19.05 cm

### 351. Drummer

Often the leader in his community, the drummer with his drum has been present at all Bering Sea Eskimos' social gatherings, regardless of whether people are dancing a narrative as entertainment for an evening, calling the shades of animals during a festival, or coming under the spell of a shaman. Lawrence Ahvakana has captured the image of the ever-present drummer and his drum in a large granite, wood, and metal sculpture.

Lawrence Ahvakana (b. 1946, Fairbanks, Alaska). *The Drummer*, 1976. Granite, wood, and metal (Collection, Atlantic Richfield Company, Alaska), 83.83 cm × 68.58 cm × 22.86 cm

### 352. Platter

While Ronald Senungetuk's silversmithing reveals little Eskimo cultural heritage, this platter is clearly conceptually based on nineteenth-century bent-wood tray decorations which have strong negative-positive images, lifelines, and skeletal motifs. The overall form of the platter and form of the creature are clearly the work of a fine contemporary artist.

Ronald Senungetuk (b. 1933, Wales, Alaska). *Silver Salmon Platter*, 1979. Hardwood, red pigment (Collection, Anchorage Historical and Fine Arts Museum, 79.90.2), 3.32 cm × 31.75 cm × 76.5 cm

### 353. Predator and Prey

Nineteenth-century carvings and symbolism have dealt with predator-prey relationships. Hunting implements were carved in the shape of or contained the image of a major predator of the animal or fish being hunted. *Inua* masks were often carved with the animal in question eating or catching its food. Earl Mayac has also dealt with the predator-prey relationship by intertwining seal and fish in a large alabaster sculpture.

Earl Mayac (b. 1938, King Island, Alaska). *Seal with Fish*, 1974. Alabaster (Private Collection), 40.64 cm × 40.64 cm × 20.32 cm

280

**354. Jewelry**

Nineteenth-century Eskimos delighted in wearing earrings, bracelets, and hair ornaments covered with whimsical, geometric, or spiritual designs. Ronald Senungetuk's jewelry only rarely reflects evidence of this heritage. Rather, his work is international in materials, design, and quality. His exposure to contemporary art styles outside of Alaska came initially through his training at the School for American Craftsmen at Rochester, New York, and his studies in Norway as a Fulbright scholar.

Ronald Senungetuk (b. 1933, Wales, Alaska). Untitled pendant, ca. 1969. Cast silver with pearl (Private Collection), 6.35 cm × 1.9 cm; Untitled pendant, 1975. Sterling silver and agate (Permanent Collection, Visual Arts Center of Alaska, Anchorage), each section 4.74 cm × 4.74 cm

## Leading Artists Today

A close look at the successful artists reveals one man who has influenced their lives, encouraged them, arranged for advanced schooling, provided jobs in some instances, and, by his own example, enlarged their vision of art. He is George Fedoroff, former field representative, Indian Arts and Crafts Board, U.S. Department of the Interior.

Certainly the most widely recognized and most influential artist of Eskimo heritage is Ronald Senungetuk, professor of art, University of Alaska, Fairbanks. He is a graduate of the School for American Craftsmen, Rochester Institute of Technology, New York, and recipient of a Fulbright Fellowship to study metalsmithing and design in Norway. His silver and gold jewelry and his finely crafted wooden trays have been exhibited in designer-craftsmen shows from coast to coast and abroad. Much of his work is international in style. Rarely is there evidence of his Eskimo origin.

Joseph Senungetuk is a foremost printmaker and one of the best sculptors at present. With a degree from the San Francisco Art Institute, he has distinguished himself as a teacher, writer, and activist. Several of his prints might be classified as social protest art.

Two of Alaska's important Eskimo artists now reside in the Pacific Northwest. Both have exhibitions in Alaska on a regular basis and receive substantial sums for their art. Melvin Olanna, trained at the Institute of American Indian Arts Museum in Santa Fe and the University of Alaska, has produced work ranging from the traditional to pop art. Lawrence Ahvakana, a graduate of the Rhode Island School of Design, has also been exposed to strong outside influences reflected in his hard edge paintings, skillfully blown glass, sensitive pottery, and welded steel sculpture.

Among the older Eskimos, Bernard Katexac is respected for his woodblock prints which depict traditional subjects. John Kailukiak, also a graduate of the Rhode Island School of Design, is versatile as a sculptor, printmaker, and painter. His large paintings are particularly strong. Another trained artist whose work can be highly creative is Sylvester Ayek, sculptor and printmaker. One of the most promising young artists, Peter Seeganna died at the age of thirty-five; he left behind distinguished sculpture and prints. Richard Seeganna has studied at the University of Alaska; his sculpture reflects considerable talent. Recognized as one of the best ivory carvers in the state, Earl Mayac has also demonstrated noteworthy ability in handling larger stone compositions.

### 355. Walrus on Ice

Florence Malewotkuk has used a bleached seal skin as the canvas for her depiction of walrus gathered on ice floes. Her study is reminiscent of nineteenth-century engravers' portrayals of walrus on drill bows and trade pipes. Malewotkuk's careful drawing and accurate perspective testify to her expert draftsmanship and preference for realism.

Florence Nupok (Chauncey) Malewotkuk (b. 1906, Gambell, St. Lawrence Island, Alaska). *Walruses on Ice Floe*. Ink on bleached seal skin (Collection, Anchorage Historical and Fine Arts Museum, 75.56.1), 134.62 cm × 104.14 cm

### 356. Walrus Inua

Nelson collected this tiny walrus in the late 1870s. Since a semihuman face, interpreted as being the walrus's *inua*, appears on its breast, and the piece has no obvious mechanical function, its seems likely that it was a fetish, possibly carried by a hunter to insure success of the walrus hunt. As such it would have been a treasured personal possession.

No such reference to the personal or supernatural appears in the much larger images of walrus produced by artists working in the twentieth century. Their work is produced for commercial sale rather than for personal use, and they have all made the form of the animal or its habitat the subject of their work.

Cape Vancouver 43564, 4.51 cm long

### 357. Walrus Gathering

Bernard Katexac's walrus are shown gathered on the ice, resting one on top of the other, the way walrus often do. Katexac pulls the viewer close to animals and emphasizes the animals' enormous bulk.

Bernard Katexac (b. 1922, King Island, Alaska). *Walruses*, 1969. Woodblock (Collection, Anchorage Historical and Fine Arts Museum, 70.152.6), 27.94 cm × 45.72 cm

### 358. Resting Walrus

Peter Seeganna has studied an individual walrus and has carved him in a resting pose, with his head turned to one side. His animal has elegant streamlined curves and is therefore quite unlike the bulky mammals illustrated by Florence Malewotkuk and Bernard Katexac.

Peter Seeganna (b. 1938, King Island, Alaska). *Walrus*, 1960s. White marble (Collection, Alaska State Museum, Juneau, VA 357), 12.7 cm × 22.86 cm × 12.06 cm

Finally, the sculptures John Penatac produced while in residence at the Visual Arts Center of Alaska exhibit a rare ability to capture the essence of sea mammal forms in large compositions. Except for Peter Seeganna, no other native sculptor in Alaska has achieved the level of Penatac's visually exciting conceptions of the animal world.

These artists, like their forebears, possess the talents of keen observation and imaginative abstraction. As can be recognized, they depict not just what their eyes see but also what their minds know—mythical beings, skeletal views, ancient symbols. Some of their art would not immediately be identified as the achievement of an Eskimo; indeed, in the future their

### 359. Walrus Abstraction

John Penatac has made the most abstract statement concerning walrus of any of the artists presented here. His work is a study of the animal's huge folds of flesh and flippers. Penatac's sculpture, along with works of other twentieth-century artists, indicates that although the nineteenth-century subject matter still remains popular, new raw materials and techniques have brought about profound changes in the area of Alaskan Eskimo art. Artists, in addition to having new tools with which to work, are no longer bound by the cultural context in which an object must function. Reflecting the changing functions of the objects and the international training of the artists, many of these pieces are not immediately recognizable as being the work of Eskimo artists. Rather, the sculptures, prints, and drawings are created by well-trained creative individuals who happen to be of Eskimo heritage.

John Penatac (b. 1940, King Island, Alaska). *Walrus II*, 1976. Alabaster (Permanent Collection, Visual Arts Center of Alaska, Anchorage, 77.9.1), 38.1 cm × 50.8 cm × 15.24 cm

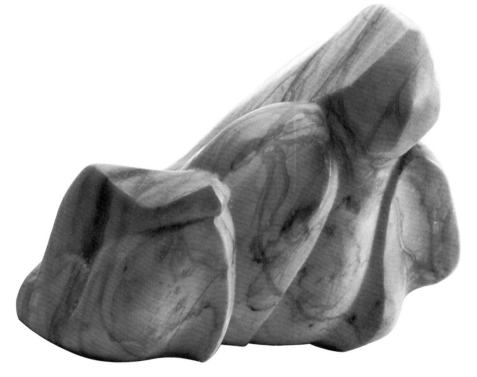

**360. Covered Basket with Birds' Feet**

Figures defined by coiled dyed grass parade around this twentieth-century piece. Lizzie Tirchick has added seed beads and birds' feet as decorative elements. The dangling birds' feet bring to mind a similarly decorated basket collected by Nelson (fig. 136).

The nineteenth-century weaver, who was still experimenting with the coiling method, could liven up her basket with European yarns and beads, as well as blackened sinew or grass. Today, Eskimo baskets are extremely colorful, for women color strips of gut skin or grass with commercial dyes. They also soak or boil candy wrappers and other materials, and use this infusion to add color to their work.

Lizzie Tirchick (Chefornak, Alaska). *Covered Coiled Basket*, ca. 1980. Beach grass, seed beads, dyed grass, and birds' feet (Private Collection), 24.76 cm × 27.3 cm

**361. Lidded Basket**

During the time of Nelson's visit to Alaska, some baskets had flat lids hinged to the containers with braided sinew or strips of rawhide. Coiled baskets were minimally decorated with tufts of wool, blackened grass or sinew, baleen, strips of dyed rawhide, and birds' toes. By the early twentieth century, when this basket was collected, baskets were being made with tightly fitted knobbed lids, and strips of dyed gutskin were wrapped around the coil bundle, creating geometric designs.

Kwinhgak (Collection, University of Alaska Museum, Fairbanks, UA 236–4048AB), 14.6 cm high

## 362. Modern Work Basket

Twined baskets are strong, flexible, and durable containers. Throughout the nineteenth century they were used to carry clothing and to store fish. Twined baskets are still used today for many of the same functions. The baskets are still open twined and their rims are finished with open-braided work.

Neva Rivers (Hooper Bay, Alaska). *Work Basket*, 1981. Beach grass (Private Collection), 26.03 cm × 39.37 cm

## 363. Open-twined Basket

Throughout the nineteenth century Eskimos were quick to incorporate exotic materials into their tool kits if they perceived advantages to the materials. This process is still in operation. Pansy Jones has used remnants of a Japanese fishing net as the base for her open basket. She has handled the polypropylene the same way women have handled grasses when making fish bags, creating an open-twined basket with a braided rim.

Pansy Jones (Mekoryuk, Nunivak Island, Alaska). *Open Basket*, 1969. Polypropylene, blue-purple yarn (Collection, University of Alaska Museum, Fairbanks, UA 69–20–1), 27.94 cm × 35.56 cm

mature styles, responding to diverse world influences, may so closely resemble those of other contemporary American artists that the "roots in the past" will disappear. Today those roots inspire some of the most highly creative work. Properly motivated, these artists are capable of producing a new twentieth-century "Eskimo" style which is the amalgam of their own creative urges, their Eskimo heritage, and the sum of their personal experiences and training. What type of art will emerge cannot be forecast. Only one prediction seems valid. It will not fit the neat stereotypes of what is known as "Eskimo art" today.

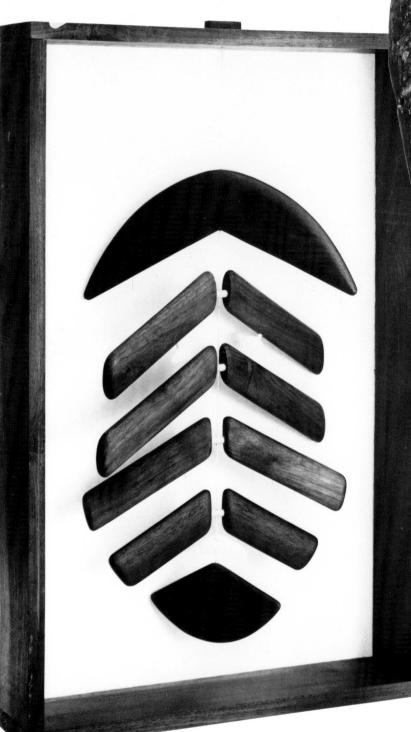

### 364. Point Hope Mask

The original motivation behind the carving of this nineteenth-century mask is unknown, as the piece was uncovered in an abandoned men's house in Point Hope in 1935. The chevron pattern may represent tattooing or blackening of the face, or the pattern may be an abstraction of whale flukes, which often appeared instead of a nose on northern masks.

Point Hope (Collection, The National Museum of Denmark, Copenhagen, P 6386), 21.2 cm × 13.97 cm

### 365. Mobile

The Point Hope man who carved the mask illustrated in figure 364 created a powerful image. Sylvester Ayek, in a creative leap of his own imagination, envisioned a mobile based on this form. Ayek carved the lowest section of the mask in the shape of an ulu blade.

Sylvester Ayek (b. 1941, King Island, Alaska). *Mobile Mask*, 1974. Wood, sinew, and ivory (Collection, Anchorage Historical and Fine Arts Museum, 75.49.1), 86.99 cm × 57 cm

## 366. Mountain Spirits

The handsome late–nineteenth-century mask collected by Henry Neumann and made out of wood, strips of dyed gut skin, gull feathers, and eagle down was the inspiration for Lawrence Ahvakana's large wrought iron mask created in this century. Eskimos of previous generations believed that both animate and inanimate objects possessed spirits. The portrayal of these spirits challenged the imagination of the mask maker and resulted in an endless variety of artistic forms. The earlier mask was made to be worn, and had it not been collected the mask would have been discarded after its spiritual utility had been exhausted. Ahvakana's mask is designed as a wall-hung piece of art and is made out of metal rather than organic materials.

St. Michael (Collection, Sheldon Jackson Museum, Sheldon Jackson College, Sitka, II.G.7), 70 cm high; Lawrence Ahvakana (b. 1946, Fairbanks, Alaska). *Mountain Spirit*, 1969. Wrought iron (Collection, Anchorage Historical and Fine Arts Museum, 71.213.1), 104.14 cm × 86.36 cm

# references

Ager, Lynn Price
    1971    The Eskimo Storyknife Complex of Southwestern Alaska. Unpublished M.A. thesis, Department of Anthropology, University of Alaska, Fairbanks.
    1974    Storyknifing: An Alaskan Eskimo Girls' Game. *Journal of the Folklore Institute* 11(3):187–98.
  1979/80  Illustrated Oral Literature from Southwestern Alaska: Storyknifing, Storyknives, Knifestories. Part I, II. *Arts and Culture of the North* 4(1):199–202.

Ager, Thomas A.
    1982a  Vegetational History of Western Alaska during Wisconsonian Glacial Interval and the Holocene. In *Paleoecology of Beringia*. Hopkins, Matthews, Schweger and Young, eds. New York: Academic Press, in press.
    1982b  Holocene Vegetational History of Alaska. In *Holocene of the United States*. H. E. Wright, ed. Minneapolis: University of Minnesota, in press.

Ager, Thomas A. and Ager, Lynn Price
    1980    Ethnobotany of the Eskimos of Nelson Island, Alaska. *Arctic Anthropology* 17(1):27–48.

Alaska Geographic Society
    1979    Yukon-Kuskokwim Delta. *Alaska Geographic* 6(1).

Alaska Planning Group
    Final Environmental Statement for Proposed Chukchi-Imuruk National Reserve. Washington, D.C.: U. S. Department of the Interior. (n.d.)

*Amerikas Nordwest-Kunste neueste Ergebnisse Ethnologischer Reisen*
    1883    Catalog of artifacts collected by J. A. Jacobsen in Alaska, 1881–1883. Berlin: A. Asher and Company.

Anderson, Douglas D.
    1978    Western Arctic and Sub-Arctic. In *Chronologies in New World Archeology*, R. E. Taylor and C. W. Meighan, eds., pp. 29–50. Academic Press.

Bauman, Margie
    1972    Anchorage's Busy Ceramics Factory. *Anchorage Daily News*, July 2.

Beaglehole, J. C., ed.
    1967    *The Journals of Captain James Cook on His Voyages of Discovery*, vol 3: *The Voyage of the Resolution and the Discovery, 1776–1789*. Cambridge: Cambridge University Press for the Hakluyt Society.

Beechey, Frederick W.
    1831    *Narrative of a Voyage to the Pacific and Bering's Strait, 1825–1828*. London: Henry Colburn and Richard Bentley.

Blodgett, Jean
    1979    *The Coming and Going of the Shaman: Eskimo Shamanism and Art*. Winnipeg: Winnipeg Art Gallery.

Bockstoce, John R.
    1977    *Eskimos of Northwest Alaska in the Early Nineteenth Century*. Oxford: Pitt Rivers Museum.
    1979    The Archaeology of Cape Nome, Alaska. *University Museum Monograph* 38:1–133. Philadelphia: University Museum, University of Pennsylvania.

Bogoras, Vladimir G.
    1907    *The Chukchee*. Memoirs of the American Museum of Natural History, Vol. 11, part 2. New York.

Burch, Ernest S.
  1972  The Caribou/Wild Reindeer as a Human Resource. *American Antiquity* 37(3):339–68.
  1981  *The Traditional Eskimo Hunters of Point Hope, Alaska, 1800–1975.* North Slope Borough.

Canadian Eskimo Arts Council
  1971  *Sculpture/Inuit: Masterworks of the Canadian Arctic.* Toronto: University of Toronto Press.

Carpenter, Edmund P.
  1973  *Eskimo Realities.* Holt, Rinehart and Winston.

Choris, Ludovik
  1822  *Voyage Pittoresque Autour du Monde.* Paris: Fermin Didot.

Colinvaux, Paul A.
  1964  The Environment of the Bering Land Bridge. *Ecological Monographs* 34:297–329.
  1967  Bering Land Bridge: Evidence of Spruce in Late Wisconsin Times. *Science* 156:380–83.
  1967  A Long Pollen Record from St. Lawrence, Bering Sea, Alaska. *Palaeogeography, Palaeoclimatology, and Palaeoecology* 3:29–48.
  1981  Historical Ecology in Beringia: The South Land Bridge Coast at St. Paul Island. *Quarterly Research* 16:18–36.

Collins, Henry B.
  1928  Check-Stamped Pottery from Alaska. *Journal of the Washington Academy of Sciences* 18(9): 254–56.
  1937  Archeology of St. Lawrence Island, Alaska. *Smithsonian Miscellaneous Collections* 96(1):1–431.
  1959  An Okvik Artifact from Southwest Alaska and Stylistic Resemblances between Early Eskimo and Paleolithic Art. *Polar Notes* 1:13–27. Hanover, New Hampshire.
  1962  Eskimo Cultures. *Encyclopedia of World Art* 5, Vols. 1–28. McGraw-Hill.
  1971  Composite Masks: Chinese and Eskimo. *Anthropologica* 11(1–2):271–78.
  1973  Eskimo Art. In *The Far North: 2000 Years of American Eskimo and Indian Art*, pp. 1–131. Washington, D.C.: National Gallery of Art.
  1975  Archaeological Investigations at Bering Strait, 1936. *National Geographic Society Research Reports*, 1890–1954 Projects. Washington, D.C.: National Geographic Society.

Curtis, Edward S.
  1930  *The North American Indian*, Vol. 20. New York: Johnson Reprint Company (reprinted 1976).

Dall, W. H.
  1870  *Alaska and Its Resources.* Boston: Lee and Shepard (reprinted by Arno Press, Inc., 1970).

Driscoll, Bernadette
  1980  *The Inuit Amautik: I Like My Hood to be Full.* Winnipeg: Winnipeg Art Gallery.

Fagg, William, ed.
  1972  *Eskimo Art in the British Museum.* London: British Museum.

Fries, J. A.
  1977  *The Vascular Plants of Nunivak Island, Alaska.* Unpublished senior thesis, Middlebury College.

Giddings, James Louis
  1964  *The Archaeology of Cape Denbigh.* Providence, Rhode Island: Brown University Press.
  1967  *Ancient Men of the Arctic.* New York: Alfred A. Knopf.

Goetz, Helga
  1977  *The Inuit Print.* Ottawa: National Museum of Canada.

Goldman, E. A.
  1935  Edward William Nelson—Naturalist, 1855–1934. *Auk* 52(2):135–48.

Gordon, George Byron
  1917  *In the Alaskan Wilderness.* Philadelphia: John C. Winston Co.

Harington, C.R.
    1978    Quaternary Vertebrate Faunas of Canada and Alaska and their Suggested Chronological Sequence. *Syllogeus* 15:1–105.

Harris, Dale B.
    1963    *Children's Drawings as Measures of Intellectual Maturity*. New York: Harcourt, Brace, and World.

Hawks, E. W.
    1913    The "Inviting-In" Feast of the Alaska Eskimo. *Geological Survey Memoir 45, Anthropological Series No. 3*. Ottawa: Canada Department of Mines.
    1914    The Dance Festivals of the Alaskan Eskimo. *University Museum Anthropological Publication* 6(2). Philadelphia: University of Pennsylvania.

Heller, Christine
    1966    *Wild, Edible and Poisonous Plants of Alaska*. Fairbanks: University of Alaska, Division of Statewide Services Cooperative Extension Service.

Henry, Agnes
    1981    Yupik Philosophy of Life. In *Yupik Lore, Oral Traditions of an Eskimo People*. Edward A. Tennant and Joseph N. Bitar, eds. Bethel, Alaska: Lower Kuskokwim School District.

Himmelheber, Hans
    1953    *Eskimokunstler, Ergebnisse einer Reise pin Alaska* Eisenach: Erich Roth-Verlag.

Hoffman, Walter James
    1897    The Graphic Art of the Eskimos. *United States National Museum Annual Report for 1895*, pp. 739–968. Washington, D.C.: U. S. Government Printing Office.

Hooper, Calvin Leighton
    1884    *Report of the Cruise of the U. S. Revenue Steamer Thomas Corwin, in the Arctic Ocean, 1881*. Washington, D.C.: U. S. Government Printing Office.

Hopkins, David M.
    1973    Sea Level History in Beringia during the Last 250,000 Years. *Quaternary Research* 520–40.
    1979    Landscape and Climate of Beringia during Late Pleistocene and Holocene Time. In *The First Americans: Affinities, and Adaptations*, W. S. Laughlin and A. B. Harper, eds., pp. 15–41. New York: Gustav Fisher.

Hopkins, David M., ed.
    1967    *The Bering Land Bridge*. Stanford: Stanford University Press.

Hopkins, David M., Matthews, J. V., Jr., Schweger, Charles E., and Young, Steven B., eds.
    1982    *Paleoecology of Beringia*. New York: Academic Press, in press.

Hughes, Charles C.
    1965    Under Four Flags: Recent Culture Change Among the Eskimos. *Current Anthropology* 5(1).

Hulten, Eric
    1968    *Flora of Alaska and Neighboring Territories: A Manual of Vascular Plants*. Stanford: Stanford University Press.

Indian Arts and Crafts Board
    1966    *Smoke Signals*. Circular for Indian Artists and Craftsmen Issued by Indian Arts and Crafts Board of the U. S. Department of the Interior, No. 50–51. Washington, D.C.: Indian Arts and Crafts Board.

Irving, William N.
    1968    The Arctic Small Tool Tradition. *Proceedings of the VIII International Congress of Anthropological and Ethnological Sciences* 3:340–42. Tokyo and Kyoto.

Jenness, Diamond
    1928    Ethnological Problems of Arctic America. *America Geographical Society Special Publication* 7:167–75.

King, Jonathan C. H.
    1981    *Artifical Curiosities from the Northwest Coast of America*. London: British Museum Publications.

Klein, David R.
    1966    Waterfowl in the Economy of the Eskimos on the Yukon-Kuskokwim Delta, Alaska. *Arctic* 19:319–36.

Kleinfeld, Judith
    1970    Cognitive Strengths of Eskimos and Implications for Education. *ISEGR Occasional Paper No. 3.* Fairbanks: Institute of Social, Economic and Government Research, University of Alaska.

Kotzebue, Otto von
    1821    *Voyage of Discovery in the South Sea, and to Behrings Straits, in Search of a Northwest Passage; undertaken in the years 1815–18, in the ship Rurick*, Vol. 1. London: Longman, Hurst, Rees, Orme, and Brown.

Koutsky, Kathryn
    1981    *Early Days on Norton Sound and Bering Strait. Vol. 2, The Wales Area.* Occasional Paper No. 29. Fairbanks: Anthropology and Historic Preservation Cooperative Park Studies Unit, University of Alaska.

Lantis, Margaret
    1946    The Social Culture of the Nunivak Eskimo. *Transactions of the American Philosophical Society.* Philadelphia: The American Philosophical Society.
    1947    Alaskan Eskimo Ceremonialism. In *Monographs of the American Ethnological Society*, XI, Marian W. Smith, ed. New York: J. J. Augustin Publisher.
    1954    Edward William Nelson. *Anthropological Papers of the University of Alaska* 3(1):5–16.
    1959    Folk Medicine and Hygiene: Lower Kuskokwim and Nunivak-Nelson Island Areas. *Anthropological Papers of the University of Alaska* 8:1–75.
    1960    *Eskimo Childhood and Interpersonal Relationships.* Seattle: University of Washington Press.

Larsen, Helge and Rainey, Froelich
    1948    Ipiutak and the Arctic Whale Hunting Culture. *Anthropological Papers of the American Museum of Natural History*, Vol. 42. New York: American Museum of Natural History.

Laughlin, William S.
    1963    Eskimos and Aleuts: Their Origins and Evolution. *Science* 142(3503):633–45. Washington, D.C.

Mason, J. Alden
    1927    Eskimo Pictorial Art. *The Museum Journal*, University of Pennsylvania 18(3):248–83.

Matthews, John V., Jr.
    1974    Quaternary Environments at Cape Deceit (Seward Peninsula, Alaska): Evolution of a Tundra Ecosystem. *Geological Society of America*, Bulletin 85:1353–84.

Meldgaard, Jorgen
    1959    *Eskimo Sculpture.* London: Methuen.

Miller, Maurine
    1978    *Alaskameut.* Alaskaland—Bear Gallery. Alaska Association for the Arts.

Morrow, James E.
    1974    *Illustrated Keys to the Freshwater Fishes of Alaska.* Anchorage: Alaska Northwest Publishing Co.

Muir, John
    1917    *The Cruise of the Corwin: Journal of the Arctic Expedition of DeLong and the Jeannette.* Boston: Houghton-Mifflin Co.

Murdoch, John
    1892    Ethnological Results of the Point Barrow Expedition. *United States Bureau of Ethnology, Ninth Annual Report (for) 1887–1888.* Washington, D.C.: U. S. Government Printing Office.

Nelson, C. H.
    1980    Late Pleistocene-Holocene Transgressive Sedimentation in Deltaic and Non-deltaic Areas of the Bering Epicontinental Shelf. In *Geological,*

*Geochemical and Geotechnical Observations on the Bering Shelf, Alaska,* M. C. Larson, C. H. Nelson, and D. R. Thor, eds. *U. S. Geological Survey Open-File Report 80–979.*

Nelson, Edward W.
    1879    Letter to Robert Ridgway of June 26, 1979. Smithsonian Archives. Washington, D.C.: Smithsonian Institution.
              List of Ethnological Specimens Obtained in Alaska with notes. 3 vols. Manuscripts, National Anthropological Archives, Smithsonian Institution. (n.d.)
    1882    A Sledge Journey in the Delta of the Yukon, Northern Alaska. *Proceedings of the Royal Geographical Society and Monthly Record of Geography,* New Series 4:667.
    1884    Birds of the Bering Sea and the Arctic Ocean. In *Cruise of the Revenue Steamer Corwin in Alaska and the N.W. Arctic Ocean in 1881.* Washington, D.C.: U. S. Government Printing Office.
    1884    Blackfish. In *The Fisheries and Fishery Industries,* G. B. Goode. U. S. Section I. United States Department of the Interior. Washington, D.C.: U. S. Government Printing Office.
    1887    *Report upon Natural History Collections made in Alaska Between the Years 1877–1881.* Washington, D.C.: Arctic Series of Publications, U. S. Army Signal Service, III.
    1899    The Eskimo About Bering Strait. *Bureau of American Ethnology Annual Report,* Vol. 1, pp. 1–518 Washington, D.C.: Smithsonian Institution.

Nowak, Michael
    1970    A Preliminary Report on the Archaeology of Nunivak Island, Alaska. *Anthropological Papers of the University of Alaska* 15(1):19–32. Fairbanks.

Oswalt, Wendell, H.
    1952    The Archaeology of Hooper Bay Village, Alaska. *Anthropological Papers of the University of Alaska* 1(1):47–91. Fairbanks.
    1957    A Western Eskimo Ethnobotany. *Anthropological Papers of the University of Alaska* 6:16–36.
    1964a   Traditional Storyknife Tales of Yuk Girls. *Proceedings of the American Philosophical Society* 108(4):310–66.
    1964b   *Napaskiak: An Alaskan Eskimo Community.* Tucson: University of Arizona Press.
    1980    *Kolmakovskiy Redoubt: The Ethnoarchaeology of a Russian Fort in Alaska.* Monumenta Archaeologica 8. Los Angeles: Institute of Archaeology, University of California.

Pearce, Susan M.
    1975    Towards the Pole. *Exeter Museums Publications* No. 82. Exeter, England: Royal Albert Memorial Museum.

Pennant, Thomas
    1792    *Arctic Zoology.* (Second Edition, first edition, 1784.) London: Printed for Robert Faulder.

Petroff, Ivan
    1884    *Report on the Population, Industries, and Resources of Alaska.* Washington, D.C.: U. S. Government Printing Office.

Péwé, Troy
    1975    Quaternary Geology of Alaska. *U. S. Geological Survey Professional Paper* 835.

Porter, Robert B., ed.
    1893    *Report on Population and Resources of Alaska. U. S. Eleventh Census, 1890.* Washington, D.C.: U. S. Government Printing Office.

Rainey, Froelich
    1941    Eskimo Prehistory: The Okvik Site on the Punuk Islands. *Anthropological Papers of the American Museum of Natural History* 37(4):453–569. New York.

Ray, Dorothy Jean
    1964    Nineteenth Century Settlement and Subsistence Patterns in Bering Strait. *Arctic Anthropology* 2(2):61–91.
    1967    *Eskimo Masks: Art and Ceremony.* Seattle: University of Washington Press.

1969    *Graphic Arts of the Alaskan Eskimo.* U. S. Department of the Interior, Indian Arts and Crafts Board. Washington, D.C.: U. S. Government Printing Office.

1975    *The Eskimos of Bering Strait, 1650–1898.* Seattle: University of Washington Press.

1977    *Eskimo Art: Tradition and Innovation in North Alaska.* Seattle: University of Washington Press.

1981    *Aleut and Eskimo Art: Tradition and Innovation in South Alaska.* Seattle: University of Washington Press.

Ray, P. Henry
    1885    Ethnographic Sketch of the Natives of Point Barrow. *U.S. Signal Service Report of the International Polar Expedition to Point Barrow, Alaska.* Washington, D.C.: U. S. Government Printing Office.

Selkregg, Lidia L., ed.
    1974    *Alaska Regional Profiles,* Vol. 2 (Arctic Region), Vol. 3 (Southwest Region), Vol. 5 (Northwest Region), Vol. 6 (Yukon Region). University of Alaska, Arctic Environmental Information and Data Center for the State of Alaska and the Joint Federal-State Land Use Planning Commission for Alaska.

Senungetuk, Joseph E.
    1971    *Give or Take Century: An Eskimo Chronicle.* San Francisco: The Indian Historian Press.

Smith, James G. E.
    1980    *Arctic Art: Eskimo Ivory.* New York: Museum of the American Indian, Heye Foundation. Exhibition catalogue.

Swadesh, Morris
    1951    Kleinschmidt Centennial III: Unaaliq and Proto Eskimo. *International Journal of American Linguistics* 17:66–70.

Tennant, Edward A. and Bitar, Joseph N., eds.
    1981    *Yupik Lore: Oral Traditions of an Eskimo People.* Bethel, Alaska: Lower Kuskokwim School District.

Turner, L. M.
    1886    *Contributions to the Natural History of Alaska.* Washington, D.C.: U. S. Department of Agriculture, Soil Conservation Service.

VanStone, James W.
    1957    An Archaeological Reconnaissance of Nunivak Island, Alaska. *Anthropological Papers of the University of Alaska* 5(2):97–117. Fairbanks.

    1976    The Bruce Collection of Eskimo Material Culture from Port Clarence, Alaska. *Fieldiana: Anthropology,* Vol. 67.

    1980    The Bruce Collection of Eskimo Material Culture from Kotzebue Sound, Alaska. *Fieldiana: Anthropology,* New Series, No. 1.

VanStone, James W., ed.
    1978    E. W. Nelson's Notes on the Indians of the Yukon and Innoko Rivers, Alaska. *Fieldiana: Anthropology,* Vol. 70.

Viereck, Leslie A. and Little, Elbert L.
    1972    *Alaska Trees and Shrubs.* Agriculture Handbook No. 410. Washington, D.C.: U. S. Department of Agriculture Forest Service.

Woodbury, Anthony C., ed.
    *Narratives and Tales from Chevak, Alaska.* Bethel, Alaska: Yupik Language Center, Kuskokwim Community College, in press.

Wright, Herbert E., Jr.
    1982    *Holocene of the United States.* Minneapolis: University of Minnesota Press, in press.

Young, Steven B. and Hall, Edwin S., Jr.
    1969    Contributions to the Ethnobotany of the St. Lawrence Island Eskimo. *Anthropological Papers of the University of Alaska* 14(2):43–53.

Zagoskin, Lavrentii A.
    1967    *Lieutenant Zagoskin's Travels in Russian America, 1842–1844.* Penelope Rainey, translator; Henry N. Michael, ed. Toronto: University of Toronto Press.

**Photographic and Illustration Credits**

All photographs by Joel Breger, all maps and charts by Molly Ryan, and all drawings by Jo Ann Moore, with the exception of:

Lynn Price Ager, Juneau, Alaska: figs. 192–94

James H. Barker, Bethel, Alaska: pp. 26–27, fig. 131

Alfred H. Blaker: fig. 331

Henry B. Collins: pp. 2–3, 4–5, 114–15, 160–61

Anne Hartmann, Anchorage, Alaska: fig. 303

Henry E. Huntington Library and Art Gallery, San Marino, California: fig. 7

Sam Kimura, Anchorage, Alaska: figs. 336, 338–40, 345–48, 350–52, 354–55, 357, 359–60, 362, 365 (Mountain Spirit), 366

Victor Krantz, Smithsonian Institution: figs. 309–10

National Museum of Denmark: fig. 364

Mark Perrott, Pittsburgh, Pennsylvania: fig. 353

Ken Pratt, Cooperative Park Studies Unit, University of Alaska: fig. 289

Dorothy Jean Ray, Port Townsend, Washington: fig. 313, 332

United States Department of the Interior, Indian Arts and Crafts Board, Washington, D.C.: figs. 335, 337, 341–42, 349

University of Alaska Museum, Fairbanks, Alaska: figs. 361, 363


Cover: Horned Puffin Eating Walrus, South of Lower Yukon, 33107; photograph courtesy of American Museum of Natural History, New York

**Library of Congress Cataloging in Publication Data**

Fitzhugh, William W., 1943–
  Inua : spirit world of the Bering Sea Eskimo.

  Prepared in conjunction with an exhibit of the
Edward William Nelson Bering Sea Eskimo ethnology
collection of the National Museum of Natural History.
  Bibliography: p.
  1. Eskimos—Alaska—Exhibitions.  2. Nelson, Edward
William, 1855–1934—Ethnological collections—Exhibi-
tions.  3. National Museum of Natural History (U.S.)—
Catalogs.  I. Kaplan, Susan A.  II. Collins, Henry Bascom,
1899–     .  III. National Museum of Natural History
(U.S.)  IV. Title.
E99.E7F55           306'.08997          82–5542
ISBN 0–87474–429–6 (pbk.)           AACR2
ISBN 0–87474–430–X

The paper in this book meets the guidelines for permanence and
durability of the Committee on Production Guidelines for Book
Longevity of the Council on Library Resources.

*"Drink well, spirits of those of whom I have told."*

# inua

This book was set in Trump Medieval by
FotoTypesetters Incorporated, Baltimore, Maryland, and
printed by Eastern Press, Inc., New Haven, Connecticut

Book design by Alex Castro